The Guatemalan Military Project

Pennsylvania Studies in Human Rights

Bert B. Lockwood, Jr., Series Editor

A complete list of books in the series is available from the publisher.

The Guatemalan Military Project

A Violence Called Democracy

Jennifer Schirmer

PENN

University of Pennsylvania Press

Philadelphia

10 9 8 7 6 5 4 3 2 1

Published by
University of Pennsylvania Press
Philadelphia, Pennsylvania 19104-4011

Library of Congress Cataloging-in-Publication Data
Schirmer, Jennifer G.
    The Guatemalan military project : a violence called democracy /
Jennifer Schirmer.
        p.   cm.   (Pennsylvania Studies in Human Rights)
    Includes bibliographical references and index.
    ISBN 0-8122-3325-5 (alk. paper)
    1. Guatemala — Politics and government — 1945–1985.   2. Guatemala —
Politics and government — 1985–   .   3. Guatemala — Armed Forces —
Political activity — History — 20th century.   4. Guatemala — Military
policy.   5. Political persecution — Guatemala — History — 20th century.
6. Indians of Central America — Guatemala — Government relations.
7. Civil-military relations — Guatemala — History — 20th century.   I. Title.
F1466.5.S33   1998
972.8105′2 — dc21   98-28114
                                                                          CIP

Contents

Acknowledgments

Many people at Harvard University have generously provided me with an intellectual home since the early 1980s; I deeply appreciate the encouragement and steadfast support for my work, especially from Stanley Hoffmann and Peter Hall at the Center for European Studies. The Human Rights Program of the Harvard Law School, too, served as a haven from 1983 to 1986 with the support of the Ella Lyman Cabot Trust Award. During this time I developed the thesis for the book and began my interviews, first with Chilean and Guatemalan judges, lawyers, and journalists and later with military officers. C. Clyde Ferguson, wholly dedicated to human rights, first had confidence in my research; Fred Snyder, generous to a fault, invited me to lecture his classes. Both, sadly, have passed away. Phil Heymann, David Smith, Phil Alston, and Hugo Fruhling all deserve thanks for giving me their time, comments, and support. Early on, Donald Fox, Aryeh Neier, Allan Nairn, Jean-Marie Simon, and George Black were generous with their advice, analysis and contacts; I also thank George for sharing his copies of *Revista Militar* and for first encouraging me to speak with military officers about the war. Guatemalan colleagues in Washington and Costa Rica at the time, Frank LaRue and Edelberto Torres-Rivas, have always provided succinct intellectual analyses of *la situación,* and remain invaluable friends. Gabriel Aguilera Peralta is to be thanked for his generosity in enhancing and encouraging my work on the military. In Guatemala, Héctor Rosada Granados, the late Lieutenant Colonel José Luis Cruz Salazar, and Miguel Balcárcel generously provided me with office space, interviews, and cogent analyses during the torrential months of August and September 1988 at the research institute ASIES. Several of the staff at *Inforpress Centroamericana,* along with a number of journalists who cannot be named, were most generous with their sources and archives throughout the 1980s. I thank you profusely and remain in awe of your courage.

Fred Halliday of the Centre for International Studies at the London School of Politics and Economics deserves my sincere thanks for providing me with a refuge in the spring of 1991 for writing up my interviews. Lars Schoultz, Sam Fitch, and Robert Fishman all provided invaluable intellectual encouragement and advice that sometimes went unheeded. Martin Diskin, with his thoughtful and persistently keen eye for the overall picture and his dogged commitment to justice, was an invaluable source of intellectual support and inspiration; he will be much missed. Bert Lockwood is to be thanked for having faith in the book and seeing it through to publication. Margaret Thomas provided me firm guidance during my first anthropological fieldwork in Guatemala in 1970, establishing in my mind a respect for and dedication to anthropological methods as well as to Guatemala; I value her loyal and generous friendship.

Susana Beatriz Herrera has made an inestimable contribution to this book by providing flawless and prompt bilingual transcriptions; Iris Gomez must be thanked for her good humor and patience during our sessions of bilingual editing of the interviews. Keith O'Connor patiently created the superb detailed maps in the book; Keith Garner skillfully crafted the intelligence charts; Stephanie Hollyman generously provided her photograph for the front cover; and I thank Doug Cogger for lending his excellent photographic skills to make the illustrations camera-ready.

Most important of all, Eddie Robbins's constant intellectual (and editorial) challenges and wonderful companionship (together with Kiné and Apurimac), helped sustain me in the research and writing of this book.

Finally, I would like to thank General Gramajo and the late Colonel Girón Tánchez in particular, and the dozens of other officers and *especialistas* who were generous with their time to speak with me about their perspective on the war, about the civil-military *proyecto,* and about their worldview in general, especially for a book over which they had no control. Regrettably, there are many, many more Guatemalans who cannot be named. This book is dedicated to their commitment to create, against all odds, an authentic democracy in Guatemala.

Maps and Chart

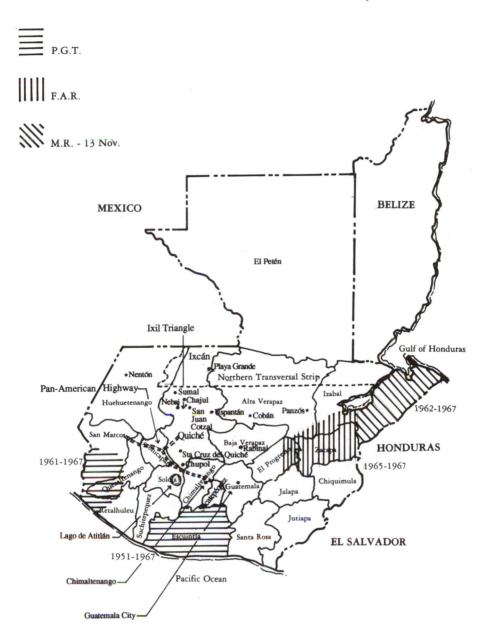

Figure 1. Geography of insurgency, 1961–67, from the Guatemalan Army's perspective.

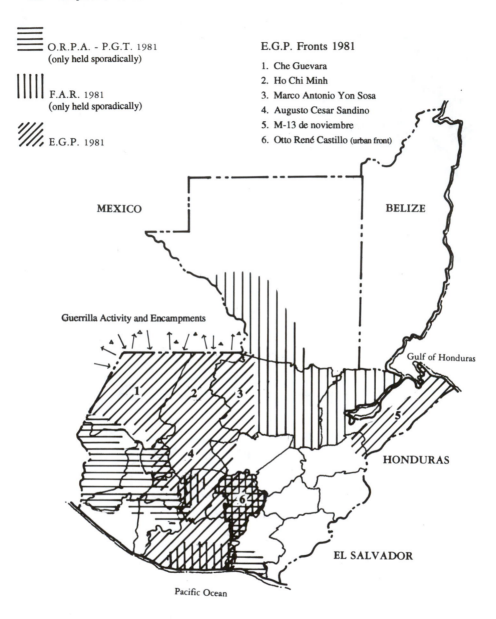

MEXICO

BELIZE

Guerrilla Activity and Encampments

Gulf of Honduras

HONDURAS

EL SALVADOR

Pacific Ocean

Figure 2. Geography of insurgency, November 1981, from the Guatemalan Army's perspective.

STAGE I October 1981 - March 1982

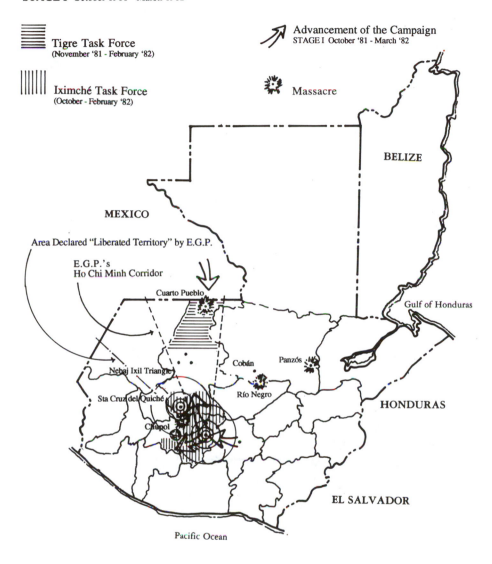

Figure 3. The October 1981–March 1982 Counterinsurgency Campaign of Lucas García.

STAGES II & III April 1982 - May 1983

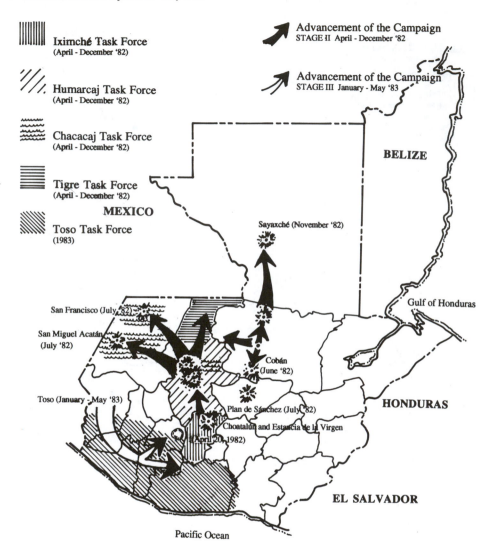

Figure 4. The 1982–1983 Counterinsurgency Campaign of Ríos Montt.

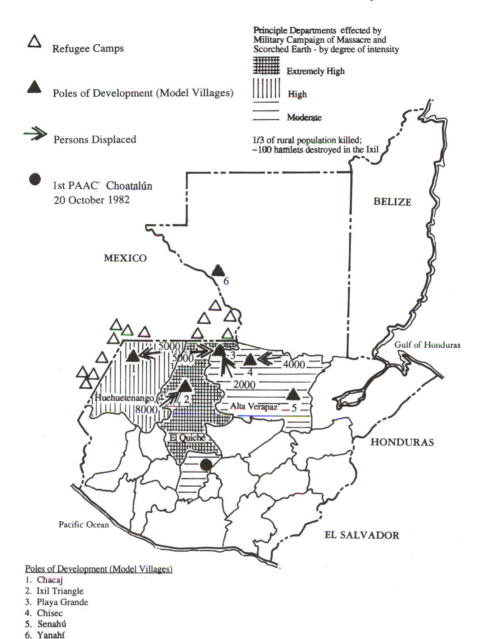

Figure 5. Army figures and locations of the displaced, refugee camps, and Poles of Development, 1982–84.

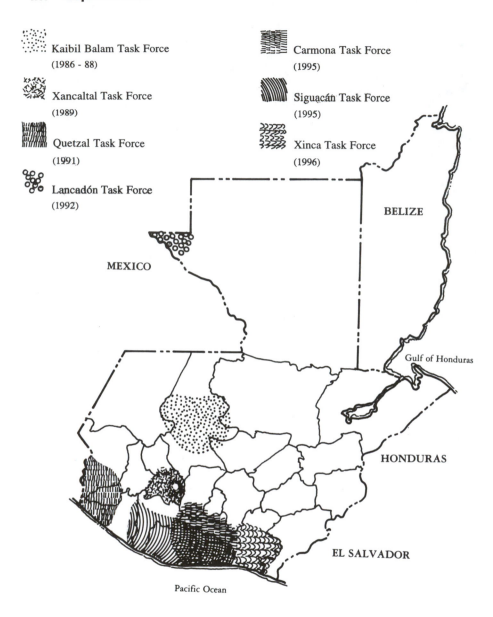

Kaibil Balam Task Force
(1986 - 88)

Xancaltal Task Force
(1989)

Quetzal Task Force
(1991)

Lancadón Task Force
(1992)

Carmona Task Force
(1995)

Siguacán Task Force
(1995)

Xinca Task Force
(1996)

BELIZE

MEXICO

Gulf of Honduras

HONDURAS

EL SALVADOR

Pacific Ocean

Figure 6. Army Task Forces for offensives between 1986 and 1996.

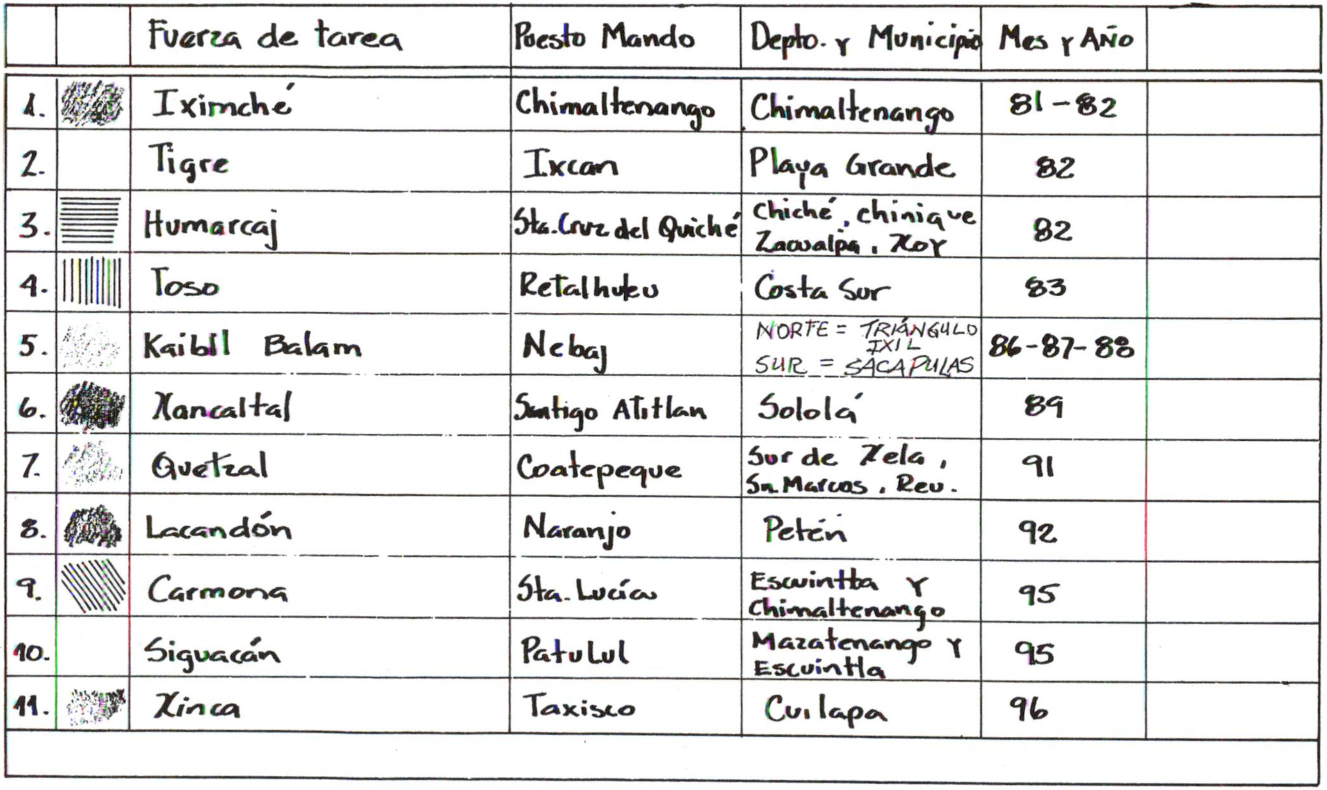

	Fuerza de tarea	Puesto Mando	Depto. y Municipio	Mes y Año	
1.	Iximché	Chimaltenango	Chimaltenango	81 – 82	
2.	Tigre	Ixcan	Playa Grande	82	
3.	Humarcaj	Sta. Cruz del Quiché	Chiché, chinique Zacualpa, Xoy	82	
4.	Ioso	Retalhuleu	Costa Sur	83	
5.	Kaibil Balam	Nebaj	NORTE = TRIÁNGULO IXIL SUR = SACAPULAS	86-87-88	
6.	Xancaltaj	Santiago Atitlan	Sololá	89	
7.	Quetzal	Coatepeque	Sur de Zela, Sn.Marcos, Reu.	91	
8.	Lacandón	Naranjo	Petén	92	
9.	Carmona	Sta. Lucía	Escuintla Y Chimaltenango	95	
10.	Siguacán	Patulul	Mazatenango Y Escuintla	95	
11.	Xinca	Taxisco	Cuilapa	96	

Figure 7. Army Task Force chart as drawn by officers, November 1997, an incomplete mapping of its task forces between 1981 and 1996.

Introduction

Our strategic goal has been to reverse Clausewitz's philosophy of war to state that in Guatemala, politics must be the continuation of war. But that does not mean that we are abandoning war; we are fighting it from a much broader horizon within a democratic framework. We may be renovating our methods of warfare but we are not abandoning them. . . . We are continuing our [counterinsurgency] operations [against] international subversion because the Constitution demands it.
— General Héctor Alejandro Gramajo Morales, Minister of Defense

Statecrafting through political violence can take a variety of forms. In Guatemala, a democracy was "born" out of the womb of a counterinsurgency campaign in 1982 that killed an estimated 75,000, razed a proclaimed 440 villages, and displaced over one million refugees. "To achieve democracy, the country first needed to be at peace" (General Gramajo, interview; 1995: 193). By tracing the military's ascendance to power by way of state violence through the eyes of Guatemalan officers themselves, this book serves as a window onto the internal workings and thinking of the most powerful, least researched, and least understood institution in Guatemala.

It has become axiomatic to say that the military has been a dominant actor in Guatemala for decades. Little, however, is known about its precise thinking and strategy. In this book, officers reveal in their own words their habits of mind regarding opposition, national security doctrine, democracy, human rights, and law. Interviews with fifty military officers (including six Defense Ministers and Heads of State), most of whom have played key roles in the recomposition of the State ideologically, militarily, and legally, reveal the thinking of the officer corps as a specific contemporary instance of an institution that has learned to play its electoral-constitutional cards internationally while continuing to practice its sui generis counterinsurgency campaign domestically. Interviews with a former president, twelve congressional deputies, and more than thirty Guatemalan lawyers, journalists, and social scientists between 1984 and 1996 further reveal the specific logics and actions internal to this uniquely civil-military hybrid of statecrafting. Interviews with the military provide us with a detailed account of organizational structures they have set up that allow them to undertake the dual objectives of repression and consolidation, of warmaking and statecrafting, and of strengthening internal repressive capacities (to protect the State's repressive coherence) while self-consciously speaking about autonomy from the oligarchy and lack of responsibility for human rights violations. The unevenness of a State's capacities to govern by political repression at particular moments and over time may be the most important structural feature of a State institution to understand: how it confronts domestic and international challenges, learns from its mistakes, and in response, continually reconstitutes its strategies and reshapes its objectives. Through these interviews, the shifting logics of power within the Guatemalan military High Command and, by extension, the State in its capacity to deploy violence and maintain itself institutionally, are graphically delineated.

But rather than naked military rule based on emergency measures, juntas, and coups—instruments of power that have lost their legitimacy internationally—it is the appropriation of the imagery of the rule of law, of the mechanisms and procedures of electoral democracy, that is perilous to the human rights of Guatemalans. The immersion of a security doctrine within a traditional constitutional order signifies the *structured* and violent denial of human rights and dissent. This book rests on the assumption that if a thoroughgoing and authentic democratization of a society in which the military holds political power requires a major erosion and disarming of that power, then an understanding of the reasoning of those who hold such power is also required.

New Directions of Research

Conceptions and paradigms of "the State" are often based on grand theorizing, received theoretical frameworks, and idealized notions of either omniscient or powerless states. More finely tuned, contextualized analyses that probe the actual organization, uses, and logics of state power by both civilian and military projects help us to better understand the cultural logics of power. Reassessments of democratizing processes in Latin American countries with strong militaries, too, demand a more finegrained and less unilinear interpretation of military institutional studies, along with a more nuanced typology. There is much discussion, for example, about whether a return to the barracks in fact signifies a demilitarization and a recivilization of institutions. Some analysts contend that a return to the barracks is never definitive and that the postmilitary state, whatever its degree of democratization, lives in the shadow of the barracks door. As Alain Rouquié remarks: "In the recent history of Latin America, noninstitutionalized military governments have generally agreed to withdraw from power only in the context of certain guarantees. They have endeavored to fix the subsequent rules of the game. What is more, they have not hesitated, when the situation permitted it, to demand a place for the military institutions in the constitutional structure of the emergent democracy, and thus a permanent right to supervise ensuing political decisions" (1986: 121). Given this fixing of the subsequent rules, as in the case of Guatemala, how does one measure the extent and levels to which demilitarization is accomplished? An approach that is not informed by a priori assumptions or "reassuring generalizations" (Rouquié 1986: 110) but more by empirical studies of the outcome of a "postmilitarism" is needed. Terry Karl, too, suggests that it is no longer adequate to examine regime transitions "writ large" from a general category of authoritarian rule to democracy. "Such broad-gauged efforts," she states, "must be complemented by the identification of different types of democracies from distinctive modes of regime transition." She goes on to identify "electoralism" as "the faith that merely holding elections will channel political action into peaceful contests among elites and accord public legitimacy to the winners in these contests," adding that democratic theorists see the need to shift their attention to the particular strategic calculations involved in moving from one type of political regime to another, with the absence of predictable "rules of the game" (1990: 15).

This book complements institutional approaches to the military (Rouquié 1984, 1986; Fitch and Fontana 1990), as well as the reassessment literature on redemocratization (Karl 1990; O'Donnell et al. 1986; Mainwaring et al. 1992). But it also stands in contrast to many of the political science studies of the military that have focused primarily on the strategies of state actors by using categories from the political scientist's "outside" frame of reference. Although contributing to an institutional understanding of the armed forces, these methods often fail to capture crucial subtleties, such as political actors' convictions (or lack thereof), or fail to pose questions that yield a better understanding of processes of transition and difficulties for democratic consolidation. Stepan, for one, argues for a "much closer critical inquiry" of military discourse (1988: 45). Ethnography is a methodology that tries to capture, by way of lengthy, systematic interviews, the perceptions, categories of thought, and systems of meanings of the informants themselves rather than imposing an outside frame of reference. While such a methodology, unique to anthropology, has normally focused on the meanings and terms employed by the popular classes and civil society—with many important ethnographic studies on the impact of violence on the indigenous population in Guatemala, for example (cf. Stoll 1993; Warren 1993; Wilson 1991; Smith 1990a, b), there are very few similar studies on military thinking. I have utilized the ethnographic method here to capture the *mentalité* of the military officer. These interviews thus serve as both a complement and a counterpoint to scholars working on the legacies of political violence on civil society.

Although national security has been viewed as a tailor-made rationalization for the overthrow of civilian governments (O'Donnell et al. 1986: 370), or as a justification for using exceptional law as a form of law enforcement,[1] little has been written about how this doctrine actually becomes an integral part of *traditional, democratic,* and *legal* structures and discourse, such that coups d'état may be needed only in the form of rumor, and states of emergency need no longer be declared for official lawlessness to be rife. While many have argued that there is a rise of democracy throughout the world, and fewer have declared an end to ideological history,[2] there is much less discussion of the role that national security establishments and intelligence communities — the military, the secret security apparatuses — have played in the past and should play in the future within such democracies. Are some democracies more bounded by national security priorities than others? Where do and should such boundaries lie? How much executive power does and should extend over national security and intelligence apparatuses and vice versa?[3] Finally, is a democracy that is thoroughly penetrated by national security concepts and practices indeed as "stable" and "nonviolent" as contended? Rather than see the issue as democracy *or* national security, then, we need to examine precisely how national security becomes, and remains, structured within various kinds of quasi- and fully democratic orders of governance.[4]

State violence, too, has tended to be characterized as "irrational in some sense" (O'Donnell et al. 1986: 356), with that sense rarely specified. A similarly ill-defined irrationality of massive human rights abuse is assumed by many within the human rights movement: military regimes are seen as not just irrational and evil, but crazy as well. Without a structural analysis of violence as intrinsic to the logic of counterinsurgency, a regime that violates human rights seems to occur simply because of uncontrollable, bloodlusting commanders or poorly disciplined peasant recruits who need to be given a code of conduct — a view that ironically serves as an essentialist rationale by militaries for why they cannot control their own forces. Rather than being irrational and out of control, many of these Latin American militaries are precisely in control and acting in their own best interests. Yet historically, neither a professionalization of a military nor an institutionalization of its activities appears to have stunted systematic repression; it has merely restructured violence to make it more selective.

Finally, the liberal, legalistic conception of human rights assumes that no matter how widespread and systematic the abuses, "they are still *deviations* from the legal norm and are not the norm itself" (Anderson and Anderson 1985: 95–96), with an emphasis upon individuals rather than State policy or collective interests. Thus, many human rights lawyers and U.S. State Department personnel tenure a view that repression is "merely" a consequence of corruption of power, or of a lack of "talented jurists," or of individual police-men who need to be reeducated in North American administration of jus-tice methods (e.g., AA for ICJ 1987: 13 and passim). Without an understand-ing of how deeply entrenched and inexorable human rights violations are to the justificatory narratives and mentalities of the Guatemalan military, no "positive will" to make human dignity and life of international concern, or humanitarian enunciations and denunciations by human rights activists, more often inspired by sympathy than realism, can counter such structural repression (Torres-Rivas 1986: 470, 478). Nor are they able to counter the disguising of human rights abuses, such as the Reagan administration's regard for improvement-on-the-basis-of-numbers or its outright embrace of repressive states, such as President Reagan's comment that President Ríos Montt had gotten a "bum rap" (Weekly Compilation of Presidential State-ments, 13 December 1982).

Not only must human rights and political science arguments regard-ing authoritarianism versus democracy be more specifically and carefully grounded within Central American social and political realities, but viola-tions and their "interpretation" (or spin) internationally must be under-stood as being frequently within the rational self-interest of the perpetrator. Until this *structured* inexorability within a juridical national security order is made explicit within human rights analyses, the cultural and political con-ceit remains as to the "backwardness" of Latin American legal structures, the "unprofessionalism" of the military institutions, and the congenital affinity of Latin Americans for "authoritarianism" — three characteristics claimed by such critics of human rights as Wiarda (1982), Kirkpatrick (1979, 1982), and Leiken and Rubin (1987). As a study of state security, this book seeks to expand the evaluation of human rights beyond the counting of bodies and the exercise of rule of law beyond electoral contests and talented jurists to one that examines the structural nature and logic of repression itself.

The Interviews

Interviews with officers were begun in January 1986 and continued through November 1996. Why is General Gramajo so prominent among the inter-viewees? One reason is that the opportunity presented itself: a series of fourteen taped interviews were conducted beginning in June 1990 (imme-diately after his retirement) and continued almost monthly until January 1991; two more were conducted over the telephone long distance in spring 1991, and two more in his office in Guatemala City in January 1994. Why is his vision of events from within the military so significant? His career spans counterinsurgency in Guatemala: between 1965 and 1970, he and other officers trained with U.S. Special Forces from the Eighth Special Forces

Group brought in from Panama. In 1965–66, he commanded an expanded special forces company in the counterinsurgency campaign in Zacapa, with a small cabal of officers he led who call themselves the Arrows (Las Flechas). (The insignia for Civil Affairs today is an arrow between two hands shaking, based on Las Flechas.) They were a tight-knit group, of mostly, if not all, intelligence officers, with many of the Flechas later holding high positions of leadership within the Guatemalan armed forces during the 1980s and 1990s. These include three ministers of defense, three chiefs of the National Defense Staff, and several generals and influential colonels: General Mario René Enríquez Morales (minister of defense), General José Luis Quilo Ayuso (chief of the National Defense staff), General Roberto Matta Gálvez (deputy chief of the National Defense staff and chief of the powerful Estado Mayor Presidencial, or Presidential General Staff), Generals Julio Balconi Turcios (defense minister), Colonel Mario Roberto García Catalán, and Colonel Mario Rolando Terraza-Pinot (Civil Affairs/Intelligence). The Defense Intelligence Agency's brief biography of Gramajo calls these officers "Gramajo's boys," and Gramajo recounts with pride how he arranged promotions for Las Flechas during his tenure as Defense Minister. In addition, in the counterinsurgency offensive of 1982, then Colonel Gramajo served as Deputy Chief of Staff, helping to plan and implement all combat operations, intelligence, and civil affairs in the western theater of the highlands, where most of the massacres occurred. He served as Toso theater commander in 1983; he refers to the Pacification campaign as his "baby." As an architect of the 30/70 percent formula of Beans and Bullets set out in the National Plan for Security and Development, he also served as the "liaison man" between the Beans and the Bullets. Finally, Gramajo's role in military intelligence (G-2) has been central; he claims to be the "granddaddy of G-2" in 1966–70, when the intelligence apparatus was first systematically assembled by the United States;[5] he also claims to have brought psychological warfare to Guatemala while he was part of the U.S. Special Forces training (1965–70). He served as the "de facto G-2 chief of intelligence" during the 1982–83 offensive, and as Mejía Víctores's "informal liaison man" with the CIA, U.S. Army and U.S. Embassy while Military Zone Commander of the General Headquarters in Guatemala City in 1983. Finally, throughout the 1980s, if not during his entire career, he worked with the CIA — "the best of all the institutions in the United States" — to establish a new intelligence methodology and build a new intelligence school in 1987, which initially placed a plaque at its entrance thanking both Gramajo and the CIA (the latter has since been removed).

In short, Gramajo's career is a window onto the political *mentalité* and cultural logics of institutionalist officers who, despite the U.S. State Department and U.S. Embassy's title of "moderates," maintain a counterinsurgency threat mentality against "Opponents of the State." In contrast, an interview in Chapter 9 with officers who staged at least four unsuccessful coup attempts in 1988 and 1989, who refer to themselves as the Officers of the Mountain, together with two of their translated *comunicados*, reveals their thinking.

Mainly higher-ranking and middle-ranking officers were interviewed to understand (1) what the 30/70 thinking of the institutionalist officers was and who crafted it; (2) whether it prevails after Gramajo's retirement (it is but sotto voce, as one colonel explained, with some changes); and, (3) how likely it is for the threat mentality of the military (with the distrust of and disdain for "opponents") and its close cousin, assumed impunity for human rights violations, to be transformed into positive attitudes and allegiance to participatory democracy? In short, how inexorably antidemocratic are the Guatemalan armed forces, and what hope is there for a genuine guarantee of human rights protections in the near future?

Interviews by the author are indicated as (interview); interviews by others are so cited. A list of officers and civilians interviewed is to be found in Appendix 1.

A Note on the Military

Although those involved in the *proyecto* include navy and air force officers, as well as civilians, the Guatemalan Army is by far the most prominent and most powerful of the three branches of the armed forces, with the air force and navy considered integral parts of it. Thus, the terms "army" and "military" are used interchangeably throughout the book to faithfully represent officers' use of the terms in interviews. "Military" most often is used when referring to the broad reach of the armed forces, including civil-military relations. But, given the powerful reach of army intelligence, "army" also serves to represent the armed forces. In 1983, the navy and air force each had a few hundred men and officers, whereas the army had about 30,000. As of 1996, the total figure stood at 38,000, with 2,100 officers, 1000 Kaibils/Special Forces, about 500 civilians (doctors, dentists, etc.), and innumerable technical *especialistas*; the rest are troops. Of the officers, there were 10 to 14 generals, 60 colonels, 160 lieutenant colonels, and 190 majors. With the Peace Accords, in which the army is expected to reduce its forces by one-third by December 1997, the army has attempted to inflate this total figure to 50,000 by adding personnel, military school alumni, and civilians who work for the army only a few days a year.

Organization of the Book

The book has been organized episodically to help the reader understand the intellectual evolutions and strategic transitions of the Guatemalan military that have occurred on several levels. From a backdrop of chronology beginning with the 1944 revolution and moving into the 1970s, these transitions include the shifts from a military that served for purposes of internal and external defense to one that becomes the locus of state power — "running the State," as one intelligence officer boasts (interview); from a counterinsurgency strategy of occupation in the 1970s to one in the 1980s of integration with Civil Affairs and "minimum force"; a rejection of National Security Doctrine for a nationalistic Thesis of National Stability, as well as a shift away from outright careerism dependent upon rightwing elites toward a more autonomous professionalism called "fundamentalism."

Chapter 1 begins with a brief history of the Guatemalan military's rise to power, outlining the crises that incrementally converted the armed forces into the site of State power by the 1980s. Chapter 2 reconstructs the pacification campaign of 1982–84 and provides an anatomy of counterinsurgency. Chapter 3 continues the narrative of the counterinsurgency by examining the restructuring of indigenous life with model villages, Inter-institutional coordinators, and Poles of Development. Chapter 4 delineates the looting of the guerrilla Fuerzas Irregulares Locales network by the military to establish Civil Patrols and companies of Indian soldiers to force the indigenous community to "choose between two armies." Chapter 5 discusses the ideological underpinnings of Civil Affairs with its utilization of psychological warfare and social intelligence and its creation of the Sanctioned Mayan. The military's perception of being at once within and outside the law, as outlined in Chapter 6, allows us to see how it relied upon and looted preexisting institutions (Congress and the Supreme Court) for its project. Chapter 7 details the intelligence apparatus and the role of the CIA in Guatemala. The extent of the collaboration between the Christian Democratic President Cerezo and the Defense Minister Gramajo is revealed in Chapter 8, to the point of seriously militarizing, undermining, and making complicitous the presidency, as per the military's strategy. Chapter 9 deals with the contradictions of the politico-military project articulated as coup attempts by Oficiales de la Montaña — middle-ranking officers and *latifundista* (wealthy landowners) elements in 1988 and by an internal coup in 1989. Finally, Chapter 10 discusses the sui generis Thesis of National Stability with its Opponents of the State schema. As the military's expansive and entrenched threat mentality toward dissent and opposition into the remote future is revealed, it becomes clear that repression is viewed by officers as an intrinsic and inevitable part of the "20- to 25-year transition" to democracy.

Chapter 1
A Brief History of the Guatemalan Military's Rise to Power

> From this day forward the Guatemalan army will be an institution of impeccable professionalism. Led by men who have proven their patriotism and their love of the Guatemalan people, it will be the guardian of our domestic peace, and it will join in the great cultural awakening of our country.
>
> — President Arévalo's 1944 inaugural address

Historically, specific threats have caused the Guatemalan military to defend itself increasingly as a corporate entity. These threats include attempts to establish a civilian militia, a failed coup attempt by officers, some of whom proceeded to establish a guerrilla movement, and the near success of that guerrilla insurgency some twenty years later. With each crisis, the military's role in public affairs "has changed steadily, and the change has been in one direction. While it has broadened its position in society at large, it has consistently consolidated its mechanisms and bases of control" (Adams 1970: 277).

In a series of crises, beginning in 1944, the Guatemalan military learned to replace the personalistic caudillo model with the military as an institution, and to reformulate its identification as an institution within the State, until it gained the power to recast the State in the military's own image, implanting counterinsurgency into the very constitutional, administrative, and juridical foundations of the State. In short, each threat came to represent an opportunity for the military to consolidate as an institution and to expand its power.

Examining the history of this period illustrates the incremental growth of the military's politico-legal participation and institutional ascendancy, and its claim of a constitutional mandate to protect the nation by waging war and increasing its autonomy—at the expense over time of its political effectiveness. Finally, in 1982, understanding that it could never finally win a war against insurgents, the military learned to conduct political wars in order to maintain its historical regnancy: "For the last 17 years, the Army has been involved in government, and not in the part that corresponds to the State. Then we participated in matters of State security, staging military actions against the subversion. Now we participate within the State as a normal thing" stated Gramajo 1987 (Ejército, Foro nacional 1987b: 126).

In pre-1944 Guatemala, as in the rest of Central America, the military was a ragtag army used as an instrument by its dictator to "divide and conquer": General Jorge Ubico (1931–44) was to be the last military strongman whose power was personalistic. In 1944, after fourteen years of Ubico's ruthlessness, urban workers, middle-class students and teachers, the landed elite, and the officer corps joined temporarily to demand first Ubico's resignation and then that of General Federico Ponce, the self-appointed provisional president from a defunct three-general junta. Juan José Arévalo, the country's first democratically elected president, was a philosophy professor. Retired Colonel-lawyer Diéguez Pilón, who served in the Chief of Staff's office under Arévalo, remembers the time fondly:

The opportunity arose after the 20 October 1944 revolution. We officers were constantly with students: they came to the Presidential Palace, they opened the doors to the military barracks, they spoke with the ministers and with military officers. We officers began to gain new knowledge about civilian life as well as about ourselves. (interview)

Ironically, the political consolidation of the Guatemalan military first began during this period, known as the country's "ten years of spring," between 1944 and 1954, under Arévalo and the more revolutionary administration of his successor, Jacobo Arbenz, himself a military academy graduate and army captain. Under President Arbenz's regime, officers—who had first recognized their ability to make national political decisions by joining with civilians in the 1944 Revolution—held public administration and ministerial posts, including eight military congressional deputies. The institutionalization of military autonomy can also be traced to this period: the 1945 Constitution converted the army into an indispensable political and administrative institution, establishing a Superior Council of National Defense (Consejo Superior de Defensa Nacional). Inauspiciously, this formally separated the army from the executive and gave it autonomy in both its command and its mission.

The military has its roots in the very beginning of the modern Guatemalan state, the Revolution of 1871, when Generals Miguel García Granados and Justo Rufino Barrios presided over the development of the new nation and its armed forces. One of their reforms was to create a military academy in 1873, the Escuela Politécnica. The academy has played an important part in both Guatemalan politics and the development of its military leaders ever since, but the academy did not emphasize equipping officer candidates for participation in national political life until after 1944 (Adams 1970: 254). The post-1944 army, particularly under the direction of Escuela Politécnica graduate Arbenz, was proud of its efficiency and learned to consolidate itself into more of a professional institution that identified itself with the nation.[1]

Among the first items of the 1944 revolutionary legislation was Decree 17, which opened the doors for markedly increased political intervention in national affairs by the military—which even took the name the Army of the October Revolution. This decree laid the legal foundation for the autonomy of the military, protecting it from "the whims of government." Decree 17 was sanctioned by Article 156 of the 1945 Constitution, which created the Consejo Superior de Defensa Nacional as a "consulting organization charged with resolving the issues related to the functioning of the army and will act as the Superior Tribunal of the army. . . . to judge and know matters convocated by the President, Defense Minister or Chief of the Armed Forces."[2] The twenty-one member Council consisted of ten permanent members (seven chiefs of military zones, the Minister of Defense, Chief of the Air Force, and Chief of the Army) and eleven officers elected every three years by all active duty officers, headed by the Chief of the Armed Forces.

Major Francisco Arana, a member of the 1944 junta, was responsible for the creation of this new position, more powerful than that of Defense Minister. He demanded that the new constitution guarantee his dominant position in the army in exchange for allowing the duly elected Arévalo to take office (1988 interview with Cruz Salazar; Gleijeses 1991: 53). As head of the all-military Council, the Chief of the Armed Forces began his six-year tenure at the same time as the new President, effectively creating a parallel president elected by all military commanders and high-ranking officers: "patently absurd in an army of a few thousand men" (Gleijeses 1991: 53). As it was the Army's task "to watch over the democratic process and the laws" (Cruz Salazar 1970: 82), constitutional debates would rage in the Consejo as to whether the executive had violated the Constitution, which sometimes led to secret meetings with President Arévalo. "At one discussion," Cruz Salazar recounts, "one officer accused Arévalo of violating the constitution, explaining that since it had outlawed exile, how would he explain the 3000 exiles?" (1988 interview). The Consejo thus, paradoxically, both served authoritarian interests of the army to consolidate its position and at the same time worked to democratize ranks, as a "species of collegial body within the army composed of elected representatives" (Beltranena 1992: 103).

This new liberal legal-political culture within the military helped initiate a new kind of political thinking among career officers, as one officer describes:

Subordination and hierarchy were respected within the army. But in these meetings during the revolution, we needed to create a new class of officers for the Chief of Staff and presidential service who could take the initiative, make decisions on their own. We believed that an officer of the Chief of Staff must be exercising his disquiet, his thinking, his intelligence so that at any given moment he could act. This was a central part of our discussions as officers at the time to make the army more professional. (Diéguez Pilón, interview)[3]

But, as we shall see, this "ten years of spring" had a profound effect on cadets and younger officers who found themselves for the first time "exercising their disquiet" in a new society where liberal ideas and ideals were taken seriously.

For the army's ascendancy, moreover, "the intervention of the *Consejo* into such complex, varied and delicate matters was not a matter of mere meddling," wrote Cruz Salazar. "On the contrary, *its intervention into government matters was legislated*," opening the gates for arbitrary political actions and, in turn, legally blocking the government's meddling with the military's institutionality after the 1954 coup (1970: 83, emphasis added).

To further ensure the military's autonomy and political power, the General Staff of the Armed Forces (Jefatura de las Fuerzas Armadas) was established in 1945. Article 152 of the 1945 Constitution indicates its political importance: only Congress could remove the Chief of the General Staff. Article 157 states that "military nominations [for the Consejo] will be made by the Chief of Staff through the Defense Minister." In short, it was "an impenetrable circle" in which nominations rested "on the only organism that has the faculty to object to such nominations. It is pure romanticism to believe Congress has any say, given that the majority of the permanent representatives owe their position to the Chief of the General Staff" (Cruz Salazar 1970: 83). Such a consolidation of military and political power in the hands of the army made it all but impossible for Congress to oppose a demotion of the Chief of Staff, or to encroach in any way on the army's political territory.

Under the 1945 constitution, a military officer could be elected president but only if he had left active duty at least six months before election day. Arana ignored this provision and ran his campaign, using government funds while still in office. Had he stepped down, his successor would have been selected by the Guatemalan Congress from a list of three names submitted by the Consejo. Gleijeses writes of the "quiet tug of war" waged in 1949 within the Consejo between *aranista* officers, who wanted to ensure that commanders of the Military Zones and unit commanders controlled the balloting, and *arbencista* officers, who wanted to ensure a secret vote among the more than seven hundred active-duty officers at the time (1991: 61).

On 18 July 1949, Chief of Staff Arana, who had been plotting a coup, was assassinated by *arbencistas*. Nevertheless, the General Staff of the Armed Forces remained intact as an institutional force and in direct competition for political power with the civilian president (Cruz Salazar 1970: 84). Colonel Carlos Paz Tejada, who replaced Arana as Chief of Staff, explains in an interview forty years later:

In practice, the Consejo was deliberative, a species of assembly where the military made politics — the politics of the Army. Such a reality contradicted the very same constitution which established that the Army had to be apolitical, obedient, and nondeliberative.[4]

Thus, despite the military's repeated insistence over the years on being "essentially apolitical and nondeliberative," the constitutional article that created the Consejo as a "consulting organization to resolve matters related to the functioning of the army" is quite straightforward: in practice, "functioning of the army" means the fulfillment of the Constitution, which in turn (according to article 154) means defending "the rights and freedom of the nation," "guaranteeing democracy," and defending "laws and social and political institutions of the country." These provisions (which also appear in the 1985 Constitution), are so abstract, so nonelaborated as to allow arbitrary and even contradictory application.

Furthermore, because the General Staff was added to the 1945 Constitution post hoc, it came to be seen as autonomous from and effectively *above* civilian law. Later, we will see how this vision of being both within and above the law is still very much a part of the military's worldview and how the project begun in 1982 is a direct consequence of such thinking.

Presidents Arévalo and Arbenz developed a strong modus vivendi with the six-thousand-man army to assure its loyalty to the revolution: they increased salaries, created well-paid governorship positions throughout the country for colonels (the highest rank at the time), and provided generous scholarships abroad at least until early 1954. Arbenz — whom many officers saw as *their* president — somehow convinced his ultraconservative officers to accept the most sweeping agrarian reform in the history of Central America (1952 Decree 900): between January 1953 and June 1954, over half a million hectares of land were expropriated and distributed to roughly 100,000 peasant families. These benefits, together with the agrarian reform, and a general liberalization of Guatemalan society at the time, established a military career as an option for the children of middle-class and lower-middle-class families. This, in turn, led to a diverse student body of cadets, some of whom, growing up in the midst of this social democratic–communist experiment, would later emerge as the vanguard of the idealism of social justice and collective economic rights of the *revolución de octubre* in the guise of future guerrilla leaders (Beltranena 1992: 103).

However, in 1954 Arbenz antagonized the older and more traditional officers (and wealthy landowners) with his attempt to create a civilian militia to protect this agrarian reform process. Fully aware of the army's increasing uneasiness with the communist flavor of his government and fearful of a

U.S. invasion, Arbenz secretly contracted for a shipment of weapons from Czechoslovakia. This shipment was discovered, fraying the already tenuous bond between the President and his army (Adams 1970: 266).

In June 1954, a motley group of 150 émigrés and mercenaries, the self-styled *liberacionista* army, under the nominal control of the fugitive colonel Castillo Armas, aided and equipped by the CIA, invaded Guatemala (cf. Schlesinger and Kinzer 1983; Immerman 1982). Fearful that resistance would bring repercussions from the United States, the army high command acquiesced, forcing Arbenz to resign and go into exile. In response, cadets and younger officers at the Escuela Politécnica, demanding an "end to the insults," fired upon the *liberacionistas*, only to surrender the following day in exchange for a guarantee that they would not be punished. Jeered by both the victors and the defeated in a military parade on 1 August 1954, officers vowed never again to be humiliated: on 2 August a coup was attempted and failed. This was followed by another in 1957, in which two colonels died[5] and yet another in July 1960 that was led by young Lieutenant Guillermo Lavagnino, who was the "insurrection precursor" to Lieutenant Yon Sosa. These uprisings prompt Beltranena to posit that if the army had indeed decided to oppose it, the invasion would not have been possible (1992: 105). Gleijeses, in contrast, argues that "opportunism proved stronger than honor; fear of Washington more powerful than national pride" (1991: 360).

In the months that followed, thousands of civilians were arrested, tortured, and killed, while many of the officers who had supported Arbenz were demoted, retired, or exiled. The agrarian reform was "not only stopped but positively reversed": by the end of 1956, only 0.4 percent of those supposed to benefit from the reform still retained their lands, leaving many peasants with only memories of their earlier gains (Wickham-Crowley 1992: 121).[6]

The army that arose after the U.S.-financed invasion of 1954 was fiercely anticommunist and bound to the Cold War fears of both Guatemala's upper class and Big Brother to the north. U.S. officers once again directed the Escuela Politécnica as they had before 1944. (Under Ubico, U.S. military involvement in training Guatemalan officers had reached such a level that five directors of the Escuela had been U.S. army officers.)

Lacking a political constituency and dependent upon only elements in the army to put down both civilian and military protests against the *liberacionistas*, Castillo Armas and his counterrevolutionary forces dissolved both the Consejo and Jefatura in the 1954 coup. Nonetheless, the army's legal autonomy was ensured in the 1956 constitution, and doubly guaranteed in the Army's Constitutive Law of 1956 (Ley Constitutiva del Ejército). As Cruz Salazar states:

> The legality planned in the 1956 Constitution was imitated in the 1956 Constitutive Law of the Army, with the result that the 1965 Constitution merely refers the

reader to this [same] Constitutive Law. *This signifies that the Constitution itself neither determines nor regulates anything about the Army.* Only the Constitutive Law can change the Army's status, which means that the army is completely autonomous [from the Constitution].[7] (1970: 96; his emphasis)

In short, the paradoxical legacy of the 1944 liberal revolution was, on the one hand, to provide a firm constitutional basis for the army's political ascendancy and, on the other, to produce an officer-led guerrilla insurgency as the vanguard of social and economic justice. The army also maintained the political gains garnered in 1944, with more officers in public administration posts after 1954.

The years after the 1956 Constitution were tumultuous ones, with the army openly intervening in an electoral contest for the first time in 1958, effectively impeding the voting for candidates other than General Miguel Ydígoras Fuentes. On 13 November 1960, some 120 left-leaning junior officers attempted a coup in the name of "social justice, a just distribution of national wealth" and against *los gringos imperialistas* (see Appendix 2).[8] The layers of motivation for this coup attempt help us to understand not only the significance of the postrevolutionary period for the army, but the resultant thirty-six years of armed conflict: there was hatred, some officers argue, between the younger officers and the older officers because of the High Command's betrayal of Arbenz, because of the rampant corruption within the upper ranks of the army, because of older officers' reluctance to embrace the new irregular warfare combat training younger officers were first receiving in the United States in 1959 (later to be taught at the Escuela Politécnica as a Tactic IV course, Guerrillas y Contra-guerrillas in 1961), and because of the "efficient clandestine activity of the Asociación del Niño Dios" made up of officers who opposed the presence of the *antifidelista* Brigade 2506 on Guatemalan soil (Ejército n.d.: 23). President Miguel Ydígoras Fuentes permitted the CIA's secret contracting of Guatemalan officers at high salaries to train Cuban troops at the Campo Trax, located on the estate, Finca Helvetia de Retalhuleu, for the ill-fated Bay of Pigs invasion. Navy Captain Cifuentes argues that this difference in salary was far more important to the rebel officers than the presence of a powerful army on national territory, especially when salaries had not been paid for two months (1993: 34). The coup was suppressed (ironically, with bomber planes used to train Cuban pilots at the *finca*), and sixty or so, or roughly 21 percent of all officers at the time, were court-martialed (Gramajo, interview). But several army officers escaped capture, among them 2d Lieutenant Luis Augusto Turcios Lima and Lieutenant Marco Antonio Yon Sosa, both of whom had recently returned from counterinsurgency training at Fort Glick in the Panama Canal Zone and Fort Benning, Georgia, respectively. In August 1961, Yon Sosa announced the formation of the MR-13 guerrilla movement (Movimiento Revolucionario 13 de noviembre) (see

Appendix 2), later integrated (in December 1962) with FAR (Fuerzas Armadas Rebeldes), the military wing of the Guatemalan Labor (Communist) Party or PGT, and with students of the Frente Revolucionario 12 de abril. All three *frentes* of MR13Nov-FAR-PGT combatants, never numbering more than five hundred, were directed by these former officers trained by the U.S. military in special forces mountain and jungle warfare antiguerrilla operations (see Figure 1). The fleeing rebels were openly welcomed by ladino peasants in the eastern departments of Izabal and Zacapa, where Guatemalan communists had organized locals in the banana region. But, by the end of 1966, they had been practically eliminated, while others (including the son of Nobel Prize laureate, Miguel Angel Asturias) were released from prison and exiled. Turcios Lima, who died in 1967, had begun to forge links with Kekchí Indians, while the other disaffected army officers, for their part, like the 1944–54 reformers, believed in Indian "cultural backwardness" and thus did not gain strong popular support anywhere (Dunckerley 1988: 508, 454).

During the first few years of insurgency, guerrilla leaders maintained close contacts with their old junior-officer cohorts, even appearing in the capital at parties for officers of the same *promoción* (graduating class) in the Escuela Politécnica (Adams 1970: 258).[9] General Gramajo was of the same *promoción*, and recalls being pulled into a car on Sixth Avenue in Guatemala City in 1962 to find himself face-to-face with Luis Turcios Lima and other rebel officers. They took him to an all-night restaurant, where they traded stories about the old days but shied clear of politics. Gramajo had worked with Yon Sosa on special warfare tactics at the Santa Cruz del Quiché military base: "They were my fellow officers, not criminals."[10] The rebel officers were indulged even to the point of being sold weapons by soldiers in order to force the downfall of the hated Ydígoras regime. Bombs were exploded in the city and the secret police chief, Ranulfo González (alias Siete Litros), was assassinated by MR-13.

This willingness to fraternize with the enemy ended abruptly in May 1965, when the guerrillas (who had been arming the peasantry) ambushed seventeen soldiers and a lieutenant, killing them all. For Gramajo, this event "forced us to decide" about the seriousness of the threat. "After that, we who had friends in the guerrilla movement decided that the deaths were such a big thing that we had to take sides" (interview).

Declaring a "Cuba-inspired threat," the government launched a massive counterinsurgency program that modernized military weaponry and established a vast intelligence network that included the use of military *comisionados*, a mobile military police, paramilitary death squads, and sophisticated torture techniques (McClintock 1985: 64). With training and guidance from the U.S. Army Eighth Special Forces Group, brought in from Panama, Colonel Carlos Arana Osorio (Escuela Politécnica director after the 1954 coup) was placed in charge of this brutal campaign between 1966 and 1967 in which thousands of poor rural *ladinos* (mestizos), along with most of the guerrilla leadership, succumbed (cf. Wickham-Crowley 1992: 67, 80, and 83). Remnants of FAR were reincarnated as the new Guerrilla Army of the Poor, Ejército Guerrillero del Pueblo (EGP), which was to reenter the Ixcán from Mexico in 1972.

The Military's Experiments at Governing, 1963–1982

In the years after the failed 1960 coup, the army experimented with state governance. In 1961, the military's influence in national affairs was so strong that President-General Ydígoras reorganized his cabinet so that the only civilian member was the Minister of Foreign Relations. On 25 November 1962, there was an uprising by Air Force officers; three hundred were taken prisoner by Ydígoras's forces. Then on 30 March 1963, Ydígoras's Defense Minister, Colonel Enrique Peralta Azurdia, and the heads of military bases staged a coup, issuing a statement that it was

impossible to resolve [the country's] grave problems within the constitutional framework, since the communists take advantage of the broad freedoms which the present constitution concedes; they have infiltrated the government and the different political parties, creating splits in the democratic forces at the same time as they unite their own resources, with the logical result that they are empowered by the government within an apparent legality, in order to implant a communist regime as they have in other countries (Cruz Salazar 1970: 95)

This moved the army into a decisive political position *in the name of the armed forces*, resulting in a state of siege, suspension of all rights (including habeas corpus), as well as assassinations, kidnappings, and "the calvary of terror" (96); the army moved from being a determinant presence within the civilian state structure to assuming control of the State itself. The military began to function as a political force, "giving orders" and growing "accustomed to making political decisions within a special framework directed by the concept of national security. . . . From this, no government could escape, especially the civilian ones" (Cruz Salazar, 1986 interview).

The regime of Colonel Peralta Azurdia (1963–66) established a political strategy that effectively prevented opposition reformist parties from participating in politics for the next fifteen years by waging "counter-terror" campaigns through clandestine groups "designed to prevent any alteration — however minor — of the social and economic structure of the country" (Handy 1984: 394). The Institutional Democratic Party (PID) was established at this time, dominated by the military. In 1970, Colonel Carlos Arana Osorio reclaimed the presidency for the PID in the *electoral folklórico* of this period from civilian Julio César Méndez Montenegro (who had had to sign an agreement "to give the military a free hand in counterinsurgency and autonomy in. . . . [the] selection of the defense minister, chief of staff, budgets, etc." before taking office) (Trudeau 1989: 94). A political scheme (described by officers in interviews as "elected-but-appointed," *electos pero mandados*) was firmly established, with "tacit understandings among the military institution, the private sector and the political parties to create a facade of democratic politics, marked by periodic elections" (González, quoted in Rosenthal 1992: 32).

The counterinsurgency campaigns of the 1970s permitted the military to deepen its control over state and civilian institutions, and to strengthen and make permanent its presence in the western highlands, where it had traditionally been weak or absent. A new wave of repression began to be used selectively in 1975 under President-General Kjell Eugenio Laugerud García (1974–78), after guerrillas publicly executed an unpopular landowner, the "Tiger of the Ixcán" (cf. Payeras 1983), but it had little success in stemming either guerrilla activity or popular organizing; hence, repression became increasingly blind, random, and massive under President-General Romeo Lucas García (1978–82) — which, in turn, swelled the ranks of the guerrillas. The regime did not "distinguish its targeting of state authorities, the army's hierarchy, the political leaders [or], an entrenched bureaucracy" (Gramajo, 1991b: 6). Even military families were not exempt from the violence, as Gramajo explains: "There was such fear of [Interior Minister] Donaldo Alvarez Ruíz and [police chief] Colonel Germán Chupina Barahona who together had control over all the army and police forces" (interview).[11] "It's everyone for himself," Alvarez stated in 1979 (Black et al. 1984: 41).

This pattern of explicitly military elections and governance eviscerated political institutions and political life through the 1970s and into the 1980s. But during the Lucas García regime, repression by state-controlled death squads and counterinsurgency patrols rapidly began to have a negative effect on the military as an institution as well. Arbitrary slaughter — paramilitary activity, summary executions, kidnappings, and forced disappearances, leaving eight hundred bodies a month on the streets — was becoming increasingly counterproductive. The military began to realize that strictly military solutions and international denunciations would lead them into "a Salvador-type civil war," as one colonel of the 1982 junta later admitted. "The fact is, we were without power during this period and deteriorating rapidly internationally" (Colonel Gordillo, interview). Gramajo describes the situation in 1980: "Our country was on the verge of collapse — a polarized, intolerant society with decadent political institutions, an economy debilitated by capital flight, and isolated internationally."[12] As Fernando Andrade Díaz-Durán, who would be Foreign Minister in 1983–86, later said in a speech, "Guatemala had fallen into an abyss of very deep crisis . . . and needed political re-ordering" (1988: 128–29). By early 1982, allegations of massive corruption against a group of civilians and officers whom Lucas García treated as favorites,[13] increasing fatalities among soldiers and junior officers, a growing guerrilla threat, and international isolation because of a deplorable human rights record produced a crisis within the military that threatened its hierarchical structure of command and, ultimately, its political dominance (Keefe 1984: 134).

As George Black describes the situation, a "clique of high-ranking officers functioned as a central committee in all but name, carving huge fortunes . . . out of the opportunities almost unlimited power provided them." For example, they took charge of some forty-three semiautonomous state institutions, created their own Department of Radio and Television (purchasing TV Channel 5), and created a financial network that today still includes a publishing house, credit institutions, cement works, parking garages, the Institute for Military Social Security, and the Army Bank—"a financial monster with active capital of $119.2 million in 1981" (1989: 509–12). By the 1980s, this economic institutionalization of the army had become so fused with the state that members of military intelligence "sometimes receive their paychecks from the government agencies responsible for electric power or tourism."[14] (By the mid-1990s, businesses like import-export and fish farming as well as sweatshops had been added to the list of lucrative military ventures.) Some army officers, such as General Ricardo Peralta Méndez, 1970–75 director of the Center for Military Studies, and General Efraín Ríos Montt, also a former director of CEM, warned of the imminent collapse of the armed forces in 1981: "There are generals who aspire to sit in two chairs: that of a general and that of a businessman" (Soto, quoted in Beltranena 1992: 119–20). An appraisal of the national situation by the High Command and General Staff in 1980, presented unofficially to President Lucas, read: "To convince the citizen to vote, it is necessary to guarantee him that his will, articulated in ballot form, is a powerful democratic tool that will be respected. This would be much easier if a military officer did not participate as a presidential candidate in the next election" (Gramajo 1991a: 7; see Appendix 2).[15] Acting on this advice, Lucas García offered the 1982 presidential candidacy to several loyal "partyless" civilian national figures, but they all turned him down.[16] Lucas's hesitation opened the floodgates of internal army intrigue and the reactionary PID and Partido Revolucionario (Revolutionary Party) leaders offered him one candidate: his own Defense Minister, General Angel Aníbal Guevara. His campaign was based on the illusion that the army was winning the war. The president's brother "Chief of Staff Benedicto Lucas García would come into a conflict zone by helicopter, first flying over to check that there was no fighting [going on] and in full combat dress he'd be interviewed by the press as a publicity stunt," one officer remembered bitterly; in contrast, loyal *luquista* officers remember the general as being extremely concerned for "his" troops (interviews). But what many officers feared was that the insurgents, working for a final insurrection, were asking the rural population to vote for Guevara (Gramajo 1991a: 7 and 8). When Guevara was declared the winner in the 7 March 1982 elections, the three opposing candidates staged a public protest of electoral fraud; all three were beaten and thrown in jail (together with international and national journalists).

So it was in 1982 — against the turbulence that followed Guevara's fraudulent victory, against international isolation because of highly repressive actions that had violated the Carter administration's human-rights-centered policy, against "a credit scandal in the midst of an acute shortage of foreign currency, a plunge of the GNP and capital flight, high unemployment, a weakened hierarchical structure of army command, a surprisingly effective campaign by insurgents in organizing the indigenous population in the central and western Highlands" (Gramajo 1991a: 5–6), and against a rapidly growing popular movement that had gained the sympathy of many working and unemployed poor urban dwellers — that military officers began to conspire with traditional allies from the extreme right, the landed and business elite, to depose the government.

One week before the 1982 coup, Colonel Manuel Antonio Callejas y Callejas, the "efficient head of military intelligence," detected the coup preparations and provided President Lucas García and the High Command with details of the conspiracy. With his Presidential Chief of Staff, Colonel Héctor Montalván Batres, telling him the contrary, the president labeled this information as "exaggeration" and his brother, chief of the Army General Staff, General Benedicto Lucas, accused Callejas of "irrational thinking due to stress" (Gramajo 1991a: 9; interview). The new Defense Minister General Luis René Mendoza Paloma, not a member of the Lucas family, remained mute, but later told Callejas that the young officers "without a colonel couldn't pull it off" (intelligence source, 1990 interview). When the time came, the preparations were so strong and the discontent so high that Lucas was incapable of reacting violently and forced to resign.

On 23 March 1982, at least two, if not three, coup plots were afoot. One account details how two lieutenants, twenty and twenty-one years old, had approached Captain Rodolfo Muñoz Pilona, G-2 officer of the Mariscal Zavala Brigade in Guatemala City, the day the presidential candidates were physically beaten by *luquista* forces. Within a week, most of the lieutenants and second lieutenants at the Grupo Táctico of La Aurora air base, all the lieutenants at the military school Adolfo Hall, and a captain at the Guardia de Honor (Honor Guard) were behind the coup; General Ríos Montt agreed to participate. Also, National Liberation Movement (MLN) party leader, Mario Sandoval Alarcón, together with the MLN Vice Presidential candidate Leonel Sisniega Otero (who spoke on the radio during the coup just as he had for Radio Liberación in 1954), and journalist Danilo Roca, were actively organizing against Lucas. Captain Muñoz, with the backing of senior and retired air force officers, moved in tanks to surround the National Palace; after hours of negotiations Lucas agreed to step down as long as his successor was a general. General Ríos Montt[17] was asked to head a military junta that initially consisted of the young officers who had engineered the coup: Colonel Victor Manuel Argueta Villalta, Lieutenant Colonel Mario René Enríquez, Maj. Angel Arturo Sánchez Gudiel, and Captain Muñoz. Several hours later, the second "junta" included Ríos Montt, General Horacio Maldonado Schaad (a close friend of President Lucas and Honor Guard Commander), and Colonel Luis Gordillo Martínez (another close friend of President Lucas and Commander of the Cuartel General). Gordillo served as the liaison officer between the army hardliners and the ultraconservative *latifundistas*. Air Force Captain Mario Rivas García Ríos and Second Lieutenant Héctor Mauricio López Bonilla were added to the original four "*golpistas*" in the Young Officers Advisory Group (Grupo Asesor), known derisively by more senior officers as "La Juntita" or the "Little Junta." Ríos Montt has stated, "I was called to put everything in order" (interview).[18] Sereseres argues that the young officers, demoralized by the prospect of more corruption and violence, "acted in the name of their institution and the nation apart (though possibly with encouragement) from any political party or civilian faction" (1982).

Another account offered by Gramajo insists that it was not young officers but "a conspiracy" by members of the extreme rightwing (MLN) who paid Ríos Montt to take control

because they always go for the safe alternative: "If we don't win the elections, let's take over the government with a coup!" So they approached Efraín Ríos Montt and said, "Here's the money, prepare a revolt."[19] The day of the coup, Sisniega Otero and Danilo Roca were on the radio, saying this was a coup of young officers. They just invented the phrase "*oficiales jóvenes*" (young officers). And Efraín Ríos arrived pretending he didn't know anything about it, even though he was in on the negotiations; then he got rid of the politicians and remained in the junta with the young officers who had been his students. So there had been no such movement of young officers. What it was, was a political conspiracy they took advantage of. (interview)[20]

Several intelligence informants, both civilian and military, have stated that the CIA was deeply involved in encouraging and underwriting the 1982 Guatemalan coup, which represented "a fortuitous event," given the instability in the region following the July 1979 fall of General Somoza in Nicaragua, the October 1979 fall of General Romero in El Salvador, and the "chaos" of the Lucas regime in 1981. One source stated he knew that U.S. MilGroup officers had approached two young lieutenants from the *servicio de transmisiones* in the Army General Staff with cash, and then contacted MLN party leader Sandoval Alarcón. These lieutenants together with two captains (including Ríos Montt's son) would serve as "*inspectores*," "exercising a great deal of influence within the administration and performance of the government" (Gramajo 1995: 171). These three accounts are not contradictory but may detail parts of the whole: a young officers' revolt, an MLN conspiracy, with CIA money fueling both.

After the March coup, a state of siege was proclaimed that suspended all constitutional guarantees and made it a capital offense "to betray the nation [or to] act against the integrity of the state." Special secret tribunals were set up to try a variety of crimes, and Congress and political parties were banned. The Army General Staff, which included officers from the Escuela Politécnica, the elite unit of Paratroopers, and the Center for Military Studies, proposed a more flexible strategy to fight a "prolonged war" against the guerrillas. The insurgent threat of the 1960s had been wiped out by a brutal rural and urban counterinsurgency campaign; by this time, however, the insurgency in the highlands extended into sixteen of the twenty-two *departamentos* (provinces), and had, by public army estimates in 1981, 276,000 (and by internal military intelligence estimates in 1982, 350,000) supporters in the population (Cifuentes 1982; interviews). As it became clearer that there was no long-term military solution to the insurgency, impetus for change emerged from within the armed forces. The military believed that to be able to maintain its very existence there had to be at least the appearance of a democracy in which certain elite civilian sectors were able to function — a complete reversal of the situation of 1944, when the army made itself part of the civilian October Revolution to increase its own political ascendancy. It set about remodeling the military and intelligence apparatus into hierarchical, disciplined institutions with plans for an outreach to civilian allies, as well as to the guerrilla.[21] As Gramajo states:

During these critical moments, the national problem was analyzed in depth and a new strategy was designed that did not change objectives but developed new and incredibly flexible tactics that formed part of the new military thinking, thinking that we should be proud of, not the product of arbitrary capriciousness or the illuminations of only one man, but on the contrary, the result of a joint effort by the Army General Staff which had the moral courage to commit themselves to the process of national reconstruction, knowing all along the risk they ran in helping de facto governments.[22]

In 1991, he would write,

We had to learn the strategies of the opponents of the State. We had to analyze our weaknesses and capabilities in the army and within the government. It was clear to us in the Army General Staff that a paradox existed in the use of force (repression) to bring peace to the country. There was a clear need to produce peace by other means, perhaps more complicated, more sophisticated, more elaborated, and more time-consuming, but at the same time, more humanitarian, directed toward solving, alleviating or eliminating the causes affecting peace. (1991a: 13)

Three colonels with experience in military strategy were put in charge of crafting a Strategic Plan: Colonel Rodolfo Lobos Zamora, Colonel César Augusto Cáceres Rojas, and Colonel Héctor Gramajo Morales. These three military architects from the Defense Ministry, the Army General Staff, and the Center for Military Studies under orders from General Ríos Montt, together with some hand-picked civilian professionals and administrators,[23] consciously set out to update the 1980 Center for Military Studies' Strategic Appraisal, reconstruct military strategy, and create, with an elaborate counterinsurgency campaign, a long-term, multiple-stage Plan Nacional de Seguridad y Desarrollo (National Plan of Security and Development).

The problems of the country were identified in a fourteen-point list of "Current National Objectives" (see Appendix 2). These were meant to restore a spirit of national identity, starting with point 1 (added to the original thirteen points "to overcome Ríos Montt's superstition about number 13"): "To make the citizen feel that the authorities are at the service of the people and not that the people are at the service of the authorities." In addition, point 9 was meant "to stimulate among the various pressure groups which represent the activity of the nation a new way of thinking, developmentalist, reformist and nationalist." This policy of "pacification and reconciliation" entailed a shift from a national security strategy that framed the conflict as a total (100 percent) polarization of the population—you're either with us or against us—to one that focused 70 percent of its effort on recovering war refugees through development projects ("Beans") while using 30 percent of the effort for repressive measures ("Bullets") against those the army viewed as "lost." Gramajo explains:

The first thing we did was very valuable: to recognize that the problem was the Army's participation in political and economic decisions or in the social organization of the country. This was bad: it helped to maintain the status quo and didn't help to develop the country. . . . It was not precisely this that inspired the '82 coup; nonetheless the system that existed exploded in 1982 and the army came to its rescue and had the opportunity to implement revision. . . . Without announcing that we were creating political space for everyone, we only said that there were economic, social, and political problems that we must prevent. We said, "We're going to pacify the country so that the political sectors act with legitimacy in order to make economic decisions and resolve social problems." And the strategy of pacification was 30 percent of bullets and 70 percent of beans in order to adjust the economic problems. . . . *We made an analysis about how to combat a terrorist insurgency within a democracy*, and use a less costly, more humanitarian strategy, to be more compatible with the democratic system. (interview; emphasis added)

The Army General Staff planned the 30/70 percent counterinsurgency campaign in five different phases, according to Gramajo:

1. Victoria 82, or Operación Ceniza (Operation Ashes)—the scorched-earth "pacification campaign" headed by Colonels Lobos, Cáceres, and Gramajo.
2. Firmeza 83 (Firmness), or Plan G—for the redeployment of troops and the establishment of Civil Patrols and Plan of Assistance to Conflict Areas (PAAC) in order to disrupt guerrilla actions and achieve the specific objectives of providing "Shelter, Work, and Food" (*Techo, Trabajo, y Tortilla*); overseen by Colonels Lobos and Gramajo.

3. Re-Encuentro Institucional 84 (Institutional Re-Encounter) — the reconstruction of that which had been "destroyed by the subversion" with the establishment of Poles of Development and Model Villages; work for the "return to constitutionality" and "guarantee the purity and legality" of the Constituent Assembly elections in July 1984, with the Commission of 30 (consisting of the new Assembly deputies) undertaking the writing of a new constitution; overseen by Colonel Lobos.

4. Estabilidad Nacional 85 (National Stability) — the intensification of military operations throughout the country, the expansion of government institutions into rural socioeconomic programs, and the use of the army to directly oversee the presidential elections of 1985 and "encourage massive civic participation" (Beltranena 1992: 172); overseen by Colonel Gramajo.

5. Avance (Advance) in 1986 — the transition: the military government headed by General Humberto Mejía Víctores exits and the civilian President Vinicio Cerezo enters office.

The campaigns were planned and begun in the northwestern part of the highlands: Chimaltenango in late April and May, begun again in June in El Quiché, and continued in July–December into Huehuetenango, the Ixcán and the Alta and Baja Verapaces. Experiments of strategic-hamlet, Civil Patrols, and Civil Affairs were also included during this period. The campaign ended because "the results were more rapid than we had expected. We revised it [to include] another phase of changes," Gramajo explained, referring to the zonification and intensification of the campaign into the southwestern highland region. In the Victoria phase, the tactics to be employed, according to its "Appendix H: Standing Orders for the Development of Anti-Subversive Operations" included,

The war must be fought on all fronts: military, political but above all socio-economic. The minds of the population are our main target. . . . B. Military Strategy: To increase the size of the Army, especially of commands in rural areas as well as rely on Civil Defense Units to a) deny the subversives access to the population who constitute their social and political support base. . . . Tactics to be employed: 1. Trick them, 2. Find them, 3. Attack them and 4. Annihilate them. (Ejército 1982b; see Appendix 2)

After referring to the crisis in the country, with the "subversion having caused great damage to the infrastructure, family and social integrity" due to the army's insufficient manpower and equipment to cover all the different fronts, the Plan calls for nothing less than the reorganization of the state to make it more "efficient" and to create a climate of "political stability." The main objective of the Plan is to provide "development within a context of rational and effective security." To do so, it designates four areas for action: (1) *Political Stability*: to consolidate the legitimacy of the governments at the national and international level by planning the return to a regime of legality with the restoration of the electoral system and political parties; (2) *Economic Stability*: to reverse the economic hardships that have contributed to the subversion; to watch over forces of production to eliminate its vulnerability to subversion; (3) *Psycho-social Stability*: to educate the population in a doctrine opposed to communism, to contain the advances achieved by the "subversion" among the peasants, *indígenas* (Indians), and illiterate; and (4) *Military Stability*: to identify and destroy the "armed subversion"; improve central intelligence and secure international intelligence and assistance (Ejército National Plan of Security and Development 1982a:2).

With Plan in hand, the military proceeded to penetrate the executive, juridical, administrative, and economic branches: it suspended the National Assembly and established a Council of State; suspended the Constitution and implemented a Fundamental Statute of Government; imposed a State of Siege to prevent political activities (Decree-Law 24-82), with Article 4 of this decree militarizing transport and education; and set up Special Tribunals (Decree-Law 46-82). The National Plan of Security and Development recognized, as one colonel stated bluntly, that "the army can no longer win with only guns" (1986 interview). Nevertheless, a government accord placed the National Police under the control of the defense ministry, thus militarizing the Interior Ministry. And in a July 1982 decree, Ríos Montt appointed rural mayors under threat just in case some refused to accept their new status. This concept of integrating security and development will play a major role in General Gramajo's formulation of a Thesis of National Stability and the subsequent military project, drawn up between 1984 and 1986 and published as an army booklet in 1989.

While this Plan was a reaction to the old order, it was not a progressive statement; indeed, it was designed to effect a "return to constitutionality" while diligently and brutally pursuing the guerrilla through pacification and scorched-earth techniques. This Plan called for reorganizing the state to resolve the country's economic, political, and military crises and yet sought to maintain existing state structures by introducing only certain kinds of reforms, such as reversing the economic recession (but without tax reform at this early period), and restoring a regime of electoral and constitutional legality (but without land reform). Its "Basic Strategic Concept" was directed at "coordinat[ing] and integrat[ing] antisubversive programs at the level of all political bodies of the nation"; yet this group's major efforts were to maintain the institutional unity and integrity of the armed forces. By 20 April 1982, a general mobilization of counterinsurgency operations was underway; by 20 May, Civil Affairs Units had been organized and dispersed to the "conflict zones" to "liquidate the local clandestine committees (CCL) and recuperate the local irregular forces (FIL)" (Letona 1989: 5).

The 1982 Palace Coup

Another part of the strategic analysis by which to counter "one of the principal enemies of the system — revolutionary Catholic priests and their agents, the catechists" (*curas revolucionarios y sus catequistas que son sus agentes*) — was with the use of evangelicalism. Born-again General Ríos Montt "served a useful purpose" in fulfilling this role (Beltranena, 1990 interview). Thus a decision was taken by the Estado Mayor that on 9 June, Ríos Montt with his Juntita of ten officers (representing all ranks to serve as conduits to younger officers) would oust Lucas-identified officers General Maldonado Schaad and Colonel Gordillo in what is known as the "Palace Coup." "A *dictadura* in which all power is consolidated in the High Command replaced the *dictablanda* period of accommodation" of extreme hard-liners both within and outside the military (Beltranena 1992: 150). Protests by Gordillo and Schaad, it is reported, were squelched with checks for fifty thousand dollars (*Latin American Weekly Report*, 30 July 1982).

While the details vary slightly according to the informant, the main lines of what took place are clear: rather than engage in the wholesale expulsion of officers (as Guatemalan officers see as the major mistake of the young rebel officers in El Salvador in 1979), the Army General Staff also gradually exiled some of the more ambitious officers who served during the Lucas regime. (The same tactic of exile and "self-purge" of the "more intransigent" officers was utilized by the High Command in 1995 and 1996 to maintain the army's *proyecto* after the signing of the Peace Accords.) At the major military base and cemetery in Guatemala City, Secret Tribunal executions were held of police and civilian "authorities who had not respected the law" during the Lucas years, or prisoners initially captured during the coup were released, only later to be assassinated "because they were dangerous. The fruit of justice is called peace" (Ríos Montt, 1991 interview). In this way, the military attempted to remain in full control of the reorganization of government, the armed forces, and the police, as well as the political life of civil society. Not surprisingly, a fissure within the officer corps developed: those associated with Lucas were sent into field commands, while those who backed Ríos took the choice Defense Ministry and Army General Staff positions. This fissure meant that Ríos Montt's first year saw several coup attempts: one in August involving Sisniega and others of the extreme rightwing with a small but loyal following among hardline junior officers who had enjoyed immense power between 1970 and 1982; another coup attempt in October involved Colonel Gordillo, who was arrested and discharged from the army. Moreover, General Maldonado Schaad was accused of protecting *luquista* military officers and "interfering with law enforcement efforts to bring punitive sanctions against the corrupted and human rights violators" (Gramajo 1991a:10). While it is estimated that at least "110 officers were relieved of their duties" during the year (Sereseres, interview), the purge focused on police officers; military officers, as customary, were exempt (Beltranena 1992: 150).

This new strategy demanded an even more disciplined command structure, and could not accommodate the example of insubordination that the Young Officers had effectively set for the lower ranks (as in 1944 when the elected Consejo Nacional de la Defensa provided opportunities for "lieutenants to rise and discuss with the Defense Minister the destiny of the Armed Forces"). This insubordination was exacerbated when several young officers moved into powerful positions within the Presidential General Staff. More senior officers in the Army General Staff, including Colonel Gramajo, were concerned about instilling hierarchical discipline "for the institutionality of the army": "Access to power had to be structured so that it could only be obtained through the High Command" (Sereseres, interview). Many voiced concern with "*La Juntita*":

> The young officers put Ríos in power, so Ríos designated them commanders. But if you are put in command because of the [army's hierarchical] law, you are legal and you have the right [to exercise that command]. But if you are put in command because of a coup, it is a very fragile position and you need the consent of the juniors. (Gramajo, interview)

This fragility would manifest itself in mini-rebellions during the Pacification campaign throughout 1982 and 1983. It was only later, in mid-1983, that Ríos Montt began to detour from the Plan and had himself to be deposed. Other officers who refused to go along either with the *proyecto* or the Pacification campaign met with "accidents." (Many officers vividly recalled the case of Colonel Luis Alfonso Rébulli Capelli, Second Commander of Quezaltenango under Colonel Lobos Zamora and Commander of Sololá, who was killed by a civilian-dressed man with an M-16 rifle while walking along the Pan American Highway). "There are many 'accidents' in the army," said one intelligence colonel cynically (1990 interview).

In 1983, army and security forces were united under one command (Decree-Law 149-83) and in 1984, all levels of municipal, departmental, and national governmental institutions were integrated into the counterinsurgency coordinating efforts of Poles of Development (the National System of Inter-Institutional Coordinators [IICs]; Decree-Law 111-84). The military targeted the hearts, minds, and stomachs of the highland population.

Besides the Grupo Asesor, consisting of seven advisors appointed to counsel Ríos Montt on political matters, a Council of State (Consejo de Estado), which replaced the National Assembly, was established by Ríos Montt, and Jorge Serrano was appointed its President. The thirty-four-member Council was to advise the President and select members of the new Supreme Electoral Tribunal, an arrangement "creating the impression," Andrade Díaz-Durán explains, that there existed powers autonomous from the State and that they were functioning practically in a state of legality, while the truth is that the governments before and after August 8 [the 1983 coup], were *de facto* governments, military governments, whose political responsibility was . . . pledged to guarantee to all Guatemalans a return to democratic institutionality within reasonable limits, . . . with a genuine and authentic *apertura*. (1988: 127, 132)

The Council members were to include four handpicked representatives of the economic elite, seven from professional and civil servant associations (the university, bar, press, municipalities), ten *indígena* representatives, and one from each of the five legally registered political parties. Four of the five parties, however, boycotted the Council.[24] The inclusion of *indígenas* served a dual purpose: internationally, the Guatemalan government proffered it as proof of democratic magnanimity toward the indigenous population; domestically, it proved useful as part of the army's amnesty program for guerrillas, as we will see in a later chapter.

Part of the effort under the Plan was to "re-structure the electoral system [and] to re-establish constitutional order in the country as a matter of urgency." Law was not only a central part of this *proceso*, but it was so intermixed with security that the two became one and the same. The Fundamental Statute of Government intended "to implement a juridical-political structure in the Nation . . . based on honesty, stability, legality, and security" in order to "juridically normalize the country." Colonel-lawyer Girón Tánchez, the legal architect of the Statute, explained:

If you read the Statute, you will see that law serves everything; it had fundamentally one political goal: to prepare the environment of the country in order to carry through with free elections and to silence the political order in the country into a constitutional regime. (1986 interview)[25]

The Statute was, in fact, only a legal dress rehearsal for the 1985 constitution.
Born-again General Ríos Montt's loquacious personality (in marked contrast to Lucas García's shyness) in his televised evangelical messages provided the psychological and moral backdrop during the first ten months of the campaign. In the urban centers with access to television, Ríos Montt, extolling his Iglesia del Verbo (Church of the Word), played his role to the hilt, giving the Plan names like Beans and Bullets (*Frijoles y Fusiles*) and "Shelter, Work, and Food" (*Techo, Trabajo y Tortilla*).[26] However, by late spring 1983, it became increasingly clear that Ríos Montt and his clique of officers had lost control of the army in the field, and his harangues on national television were becoming embarrassing and politically destabilizing for the officer corps: "He did not have a clear sense of where his power derived from. It came from the armed forces, clearly, but he thought that Guatemala was his church, and he would refer to people, who he thought to be simpletons, as dogs and bitches. It was insulting" (Gramajo, interview).

Officers refer to the 1983 internal coup as a relief (*relevo*) from the "Government of the Word" (*el Gobierno del Verbo*).

The 1983 *Relevo* and Political Reordering

The Pacification campaign based on the scorched-earth strategy of "killing zones" had succeeded in undermining guerrilla support in the highlands by December 1982.[27] Still, pressures from the ultraconservative business sector, especially from his advisor, Manuel Ayau, a follower of Pinochet's Chicago Boys' neoliberal economic plan,[28] led Ríos Montt to announce to military commanders that it would take "at least seven more years" of military government to "consolidate" Guatemala and that he was disrupting *el proceso* toward elections by focusing on economic issues first rather than on the political. Because Ríos Montt began "reacting in the orthodox manner of pure careerism and not professionalism, of wanting to be a Pinochet in Guatemala," the Army High Command decided to "relieve" him of the presidency.[29] Attacks by former Colonel Gordillo and Leonel Sisniega Otero on a popular television program raised concerns within the officer corps of potential army disunity. In response to these pressures, as well as demands by officers during a "coup rehearsal" at the Huehuetenango military base on 29 June 1983,[30] Ríos Montt agreed to fix the date for constituent assembly elections for 1 July 1984 (formally inaugurating the Supreme Electoral Tribunal on 30 June), to reimpose a state of alarm (that had been lifted on 22 March 1983) that restricted civil liberties, and to dissolve the Young Officers Advisory Council of the Estado Mayor Presidencial (although three of the six officers stayed on as aides) (Keefe 1984: 140).

According to General Mejía, he and the coup plotters used the scheduled meeting of Ríos Montt with the U.S. military at Southern Command (SOUTHCOM) together with the Salvadoran and Honduran presidents aboard the U.S. aircraft carrier, the USS *Ranger*, off the Pacific coast on 8 August as a diversion to "relieve" Ríos Montt of his command as president (1990 interview). (Mejía himself had met with SOUTHCOM and Salvadoran and Honduran Defense Ministers two days earlier.) Mejía called a meeting with his new Council of Commanders at 9 A.M. on 8 August — precisely the time Ríos Montt was to board the carrier. But with information in hand from army intelligence, detecting Mejía's maneuvers, Ríos Montt stopped off to greet the colonels at 8 A.M. on his way to the airport. While Ríos was present, Mejía asked each commander for his vote, and within a matter of minutes, Defense Minister Mejía "relieved" Ríos Montt of his command. Allowed to return to the palace, Ríos attempted to organize resistance: several soldiers were wounded, and Ríos's personal guard was killed in exchanges of gunfire around the National Palace. Two hours later, Ríos was escorted from his office in civilian clothes. The military had managed to retain its institutionality against its first caudillo crisis since Ubico.

And despite categorical denials by the U.S. government, U.S. involvement in Ríos Montt's overthrow was widely reported in the Guatemalan press.

The Council of Commanders selected General Mejía for both institutional and ideological continuity: as a general, he would not only maintain the continuity of the Pacification campaign, but "return Guatemala to a regime of legality" (Andrade, 1991 interview); also, he represented an ultraconservative tendency within the army that tried (unsuccessfully) to repair the damaged ties with the *latifundistas*. "We felt with Mejía we would have no argument from the rest of the colonels" (Gramajo, interview). Mejía replaced Ríos's Juntita with the Council of Commanders, which had four "outspoken military commanders," including Cuartel General commander General Gramajo, serving as key strategists and "advisors" during this period.[31]

After the 1983 *relevo*, more officers were willing to accept this new montage of political-military thinking, which assured them the counterinsurgency war would continue no matter who won the 1985 elections. As the imagery of democratic constitutionalism was slowly being forged, the armed forces began to disengage from government administration as a way to guard against being blamed for civilian incompetence or human rights abuses. A "phaseout" program was implemented on 31 May 1985 so that the only active duty or retired military officer in government administration was General Mejía. Six months before the inauguration of the new president, "We threw everyone [military] out of government. So much so that we left the National Police to a policeman and everything there fell apart. He became so corrupt, losing proceedings, that we had to replace him with a military officer" (Gramajo, interview).

In its proclamation of 8 August 1983, the Army reiterated its pledge to "restructure" Guatemalan society,[32] and respect "the juridical boundaries" established by the Fundamental Statute, and provide for "juridical security," as Lic. Andrade states:

> The only modification we made was in regard to who appointed the First Magistrate [the Supreme Court Justice] and this decision was made by the Army itself. . . . We also lifted the state of emergency. A state of siege had previously been in effect and this [lifting] was very important because these states restructure the rights of citizens . . . and limit in some way, the free political game. . . . The dissolution of the Special Tribunals — a juridical aberration of the twentieth century that judged the accused by an unknown judge and kept the evidence used secret — was also undertaken. (1988: 133)

The 1984 National Assembly and 1985 presidential elections were "ordered" by Mejía by way of an army bulletin. "In other words, it was the fulfillment of a solemn and public pledge," according to Andrade. "Clean and unquestioned" elections attended by international observers were seen as the solution to "purify" *el pueblo* at the polls (1991 interview). Not only were elections "ordered" by the military, but they were scheduled to comply with

military objectives of the National Plan for a civilian president. The years 1984–85, then, were the two years of the military *proceso* during which time, as one Guatemalan intellectual has asserted,

the military's strategies were consolidated with respect to civilian participation in terms of a Constitution, Congress, a Constitutional Court, and a civilian President. If these institutions exist, it is only because the military want them to exist. There is no political terrain gained by the civilians. This is not a democratizing process for participation; it is a function, a political space for civilians. But if it is a space, it is granted by the military. (1988 anonymous interview)

The only worrisome issue for the military was what a civilian presidency would mean for their National Plan. Concerned about the civilian candidates, it attempted at one point to create new political parties that could be more easily controlled. According to Colonel Gordillo, "We committed the mistake of allowing the traditional parties, with their hegemony over and monopoly of political skills, to retain their traditional names and labels. Well, it was like competing with Coca-Cola!" (1988 interview). The High Command under Mejía also tried, despite their "nondeliberative" stance, to support their favorite presidential candidate, as Gramajo explains: "Mejía wanted to support [UCN candidate Jorge] Carpio, but when a poll was taken which told us that he didn't have a chance, we didn't help anyone and the elections were clean. . . . The army continued its position of not interfering. Whoever won, won" (interview). *El proyecto político-militar* assured the military and the politico-economic elite, that the counterinsurgency war was *independent of whomever won the 1985 elections* (Sarti Castañeda 1986: 27; emphasis added). Providing legal means to maintain *el proyecto*, the Defense Minister Jaime Hernández stated to the press and the National Assembly in December 1985 that, before anything else, civilians must respect the military project, and that sixteen new decree-laws had been emitted only a few days previous to the inauguration of the newly elected civilian President, Vinicio Cerezo. As one Guatemalan intellectual put it,

One was given to understand that the IICs [Inter Institutional Coordinators] and the PACs [Civil Patrols] could not be eliminated whatsoever. The military government was to be changed to a civilian one, with the military remaining as the structure of power, passing to the civilians only the external part of politics. That is, change the harmony but keep to the same old tune. The appearance is different, but inside it is the same old thing. (1988 anonymous interview)

Planned in 1982 and brought to fruition with the election of civilian President Cerezo in 1985 — "three years, nine months, eleven days," as Gramajo recalled precisely — the politico-military project had managed to implant security issues within the political and legal framework of Guatemala. But it was to be a security — and a formal electoral democracy — on the military's terms. For example, "The first thing President Cerezo did on his first day in

office, 16 January, was to establish the Council of National Security [Consejo de Seguridad Nacional] to hold discussions and give talks, and so forth. He was summarily told, 'No *señor*, you have been given the freedom to act, but to act only within the Plan.' This intelligence analyst added, "If civilians occupy their assigned places (*los lugares asignados*), then the success [of *el proyecto*] is assured" (interview).

Why the Shift?

What were their reasons for the strategic shift to a democratic transition in 1982? One of the most pressing concerns was that the institution of the military itself was in danger. To distinguish this military quickly from the corrupt Lucas García-Alvarez-Chupina model, military discipline and hierarchy were reinstated. But the command structure based on the consent of junior officers (vulnerable to the corrupting influence of the extreme right and the CIA) was fragile. It was not until the third internal coup in 1983 that senior officers regained full command, and the military-directed *proyecto* that also sought to depoliticize the ranks, was back on course. By 1985 the military was in a far more powerful position in relation to the oligarchy and other political actors than ever before.

Some analysts have suggested that the partial cutoff of U.S. military aid and the dramatic reduction of economic aid were also instrumental in encouraging the Guatemalan military to hold elections. As Girón Tánchez admitted,

[It was] to guarantee respect before the international community. It is at once an internal and external juridical regime with the objective of making the international community aware and secure that Guatemala is fulfilling the international agreements and so one cannot say that there is a de facto but a de jure regime here. One must run down constitutional corridors. (1986 interviews)

And Cruz Salazar, when asked the reason for the transition, similarly responded,

I believe that there was much external pressure which forced the political opening in Guatemala, not the [economic] crisis. It was an international political necessity. . . . The U.S. decided to liquidate these military regimes [in Latin America] and demand [democratic ones] through limited pressure. Thus, it was not so much the will [of the military to change] or the crisis, but tremendous external pressure. (1988 interview)

Lic. Andrade agreed that "more than [direct] pressures, what was done was to isolate Guatemala, saying publicly that Guatemala is a violent country with a government totally distinguished by human rights violations, without any legitimacy whatsoever. A scheme completely unacceptable for the international community, but it is part of the disgraceful and unfortunate history

of Guatemala. Thus, [given such pressures], changes were made" (1990 interview).

The Reagan administration did apply some pressure, as this comment by the Guatemalan desk officer at the U.S. State Department in a March 1986 interview suggests: "We told [the Guatemalans] we wanted three things — and this is what was essentially said: (1) rule of law, (2) straighten up the economy and (3) practice of democracy — you know, the good relations between the state and individual. But, as you know, such countries often use thugs in order to establish the rule of law."[33] Nonetheless, once Ríos Montt became president, President Reagan described him as "a man of great personal integrity and commitment" who is "totally dedicated to democracy. . . . And frankly, I'm inclined to believe they've been getting a bum rap. His country is facing a brutal challenge from guerrillas that is supported by others outside Guatemala" (Weekly Compilation of Presidential Statements, 13 December 1982). Yet before the 1982 coup, we know that *golpista* officers pondered three options:

The first possibility was no change: military rule. The second was to control the structure, combining it with the army, so that while the authoritarian structure of the army is relieved, the army is given the flexibility to use it [whenever necessary]. The third is to make these structures totally civilian and leave them only to the civilians to run. The first means significant problems for the government with a logical reaction from social sectors that are against the [Civil] Patrols and Poles [of Development] and are going to demand changes. The second, or mixed solution of both civilians and military, is the most realistic and effective. To put in a civilian authority but to allow the military to destroy the guerrilla! (Cruz Salazar, 1986 interview)

This "mixed solution" extended to foreign policy: the military was very sensitive about its "pariah human rights status." Legitimation was sought by demonstrating that the Cerezo regime newly elected in 1986 had "prestige and respectability internationally," although they had to "have their domestic camp perfectly controlled, or at least well controlled. And that is the issue; this can only be done in a 'mixed way.' . . . This new government doesn't exist without economic collaboration from abroad: the renegotiation of the debt, and economic aid" (Cruz Salazar, 1986 interview).

Equally important was President Cerezo's "Active Neutrality" policy, openly enunciated in August 1987 (and committed in the Esquipulas II accords), which directed Central American governments to begin direct talks with armed insurgencies in support of President Cerezo's efforts to "improve the image of the country and seek support for his foreign policy of active neutrality to gain the credibility of the international community" (*La Hora*, 26 September 1986, p. 1). In this mixed solution, political parties served both as external legitimators to absorb international pressures regarding human rights violations and U.S. pressures to participate in the *contra* war, and as internal mediators to absorb social demands and protests.

Preempting the politico-military demands by guerrilla forces in 1982 made it unnecessary for the military to alter its "essential and permanent characteristics" as the foremost power of the state (Sarti Castañeda 1986: 24). Nor did the Guatemalan army have to compromise with the guerrilla, as did its counterpart in El Salvador one decade later. A civilian government, as Gramajo made clear in 1988 (during another counterinsurgency offensive), "allowed the army to carry out much broader and more intensified operations because the legitimacy of the government, in contrast to the illegitimacy of the previous military governments, doesn't allow the insurgency to mobilize public opinion internationally—something which proved to be an obstacle in fighting the guerrilla" (Cruz Salazar 1988a: n.p.).

The mixed solution, then, has entailed the continuation of war during a constitutional and electoral transition. A "return to constitutionality" was one dimension of *el proyecto político-militar*; Pacification and the creation of a nationalist doctrine of Civil Affairs was the other. How the 30/70 percent strategy was implemented is the subject of the next few chapters.

Chapter 2
Anatomy of the Counterinsurgency I

From Tactical to Strategic Pacification

> Listen well: the subversion or the guerrilla is not a military problem. It is an eminently political one. And as a consequence, all of the apparatuses of the state must work because there is subversion where there is a political vacuum. Knowing that, we embraced the whole problem in 1982: justice, beans, and guns.
>
> — General Ríos Montt, interview

> So we had 70 percent Beans and 30 percent Bullets [as our strategy in 1982]. That is, rather than killing 100 percent, we provided food for 70 percent. Before, you see, the doctrine was 100 percent, we killed 100 percent before this.
>
> — General Gramajo, interview[1]

After the 23 March 1982 coup, the Guatemalan army combined civil-military activity, focusing 30 percent of the effort toward killing and 70 percent of the effort toward providing food and shelter to the survivors — first referred to as Beans and Bullets and later as "Shelter, Work and Food." Additionally, it implemented a five-part strategy that included: (1) an increase in the number of soldiers by a call-up of reserve forces and by forced recruitment of captured indigenous men for soldiering as well as for paramilitary civil patrolling, (2) a campaign of pacification that initially concentrated troops for intensified "killing zone" (*matazonas*) operations (and later expanded to other areas), (3) the establishment of Civil Affairs companies to organize Civil Patrols and to concentrate refugees into model villages, (4) the expansion of the legal justification of counterinsurgency through expanded decree-laws, secret tribunals, and censorship of the media, and (5) a campaign of psychological warfare to win popular support for the army. The Beans symbolized the military government's aid to loyal Guatemalans; the Bullets symbolized the struggle against the insurgency.

This chapter will reconstruct the military's conceptions of, implementations of, and justifications for the Pacification campaign, or the Bullets, and for the beginnings of the Beans.

Antecedents of Change: Civic Action of the 1960s and 1970s and the Committee of National Reconstruction

Although there was initial resentment of U.S. intervention among the Guatemalan officer corps during the Ydígoras and Peralta Azurdia governments (1958–66) (to the point where U.S. military advisors were not provided full access to Guatemalan military intelligence reports), the U.S. model of special warfare and pacification taken directly from Vietnam was established in Guatemala during the civilian regime of President Méndez Montenegro. Government death squads inflicted massive repression in the city and in the countryside, a brutal pacification program in Zacapa and Chiquimula directed by an estimated 1000 Green Berets, took the lives of between 5000 and 10,000 peasants. At the same time, under the direction of a U.S. Army colonel and with $5 million emergency US-AID (Agency for International Development) funding, the Guatemalan Army began to establish small "civic action" (Acción Cívica Mílitar) projects in the highlands entitled Operación Honestidad (Operation Honesty), with the slogan *Seguridad y Progreso* (Security and Progress) to facilitate the pacification process and win over the population through "social works," according to retired General Ricardo Peralta Méndez, a central figure in these projects (1991 interviews; Cruz Salazar, 1988 interview). Beginning in the 1970s, the government also began to support development plans for the small agricultural sector within the framework of the Plan for National Development, working closely with civilian agencies and the private sector, but keeping the military in command. By the middle to late 1970s, the Committee on National Reconstruction (CRN) served as a model of civil-military integration in planning development in the highlands. After the 1976 earthquake, especially, the CRN became the vehicle for cross-bureaucratic, inter-institutional coordination, focusing on the most isolated communities where no other institutional organization would go. The Director of Operations of CRN in 1976 (as well as immediately after the 1982 March coup), General Peralta Méndez, describes it as

an integration of a group of Army officers, civil functionaries, and civilians from the private sector, the business sector, workers, students, and cooperatives, and so forth. These latter two groups were especially integrated into the Committee to direct the resources used in reconstruction. We wanted [to create] trust in order to provide loans to those in the countryside to be able to recuperate their homes, their work. . . . We sought to promote active participation of all Guatemalans in the process of reconstruction—not just in terms of material distribution but also in terms of who decided how the reconstruction should proceed. We thus created small committees of reconstruction in the rural areas at the level of villages, of municipalities, of departments . . . and they began to function in promoting broad popular participation, which was the real success of the reconstruction. (interview)

During this period, two opposing dynamics were operating within the military: on the one hand, the more fiercely anticommunist counterinsurgent officers, who believed "good works" to be far less effective than 100 percent brute force in countering insurgency; on the other hand, civic-action counterinsurgent officers who believed in combining the two. During the last year of President-General Kjell Laugerud's government, in 1977–78, the "100 percent" counterinsurgent officers won out. Indiscriminate repression mounted and became more acute under the regime of Lucas García (1978– 82). He "destroyed these [CRN] committees and began to accuse civic action of being communism. I had stimulated leadership in the countryside, and he dedicated himself to persecuting these 'communists' " (Peralta Méndez, interviews). This 100 percent model of scorched-earth warfare, as several *desarrollista* (developmentalist) officers pointed out, "doesn't think very much of development and believes you must kill everyone to get the job done" (interview). In this instance, "the job" only continued to grow and worsen. Despite such setbacks, the legacies of these participatory developmentalist projects were to reassert themselves in the 1982 Civil Affairs Doctrine, in which development qua pacification was designed with the dual goal of destroying the infrastructure of Indian life while buying the survivors' loyalties with food and work. Army penetration of the rural areas, begun in the mid-1960s and institutionalized under President-General Kjell Laugerud in the mid-1970s, laid the groundwork for permanent militarization in the 1980s.

With the partial cutoff of military aid by the Carter administration in 1978 and the failure of the army to successfully defeat the guerrilla, civic action officers by 1980 began to recognize the limitations of the "occupying army syndrome which had been very costly for Americans in Vietnam," with its inherent paternalism. Air Force Colonel Eduardo Wohlers, the director of Plan of Assistance to Conflict Areas in 1982–83, explained, "By trying to be the good guys we are paternalistic [to the civilian population], reinforcing a relation of dependency that we don't want to encourage" (1986 interview). In response, civic action slowly became recast as national developmentalism, which fused security with development and was renamed Civil Affairs in 1982. In a 1986 interview, Army Reservist Major-Dr. Luis Sieckavizza, a Civil Affairs spokesman, recounts this shift:

In the matter of counter-subversion, we came to realize that we were unconsciously acting like an army invading its own territory. At the root of the terms of military aid, the Guatemalan army had treated this as an area of specialization at the different U.S. centers of military formation, and we applied the famous plan of civic-military action. This plan was nothing more than the manuals which the U.S. had condensed from the lessons it had learned from its fight in Vietnam where the U.S. Army was an *invading* army. We learned this lesson, we brought it back to Guatemala, we applied it here and indirectly, we were acting like a foreign army in our own country. When [the United States] terminated our aid [in 1978], we were obligated to generate our own philosophy and our own invention of military science, and we created a military thesis known as the *tesis desarrollista* (developmentalist thesis). (interview)

By 1981, many officers had also begun to realize that the prolonged and violent repression that had been applied for two decades had not met its objective of defeating either the popular movements or the revolutionary forces (which, in their minds, were one and the same). In fact, the insurgents had improved their military capacities to such an extent that officers were estimating that they would win their "prolonged popular war" within two to three years. With the 1982 coup, the military set out to "regain" the indigenous population and "rescue their mentality" from the guerrilla. At this precise moment, insurgency and counterinsurgency operations converged for the first time in Guatemalan history: both the guerrilla and the army sought to gain the hearts and minds of the indigenous population. "They were between two fires" stated General Gramajo in a 1990 interview. As a colonel, he was part of the theater of operations in the northwestern highlands between 1982 and 1983. "And we made them choose sides." The shift from counterinsurgency tactics to more massive and intensified strategic "sweeps" is considered a pivotal moment in the minds of many officers. It implied a shift away from the U.S. Army "occupational-force" model with its "paternalistic civic action," in which little attention was given to guerrilla warfare or to local populations to one that entailed an analysis of guerrilla war that both "annihilates the guerrilla and recuperates the population." For all intents and purposes, the use of small Civil Affairs Units that permanently positioned themselves within the population meant that "occupation" not only continued but was stepped up as part of the larger political-military strategy. It entailed a shift away from the individual, sporadic and "reactive" counterinsurgency attacks on villages employed by the Grupo Lucas—officers who believe in the 100-percent strategy (*los tácticos*)—who made little attempt to "control the population." In contrast, officers who believe in utilizing state apparatuses to implement their 30/70 percent strategy of massacre and elections, of security and development, are called the *estratégicos* or institutionalist counterinsurgents. After the March 1982 coup, the *estratégicos* permanently positioned troops directly within the guerrilla zones and denied the rebels social and military support from the population, linking development directly with security, or "Beans with Bullets." It is for this reason that the Guatemalan military is viewed by U.S. counterinsurgency experts as having implemented in 1982 a "repressive yet often enlightened" strategy that combined brutal combat operations of torture, assassination, and massacre with the "soft" elements of warfare: civic action, civil defense, psychological operations, and the control of population, resources, and refugees

(Sheehan 1989: 128). Before we proceed to a reconstruction of the Pacification Campaign in 1982–83, we first need to consider the guerrilla actions and the extent of incorporation of the indigenous population into the war.

The Incorporation of Indians into the Prolonged Popular War and the Army's Counterinsurgency Operations, 1978–1982

In 1978, the army, under pressure from local landowners and labor contractors, mounted a massive wave of repression against the popular mobilization of the Indian population, with the May 1978 Panzós massacre marking the use of massacre as a counterinsurgency tactic (Vargas, cited in Richards 1985: 94). By late 1979, the EGP (the Guerrilla Army of the Poor) controlled a considerable amount of territory in the Ixil Triangle in El Quiché, holding periodic demonstrations in the major towns of Nebaj, Chajul, and Cotzal (Richards 1985: 94). By 1981, an estimated 250,000 to 500,000 in the Indian community supported the guerrillas (Arias 1990: 255); Army intelligence estimated 360,000 for the EGP alone. This revolutionary crisis had resulted from modernization efforts by the State in the 1960s and 1970s, raising developmental and electoral expectations within Indian communities and "unsettling [the] traditional order" (256). At the same time, the State blocked change in both a fraudulent and repressive manner (cf. Porras 1978). By the mid-1970s, Indian communities were divided into three groups: (1) the *costumbristas*, or orthodox "traditionalists"; (2) the Indian commercial middle class who joined with extreme rightwing groups; and (3) the younger, educated Indian *campesinos* who no longer recognized the traditionalists or the merchants as their "natural leaders" and who joined first ladino mass organizations and later the revolutionary movement. In its attempts to quell organizing activities and eliminate the leadership, the army's repression exacerbated tensions among these groups, with these younger, radicalized Indian peasants incrementally swelling the guerrilla columns. "Until late 1978, indigenous ethnic groups had favored mass organizations over armed struggle, but in early 1979, the army's active presence began to be felt throughout the highlands, and this began to generate changes in that judgment" (Arias 1990: 251–52). Falla (1983, 1994) and Stoll (1993) state that each massacre resulted in hundreds of recruits moving into the guerrilla camp "to protect themselves against the army." Indiscriminate bloody attacks on peasant villages in the western highlands as well as kidnappings and assassinations of workers, professionals, and the poor in the urban areas managed to mobilize peasant resistance "far more successfully than any leaflets distributed by leftists" (Smith 1984: 221). In short, the army's indiscriminate and brutal repression had unwittingly created far more resistance than it had destroyed.

As mentioned earlier, the "first generation" of Guatemalan insurgents was founded by two renegade army officers who fled after a 1960 reformist coup attempt. As Sheehan remarks, these early insurgents, primarily an educated ladino elite, "forgot the lessons of prolonged war proselytized by Mao in China and Giap in Vietnam" and, inspired by Castro's relatively easy victory, adapted the "*foco* theory" of Che Guevara and Regis Debray. They believed that after lighting "the brush fire of revolution" in one isolated section of Guatemala (*el foco*), the flames of revolution would rapidly spread (1989: 133).

The second generation of insurgents, represented by three main guerrilla groups — the Guerrilla Army of the Poor (EGP) "with a Che Guevara Front in Huehuetenango, and Ho Chi Minh and Augusto César Sandino Fronts in northern and southern Quiché, among others"; the Rebel Armed Forces (FAR), "active in Petén and northwestern San Marcos"; and the Organization of the People in Arms (ORPA), "with both an urban and mountain front, especially south of Lake Atitlán," according to several officers interviewed, took painstaking efforts to organize clandestinely at the grass-roots level for a "prolonged popular war" (see Figure 2). In mobilization national support for revolution, these groups — some more than others — opened up the organization to Indian participation throughout the chain of command — something even the military appreciated in May 1981: When the EGP reasons that "the enemy of the poor is the rich and that the poor form part of a large army which will achieve justice," then the EGP is "successful by offering the Guatemalan *indígena* a hope of dignity that had not been offered him during more than 400 years of humiliation and misery" (Cifuentes 1982: 27). This particular article, "Operación Ixil," in the military journal *Revista Militar* is significant because it recognizes that the revolution is poverty-induced, not communist induced. "The Bolshevik doctrine is strange to the *indígena*; he does not identify with the proletariat, but what he does understand is that he is poor and lives miserably, his work days are exhausting and the exhausted land yields little (remember that the *indígena* is anti-communist by tradition and doesn't understand the Marxist dialectic)" (27).

From his own readings of Mao, Giap, and U.S. army strategists in Vietnam, Colonel Gramajo understood as early in 1977–78, as Chief of Operations at the Army General Staff under President-General Kjell Laugerud, that the army faced "a people's war." But it was only in 1979, as deputy commander of the military base in Jutiapa, that he understood how much it had become an ethnic conflict: "At four in the morning, I was awakened to receive nine soldiers' bodies that came from the western highlands. The officers in the western part of the country would rely only on the ladino soldiers from the eastern part . . . to go and fight the Indians. So, I saw an ethnic strategy of the EGP, and I said, this is very dangerous because it is becoming an ethnic conflict" (interview). For the military and *latifundistas*, with their historic fears of Indian rebellion, the very fact that Indians were being drawn into *any* vision of struggle was an extraordinarily frightening prospect.

Beginning in 1975, the army began repressive moves against peasants in the northern transversal area called "zones of the generals," where much of the mineral- and oil-rich land was being claimed by high-ranking military officers and presidents. The killing of La Perla finca owner Luis Arenas (known as the "Tiger of Ixcán" because of his cruelty toward workers) by the EGP was "like a declaration of war" (Falla 1994: 18), and the army under Kjell Laugerud reacted immediately with the abduction of peasants in the area. It launched a counterinsurgency offensive in northern El Quiché in March 1976 in which church and cooperative workers were forcibly disappeared. Under President-General Lucas García, this pattern of repression continued and was directed against actual and potential popular indigenous leadership in Catholic Action organizations, army-directed Civic Action groups, as well as guerrilla columns in the rural areas. Unable to "eradicate the root of subversion," however, the army moved steadily from selective repression in 1978–79 to massive killings. The Panzós massacre in May 1978 of 150 Kekchí Indians resisting land expropriation carried out by a Guatemalan Special Forces unit was only the beginning in a series of massacres (cf. Aguilera Peralta 1979).

Such systematic repression began to generate reluctant changes in indigenous thinking from electoral and mass organizing to armed struggle, especially in 1980 with the firebombing of the Spanish Embassy in Guatemala City by the *luquista* security forces.[2] By early 1982, in a region where few Indians had ever volunteered for military service, the EGP alone had grown to major proportions in the Ixil Triangle: regular fighters numbered 4000 to 6000; local irregular forces (*fuerzas irregulares locales*, FIL) 10,000 (those who would serve on self-defense committees, cut telegraph lines, blockade highways with nails, barricades, and fallen trees in both directions to prevent the army from reacting in time when EGP guerrillas occupied a village); and sympathizers within EGP-base areas, 60,000 (those who would provide food and clothing for the permanent guerrilla units) (Sereseres 1984: 37). The army, for its part, initially estimated 6000–7000 combatants altogether, which it later revised to 10,000–12,000 irregulars "better armed than the army" (Gramajo, interview), with 100,000 serving as part of the guerrilla "infrastructure" and another 260,000 in areas under guerrilla control. Guerrilla forces had gained support or control of eight of the twenty-two provinces by way of sabotage (placing claymore mines, building trenches, ambushing military convoys, and intercepting traffic to demand "war tax" along the western part of the Pan American Highway), killing a significant number of troops and junior officers (57 captains, lieutenants, second lieutenants, and *especialistas* were killed in 1981, according to army reports), selectively killing mayors and military commissioners/informants, and temporarily occupying villages and towns with units as large as 250 in the northwestern departments of Huehuetenango, Quiché, Alta Verapaz, Chimaltenango, and Sololá, as well as parts of Quezaltenango, Totonicapán, and San

Marcos. Buoyed by the success of the Nicaraguan revolutionary forces in 1979, and by their initial military gains, the guerrilla forces seriously misread the army's loss of territory and troops as "strategic equilibrium" of military force, and believed victory to be at hand (cf. Aguilera 1986). The inability of the guerrillas to defend the peasant population against a brutal military offensive was to be a major miscalculation on their part (cf. Payeras 1991).

By early 1982, the guerrilla forces, now united as the Unidad Revolucionaria Nacional Guatemalteca (Guatemalan National Revolutionary Unity or URNG), formulated a plan to declare a portion of Guatemala liberated territory (*territorios liberados*), with an insurgent government (the EGP handed out its own identity cards), and prepared for a major offensive in the departments of Huehuetenango, Quiché, and Chimaltenango. According to the army, the FIL fortified villages, dug trenches, built traps, and established cavernous subterranean hospitals, printing presses, and claymore-mine and uniform-making workshops.

"This was a great threat to Guatemala. The guerrillas were well-entrenched and intended to declare a portion of the highlands (*altiplano*) liberated territory and obtain international recognition as a governing body," Defense Minister Bolaños recounted in a 1990 interview. Up until this time, Lucas García's commanders had been conducting individual, sporadic attacks on villages with little attempt to control the refugee population. But with guerrilla fronts present in sixteen of the twenty-two departments, many of the areas had been converted into "*no ir*" (off limits) zones not only for the U.S. Embassy and US-AID staff (who were not permitted beyond Antigua in their heavy, bulletproof vehicles), but for the army as well. In Nebaj, El Quiché, for example, "You didn't have to go up into the mountains to combat the guerrilla. They had machine guns poking out of windows in the municipality!" (Colonel Noack, 1995 interview).

In Guatemala City, the army felt as though "we were up against the wall because the guerrillas were as close as Chimaltenango. I mean, you couldn't even drive out on a Sunday to Antigua without running into guerrillas at Amatitlán!" Cruz Salazar relates (1986 interview).[3] In a desperate move, General Benedicto Lucas García (the president's brother), stepped in as Army Chief of Staff to make the army "an aggressive, flexible and highly mobile army that will hit the guerrillas in their strongholds rather than their hitting us in ours" (*Latin American Regional Reports*, 12 February 1982). To pre-empt this action by the guerrilla, "General Benny" launched a massive scorched-earth "sweep" on 1 October 1981 in Chimaltenango with Task Force Iximché that later moved north into Quiché and west into Solelá. (Like Ríos Montt in the 1966–67 Zacapa campaign, General Benny "personally directed [some of] the tactical maneuvers in Chimaltenango in 1981" [Gramajo, interview].) The intensive series of massacres and burnings of villages and hamlets such as at Chupol, Quiché, which "was very very harsh (*muy, muy, duro*)" (col., interview), caused thousands to flee into the mountains and across the border (see Figure 3). Chimaltenango was chosen for several reasons. From the discovery and dismantling of ORPA's safe houses (*casas de seguridad*), in Guatemala City during the summer of that year, arms caches were tracked to Chimaltenango, according to army intelligence officers (interviews). It was also the region where the unique Operación Xibalbá (Xibalbá being equivalent to hell in the major Mayan religious text *Popul Vuh*) was launched by an Army Special Operations comando headed by Lieutenant Héctor Mauricio López Bonilla. This comando successfully infiltrated a 28-man EGP unit of the Augusto César Sandino Front: "The military strategy was to simulate being a guerrilla unit passing through the area. The EGP unit was completely neutralized," according to Beltranena. All 28 were killed after information had been obtained. Chimaltenango was also "a strategic department" where ladino-Indian relations were most polarized and where "the methods of the prolonged popular war" had resulted in such effective self-defense "that the army could not penetrate or walk through villages without being detected and intercepted by local vigilantes. . . . For the Army, this was an anomalous situation that officially it could not permit," according to Gramajo (1995: 201). In the Ixil Triangle, too, there was a lack of surprise on the part of villagers in the army's approach: "We would arrive at a village," explained a G-2 colonel who was a captain in the Ixil under Lucas, "and despite the shelling, we would find no dead, no wounded, *nobody*. Fires would still be burning but they had all been alerted to the army's arrival by the guerrillas' own advance-warning system: *fuerzas irregulares locales*. This was incredibly psychologically demoralizing for our troops. Later, we found out that the wounded or dead had been hurriedly carried by back up to the subterranean guerrilla hospital in the hills" (interview).

In response, Benedicto Lucas "assembled all troops, especially those from the Ixcán area, Jutiapa, and Cobán, in a very desperate move, and launched an offensive using mass tactics" — leaving the Ixcán area unguarded (Gramajo, interview). The army, he said, was going to be on the offensive as long as it was necessary to do so. The objective of these operations, however, was only secondarily to fight the rebels: most of those killed were unarmed civilians fleeing the army and thus considered, by definition, *subversivos*. Even with General Benny's French counterinsurgency training at Saint Cyr and in Algeria in the 1950s, military critics argue that these operations were "without any planning or logistical base, and thus indiscriminate because [the army] did not understand guerrilla warfare" (interviews). To counter guerrilla actions, for example, the Army Chief of Staff organized mobile patrols (*patrullas móbiles*) in Santa Cruz del Quiché that received instructions from the Army Chief of Staff's office to move from one place to another, surfacing forty days later in Huehuetenango: "It was supposed to give the impression that the army was winning the war." By January and February 1982, however, "resources were depleted" because most of *los tácticos* were "old, corrupt officers more interested in making money than in maintaining the institution," stated one *estratégico* officer (interview). President-General Romeo Lucas's constant rotation of commanders (to prevent coup attempts), moreover, worked at cross purposes to these operations, and troops continued to mostly react to guerrilla attacks tit for tat and then move on. Nevertheless, the Lucas regime managed to kill an estimated 35,000 on both sides as a result of the Iximché operations in the highlands as well as in Guatemala City—the majority of victims unarmed civilians. High casualty rates among junior officers from claymore mines, guerrilla offensives, and the lack of medicine at the army hospital (due to the lack of cash from corruption), the meanspirited officer pension law,[4] the systematic overuse of troops and their sense that they had been "abandoned" by a very old and stagnant High Command all contributed to low troop and officer morale and "enormous discontentment, especially among the second- and third-level *comandantes*" (intelligence source, interview). (According to one anecdote, when "General Benny" visited troops during the Christmas of 1981, he and his staff were dressed, in contrast to the tired olive-green fatigues of the troops, in new camouflage uniforms with new airborne-style boots, prompting the commander of Chimaltenango to say to him, "It seems you are the army of the rich and we are the army of the poor.") As a result, junior officers began surreptitiously preparing for a coup in late 1981, demanding new leadership and strategy to regain the army's institutionality and sense of purpose. The shift entailed an intensification and systematization of the already brutal counterinsurgency policy.

The *estratégicos* or *institucionalistas*, who were, for the most part, younger CEM and special forces-trained intelligence officers, staged a coup in March 1982 and immediately began drawing up their own plans. After purging the more corrupt officers (by exile or retirement), they centrally coordinated all intelligence forces to fight subversion: "Kamikaze" Special Reaction Military Police Battalion in the city, the Presidential Security Office (Archivos), army intelligence (G-2), an Army Public Relations office and Civil Affairs units in the highlands. This concentration of energies and forces resulted in the most closely coordinated, intensive massacre campaign in Guatemalan history, killing an estimated 75,000 in 18 months (most in the first eight months, between April and November 1982, primarily in the departments of Chimaltenango, Quiché, Huehuetenango and the Vérapaces). "One of the first things we did was draw up a document for the campaign with annexes and appendices. It was a complete job with planning down to the last detail," stated Gramajo proudly (interview).

The Pacification Campaign

As in every counterinsurgency war, the primary objective of this scorched-earth campaign—initially called by the High Command Operación Ceniza, or Operation Ashes, and then changed (at least for public relations uses) to "OPPLAN Victoria 82" or "*la pacificación*" for short—was to "separate and isolate the insurgents from the civilian population" with full military force—or in militarese, the reverse: "to rescue the noncombatant civilian population" from the guerrilla (Cifuentes 1982: 26). Ríos Montt, in his weekly television sermons, called for the need to surgically excise evil from Guatemala, and "dry up the human sea in which the guerrilla fish swim" (Richard 1985: 95). The searing contradiction of scorched-earth warfare, though, is that in order to accomplish this "separation," certain areas are targeted for massive killings: that is, the military must treat the civilians they are to "rescue" *as though they are combatants*, killing and burning all living things within the "secured area." No distinction is made between combatant and noncombatant; separation is purely rhetorical. Nor are killings accidental "abuses" or "excesses"; rather, they represent a scientifically precise, sustained orchestration of a systematic, intentional massive campaign of extermination. Indeed, the very existence of the Guatemalan Army's 30/70 percent formula indicates an attempt to make war more scientifically precise in its human costs and consequences. In Guatemala, it was primarily the indigenous population in the most highly active guerrilla zones that was targeted in order to sever the guerrillas from their civilian support network. This meant literally emptying the local population from its socio-cultural and geographic habitat in order to create logistical and recruitment difficulties of every order. Mass killing in areas called by Gramajo as "killing zones" (*matazonas*) was thus inexorable to these campaigns. The major difference with the *luquista* approach of "100 percent" extermination is the attachment of sweeps of "annihilation" to sweeps of "recuperation" (*aniquilamiento y recuperación*). The plan of the institutionalist officers was first to exterminate thousands upon thousands of indigenous noncombatants in waves of terror and then recoup any refugee-prisoners left over in order to ensure the *permanent* destruction of the combatants' infrastructure.

On the day after the coup, 24 March 1982, Colonel Gramajo was made Deputy Chief of Staff, serving by his own admission as the "coordinator and supervisor of the military commanders of operations of the western zone (Alta and Baja Verapaces, El Quiché, Huehuetenango, and Chimaltenango)." The very next day he went to Chimaltenango to "ensure troop loyalty." His job was to oversee "military operations and Civil Affairs with regard to personnel, logistics, and intelligence" during the first year of the Pacification campaign—a campaign he refers to as his "baby" (interview). Within the Army General Staff, he strategized with Colonel Rodolfo Lobos Zamora and Colonel César Augusto Cáceres Rojas to determine, with much precision, the eight departments considered geographic "areas of conflict" with major guerrilla support. On 5 April, the confidential Plan Nacional de Seguridad y Desarrollo Directive Number 0002 was formally presented to the Junta Militar de Gobierno, the Grupo Asesor, and the Ministers of State; it was formally signed by the Junta on 10 April 1982, and the campaign officially began on 20 April. The main objective of the Plan was to create a comprehensive policy for the implementation of this counterinsurgency initiative that provided "development within a context of rational and effective security." Appendix H (Standing Orders for the Development of Antisubversive Operations) was added and signed by Army Chief of Staff López Fuentes and Operations (G-3) Chief Mendoza García on 16 July 1982.

Militarily, the Plan resulted in a centralized and highly coordinated system of command for an intensification of the massacre campaign. First, the presence of a "maximum military command" (*máximo mando militar*), operating from the Army General Staff (with all its centralized communication and technical resources) was made an integral part of the structure of military zone commanders. Second, the operational strategy of the sweep campaign was organized around Task Forces (*Fuerzas de Tarea*): each was assigned a Task Force commander and given "the responsibility" of a particular conflict zone. In turn, each Task Force was internally a "structural component in which various *comandos* are integrated, and in sweeps, all units of the armed forces are involved," one G-2 colonel stated (interview). For example, the Mariscal Zavala Brigade[5] had as its primary responsibility the Ixil Triangle, which coordinated sweep operations with other Reservas Estratégicas (units without fixed jurisdictions), paratroopers, Kaibils, the Honor Guard and the Air Force Tactical Group (of the Aurora Air Base). Within El Quiché proper, Task Forces were designated certain areas: Fuerza de Tarea Operación Cumarcaj[6] consisted of elite units of paratroopers, the Air Force Tactical Group, and the Army Corps of Engineers, which together coordinated the "sweeps through Nebaj, La Perla, Chiul and San Juan Cotzal against the *19 de enero* EGP column." Another Task Force, Operación Chacacaj, headed by Colonel (and later General and Defense Minister) Luis Enrique Mendoza, commanded sweep operations through Uspantán and parts of Huehuetenango, and again included the elite paratrooper unit. In late 1982, Col. Getellá was placed in charge of Task Force Iximché in Chimaltenango, taking over from *luquista* Tactical Group commander Col. Carlos González. Units of soldiers would be made "*disponible*," or unassigned and available immediately, integrated with air support, given a commander, and ordered into an operation (anonymous colonel, interview). Large operations, such as the San Francisco, Plan de Sánchez, and Cuarto Pueblo massacres, included helicopter gunships and bombing raids in which 105 mm mortar grenades and recoilless rockets were used (Figures 3, 4).

This meant that there was significant but not carte blanche operational flexibility at the local levels for individual military commanders. Gramajo's role as inspector general and deputy chief of staff included speaking with commanders at each military zone, giving them information about which villages to attack, and traveling around the highlands by helicopter to direct the war effort. But, he added, "they, too, had a lot of leeway as there was much decentralization [of tasks]. . . . Each military field commander was disposed to their own ways of how the strategy was to be implemented at the local level. Nevertheless, they had their Objectives: protect the population, recuperate the population indoctrinated with ideas foreign to Guatemala, and neutralize the insurgents." These Objectives were maintained through strict military discipline and hierarchization of rank: Gramajo and the Army General staff were kept informed hourly and daily via radio transmission logs and intelligence reports about all details of the campaign. "There was a slight separation between theory and practice (*criterios y práctica*)" one colonel explained. "*But a comandante could not follow his own strategy against his superiors*," he went on to emphasize (interview). The command structure was later strengthened in 1983 with a new strategic deployment and an expansion of military zones from nine to nineteen, including two separate zones established in northern and southern Quiché (Sta. Cruz del Quiché [ZM 20] and Playa Grande, Ixcán [ZM 22]).

Third, local civilian populations were mobilized into patrols and with Decree-Law 44-82 (Recopilador de Leyes 1982: 175), 2000 reservists were recalled to active duty for six-month tours to augment military and civil defense forces (Sheehan 1989: 147). As Gramajo recounts, "We recalled reservists to active duty and all the doctors, teachers, civil engineers, people working for the government in Cobán [Alta Verapaz], Huehuetenango, [and] Quiché had to spend time in the areas of conflict. If they refused to go, they would be forced to join the military ranks" (interview). Air Force and Naval Reserves were created (Decree-Law 47-82) together with Civil Patrols and Ixil companies of "local soldiers." In all, the number of troops increased from 27,000 to approximately 36,000. Troops were decentralized into smaller, company-sized units of between 60 and 120 men, and put through "reconditioning: we rested, reequipped, and did a lot of things normal armies do to prepare for an offensive" in April 1982 (Gramajo, interview). Just before the offensive, Gramajo (accompanied by Presidential Chief of Staff Colonel Victor Argueta), called on the U.S. and Mexican Ambassadors to ask them "to tell the guerrillas that we want to have a dialogue"; otherwise, "a lot of blood is going to be spilled" (Gramajo interview). But as "the subversives did not heed our warning, we went ahead with our plans" (Gramajo interview, Berganza and Klussman *Prensa Libre* 1987).[7] This remark reflects the principal feature of the Pacification campaign: massacre.

To get at the guerrilla, "it was determined village by village if each was infiltrated and consciously or unconsciously involved [with the guerrilla]," Gramajo explains in an interview. The Task Force Cumarcaj intelligence report on the "Order of Battle of the Subversive Opponent," detailed, for example, how the EGP "19 de enero" column would "win or neutralize villages west of Chajul" and had villages "under their control" to the southwest; villages to the northwest were "in favor of the army" (Gramajo 1995: 182–83). On the drawing boards of the Army General Staff and in garrison headquarters, villages were assigned a colored pin. Those villages in the "red zones" were in enemy territory: no distinction was made between the *guerrilleros* and their peasant supporters. Both were to be attacked and obliterated. All villages in the Ixil were considered "red," one colonel stated matter-of-factly (interview). Those in the "pink zones" were to be attacked but left standing, and those in the "white zones" (with green pins) were "safe villages" to be left alone. The counterinsurgency war was "elaborated down to the last detail and the enemy, which had to be eliminated, very carefully defined" (officer quoted in Comité Pro-Justicia y Paz 1986: 33). The Army General Staff demarcated with a semicircle a sector in the highlands where they perceived the EGP to have the greatest support and where the Catholic Church and popular organizations had been most active. Upon studying this territory, they came to see that this region had one of the lowest indexes of basic services, education, and local development. Nonetheless, despite such levels of poverty, support for the EGP, at least in the Ixil Triangle, seems to have been more fleeting, skyrocketing only after each wave of massive repression as a form of protection from the army (cf. Stoll 1993; Falla 1994). Fully aware that the EGP had not sufficiently "ideologized" the peasants — "*Never, never* in their lives did the subversion believe in the population" (Gramajo, interview)[8] — the plan was to first "isolate and separate the civilian population from the guerrilla, forcing them to make a choice: them or us" and then proceed to loot the *fuerzas irregulares locales* civil defense system that would force the population into the same kind of murderous complicity with the military that the military accused them of having with the guerrilla. "That was what we needed to understand [to win the war]: the phenomenon of *campesinos* being between two armies and not necessarily belonging to either. . . . Not everyone was an EGP volunteer," stated Colonel Noack (1995 interview).

The Army General Staff ordered the newly established "primary" Fuerzas de Tarea into the departments with the heaviest activity of the EGP guerrillas: Chimaltenango (Task Force Iximché), El Quiché (Task Force Cumarcaj), and Huehuetenango, including the Ixcán (Task Force Chacacaj), and Baja and Alta Verapaz. "Secondary" Task Forces were later launched in the January 1983 TOSO (Teatro de Operaciónes Sur Occidental) campaign against the southwestern ORPA region. "We began in Chimaltenango," Gramajo explained, "moved into Quiché and then later on into Alta Verapaz and Baja Verapaz, and the rest of the country, from south to north and east to west," concentrating on areas where the EGP guerrillas were organizing among the indigenous population, and/or where there had been much popular organizing (see Figure 4). The campaign officially began on 20 April 1982, when "three captains, two battalions and several air force pilots" (Sereseres, interview) providing aerial (air plane and helicopter) bombardment support were sent in on a concentrated "sweep operation" to attack and destroy "the villages of Estancia de la Virgen, Choatalún and Chipila in Chimaltenango," according to Gramajo (interview). Later, it was estimated that over 250 peasants in these villages, including children and women in their homes, had been killed either by the bombardment or by ground troops opening fire on the civilian population.[9] (Estancia de la Virgen and Choatalún would later serve as one of the first strategic-hamlet/PAAC (Plan of Assistance to Conflict Areas) resettlement experiments in October 1982.) Daily orders were given to field commanders as to which villages to strike (in the red zones), and which individuals were to be eliminated (in the pink zones), and hourly radio contact was maintained for updates and body counts with zone army headquarters, which, in turn, received their orders from the Army General Staff. According to standard army operating procedures, one colonel explained, these activities were recorded in a "Diary of Operations" for inspection by Gramajo and reviewed with each field commander in his weekly meetings with them. "I coordinated and supervised all the military [field] commanders, personally overseeing the Bullets effort, traveling throughout the highlands by helicopter" (interview).

Drawing out the "pacification" campaign strategy of the army on the table, Gramajo explains how the strategy was one in which "the Army attacked: here were the villages, here is the population supporting *la guerrilla* from behind, and the Army attacked *everyone* and we continued attacking, attacking until we cornered them and we got to the point where the *población* was separated from the subversive leaders. . . . Exactly in '82 [he slams the table] this strategy began" (interview; his emphasis). The second phase of the campaign was to "saturate the area with patrols" of sixty or more men, rounding up and sweeping the refugee population into army garrisons where, effectively prisoners, they were interrogated, tortured, and either summarily shot (if suspected of guerrilla involvement) or relocated into hastily constructed strategic hamlets (compounds surrounded by barbed wire and watchtowers). "We did a 180-degree turn in strategy in which the displaced, instead of being considered a nuisance to military operations, were collected and brought to the village. Before 1982, if we did not deliberately kill the people we did not care for the people" (Gramajo, interview w/o attribution)[10] (see Figures 8 and 9). To assure that "sweep areas" remained militarily secured, small combat units were based on a strategy of presence — or "position and denial" (Sheehan 1989: 142, 150). Separated from the large garrisons, these units developed their own intelligence nets based on direct contact with the local population, who provided the military units, as did the earlier guerrilla forces, with logistical support such as food

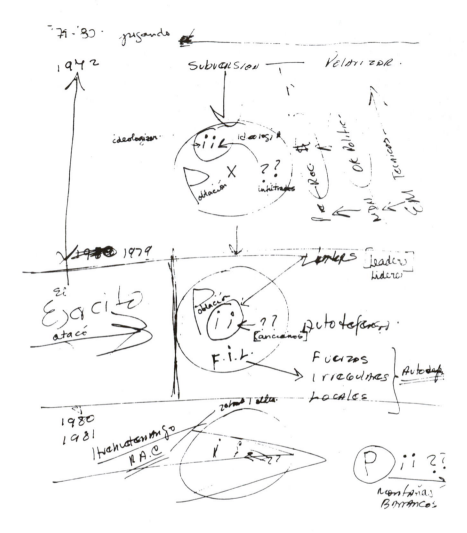

Figure 8. General Gramajo's sketch: 1972–79 guerrillas (represented as ??) infiltrating and ideologizing leaders (ii); 1979 the army attacked the population (P), confronting the Local Irregular Forces (FIL). One Civil Patrol (PAC) was organized in 1980/81 in Huehuetenango.

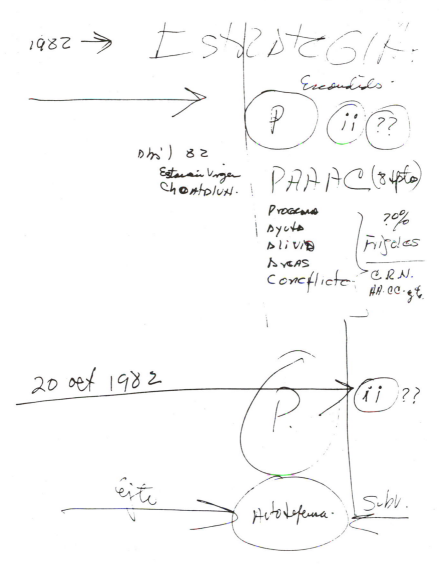

Figure 9. General Gramajo's sketch: the Strategy in 1982 was, "the army continued attacking, attacking until we cornered them and . . . the population (P) was separated from the subversive leaders" (??) (ii). The Plan of Action in Areas of Conflict (PAAC) began 20 October 1982 at Estancia de la Virgen and Choatalún, Chimaltenango.

production. In other words, these units began to duplicate guerrilla tactics, combing the rural area to "annihilate the local clandestine committees (CCL) and the guerrillas' permanent military units (UMP)" and "eliminate" those suspected of being guerrillas or complicitous with them. With the reorganization of more numerous and smaller military units, response times were shortened: army units at large garrisons could react within an hour or two to support local defense forces under attack by guerrilla forces (Letona 1989: 20). In this manner, the several tactical stages of counterinsurgency, while theoretically consequential, could be implemented simultaneously in an area where guerrilla forces were still operating (Richards 1985: 96). Moreover, according to Letona, an estimated "20,000 former enemy guerrillas and sympathizers enrolled in the amnesty program in the first year. Some were combatants, others were part of the logistical or political structure, and some belonged to the political and military leadership structure." Many would become Civil Patrols members "providing an invaluable source of information to military units" (1989: 21). Civil Patrollers familiar with an area were often used to root out survivors in the bush.

"Rules of Engagement" and a "Code of Conduct" were established as guidelines for army units after the March 1982 coup: "The rules served to emphasize respect for the civilian population and thereby obtain their respect for the government and the armed forces" (Letona 1989: 21). Asked how the army could distinguish between the *campesino* and the subversion if both were *indígena*, Gramajo responded: "He who had a gun, we responded with guns, and he who didn't, no." Navy Captain Jorge Mazariegos explained the difference on the basis of literacy: "They say, 'you are the army of the rich, we [of the EGP] are the army of the poor. I'm poor so I'm in this army. So they [the guerrillas] deceive him! *But if they aren't illiterate, then they aren't deceived"* and have joined up willingly (1990 interview; his emphasis). Other officers who served in the Ixil at this time have since admitted that unarmed civilians were routinely killed:

"*Everyone, everyone* was a guerrilla; no difference was made in killing them. The big difference" in the shift in strategy after the 1982 coup "was that we couldn't eliminate them all" (*Todos, todos, no había diferencia en matarlos. La gran diferencia fue que no podíamos eliminar a todos.*) Some were captured and their lives spared so they could serve as informers. (intelligence col., interview)

Asked how one could separate out the civilian population from the guerrilla if one could not distinguish between the two, one army intelligence colonel, who served as a captain in San Juan Cotzal in early 1982, explains how informers were created and a separation within the population made. He suggested there were "two ways: One way was by conviction: you say to the prisoner, 'You have to accept what I'm telling you. We understand the problem: here everyone is incorporated into the guerrilla. I am offering you an opportunity to work with us or them (*juegan con nosotros o juegan con ellos*). It's your choice' " (interview). When asked, what if the individual chose the guerrilla, the colonel slapped his hands together and said: "Then you are my enemy and I'm going to use weapons to combat you. If you join us, I'll help you." According to the colonel, this, in turn, generated a list of names of those principally responsible for "subversion." This came "from the same villagers who among them know who is who. So when one goes to [penetrate] the organizational levels of the local clandestine committees [CCL and FIL], they will know who is the *jefe* of another CCL and FIL, and will identify the most important leaders. . . . When [the villagers] see that this particular leader is detained, and that he may talk — 'this guy is such-and-such, his name is so-and-so, he served in the army at such-and-such a time and so forth' — and they see that you know the score (*que tiene argumentos en la mano*), then they all start to sing, pointing fingers at men lined up around the plaza, saying, 'He's a guerrilla, he's another guerrilla, him over there brought me into the organization, et cetera.' *They themselves start to create a separation between themselves and the guerrilla.* The other way to create this separation is with Civil Patrols" (intelligence col. interview; emphasis added).

To combat subversion, the Army assumes common ideological heresy: everyone is "the enemy." An arbitrary separation is made to "penetrate" and "destroy" those who are by fiat deemed "lost" to subversion and to terrorize the others into collaborating. Using the tactic of guilt reversal, villagers are massacred to save them from themselves; others are tortured to collaborate. "Combating subversion" in this manner is the principal task of army intelligence (G-2): one intelligence operative during this period was posted to various military garrisons to torture guerrillas "for all the information one can get. In the torture sessions we ask, 'Where are your *compañeros*? Where is your *campamento*? Who are the ones who give you food? medicine? money?' And this *guerrillero* (who perhaps by deceit or by force was inducted into the guerrilla), when he falls into our hands and has the opportunity to live, he gives us every little thing he knows. He informs on others even without too much of a beating. And this person is given a uniform and a rifle without bullets because when he goes out to show us where the *campamento* is, a man without uniform or rifle will be seen by the *guerrilleros* (who, by the way, always see the soldiers arrive but not vice versa) as a 'guide coming to give us up' and he is shot. But if he tells us all he knows, he becomes an army collaborator who can finger individuals working either directly or indirectly with the *guerrillera*, and that's how we capture more people [to torture for more information]" (interview). As one colonel adds, "We have learned through all these years of confrontation to beat, torture, and kill and all of that: all the interrogation techniques one learns at different schools, such as *el garrote*. [But] at certain moments some guerrillas can give in without using any force at all and provide us important information. This happened once in El Quiché when a guerrilla I had decided wasn't worth any more of my time and I was getting ready to eliminate him, this one ophthalmologist (who was serving as a psychologist *especialista* in the Ixil) got him talking and we learned about the EGP hospital in the *montaña*" (interview). The G-2 operative adds:

But, there are also individuals captured in combat, at a registration point [on the road], or taking food to the guerrilla who say to you, "No, son of so-and-so, I am a *guerrillero*, I'll give no one up." The mission of a *guerrillero* is to leave and return dead or alive but never to give anyone up. . . . So, when this person will give no information, one tortures him so unmercifully (*hasta la peor desgracia que puede existir en la vida*). Then one assassinates him and throws the body into a ravine or buries him or dumps the body by the side of the road.

This same G-2 operative stated

There are times when the *comandante* comes into the room where one is torturing in order to supervise and see what one is learning from the victim. At other times, when the *comandante* sees that one is trying to get information out of this person and they're giving us nothing, he will say, "No, this one will give us nothing" and he unlatches his 9 mm, grabs it, and shoots him right then and there in the head. Then he says, "Go throw this one away" (*Vayan a botarlo a este*). At other times he leaves it up to the *elemento* to do whatever he wants with his prisoner, that he works with what he has (*que trabaje con lo que tiene*). (interview; see Appendix 2)

Preparing for the sweeps through the *departamentos* with the heaviest guerrilla activity — Quiché and Huehuetenango — Ríos Montt announced an amnesty on 24 May for all guerrillas and collaborators who turned themselves in by 1 July; after that, he said, "a merciless struggle" would begin. These series of amnesties throughout 1982 and 1983, together with psychological warfare, would later be claimed to be key to the army's successful campaign, as it began to create a network of army informants and patrollers who "were forced to choose sides."

Having established a permanent presence in Chimaltenango, dispatching patrols of sixty men or more to continue the "sweep," the Army General Staff directed other Task Forces into Quiché and Huehuetenango, intensifying their massacre operations with bombings, burning, and looting in areas previously hard hit by the sporadic operations under Lucas García. Humarcaj "began in Sta. Cruz del Quiché by cleansing, controlling, calming, and normalizing (*pimpiar, controlar, tranquilizar, y normalizar*). Then we moved on into the Ixil Triangle [to continue our work]" (general, interview). Between April and October 1982, the "pacification" phase of carefully orchestrated massacres and sustained terror destroyed the subsistence and surveillance base for the guerrilla among the population: *hacer una matazona*, as soldiers in the field referred to it, creating "killing zones" and forcing refugees and guerrillas to flee into the mountains or to Mexico. Given this concentration of troops and resources at each operation, and the lack of any substantial self-defense in these communities, these actions resulted less in confrontations with the guerrilla and more in systematic massacre of the civilian population. As one intelligence colonel remarked, "Ever since the Conquest, there have not been conflicts in the world in which there were no abuses" (interview). That was the army's intention: unlike later offensives, the objective in this campaign was only secondarily to fight the rebels.

The military's path of destruction—following the trail of the EGP—left the greatest devastation and death in Chimaltenango, northern and southern Quiché, and northern Huehuetenango. In the more remote areas, in which the army equated isolation with access to guerrilla units, and thus as "red," entire villages (in which everyone, including and sometimes especially the elderly, women, and children were targeted) were massacred by being tortured, raped, garroted, killed with a machete, hacked or bashed to death, shot or burned alive; valuables were looted, crops burned, domestic animals slaughtered, and only the shells of buildings remained in these *matazonas*. When Gramajo was asked whether there were families and children killed by the army in this campaign, his response was, "Possibly, when we encountered a group in a ravine or something like that" (interview).[11] Villages in red zones, he admitted, were "heavily attacked" by the army with much loss of life (interview w/o attribution). An estimated forty-two rural massacres were carried out in the army's offensive in the month of July alone: On 17 July, one day after the army's Appendix H for antisubversive operations was signed by the Chief of Staff, almost an entire village of over three hundred Indian peasants was shot, hacked, choked, smashed against trees, or burned to death at San Francisco, Nentón, in the department of Huehuetenango (Falla 1983). On 18 July, 268 people (12 percent under the age of three) from thirteen villages and hamlets, including Plan de Sánchez and the municipal center of Rabinal in Alta Verapaz, were massacred by the armed forces. The majority were killed by being raped, shot, struck, and burned. On 5–6 December, Kaibils[12] and Civil Patrollers dressed as guerrillas arrived and asked for food; when they were provided food, they accused the villagers of being guerrillas. Three hundred fifty men, women, and children were shot, young girls raped, children's head smashed, and the community set fire (Guatemalan Human Rights Ombudsman 1996 Report). Two earlier massacres, a week before the March coup, were also carried out: 173 villagers had their necks broken or were shot, and children had their heads smashed against rocks at Río Negro, Baja Verapaz, on 13 March; and 324–550 villagers at Cuarto Pueblo, Ixcán, were rounded up, tortured, raped, shot, and burned alive on 14 March 1982. The entire community was razed (Equipo Antropologia Forense Guatemala 1996).

At "yellow" or "white" settlements, often closer to major roads or towns, which army intelligence perceived as less compromised by the guerrilla, more selective killings and torture were carried out, sometimes without the destruction of crops or buildings: "It depends on how far the problem gets out of hand; if it gets out of hand, then brute force is necessary," Gramajo concluded (interview).[13]

The northwestern highland offensive ended "sooner than expected," in December 1982 (Gramajo, interview), and the strategists turned to confront "the 3500 well-equipped ORPA combatants" in the southwestern quadrant of the country to "return the productive south coast to normalcy. . . . As we said in the Army General Staff at this time, 'When the analysis coincides with our desires, the analysis should be repeated' " (Gramajo 1995: 202–5). TOSO, under the command of Gramajo, entailed sweeps, massacres, patrols, and "roundups" of refugee-prisoners throughout Retalhuleu, Suchitepéquez, San Marcos, Quetzaltenango, Totonicapán, and Sololá between January and May 1983. Military zones were expanded at this time, particularly in Suchitepéquez, San Marcos, Sololá, and Retalhuleu, to provide commanders with a battalion assigned to the military base in each zone (Figure 4). This also prevented certain colonels from having too much control over large zones.[14]

As intended, this wave of tortures, burnings, rapes, garrotings, massacres, and lootings terrified the population, prompting entire villages to be abandoned and dislocating between 250,000 and 1 million people, or 10 percent of the total population;[15] the San Francisco massacre alone prompted 9000 to flee (Davis 1988: 10). One US-AID-funded report of March 1984 comments on the situation in the Department of Quiché: "Perhaps as much as 80% of the population on the village level were displaced. Our findings indicate that this displacement was due to: 10% massacres, 20% destruction of homes and 70% fear" (PAVA 1984: 79). A 1985 army public relations booklet triumphantly claims razing at least 440 villages (Ejército 1985: 62), with over 100 hamlets alone destroyed in the Ixil Triangle. The army's estimate of those killed range from 150,000 (by Ríos Montt in a newspaper interview and later disclaimed) (Nyrop 1984: 189) to "25,000 to 30,000" (by Gramajo, interview). Human rights estimates of those killed range between 50,000 and 75,000 (WOLA 1985), with 250,000 children having lost at least one parent to the violence (24,000 of these in El Quiché alone) (Guatemalan Human Rights Commission 1984). In 1986, municipal authorities in each of the three main towns in the Ixil Triangle—in which the military indiscriminately burned and attacked virtually every rural Indian settlement in the area—estimated that approximately one-third of their rural population had been killed (Smith 1990b: 18) (Figure 5). Only the towns dominated by ladinos escaped massive retaliation (cf. Stoll 1993).

Gramajo admits "there was a good deal of hardship for the population, there is no doubt; I won't deny that the army committed excesses, abuses, and undisciplined acts. . . . But, we were not killing *indígenas* [on purpose]. Now, it's true, *indígenas* died in all this in substantial numbers because there were a high number of *indígenas* in the army and because they had been carried away by the subversion" (interview). The death and destruction continue to be viewed by military officers as unfortunate but necessary consequences in their justified campaign strategy to destroy the guerrillas. They blame the guerrilla for using villagers as shields and for deceiving them, referring to the emptied and destroyed villages as "the extraction by the guerrilla of 276,000 souls from their places of origin by means of threats and acts of punishment in open violations of human rights" (Colonel Mario Rolando Terraza-Pinot, Ejército 1987b: 7); Gramajo refers to these razed villages as "pueblos fantasmas" (ghost towns) (ibid.: 22; 1995: 154). At least one American advisor to the Salvadoran army, however, recognized the Guatemalan army's responsibility for the destruction of these villages, calling it "a moral outrage as well as unnecessary and counterproductive in the long term" (Sheehan 1989: 142). (Guatemalan officers often respond to such criticisms by pointing out that that is why the Salvadoran army "lost the war: because of U.S. advisors.") The guerrillas did their share of burning town halls, shooting mayors, and, especially after the Civil Patrols were established that destroyed their surveillance and logistical base, killing uncooperative indigenous peasants, and these should be roundly condemned. But the scale and the intensity of such killings was not at all comparable to the army's systematic and perfidious policy of *matazonas*.

PAAC: The Beans

Thousands of refugees succumbed to the army's "Food for Work" program—the Beans part of the Beans and Bullets strategy—and it was a critical element of the war strategy. PAAC, or Plan of Action in Areas of Conflict, coordinated by the reincarnated National Committee for Reconstruction (CRN), was the phase of "immediate development" contiguous with the Pacification. As Gramajo narrates:

The Army continued attacking, separating the population from the subversive leaders. To escape the army attacks in October 1981, the *población* had gone into the mountains and *barrancos* (ravines), and we had a model plan to deliver food [to them]: a plan of beans and not just guns. On the 20th of October [1982], the refugees in [Choatalún], Chimaltenango came down from the hills and Iximché Task Force commander Colonel Getellá, said to them, "Peace with the army. We aren't fighting you, we are fighting the *subversivos*." And they said, "Give us food." But we didn't give them food because that is not our obligation. We said, "Go back to your village, take out the food you have hidden away or grow your crops. Go and live in peace." So the *indígenas* went back to their villages. . . . We drew them out of hiding with the Beans. (interview) (see Figure 9)

Beans, though, would always be accompanied by Bullets. A number of foreign missions of human rights inquiry into reports of killings in Chimaltenango in October 1982 concluded that peasants who had been promised by the army that they could return safely to their homes after the earlier military attacks but who were suspected of any involvement with the guerrillas were summarily executed. Of an estimated 5000 or more Cakchiquels who came down from the hills into the town of Chimaltenango, for example, the army detained and later shot dead thirty men who were accused of guerrilla involvement (Amnesty International 1982: 142). Five thousand "displaced" were brought in by patrols or arrived on their own accord in Chacaj, 7000 in Playa Grande, 4000 in Chisec (Baja Verapaz), and 8000 in Nebaj alone (Col. Wahlers, 1986 interview) (see Figure 5).

Within PAAC, Shelter, Work, and Food (*Techo, Trabajo, y Tortilla*) programs were coordinated by officers of the Civil Affairs (S-5) units established in June 1982. These programs served as the army's exchange centers in the postmassacre zones, where sometimes for food and always for intelligence on the whereabouts of the guerrilla, the refugee would be told: "If you join us, we will feed you. If not, we will kill you" (intelligence colonel, interview). Surveillance of refugees provided the army with information about the guerrilla. Gramajo, who claims to have organized and established the S-5 units in the countryside, argues that the destruction of villages went hand-in-hand with surveillance: "For example, I was watching the widows from the destroyed villages: how many there were, how much they ate, who gave them food, and where the orphans were and who attended to them" (interview).

Food for Work programs forcibly recruited peasants, primarily for intelligence purposes and soldiering, then for road construction with the Army Engineers Brigade and later for refugee model village projects. The major purpose of the refugee camps was "to sustain the success of the campaign by breaking the infrastructural support of the guerrillas and minimize the participation and killing of noncombatants, because [the army] wasn't wining the war by doing so" (Sereseres, interview).

Another fundamental tactic of the post-1982 coup campaigns (and missing in the Lucas García operations) was the sophisticated manipulation of disinformation, or war propaganda, as found in "Standing Orders for the Development of Anti-Subversive Operations: Tactics to be Employed" to the Victoria '82 Campaign: "Trick them: subversion must be fought with its own methods and techniques. A Plan of Disinformation must be in effect at all times" (Ejército 1982b, Appendix H). At the national level, while the Lucas García regime used a violent and primitive anticommunist discourse, the *estratégicos* employed a language that referred to the impoverished social reality of most Guatemalans, spoke of plans of development, offered to respect human, indigenous, and religious rights, and sought to establish an electoral democracy — thus achieving a certain level of disorientation internationally, especially after the election of a civilian president in 1986. It was at the level of war propaganda, as Aguilera has pointed out, that the discourse became more sophisticated in two respects: (1) the government is portrayed as at war by necessity with the support of the people (achieved by the legal imputation of amnesty and Civil Patrols), and (2) the guerrillas are depicted as the authors of the massacres—achieved by the Machiavellian technique of imputed blame or framing: they are the reason why we had to commit atrocities; they caused us to do so by duping villagers into collaboration with the subversives (1983: 94).

Indígenas were culpable for allowing themselves to be placed, as Gramajo notes, "between the two fires" of the subversives and the army; all that they suffered was due to their own mistakes. "People with a bias will see only the brutality of the armed forces and won't see the errors, the responsibility, of the guerrillas. . . . They would send the population out to die because they were opposing us without weapons, without anything. They were just protecting eight to ten guys with rifles of the guerrilla forces" (interview w/o attribution). It has been argued that a good deal of the Ríos Montt strategy was borrowed from the U.S. Embassy MILGroup's recommendations in the mid-1970s. Its Program of Pacification and Eradication of Communism called for "combining psychological warfare with regular and irregular military tactics . . . to confuse and create the belief that in Guatemala there is a civil war between peasants and the revolutionary forces" (Black et al. 1984: 134; Barahona 1984: 109). It is difficult to confirm just how much influence this document had on Guatemalan military thinking: U.S. counterinsurgency expert César Sereseres estimated this shift in strategy was "60 percent Guatemalan, which they themselves thought up, 20 percent was learned from U.S. strategy in Vietnam, and 20 percent was from Israeli and Taiwanese military officers who have specific experience with 'more operational' procedures. The Israelis have experience with terrorists; the Taiwanese with political warfare" (interview).

Military intelligence appears to have been quite precise as to guerrilla activity on the map, but there are some contradictions in its claims as well as indications that its cultural understandings are not only racist but surprisingly outdated. Its claim to want to reestablish the elders (*ancianos*) conflicts with reports by survivors of massacres who have related how troops and officers took especial care to kill the *costumbristas* and other local transmittors of indigenous tradition with their strong ties to the local habitat. What is more likely the case is that this military activity represents an attempt to "normalize" culture by restructuring it along lines that emanate from the military's idealized vision of frozen Mayan traditions and their desire for a loyal *indigenista*. Gramajo's and Cifuentes's Strategic Appraisals in 1980 and 1981, for example, sought to create a radically altered cultural and religious, i.e., apolitical Sanctioned Mayan (see Chapter 6). They attempt to create an *indígena* who is not so much tied to local tradition as he is loyal to national symbols, the state, and by extension, the army.

The military, moreover, may very well have been unaware of the fissures that had been occurring within many of these Indian communities since the 1960s (when elders were first replaced by cooperatives and later by religious groups) (cf. Arias 1990), or they were aware of the fissures and wanted to quickly reestablish the dominance of the *costumbristas* and merchants imbued with the values of the petty mercantilists with whom the army had maintained close relations. Or alternatively, military officers did not want to talk about just how much they understood of the Indian communities to an anthropologist. What *is* clear is that the extraordinary brutality dealt these Indian communities, together with economic and political forces, have dramatically and inexorably transformed the internal dynamics of indigenous communities vis-à-vis ethnic and class divisions and leadership (cf. Stoll 1993; Arias 1990; Smith 1990a; Warren 1992).

Divisions Within the Army

But the Pacification campaign, and especially the centralization of the command structure, had the ironic effect of creating deep divisions within the army. Gramajo is remembered by officers as a likable but strict theater commander who kept a very tight leash on his field commanders and troops, special staff, and bodyguard officers,[16] and several field commanders (many former *luquista* army general staff officers) who wanted to be able to conduct the war on their own terms. There were at least five mini-rebellions, according to Gramajo, when, as Deputy Chief of Staff, he tried to impose a "blue book," or professional code of conduct and dress code, on the soldiers and officers in the "conflictive zones. I had to go at night by helicopter," Gramajo explains, "because [El Quiché commander] Colonel Matta called me and said he was being threatened by his junior officers. They called him a 'candy ass' because he didn't want to [summarily] execute seventeen prisoners. Instead, he wanted to send them to the Special Tribunals that we'd organized.[17] They wanted to kill them and I put myself in the middle and explained why we solders do not kill people, but rather that the judges have to do this" (1995: 203; interview).

Moreover, many of the special forces, Kaibils, had been allowed under Lucas García to wear long hair, Rambo-style bandanas, beards, and civilian clothing (partly to set them apart as an elite and partly to allow them to be confused with the guerrilla). When a colonel in Chimaltenango asked them to cut their hair, he was thrown in jail. "We came and freed him and promised the officers we wouldn't prosecute them. . . . The same thing happened with other commanders; Ríos ousted one of them" (Gramajo, interview w/o attribution). (Later, during the offensives of 1988 and 1989, there was similar resistance to Gramajo's attempt to create a Comando Unido in which S-1 to S-5 would have been centralized. One colonel in charge at El Aguacate during the massacre there in 1988, José Luis Quilo Ayuso, retorted in regard to this centralization, "He cannot tell me who to kill and who not to kill; I kill whomever I want," according to an anonymous source (1988 interview). These difficulties notwithstanding, to boast, on the one hand, of one's calculated Task Force *strategy* of pacification (compared to the failure of *luquista* "tactics") and the reestablishment of hierarchy, discipline, and the command structure while shrugging off, on the other hand, one's helplessness to stop the "excesses" and "abuses" of commanders who caused 440 villages to be razed and, by the army's own estimates, thirty thousand to be killed within less than eight months, does not follow. How massive and excessive does the killing have to be before it is recognized as intentional policy?

Conclusions

If one were to sketch out this dialectic of violence without diminishing the suffering of the victims, without mystifying the actions of the guerrilla,[18] and without obscuring the Army's major responsibility for the massacre campaign, it would look something like this: the Army's lessons in counterinsurgency in 1966–67 established a Cold War threat mentality to organized unarmed dissent and armed opposition forces; guerrilla forces regrouped in the 1970s and re-thought their strategy for a prolonged, more indigenous-based struggle, and by 1975 they began sabotaging Army convoys on the Pan American Highway, assassinating mayors and a key landowner known for his brutality; in 1979 the Army under Lucas García amassed troops in the Ixil Triangle, where conservative elders had requested the Army's support in eliminating the "communists"; in October 1981, the Army amassed troops under Task Force Iximché in Chimaltenango for a strictly military scorched-earth offensive that cost 35,000 lives; the Army's spiraling and often indiscriminate violence instilled resentment and fear among Indian *campesinos*, driving many into the guerrilla camp; by February 1982 the guerrilla forces could count on over 360,000 (and possibly up to 500,000) supporters; in April 1982 the Army began to more systematically attack, escalating and intensifying its Pacification campaigns of scorched-earth killing zones of those communities perceived to be guerrilla-mobilized in order to isolate and neutralize the guerrillas, while drawing refugees down from the mountains with amnesty and food for intelligence networking purposes; between April and October 1982, massacres of thousands upon thousands of noncombatants (estimated to be 90 percent of those killed) by Task Forces were carefully planned, directed, implemented, and tabulated. The subsistence and surveillance base for the guerrilla was destroyed, obligating both the guerrilla and the population to flee to the mountains (or to Mexico), with an army estimate of 20,000 succumbing to the army's offer of amnesty and even more to the Food for Work program.

The primary shift in thinking between the Lucas García years and the Ríos Montt regime was between the counterinsurgent ideologue officers, or tacticians, on the one hand, who believed in all-out 100 percent random slaughter — "blindness and massacre," according to Gramajo — which had expeditiously fueled the insurgency, and the counterinsurgent strategists of irregular guerrilla warfare, on the other, who implemented the combination of more systematic yet still brutal 30 percent of killing zones (in which everyone and every living thing trapped is killed) with 70 percent "soft" elements of pacification in counterinsurgency strategy, utilizing Civil Affairs with its psychological operations. This shift in strategy signified the army's recognition that it was losing the war as an occupying army, and that it needed to act as a national army that killed but killed more intelligently "to get the job done." General Gramajo describes the distinction as one between the "pre-1982 Lucas military *operations* in which there was an absence of strategy — brute force and nothing more" (interview) which only caused resentment among the population, and the post-1982 military *campaigns*, which brought the resultant refugee population under control and defeated the insurgency.

But the military did more. The discovery of the impoverished majority by *desarrollista* officers in the mid-1970s raised a new consciousness about the causes of insurgency. Colonel Oscar Hugo Alvarez Gómez surmised that "subversion comes from social contradictions: there is a higher class and a lower class. . . . And there is much discrimination. We military people committed a mistake: that most of the fruits of the infrastructure, if we can use this word, came only to the capital. We might say it was a huge mistake. A disproportioned development badly planned, or better put, badly executed since it has been well-planned since 1800" (1986 interview). As a result, the 1982 National Plan of Security and Development recognized that the causes of subversion were "heterogeneous, based on social injustice, political rivalry, unequal development, and the dramas of hunger, unemployment and poverty; but it can be controlled if we attempt to solve the most pressing human problems" (Ejército 1982a: 1). The ability of the military to transform itself and create a development component of counterinsurgency combat operations reflects their institutional flexibility. But it was a development intimately tied to security; there were no Beans without the Bullets, and "we first needed to impose peace," Gramajo explained. The paternalism and authoritarianism of the military's threat mentality concerning the susceptibility of the Indian to manipulation by "foreign ideologies" would remain fundamentally intact (and would hinder the effectiveness of the Poles of Development).

Penetration of the militarized state directly into the heretofore isolated indigenous village was underway. It was the first time in Guatemalan history when both the guerrillas and the army sought to gain the hearts, minds, and stomachs of the indigenous population. With "the ability of civilian and military institutions to work together" — that is, the combination of military force with "effective political coercion," considered a critical, and winning, element for an "effective administration of counterinsurgency programs" — the Guatemalan army "demonstrated an understanding of the political nature of counterinsurgent warfare" (Sheehan 1989: 138). The next chapters show how this new strategy penetrated civilian society on all levels, such that Gramajo could proclaim, "We brought government to the village."

Chapter 3
Anatomy of the Counterinsurgency II

Restructuring Indigenous Life

> We brought government to the village.
> — General Gramajo

> War is not only won with weapons. This National Plan of Security and Development of ours means bringing life [and] revenue to a people, to a community. . . . There is a saying here in Guatemala: you get more with honey than with vinegar.
> — Colonel Alvarez Gómez

To elucidate the military's forceful social, economic, and physical reordering of indigenous life in the "well-massacred"[1] highlands, this chapter will focus on the institutionalization of civil-military strategy through Poles of Development and Inter-Institutional Coordinators and the immersion of counterinsurgency within the military's constitutional project. *El proyecto politico-militar* penetrated civil society on all levels.

Once the Victory '82 OPPLAN had been completed "earlier than expected" in December 1982, leaving behind a swathe of death and economic destruction in the northwest highlands, the army began to organize the relocation of a portion of the estimated 250,000 (50,000 families) to 1 million displaced, many of whom came down from the mountains "following periods of up to three years of wandering and scavenging for survival" (PAVA 1984: 10).[2] As we saw in Chapter 2, the first phase — *Fusiles y frijoles*, or Beans and Bullets — was to feed those displaced by the military's sweeps: they were placed in several dozen refugee camps and settlements initially called *aldeas modelos*, or model villages, sometimes at burned-out sites or in new locations under the Plan of Action in Areas of Conflict (Plan de Acción en Areas de Conflicto, PAAC). The next phase — of "predevelopment," or the "three Ts" in Ríos Montt's words, "Techo, Trabajo, y Tortilla" (Shelter, Work, and

Food) — put the survivors to work. Civil Patrols and labor gangs were organized to hack out rural roads, carry out reforestation, and build secured areas for Poles of Development, where the displaced were resettled in concentrated villages. The last phase of the military scheme was "development" in which "tamed Indian communities — no longer a political threat — would generate new income for themselves and the tottering national economy by farming and selling new cash crops" (Black et al. 1984: 141).

The new military government of General Mejía Víctores, established after the August 1983 military coup against Ríos Montt, as set out in the Plan de Campaña Firmeza '83, to forcefully "penetrate" and restructure the sociocultural, economic, and settlement patterns of the massacred highlands and at the same time, institutionalize the military's permanent presence throughout the country by decreeing two counterinsurgency structures: Inter-Institutional Coordinators (Coordinadoras Inter-Institucionales) (IICs) and Poles of Development and Services (Polos de Desarrollo y Servicios). Within its initial Plan of Action of Maximum Priority (Plan de Acción de Máxima Prioridad), slated for the Ixil Triangle between December 1983 and September 1984, the Mejía regime viewed the IICs and Poles as instrumentalizing processes of social control over minimum daily needs, such as drinking water, electric lights, and housing, of those displaced by the Pacification. They also saw these structures as guaranteeing the military full control of the national territory and major participation in the planning and "running" of the state. With the massacre campaign over, the military's national strategy was now centered on the reorganization of production and rural life for security-qua-development purposes: in the military's mind, to promote forms of "modern production" and private ownership among the indigenous peasant population was a form of "insurance" against any future threats of insurgency (Gramajo, interview). The military severely restricted movement in and out of many of these militarized settlements, including access to land and employment, and by 1983, resentment was building: "The prominence of the military presence as well as our repressive actions created opposition and hostilities within the [rural] population," Gramajo later admitted (Cruz Salazar 1988a).

The military's 1984 booklet *Polos de Desarrollo* leaves little doubt that the military recognized the urgency for prioritizing security-qua-development,

It is important to emphasize that. . . . operations of security, development, countersubversive and ideological warfare will be conducted. In other words, having once attained security, the Army penetrates the population with the incentive for development, to correct the vulnerability of abandonment in our society in which [this population] has lived and which the subversion has exploited very efficiently after 12 years of good political work in the region, and which is necessary to counter in the same way. And it is for this reason that we enter into an era of ideological and developmentalist military operations which up to now have provided very good results. (Ejército, 1984a: 57–58)

Much of this task of implementing the military strategy fell to the Civil Affairs and Local Development (S-5) companies formally assigned in 1983 to each of the nineteen military zones, with military bases constructed in each of the highland departments and with numerous army posts built in municipal capitals as well as in or near model villages. Roads were constructed primarily for counterinsurgency purposes, along with airstrips built near army bases and in regions of development poles (WOLA, Krueger and Enge 1985: vii). Civil Affairs companies were assigned to those particular areas of conflict with large numbers of displaced persons, many of whom had been relocated far from their lands. (All the settlements of the displaced had been overseen initially by eleven Civil Affairs companies assigned to as many army garrisons throughout the highlands, and expanded to more than seventeen by 1986.) Another army booklet on the Poles of Development states,

It is the division of Civil Affairs under the National Defense Staff that coordinates the whole government effort through the Inter-Institutional Coordination System in order to carry development forward in those rural areas most backward and most punished by 12 years of subversive harassment. (Ejército 1985: 126)

These S-5 companies were in charge of the civil-military action of the State at the local level: coordinating the development effort, "reeducating" the internally displaced and refugees, using psychological warfare and propaganda (PSYOPS, or OPSIC in Spanish), gathering information 'in situ' before making decisions about projects, and training reserves and civil defense units—all the duties of the "soft" aspects of the war in order to integrate local efforts into the national strategy. Not only did Civil Affairs serve at this time as the linchpin for the military's nationalist institutionalist project, but it continues today to ensure military control over security and development, as will be discussed in a later chapter.

Inter-Institutional Coordinators

Goals by the military for national development requires an enlarged, decentralized, "integrated" state apparatus that effectively utilized local and regional civilian state bureaucracy. According to the army's own documents, the IICs were institutionalized for the highlands in 1983 by Decree-Law 772-83 and made nationwide by Organic Law 111-84 in November 1984 (Ejército, *Polos de Desarrollo* 1985: 9–19). The IICs corresponded in number and pertained to the organic structure of the nineteen military zones, covering two main areas of activity: maintenance of military presence and counterinsurgency actions, including population control, and administrative work and development. Their organization was presented as a municipal level-up plan, with an assumed need for the militarization of the State bureaucracy:

1. Comite de Desarrollo Local (Committee of Local Development), sub-divided into subcommittees for special work projects and presided over by the local military official or the Civil Patrol chief; it was, in turn, integrated into the
2. Coordinadora Inter-Institucional Municipal (Municipal Inter-Institutional Coordinator), headed by the commanding officer of the military garrison, who played the principal executive role; every plan for work had to be presented for discussion, approval, and control of the military; this, in turn, was integrated with
3. Coordinadora Inter-Departmental (Inter-Departmental Coordinator), corresponding to each military zone and zone commander as the coor-dinator, working with civilian bureaucrats and planning technicians at the national level; this level was integrated with
4. Coordinadora Inter-Nacional (International Coordinator), whose members were vice-ministers frequently called to sessions with military chiefs, as well as directors of State agencies, for example, SEGEPLAN (General Secretariat of Economic Planning), and CRN (Committee of National Reconstruction).

Nonetheless, municipal mayors, appointed by the military, were "virtually uninformed about the system and/or had no resources at their disposal" (WOLA, Krueger and Enge 1985: viii). Informants at the village level indi-cated that small communities received little or no assistance, and that the only way to get anything done was to go directly to the army (PAVA 1984: 81; WOLA, Krueger and Enge 1985: viii). Thus, indications are that the IICs were in fact not local entities and that the military was still "in charge of everything," even after a civilian president was elected.

Entrenched within the IICs as the official channel for extensive interna-tional private and nongovernmental aid for development funds and proj-ects, the CRN ensured that the rebuilding of the scorched-earth regions after 1983 hardly cost the military a penny. According to Black et al., in 1982, government allocations to the PAAC were a scant $1 million — enough for fifty hamlets,[3] "freeing other monies to buy arms and invest in agri-business ventures" (1984: 141). Between 1983 and 1984, Americares Foundation, working with the conservative Order of the Knights of Malta, provided $3.4 million in medical aid to the army to distribute in the model villages. An examination of US-AID projects funded in Guatemala between 1981 and 1986 reveals that US-AID was instrumental in providing: millions of dollars in aid for "displaced persons resettlement" in 1984 (through the Salva-tion Army) "with priority to widows, orphans and families affected by the violence" in San Marcos, Huehuetenango, Quelzaltenango, and Quiché; "rural development and cooperatives" in the highland region, such as the 1984 PL480 $8–10 million in food and grains, to "increase production of diversified crops"; at least four "rural potable water and sanitation" projects in the western highlands; and three "rural electrification" projects, 80 percent in the western highlands during the 1980s "to replace rural electrical infrastructure damaged/destroyed by terrorism."[4] In 1984, the UN Food and Agriculture Organization (FAO) granted $1.9 million to the Mejía Víctores government for a project of food aid to lessen malnutrition among the most vulnerable groups—young children and pregnant and lactating women, or a total of 70,000 persons in the areas of the scorched-earth campaign (Centro de Estudios de la Realidád Guatemalteca 1985: 15). In a 1986 interview, CRN Chief Air Force Colonel Herman Grotewold spoke of "support from NGOs (nongovernmental organizations): the Mennonite Church, the Catholic Church, the Rotary Club, the Lions' Club, the Salvation Army to build schools, state funds, AID, but most substantial was aid from FAO. . . . Yet, in spite of 37 million tons of rations from FAO, we still lack sufficient food in the communities." Other foreign aid included that of "the collaborators, or the Phantom Division," which Gramajo explains consisted mainly of retired CIA officers and American conservative donors who "liaisoned with the CRN" and provided private monies mostly for medical aid and military equipment to troops in the field (interview w/o attribution).

Local department-level CRNs were also established to mobilize civilians, including doctors, teachers and civil engineers, as "specialists" to work at the Poles of Development with Civil Affairs companies. The IICs thus effectively militarized the local and regional civilian bureaucracy, mobilizing both local indigenous populations and civilian state bureaucrats for the military's own purposes, while appearing to decentralize State authority: "There was absolutely no room for any kind of autonomy by the local leaders," one Guatemalan social scientist comments. "The military presence, especially in 1982–83, created a real skepticism by these villagers to participate; they'd lost any ideological reason as to why they should participate and where it would take them. It made the military schema very easy [to implement] because there was no alternative!" (1988 interview). Charged with providing 8 percent of the national budget to support local development projects, the IICs (representing the military, state ministries, and NGOs) oversaw virtually every economic and political activity at the departmental, municipal, and local levels. Under the rigid control of local garrison commanders, the IICs even began to supplant the traditional indigenous parish councils, from granting permission to hold a dance or organizing villagers into forced "public works" labor gangs to distributing food, seed, and salaries (Black et al. 1984: 139). In conjunction with the Poles of Development, the IICs, moreover, transformed what had historically been communal lands into private property for peasant indigenous communities, to create "the incentive for modern production."

Just how much control the military had in the countryside was recognized bitterly by the patron of the anticommunist extreme right, MLN leader Mario Sandoval Alarcón, not a proponent of the 30/70 percent "mixed solution." When asked about the military's participation in the next government (of civilian politicians), he said, "They must get rid of the famous Inter-Institutional Coordinators which are something very serious as they have given military commanders of each department absolutely total control over everything. They have power over the local justice of the peace, the mayor and the governor, [over] health [and] roads. They have converted these positions into a true dictatorship, with all the consequences that that brings" (Centro de Estudios de la Realidád Guatemalteca 1985: 24). Nevertheless, the end result of the IICs and Poles of Development was what the traditional sector wanted all along: controlled, cheap labor.

Poles of Development and Services: Model Villages

Decree-Law 65-84 established Poles of Development, which are defined in the army's literature as

organized population center[s] with an infrastructure which allows for the mobilizing of subsistence elements for the rural social well-being in the poorest areas in order to radiate a new dynamic to all the region contiguous with the whole country, as a means for correcting economic-social underdevelopment, improving the standard of living of Guatemalans as a part of the countersubversive strategy, with integral participation of the Government and Army by way of the Inter-Institutional Coordinators; it is the population [that is] a fundamental factor in its own development, guaranteeing the adhesion of the population's support and participation with the Armed Institution. (Ejército 1985a: 73)

Poles of Development with model villages are best understood as high-security areas built to serve as forms of population control — moving the displaced from camps into model programs — as well as to "integrate" the local indigenous population into both the antisubversive fight and the "nationalist" security and development project. When the displaced were brought in during this period, they would be lined up in front of the army compound: men in the first row, women in the second, children in the third. Since they had walked for several days or months and had high levels of malnutrition, everyone usually was first given hot food. They were asked by the S-5 specialists if any were former solders, and these persons were asked their name, dates when they served, and so forth; these men would be made part of the mobilization of army reservists, especially in the Ixil Triangle (anonymous colonel, interview). Those who were combatants in the revolutionary cadres, if not considered "lost" to subversion, would be taken aside for "informal conversations" and given "special attention," as one Kaibil lieutenant in charge of a garrison at which a group of fifty Ixils were brought in, explains: everyone was politically "reeducated," but those who had positions of responsibility within indigenous organizations were kept "close at hand," sometimes living with their families within the army compound in a house close to the officer in charge, helping with arrangements of the group

("Guatemala: Acción cívica" 1985: 12). "Reeducation" included the authoritarian scolding of "You mustn't abandon your brothers still in the mountains; you must find a way to bring them in, to make them understand. . . .
and the friendly suggestion: Don't worry, you won't starve or freeze to death;
[the guerrillas] told you that here we kill; when you are all fat, you can go
and tell them that you are staying here and that they were wrong" (11). Yet
the discrepancy between rhetoric and reality was clear: In the model villages
of Saraxoch and New Acamal near Santa Cruz Verapaz in 1984, for example,
1300 Indians were held in conditions "which can only be described as
forced internment and political re-education" (WOLA, Krueger and Enge
1985: viii). Similar conditions existed in model villages in the Ixil Triangle
visited by the author in 1986 and 1988.

Starting from the premise that past governments had abandoned indigenous communities, the Civil Affairs companies found one of their first tasks
was the physical reorganization and reconstitution of the razed indigenous
villages. To come up with a plan, the Army General Staff, working within its
paradigm of being the final arbiter of local indigenous village life, analyzed
the indigenous social system, spatial distribution, and traditional beliefs to
determine "what could be preserved and what had to be changed" to suit the
military's security imperatives ("Guatemala: Acción cívica" 1985: 16). The
result was Poles of Development: four large areas in the western highlands
from which the insurgents had been "cleansed": the Ixil Triangle in southern Quiché, Chisec in Alta Verapaz, Chacaj in Huehuetenango, and Playa
Grande in northern Quiché (see Figure 5). Much of this work was carried out
in less than one year. Some villages, such as Acul in the Ixil Triangle, which
had been razed by the military and found abandoned, were resurrected as
model villages within six months. The military planned to have included
some forty-nine villages within these four Poles to house 100,000 indigenous
people. In the end, only half were built, housing an estimated 50,000.[5]
Different poles served different counterinsurgency objectives: the Ixil Triangle, the area of most destruction by the military, was the most restructured
of all the Poles and has served an exclusively internal function as a "demon-
strative effect" for what the military considers to be populations "in resistance." Chisec is similar in this last respect. Chacaj, on the other hand, was
conceived exclusively to "attract those who cross over into Mexico," and
would eventually serve as a defense against the guerrilla. Playa Grande is the
only Pole that serves a double function: "to alleviate the pressure in southern
Quiché to guide a part of the displaced toward the north, supporting the
strategy of repatriation," according to several Civil Affairs officers interviewed ("Guatemala: Acción cívica" 1985: 6; anonymous interviews).

Within each Pole, houses and communitarian installations were built,
with streets laid out in line with the military's counterinsurgency plans: from
the perspective of those in the montaña, cold and hungry, looking down at

the grid of newly built houses and streetlights glowing in the dark, the character of these "new villages" as described in army pamphlets was intended to be viewed as "urban" and thus "developed." They were intended to "fill those up in the mountains looking down at the Pole with questions to put to those who had told them that everything was abandoned after the massacres of the army," one officer explained (interview). Additionally, the settlements follow the Spanish colonial-town grid of the New World (as well as that of a military base) with its tightly nucleated rectangularity, in contrast to the typical asymmetry of peasant settlements, which often follow the contours of the topography. With two houses between streets, and a potable water faucet on the corners, it is easier to keep in sight those who enter and leave the houses, as well as those who congregate for water and cleaning tasks (traditionally sites for gossip and information exchange). The military garrison is usually in an area higher than the village from which the army can observe the roadways as well as communitarian buildings, such as the church and school.

Officers inform the visitor that these grid settlements are perfectly straightforward in design and purpose: the need to concentrate the population for provisioning electricity, water, education, health, and security from the guerrilla. This provisioning was possible only by designing the Poles to bring about "a constructive, productive and principally defensive" plan ("Guatemala: Acción cívica" 1985: 6). According to one U.S. counterinsurgency expert, the model villagers "were not permitted to build villages where they stood before; they had to plan out a new village with architects and engineers into one large area. The old village of Acul, for example, was spread out along the valley floor, which meant little organization. To concentrate the population means you can protect and control it better, as well as provide clean water and electricity" (Sereseres, 1986 interview).

Anticipating international criticism, the military put much effort into correctly identifying the nature of the Poles. Officers wanted to distance the model villages from the U.S. military's strategic hamlet "mistakes in Vietnam," as well as from the criticism by humanitarian organizations of masking the militarization of peasant communities. As Colonel-lawyer Girón Tánchez retorted, "They are only concentration camps in the sense that people are concentrated into one area" (1986 interview). Air Force Colonel Grotewold explained in 1986 that "the Poles of Development are just small villages which group people together for them to receive light, drinking water, and so forth. These Poles exist for two reasons: (1) for the people to become ambitious to want something more [economically], and (2) the security of the country implies that we must, up to a certain point, centralize people because the problem of continuing to underwrite such subsistence for years is enormous and our country doesn't have the capacity to sustain such conflicts. Our economy breaks very easily" (interview). He did not want to call them "Poles," but merely by the "names of the villages"; Colonel Homero García Carillo, chief of Civil Affairs in 1988, also thought "Poles" were actually just "settlements" (interview).

But development, in the army's eyes, also meant productivity. Preoccupied with the crisis of land available to the majority of peasants in the highlands, especially in the Ixil, the Ríos Montt government requested a US-AID proposal as to how to solve the agrarian crisis. This agency suggested the development of a commercial market of lands (which would prove too expensive for the peasant to buy) and the conversion of large private land-holdings into *minifundias* (small farms) that the peasant could pay off through working the land (called La Perla experiment).[6] Neither suggestion was considered appropriate by UNAGRO, the landholders association (Arias 1990: 104–5). Nonetheless, by March 1985, an estimated 2480 land titles had been given out in the Poles of Development for land parcels of 300 square meters with the provision that the land be worked; many of these recipients were Civil Patrol *Jefes* and other army collaborators.

This vision of productivity was paramount for military officers working with PAAC and development poles. Civil Affairs Director, Air Force Intelligence Colonel Eduardo Wohlers, trained in Israel and one of the architects of the model village/Poles of Development program (and later chief of the air force) stated, "The Poles are a definitive transformation of the face of the Guatemalan highlands. We foresee huge plantations of fruit and vegetables with storage and processing facilities and refrigeration plants. We aim to put in the entire infrastructure for exporting frozen broccoli, Chinese cabbage, watermelons . . . 15 new crops" (Peckenham 1983: 18). In a 1986 interview he also confided that the structure of Korean communes, Israeli kibbutzim, and Taiwanese farms formed a basis for the program, although fish ponds from Taiwan, beehives, and craft centers were not developed in any significant fashion to provide economic sustainability. While many of the model villages were not economically successful (WOLA 1988: 105–7), it is believed within the military community that the Poles accomplished what they set out to do, according to one U.S. counterinsurgency analyst: "They committed the people to the army and government" (Sheehan 1989: 145).

However, once the thousands of refugees who had fled to Mexico began to return in greater numbers in the late 1980s and early 1990s, serious tensions arose: the majority would not be returned to their original lands (since they had been given to others who would continue to collaborate with the army to hold on to them), nor could they visit their relatives in their home villages. The disintegration of the economic, social, and cultural bases of a community, especially one in which land is one's "site of origin," "to be uprooted from one's ancestral, sacred lands" is at once a military strategy and a cultural trauma. It is not only a tearing apart of established social relations to impose a new system of authority, but also a breaking of ethnic history and memory in order to rewrite it (Arias 1988: 171). As we will see in Chapter 5, this form of myth robbery has created the military's own Sanctioned Mayan. Such forceful restructuring of socio-cultural, economic, and settlement patterns of indigenous life within the Poles of Development represents the most significant reorganization of the indigenous population since the Conquest, when *pueblos de indios* were established.[7]

Food for Work as Immediate Development

Part of the counterinsurgency strategy institutionalized within the Poles was to put the survivors to work, demanding their "integration" into development projects, such as Food for Work (Alimentos por Trabajo), and thus, in the military's mind, undermining guerrilla infrastructural support by sidetracking mass revolutionary activities for local economic ones. As one officer commented, "We must show them concrete results; it doesn't matter how much or many. But we can't just leave the people there waiting to see what we'll do" ("Guatemala: Acción cívica" 1985: 5).

The nature of such mobilization has taken the form of population and labor force control, and a wage substitute. As head of Civil Affairs in 1984, Colonel Mario Paíz Bolaños, stated: "In the 4 zones [referring to the Poles of Development in existence in 1984: Playa Grande, Ixil Triangle in El Quiché, Chisec in Alta Verapaz and Chacaj in Huehuetenango], 18,000 persons are being attended to, they have been given land, security and peace; the community work projects are paid with food. Each ration contains: milk, precooked wheat, cornmeal for *atol,* besides rice, corn and beans. All of these contain vitamin supplements which have varied the diet. On the other side, the Army participated in the organization and orientation of the Civil Patrols of self-defense. Thanks to this organization, it is possible to gather 3000 or more voluntary workers to construct a highway, a school, a bridge and whatever public work in 24 hours, such is the magnitude [of this organization]."[8]

Similarly, Civil Affairs reservist Major-Dr. Luis Sieckavizza stated in 1986 that "People in the Poles receive payment in kind, an integrated salary of food and credit. It is not monetary because the peasants are used to receiving part of their wage in food. Out in the countryside, there is nothing to buy, anyway, and they'd just go directly to the *cantina* if we gave them cash. So, instead, we give them food—in contrast to the hunger caused by the guerrilla. This is how we penetrate, as planned, into these isolated communities. But we aren't 'exploiting' the Indian peasant as the opposition communist press claims; the system of food-for-work is a tradition in Guatemala. . . . These Poles are not a paternalistic system: the Indians must *work* in order to receive something" (interview; his emphasis). Gramajo, too, speaks of "forging *el pueblo,*" not "giving anything away [free]; it must earn everything [it receives]." Development for the military signifies a disciplined forging of character based on hard work in which no handouts are expected or forthcoming — a political culture that one government official from the Institute for Agrarian Transformation (INTA), described as *forzovoluntario*: enforced voluntary participation (Stoll 1993). The only way the *indígenas* can "save" themselves is to work hard for little or no remuneration.

Hence, an essential component of this "integrative" and disciplined development in the Poles is cheap, if not free, labor, and it is institutionalized in the 1985 Constitution. Article 102, sections d and f, discuss work rights: "There is an obligation of the employer to pay the employee with legal tender. Nevertheless, the worker in the countryside may voluntarily receive food products representing up to 30% of his salary. . . . Periodic fixing of minimum wage will be in conformity with the law" (Constituyente de Guatemala 1985: 17). Unlike the 1956 and 1965 Constitutions, by which workers at least rhetorically were allowed to participate in determining minimum wage, the new Constitution does not even pretend such a provision. Moreover, the right to unionize and strike is so limited by this Constitution as to be nonexistent (Linares Morales 1985). Some US-AID packages in 1983 in fact reflected an implicit acceptance of such provisions by providing funding in order for the Department of Rural Roads to add 650 kilometers of roads to be built by "cheap, unskilled labor drawn from local communities."[9] The PAVA Final Report emphasized that payment in the army's food-for-work program was made with food, but "there have been reports of workers not receiving their payment of food rations even after the project they work on has been completed" (1984: 80).

In addition, unemployment has remained severe for residents of the Poles. In the Ixil area, for example, women residents complained of the lack of vegetables and goods to sell at the local market for extra money (interviews); they also complained of the even more depressed wages for model villagers who work on the coffee and cotton plantations than before *la violencia* — often at Q1 per day in subcontracts "with regular plantation workers who received the national minimum wage of Q4.20 per day or per quintal (100 pounds) of picked ripe coffee" in 1988 (Smith 1990b: 22). Returnees to Quiché in 1984 were considering emigrating again in search of work (PAVA 1984: 81).

"Services," too, within the Poles not without cost and hardship. In interviews with inhabitants within these Poles in 1986 and 1988, it was observed that many of the villagers did not in fact use the electricity available because they could not afford to pay for it. The water spigot for several hundred inhabitants was often a distance away, and the water was not always potable. And in some Poles INTA charged residents Q250 for a model house and 130 *cuerdas* (roughly 13 acres) of local land to be paid in installments over a five- to ten-year period — which most could not hope to afford. Residents reported that many families were unable to make the payments for INTA lands near Chajul in the Ixil Triangle and ended up camping on the outskirts of the model village or living with extended family in the model village (Smith 1990b: 22). Moreover, since 1983 the distribution, via a new entitlement process of the plots abandoned as a result of the scorched-earth campaign, has helped to create a class of well-off peasants who are favorable to the status quo and, as such, useful counterrevolutionary instruments for the army. For example, the new forms of state-controlled peasant organizations, such as the Association of Peasant Businesses (Empresas Campesinas Asociativas), institutionalized with Decree-Law 67-84, meant a new form of managing and controlling productive cooperatives (Centro de Estudios de la Realidád Guatemalteco 1985: 16).

Therefore, despite the military's proclaimed preoccupation with the crisis of land in the highlands, there is a severe shortage of and lack of access to land within these Poles. Many residents interviewed in the model villages in the Ixil in 1986 said they had land but it was "a very long walk," it was not legally titled, it was not large enough for subsistence, or it was in an "unsecured area" and thus "off limits" to civilians (particularly model villagers with night curfews at the time). The staple, corn, had to be purchased at exorbitant prices, with many families complaining of eating only one meal a day (interviews).

Poles of Development then, contrary to the military's espousal of their representing an antipaternalistic forging of indigenous character, autonomy and self-sufficient economy, have served precisely as the opposite: a form of instrumentalized military control over minimum daily needs (food, drinking water, housing, electricity, credit, and fertilizers), with a denial of sufficient access to land and wage-earning jobs. They have served as "places to locate displaced refugees, *campos de servicos* offered by the army; but without a productive base [of employment or of land], they have nothing to do with 'development'" (Centro de Estudios de la Realidad Guatemalteco 1985: 16). The result has been an intensification of cheap-to-free labor both in agricultural harvests and in the new labor-intensive *maquila* (sweatshop) industries (cf. Petersen 1992).

Development within the military's plans and with the endorsement of US-AID provided the military with laborers to build roads to new military bases and installations in the highlands. These laborers remained without the right to reclaim part, and many times any, of their wages or the right to contest such legalized nonparticipation and nonremuneration (Linares Morales 1985: 24). The 1985 constitution, implanted within counterinsurgency structures, such as the Poles of Development, thus legalized the economic slavery and political repression that have been practiced in Guatemala for centuries. Grotewold explained matter-of-factly at one point in the interview that "development is war carried on by economic means."

Councils of Development

Similar to the problem of instituting structures within which to control refugees created by the massacre campaign, the military realized in 1985 that it "had no plan for government" and had to figure out how to proceed along "the same planned route of development" (Gramajo, interview). The urgent question on the minds of officers, uneasy with the election of Christian Democrat Vinicio Cerezo as president in November 1995, was whether the military could maintain its control in the highlands with the election of a civilian government. Colonel Grotewold best expressed this concern: "We are prepared to give power to civilians, but we will never hand over the country's security" (WOLA, Krueger and Enge 1985: 59). Similarly, Colonel-lawyer Girón Tánchez, the architect of most of the decree-laws between 1982 and 1986, made the military's distrust of and disdain for civilian politicians clear in 1986: ". . . at the opportune moment, the IIC law was dictated because it was necessary to *demarcate* the relations between the different elements which constitute the Coordinators. . . . Clearly, I feel that civilians are not qualified to take charge of the IICs. They should be directed by military men because we have the capacity to command, the power to command, and we have the feel for organization, order, and discipline which, unfortunately, many people of the other [civilian] government lack." Yet at the same time, he understood how that very disdain "gives way to regimes of bad repute. One must run down the constitutional corridors, isn't that so?" (interview),

To overcome officers' anxieties about civilian rule, an "oral agreement" was reached between the military and Cerezo in post-election 1985 as to how this military-to-civilian shift would take place juridically, including the passage of several decree-laws that would protect the army from possible prosecution for human rights violations. Girón Tánchez recounts:

A few days before [his inauguration in January 1986], Cerezo wanted to create three new ministries: such as Culture and Sports and Development. A delegate of Vinicio Cerezo came to speak with me [about this shift]. I told him what we [the army] wanted; he told me what Cerezo wanted, and it seemed adequate, so we emitted the Executive Order" in early 1986, in which the IICs and Poles of Development were to be renamed Councils of Development (Consejos de Desarrollo), and the military governors of each department were to be replaced by civilians, with former military heads serving as advisors. (interview)

Hence, as part of a reorganization of public administration under the newly elected Cerezo government, Councils of Development replaced the IICs, and were integrated with representatives from both the public and private sectors at the departmental and municipal levels.

During this same period, however, the government's new Plan of Development for 1986–90 was presented to the newly elected deputies and mayors by the commander of the military zone of Alta Verapaz, Colonel Edgar

Rolando Hernández, in which the basic structure that merged civil administration and military jurisdiction remained unchanged. On 9 May 1986, for
example, the minister of development, René de León Schlotter, confirmed
that the Poles of Development would not only *not* disappear, but that he
would seek external funding to reinforce them (ACEN-SIAG *Weekly Reports
Bulletin*, 3 June 1986: 2 October 1986: 3–4). It is in regard to this kind of
juridical convergence that officers believe Colonel-lawyer Girón Tánchez
showed his ingenuity by immersing counterinsurgency structures within the
1985 constitution written by the National Constituent Assembly. Gramajo
states: "In spite of having so much power as the 'legislative man' (*el hombre
legislativo*) [especially during the Mejía Víctores regime], Girón Tánchez did
things in a very balanced way. He was the liaison figure. Mejía would speak
through Girón and suggest things to [the Constituent Assembly delegates].
The Councils of Development are something honorable for the Guatemalan nation, as they signify centralization. That they, which were once our
Inter-Institutional Coordinators, *are now located within the Constitution*, is tremendous. They are now civilian and deal with local development, okay?
That [structure] is located within the constitution. That is to say, that Forjar
y Libertar [the 30/70 percent institutionalist] officers are indebted to Man-
uelito" (interview; his emphasis).

As planned, each level of the IICs was run by a civilian and the development projects were in the hands of the Ministry of Development, while Civil
Affairs and the CRN gave the military virtually a free hand in the countryside. This then is the final stage in which counterinsurgency is implanted
within the administration of the state. As one Guatemalan lawyer proclaimed at the time, "We are being swallowed by the military Leviathan"
(1988 interview).

Despite the military's planning, though, there were a series of political
confrontations in the Congress between 1986 and 1988 centering around
these Councils of Development, primarily with regard to the President's
perception of controlled development, as one Guatemalan social scientist
explained: "The new Minister of Development perceived of development as
one which begins at the local, community level and works its way up to the
national level. The President, however, believed that development trickles
down from the top to the bottom, and this latter idea held. The principal
effect was to limit any possibility for local organizing" (1988 interview).
With local initiative and autonomy diminished, the Councils thus became
institutionalized instruments for national security purposes. Indeed, if one
compares the *desarrollista* principles under Mejía Víctores with those of the
Christian Democratic Party in 1985, there is virtually little difference; this
convergence is one of the reasons why *el proyecto político-militar* is called a "co-
governance of *continuismo*." There was also a vociferous response to the
Councils of Development by the extreme right wing, fearful that the population, "organized to participate in the politics of development," as one of the

Ministry of Development administrators remarked (AVANCSO 1988a: 65), would be mobilized in the 1988 municipal and the 1990 presidential elections by the Christian Democratic party or, worse, would escape control of the party as an organized movement, placing the privileged interests of the extreme rightwing in danger. An example of this fear comes from one of the military *golpistas* of 1988, echoing MLN leader Sandoval Alarcón:

Now the government has taken over part of what the Army created. The Army created the IICs, and the government calls them Councils of Development. These Councils could be very good for the country—that is to say, they could result in developing the countryside. And if the Army had manipulated the Councils and Patrols, it is certain that this president would not be Cerezo. It would have been a rat (*un ratón*) the army wanted, but the Army allowed the people to decide upon [their president].

But now here's the contradiction: I said that the Councils could be and must be something very useful for national development. But the problem is that they have been converted into an instrument that goes in two political directions: (1) they serve the Christian Democratic Party to perpetuate itself in power, as the Councils represent a real counter to the *consejos locales* (local councils), which are dysfunctional. They control the funds; they direct the development projects, and thus the peasant population. There are six million illiterate peasants whose votes can be manipulated as the peasant doesn't know who he is voting for. In the April 1988 municipal elections,[10] the peasant was given a sack of corn, a machete, and a vote for the Christian Democratic party. But the more dangerous direction is that in all of these Councils of Development, there are 7900 social-rural *promotores* (promoters), trained by personnel who were EGP militants. Thus, this government has direct connections with the guerrilla, and all of these *promotores* are sent out all over the country. They have an enormous capacity to organize the masses not in support of a political party but in support of any subversive group. These seventy-nine hundred *promotores* then could organize an enormous army which could be at the service of the subversive. (Maj. Gustavo Díaz López, 1988 interview)

General Gramajo, too, is very critical of the Ministry of Development, but not because the Christian Democrats competed with the MLN power base; but rather for its incompetence and unwillingness to make the Councils of Development "deliver something as quickly as possible" to the rural areas to make them less susceptible to the insurgency. Gramajo is much less concerned with the social promoters, as they represent for him part of the military's "social intelligence" networking: Civil Affairs (S-5) has its own school of Promoción Social for their social promoters to provide a minimum of two to three years experience working in the rural areas in a community organization. Trained by military officers, many are military commissioners, or *personas de confianza*, of the Army (Gramajo interview by Cruz Salazar 1988a). While officials at the Ministry of Development had a negative view of S-5 — "with its own philosophy of development [that is] authoritarian in nature and is not for the development of the people" — it also recognized that the Ministry and the military were not "incompatible. . . . We now see each other in a circumstantial convergence. They (S-5) have

their own strategies, [and] we are trying now to coordinate our activities"
(Vice Minister of Development, 1988 interview).

In 1986, the Ministry of Development's small budget of Q8.0 million
($1,333,333) (Q12 million [$2,000,000] in 1987) was supplemented with a
network of nongovernmental and private organizations. In a 1986 public
bid for a contract of Q3.0 million ($500,000) to train social promoters, a
private firm under the direction of Christian Democratic staff members,
won the bid; in 1987, the Ministry of Development contracted the same firm
to promote the social organization of rural communities for Q2.4 million
($400,000). The reason given for this "new method" of contracting out by
Ministry of Development officials was to strengthen "private groups" and
avoid the State bureaucracy. But what such contracts appeared to military
officers to be doing was allowing Christian Democratic Party leader René de
León Schlotter "for whom the Ministry of Development was created," to
privatize the Councils of Development, and line his pockets in the process.
Gramajo comments:

Within the Councils, there is political ineptitude. Do you know what happened? On
the first day of civilian government, [we all met with the civilians and] we military
men had decided to meet once a week. [The civilians asked those in the room,]
"Who wants to meet every fifteen days?" [No one raises his hand.] "Every month?"
[No one raises his hand.] "Every 6 months?" [He raises both hands.] This ministry
didn't exist [in terms of work]. We taught René de León and his people in the
ministry [of Development who were in charge of the new Councils of Development]
about all the work [in the now-defunct IICs]. Everything, everything, everything!
[angrily] Free! We'd worked six months creating social promoters [of development]
and all of this. Afterward, when they knew about all of this, the family of René de
León created a company to train social promoters and the Ministry of Defense paid
the company to teach 'social promotion' — all the knowhow that we had taught *them*!
And they continued to give courses on social promotion, and more courses, using all
the money on courses, but no infrastructure was created. Later on, when they began
to matriculate numerous social promoters, [Christian Democratic Party head] Alfonso Cabrera got the National Assembly to pass a motion to shelve the Councils for
preelectoral reasons so René de León would not steal the [1990 presidential] nomi-
nation away from him by way of this popular organization. Cabrera told the Army
that he didn't want there to be civilian leadership [in the highlands] because we [the
Army] were already there. Or even better, that the military was already involved
because the Councils and Comités Voluntarios (Civil Patrols) were ours. . . . The
word for 1990 was shelve all popular organizing.
Q: But, in actuality, the army is still present [in the highlands].
Sure, but no longer in matters of development, only in matters of security. And
development now is not terribly extensive, at that. (interview).[11]

As a way of softening these tensions between the established infrastructure of the Committee for National Reconstruction and Civil Affairs, on the
one hand, and the new Ministry of Development, on the other, an agreement was quietly reached in 1987 between the Ministry of Development and
Defense Minister Gramajo that the military limit its developmentalist ac-

tions to Civil Affairs to work in unison with the CRN in those locations the Ministry of Development could not reach because of being "politically and militarily delicate or physically inaccessible." The understanding was that the Ministry of Development would attend to the communities "of over 100 families, and the CRN to those under 100 families," according to several civilian CRN officials interviewed. The army has thus continued as the authority in isolated regions of San Marcos, Huehuetenango, Petén, Alta Verapaz, Sololá, Chimaltenango, and in the northern reaches of El Quiché, and has been very much present in "delicate areas" such as at refugee repatriation camps. This does not mean, however, that frictions do not continue to exist within this "interinstitutional coordination" of development, with military officers and civilian CRN functionaries viewing the Ministry of Department as "our principal rival," duplicating what others are already doing (AVANCSO 1988: 67–69).

Despite such rivalry, however, given the military's experience in handling development affairs in rural areas and in training *promotores*, the Ministry of Development left such activities, including the functioning of regional and local councils, to the military and their confidants. For it is the case that, on the one hand, the Ministry of Development and, by extension, the civilian government have allowed the army to make certain the guerrilla does not once again gain in strength, and at the same time have provided the country with "international legitimacy" (Gramajo, interview by Cruz Salazar 1988a). On the other hand, the Ministry controls development "from the top down" in such a way as to inhibit real political participation, tempering the fears of the extreme right.

This development-qua-security approach allows us to see how short-term political interests (e.g., the electoral success of the MLN in the highlands and the presidential ambitions of Christian Democrats) could be viewed as obstacles to the larger schema of development and nation-building, as well as intelligence gathering by the army via *promotores* and S-5 units. It also reveals how the politics of the continuation of war policy formulated by institutionalist officers represents a form of State security that can accommodate itself to legal structures and government political "tendencies," yet proceed with its war management counterinsurgency strategy. "Besides being opportune, this scheme of continuing with the plans of development in line with the counterinsurgency strategy allows the Army an accommodation with the government's intentions and the law" (Gramajo, interview by Cruz Salazar 1988a).

Chapter 4
Indian Soldiers and Civil Patrols of Self-Defense

The key word in this initial strategy was "participation" because the *indígenas* participated in the war effort.

— General Gramajo

In the face of foreign aggression, the people and the army came to the battlefield; we fought; we won; we pacified.

— *Civil Defense Patrols. The Popular Response to the Process of Socio-Economic-Political Integration in the Guatemala of Today*

Nowhere else in Latin America has an army managed to mobilize and divide an indigenous population against itself to such an extent — even to the point of forcing victims to become accomplices and kill one another. The creation and utilization of special companies of Indian soldiers and Civil Patrols by the army — linchpins for the 30/70 formula in which security was linked to development as a way of controlling and separating the population from the guerrilla — did just that.

With the 1982 coup, the new regime recognized how the mobilization of indigenous former soldiers and former guerrilla irregulars (especially in the Ixil Triangle) as well as the expansion of Civil Patrols could be an especially effective weapon against the guerrilla in a number of ways. First, as we have seen, it forced the population that found itself "between two fires," to choose sides, with many aligning themselves with the army to save their own lives. Second, Indian former soldiers working as or with *especialistas* in Civil Affairs Units served as human "force multipliers" for the new military bases in the fourteen new military zones and provided "excellent human intelligence sources" (Sheehan 1989: 144). Third, it proved useful for the regular army to be able to demonstrate that a part of the population was fighting on and at their side (ICADIS 1987: 16). Finally, ethnographic accounts of Civil Patrols reveal that the army was, at times, even successful at forging a spirit of opposition to, or at least a desire for separation from, the guerrilla as a way out of the violence (Stoll 1993; Kobrak 1994).

The Civil Affairs formula of development qua security mobilized the survivors of its massacres, some of whom were reservist former soldiers and/or guerrilla supporters, for development projects (e.g., roadwork) and then utilized such mobilization for recruitment either into special Indian reservist companies or Civil Defense Patrols that patrolled their locale to maintain control of the population and to destroy the guerrilla network of irregulars. In many instances, former guerrillas were tortured and interrogated for several months and amnestied on condition that they join the army; after several months to a year of soldiering, they would be selected as *jefes* of Civil Patrols. During the height of the campaign, five thousand Ixils (most of them former soldiers and thus reservists) were reinducted into the army; between 1983 and 1984, 1,300,000 indigenous men between the ages of fifteen and sixty (or approximately 16.87 percent of the total population) were members of Civil Patrols (Ejército 1994). Neutrality for the indigenous population was thus impossible. The military championed itself as the forceful stabilizer for daily existence (with patrols, food, work, and resettlements) in contrast to the "lawless" guerrillas who had "deceived" the peasant.

Under these conditions, Civil Patrollers initially provided the indigenous population, ravaged by war and hungry for stability (or for at least a minimum level of violence and terror), a sense of local security against both the military and the guerrilla; at times they managed to garner support for the army itself. Just as international aid for "reconstruction" freed army resources for weapons, Indian companies and Civil Patrols freed army units to mobilize and augment their intelligence-gathering activities for the early 1980s campaigns and the late 1980s offensives. Into the 1990s, the patrols participated in military tasks including searches, in campaigns against the guerrilla (used as "buffers" to protect their own soldiers), and in repressive operations within their own communities as well as villages nearby (Comité Pro-Justicia y Paz 1990: 3). In extending soldiering and civil patrolling throughout much of the adult male indigenous population, the military has been remarkably adroit at not only penetrating daily village life but also at spreading around responsibility for the killing. As one officer told the first patrollers in Nebaj: "Now we're all going to get our hands dirty" (Stoll 1993: 115). Every Indian soldier and patroller became implicated in or minimally acquiesced to the new order, with the subject of "loyalty" and "support" within the climate of concealment and intimidation useful in the army's psychological war campaign. In officer's minds, Civil Patrols conveniently turned a war between the army and guerrilla into a "civil war" between Indians: "Indians are killing Indians," one Civil Affairs colonel matter-of-factly explained the war to the author (1988 interview). As we will see, with demands on the increase in the 1990s by human rights organizations for an end to the Civil Patrols and an end to Patrol killings, violent reactions have been stirred in villages.

Two historical aspects of the military's views of the usefulness of Indian soldiers are important to elucidate before we concern ourselves with the military's more contemporary mobilization of the indigenous population.

Lessons from Zacapa in 1966–67 and 1981

The uses of Civil Patrols are rooted in practices developed in the 1960s and those of 1981. Thousands of civilians were organized into part-time militias as part of the 1966 counterinsurgency campaign under the zone commander of Zacapa, Colonel Carlos Arana Osorio (to become president in 1970). Strict control of the population and a brutally repressive campaign soundly defeated the guerrillas at that time, and these lessons were expected to later be heeded by young officers serving in these campaigns. In September 1981, Army Chief of Staff, General Benedicto Lucas García, ordered the formation of the first Civil Defense Patrol (Patrulla de Autodefensa Civil). A few thousand peasants in Chimaltenango and Huehuetenango were forcibly recruited into *pelotones* (platoons), given little to no training, and armed mostly with machetes and clubs. As in Zacapa, they were to function as a rural militia, patrolling crops and villages, acting as the army's eyes and ears, and fighting la guerrilla when necessary. Despite the lessons from Zacapa, however, these first attempts were apparently not very well coordinated and were not combined with strict control of the population. "The Lucas regime didn't first get rid of the guerrilla in the area before it established the *Patrullas*" (Gramajo, interview). With Indian communities refusing to join the Patrols, the military responded by "teaching them a lesson" and massacring entire villages, such as at Plan de Sánchez and Dos Erres (officer quoted in Sereseres 1985: 116) — with such "lessons" ironically augmenting the guerrilla support network. However, the army learned from its mistakes in 1981, and a massive expansion of civil defense units, combined with Civil Affairs, was a principal means of defeating the insurgency by 1983. "Without the participation of these 'armed Guatemalans,'" states Beltranena, "this phase of the war would never have ended" (1992: 158).

Ladino Versus Indian Soldiers

The recognition that Indians were a necessary part of the military took a long time to establish. In 1872 (as in 1982), the army found itself short of personnel. At that time, obligatory military service for literate ladinos was established. But, as Adams states, "the failed [liberal] strategy" to create a literate ladino army "led to reinterpreting the nature of the Indian and what, in turn, that might mean for military service" (1994: 12). Yet it took the army another half century to accept the fact that a Guatemalan military force needed Indian soldiers, and since the early twentieth century it has practiced forced conscription and depended upon Indians for a major component of its troops. Before, instead of soldiering, Indians were employed in forced construction work within the army: El Batallón de Zapadores, for example, established in 1894 to do roadwork and build fortifications, was directly dependent on the Secretariat of War and composed solely of Indians. (The status of *zapador* was in fact so undesirable that authorities referred to them as — and in one case, escorted them along with — criminals [8–10].) What one sees is an evolutionary acceptance of the culturalist (as opposed to the racist) arguments for Indian soldiers: "No one now questions whether Indians can learn to be effective soldiers. The role of the army as a 'civilizing' agent has been widely accepted, not least among some Indians" (36). "Yet the Indian is still very much the follower, and rarely the leader"; very much a foot soldier and not an officer — an attitude still prevalent among many ladino officers: a picture-card cutout of a docile, obedient soldier and the descendant of heroic Mayan warriors, who must be "forged" and civilized. By the late 1970s, however, with the rise of insurgency among the indigenous communities in the western highlands this snapshot began to fade. It was an insurgency that repeated the army's pattern of learning: failure by rebel officers to initiate a ladino peasant revolution in the *oriente* in the 1960 campaigns led the survivors to realize by the 1970s "the importance of the Indian in the development of a serious revolutionary struggle." The difference was Indians were being recruited into the insurgency not because they were docile, but "because they were seen to have the most deepseated motivation for actively seeking social change" (37). With this new indigenously rooted insurgency, officers became increasingly suspect of indigenous recruits and (as 100 years earlier) more reliant on ladino soldiers from the eastern departments of Zacapa and Jutiapa. "With the strategy of the EGP being played out in 1979 as whites fighting Indians, we [in the army] saw in every Indian an enemy," Gramajo stated. "But we did not have a chance to deal with this ethnic conflict until the 1982 coup" (interview w/o attribution).

With the 1982 coup, the Pacification strategy established as its goal "to augment the army, particularly the commanders, in areas of conflict to support the Units of Civil Self-Defense as well as other factors of power in the public administration, in order to (1) deny access of the subversives to the population which constituted their politico-social support; (2) rescue individuals from the Irregular Local Forces (*fuerzas irregulares locales*), neutralizing or eliminating those who do not want to integrate themselves into normal life; and (3) eliminate the Permanent Military Units (UMP) [of the subversives]" (Ejército 1982a).

In his weekly television sermons, Ríos Montt called for a surgical excision of evil from Guatemala; and less than two months into the pacification campaign, on 1 June 1982, Decree-Law 33-82 established the amnesty program, citing as its goal to "obtain social peace in the Nation" and give "subversives the chance to re-enter society free from criminal responsibility." They were required to turn themselves and their weapons over to the nearest military authority within thirty days.[1] Ríos Montt promised that "whoever doesn't give up I'm going to shoot" (quoted in Keefe 1984: 213).

Ending the amnesty, Ríos Montt announced that 2000 guerrillas had surrendered; other sources say two hundred or three hundred is more accurate. Former guerrilla refugees who accepted amnesty were often tortured and interrogated at army compounds and photographed for army files so that anyone the army distrusted could later be kidnapped (interviews; Stoll 1993: 155). Many returnees would later become soldiers or civil patrollers, "thus providing an invaluable source of information to military units" (Letona 1989: 21). The use of amnesty to serve as a symbolic "integration" of Indians into national life (as the CEM Strategic Appraisals in 1980 and 1981 had espoused) is exemplified by Gramajo's description of how the Consejo de Estado established by Ríos Montt in 1982 to serve as a symbolic Congress, "included *indígenas* we had brought down from the mountains." For Gramajo, including indigenous peoples in the Council was crucial "to consolidate a Guatemalan identity." The military, he goes on to say, "had many discussions at the Center for Military Studies as to why we didn't have one Guatemalan identity. And some colonels got angry with me when I told them that we were five separate nations, that a nation means a defined territory, a common language, common customs, and a common destiny. . . . They were born in a common geography, but what did a boy who gets up at 4 A.M. to walk to Quezaltenango to sell the firewood on his back have in common with a boy who gets up in Zone 15 [a wealthy neighborhood in Guatemala City] and drives to the university in his car? They have nothing in common. [We know] that the ethnic part is treated like a minority, but they are in the majority" (interview).

"Between Two Fires": Incorporating the "Recuperated" *Indígenas* into the Army as Soldiers

With "participation" and "integration" the watchwords of the 1982 coup, *indígenas* "recuperated" from the massacre sweeps were mobilized to swell the army ranks and to deny guerrilla forces their irregulars (FIL) for surveillance and defense against the army. Integrated into various army activities, civil defense units were established in the heart of guerrilla control areas, especially among the repatriated at refugee camps. Some were located within military attachments and "integrated into the static defense and patrolling missions of the army" (Sheehan 1989: 143). While arming and training the units were important factors, these concerns were always secondary to organization, intelligence, and denial of a guerrilla presence.

The strategy for dealing with the indigenous population was to be incremental. General Gramajo speaks of the different stages of recuperation and mobilization of the indigenous population by the army after the "killing zone" operations, and how both the Indian companies and Civil Patrols were born out of the guerrilla-organized FIL. The first stage was the creation of self-defense patrols by the recuperated villages:

The *indígena* groups went back to their villages, went back to eat and organize themselves into self-defense groups and didn't let the army *or* the subversives enter. There were cases in the night when they fought the subversives because these groups wanted to speak to the peasants about mobilizing them again. And there were cases [when the patrols fought] against the army because it wanted to enter to capture those who were in the village. So they fought against both. We are talking here of October 1982. (interview)

The fact that many of the members of these army-created, FIL-based patrols had been "trained in the guerrillas' own tactics, which had been converted into being used against the subversion, made it difficult for the subversives to satisfactorily confront these organized communities," states one army document (Ejército 1994). The second stage linked development projects (PAAC) with soldier recruitment and Civil Patrols:

By November 1982, principally in El Quiché, the people became [part of] the army. We had room for five thousand new soldiers in our budget and thus we created in all the *aldeas* (villages) the patrols which [already] existed in the eight departments [denominated as zones of conflict] which had been part of the PAAC program. From these *indígenas* from the villages, we created regular soldiers.

In this way, "development" served as a pretext for organizing patrols and identifying potential recruits (cf. Montejo 1993). Finally, by 1983, with the creation of new military zones,

we didn't have enough soldiers [to fill them]. The new deployment strategy stated "Here is the commander," et cetera, and officers would say, "I don't want to be a commander of a new [military] zone because it contains nothing! I [only] have three hundred to five hundred soldiers." But what is the formula? Who is a soldier in Guatemala? The constitution states, "[A soldier] is a citizen between eighteen and fifty years of age, with active service between eighteen and thirty years of age and reserve duty between thirty and fifty years of age." So, since they had already been organized by the FIL, we recruited these *nuevos soldados lugareños* (new soldiers of the locale). (interview)

Gramajo's description of army officers' reluctance to arm these new *indígena* soldiers reveals the officers' fear of the Indian-as-enemy[2] as well as the strategic stages of the campaign of recuperation of Indian loyalty:

Colonel Lima [in Quiché] told me "I need to go to Jutiapa and Zacapa to recruit soldiers" because he would not hand over weapons to the Indians. I told him, "They are not our enemy, they are *indígenas*, they are not subversives."[3] [These officers] believed that the *indígenas* were still in the first phase [of being guerrilla sympathizers]. I had to remind them that the *indígenas* were now at this stage [between the army and the guerrilla in self-defense groups], and that we had to bring them over to our side, which we did, to receive our guns. I told the officers, "Let's make a deal. I will give you the benefit of 15 percent loss of recruits to the guerrilla within the first three months of military service. Moreover, here are the guns. If of one hundred guns, you lose fifteen, I'll be satisfied. It is an acceptable percentage [of loss of either recruits or guns] because I will gain eighty-five! And we didn't lose any, any, any!"[4]

When asked why there were no losses, Gramajo explained there had not been "solidez ideológica" (ideological solidarity) with the guerrillas:

There were only those who were being manipulated by the leaders who had jeopardized all the others by putting them at risk, compromising them in terms of the subversion. We know this because the others came to us to tell us "We want peace with you." (interview)

But more importantly, he goes on to argue,

we saw that the subversives had created their own self-defense committees — the FIL. We tolerated the FIL in order to take it away from the guerrilla, and when we gave the [new] soldiers their [own] guns, we also gave them money so that they would have a wage. We gave them weapons and a wage, and we did the same to their fathers, brothers, and whomever else. We gave them work. We built roads. Work for pay, for food, and for free. That is, communal development, civic work, something in common, okay? The result of this was that they had their guns. If [the *aldea*] was afraid of [the subversives], it didn't matter because they had their guns. . . . These were regular soldiers. (interview; see Figures 10, 11)

It has since become clear that these soldiers were also given abandoned land reclaimed years later by returning refugees, creating serious, long-term conflict in these villages.

With mobilization Decree-Law 44-82 on 1 July 1982, former soldiers who had most recently completed their service (saving the army retraining time and money) were called up, together with "public servants," such as doctors, professors, and agronomists, who "were forced to return to their places of work to provide services to the population no matter how distant or dangerous the location" (Gramajo, interview). Many of these former soldiers had been and still were part of the army's intelligence network of military commissioners throughout the highlands; they would later serve as *jefes* of civil patrols.

In a later interview, Gramajo explains how many of these new indigenous regulars, "recruited" from the original FIL by perks and by force, began working with ladino officers and troops in Civil Affairs companies in mid-1982, imparting their knowledge about the terrain, dialect, and local cus-

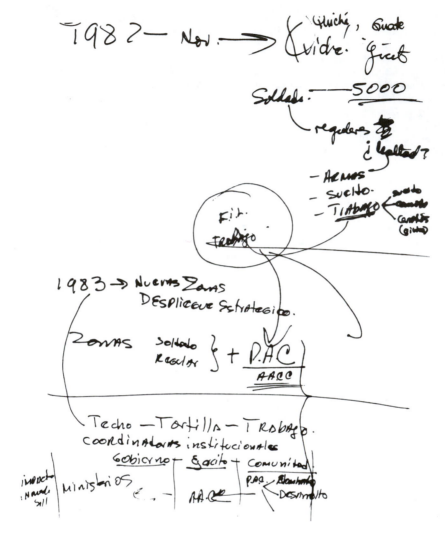

Figure 10. General Gramajo's sketch: from FIL to PAC strategy, 1982–83.

toms. For example, Ixil Companies were organized by the army in at least three towns, each consisting of 100 to 120 Ixil youths who volunteered or had previously been army conscripts (Stoll 1993: 330). They were useful in "explaining" the war to indigenous refugees with psychological warfare statements (in a Mayan dialect), as Gramajo mimics: "I'm sending a message to my cousin Juan because guerrillo Solomon is saying that I have been killed, but Solomon is telling lies because I gave myself up to the army and

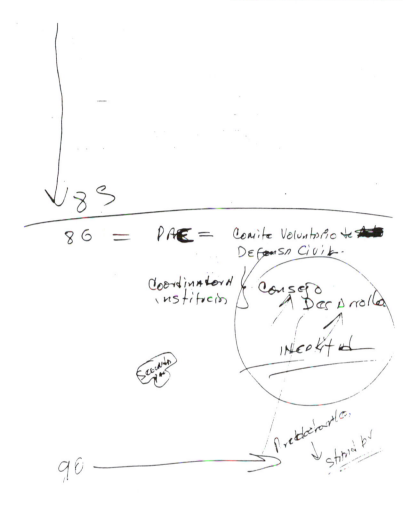

Figure 11. General Gramajo's sketch continued: from PAC to Voluntary Committees of Civil Defense, 1986–90.

not only did they not kill me but they gave me medicine and treated my sores. And now that I am free, I am asking my cousin Juan to join me" (interview). They also were useful in accompanying refugees back to their lands, making certain they did not wander too far from the model villages. Air Force Colonel Grotewold, chief of CRN, assured me in a 1986 interview that "many of these soldiers come from these very same villages that were destroyed and restructured into the Poles. They return to these villages as members of the Civil Affairs Company integrated into each infantry battalion stationed at the Poles of Development." Gramajo adds, "By recruiting from these places [in the Ixil] we figured we would better know the places we were fighting and we would cease ethnic confrontation. And besides, we were putting money into these poor places. So it was a completely integrated effort" (interview). The army's reconfiguration of the rank of sergeant into Sargento-Mayor Especialista, with more training, salary, and prestige, proved to be yet another incentive for these *nuevos soldados lugareños* to remain loyal to the institution.

Civil Patrols

Formally established by Decree-Law 160-83[5] many months after the first patrols had already been organized and directly coordinated by Civil Affairs units for the Defense Ministry, the Civil Patrols of Self-Defense have served as "the eyes and ears for the Army" in the highlands, according to the Army's own pamphlet (in both Spanish and English), *Las patrullas de autodefensa civil: La respuesta popular al proceso de integración socio-económico-político en la Guatemala actual*, "report[ing] to the authorities any persons, facts or situations that appear . . . suspicious" with "watching hours" assigned day and night (Ejército 1984c: 12–13).[6] Through the Patrols, the army learns of the community's movements, with whom it communicates, the amount of food it consumes, as well as of meetings and the content of discussions.

While technically not "soldiers" in the army, as they have received neither uniform nor a salary and many patrol without a gun, "a large number of the members of the defense patrols are persons who at one time in their life [*sic*] were enrolled in military service during a period of at least 24 months; some are therefore familiar with military life and its structure and hierarchy" (15–16). As an "auxiliary force," they must respond to the directives and commands of Civil Affairs (S-5) army officers, local military commanders, and military commissioners, as well as to the defense minister himself (Letona 1989: 22). Intended to serve as both a military and political counterpoise at the local level to the guerrillas' local FIL cadre (Sereseres 1985: 116), forced recruitment of 30,000 peasants for Civil Patrols began in April 1982, particularly in the eight "zones of conflict" where guerrilla activity was most prevalent, putting to rest the argument that the Patrols arose "spontaneously . . . by petition, by general consensus, to provide training and basic weapons to enable those peasants to defend their homes, thus making them responsible for their own defense needs" (Ejército 1984c: 16) (an argument also found in speeches made by the civilian governments). The first Patrol is said to have been formed in the town of San Nicolás, El Quiché, 7 April 1982, two days after the National Plan was formally presented to the military government. That day, a guerrilla column attacked the town, killing one man and three youths, according to an officer there at the time. Arms were delivered to the town, and when the army called a meeting, some three thousand men showed up; at the second meeting, the patrols were organized and leaders selected (anonymous colonel interview; Beltranena 1992: 158).

By the end of 1982, 300,000 of Ríos Montt's "knights of freedom" (*los paladines de la libertad*) (quoted in Vargas 1984: 91), in 850 villages were already *patrulleros*; by November 1983, the figure was 500,000 and by the end of 1984, 1,300,000 adult males were patrolling. Clearly, Civil Patrols served as a force multiplier, as Gramajo explains:

The military zones had their regular soldiers plus these "new soldiers of the locale," plus the *Patrullas* under the control of Civil Affairs. So, because there were by then enough [regular] soldiers, the Civil Patrols were begun to be organized by Civil Affairs. That is the story of the unfurling of the strategy. And what was the key word in this initial strategy? "Participation," because the *indígenas* participated in the war effort! (interview)

But "participation" is restricted: each *aldea* in Ixil country, for example, elects its own civil patrol officers except for the 3 top commanders, who were still, in the early 1990s, named by the army (Stoll 1993: 145). This figure fell to approximately 600,000 in 1986, and diminished to 202,517 by the early 1990s (with 58,114 of these latter trained in weapons) (Ejército 1994).

Civil Patrol Responsibilities

Throughout the 1980s, members of the Civil Patrols had three responsibilities: they were forced to form *pelotónes* (platoons) that patrol in and around the village in twenty-four-hour rounds, with the number of times per month each man had to march depending on both the number of men in the village and the number of those who migrate to the south coast to work on the large cotton and sugar cane *fincas*;[7] they were forced into "search operations" with the army, not knowing when or for how long, having to take along their own food; they had to undertake anything from roadwork and building construction to communal work, such as carrying firewood for the Patrol or the military commander at the nearby garrison. Between 1982 and 1985 work was paid for with food through the Food-for-Work program; however, after the Patrols became Comités Voluntarios (Voluntary Committees) in 1986, they literally served as unpaid laborers who had to supply their own food and, in some areas, pay for their own guns out of their meager earnings from laboring on the south coast.

One of the most traumatic tasks for the Civil Patrols was their "forced voluntary" complicity in killing villagers in their own or neighboring village, either based upon a list prepared by *orejas* (spies) of the army or by surprise, when coming upon refugees in the mountains on patrol with the army — or be killed themselves (cf. Montejo 1993). The consequences of creating militarized indigenous Civil Patrol *jefes* as local army commanders who serve as internal monitors of indigenous population activities — of victims becoming accomplices — has had dire consequences for human rights protections. This utilization by the army of indigenous men in both soldiering and civil patrolling actively involved civilians in the killing and sharpened village conflict: "Because of the profound involvement of local men in vigilante patrols, there are too many people implicated in the violence who want to maintain a public secret. According to one account, the army was so successful in its strategy to actively involve noncombatant civilians in the killing, now many in the community feel threatened when the military is indicted by human rights organizations" (Stoll 1993: 302).

How "Voluntary"?

The voluntary nature of these patrols has continually been asserted by the army since 1982 and is also to be found in the 1985 Constitution: "No one is obliged to associate themselves with or form part of groups or associations of civil self-defense" (Article 34, Constituyente de Guatemala 1985: 6). In comparing the language of the constitutionalization of militias since 1965, we find that it changes from "It is punishable to organize and utilize militias apart from the Army of Guatemala" (Article 215 of the 1965 constitution) to "Be it resolved that the organization of paramilitary forces or militias apart from the army of Guatemala is prohibited and punishable" (Article 89 of the 1982 Fundamental Statute of Government) to "It is punishable to organize and utilize armed groups not regulated by laws and its rules" (Article 245 of the 1985 Constitution) (Linares Morales 1985: 22). Whereas the previous articles refer to those organizations apart from the army, the more recent Constitution implicitly accepts the legal and political immersion of the security apparatus of the PACS — an example of how the military "adjusted" and "harmonized" the counterinsurgent structures with the new constitutional order. Immediately before leaving office, Chief of State Mejía Víctores passed a decree-law renaming Civil Patrols Civil Defense Committees (Comités de Defensa Civil) and redefining them civilian organizations to be assisted and coordinated by the Ministry of Defense (*Central America Report*, 26 January 1986). General Gramajo, as Defense Minister between 1986 and 1990, continued to insist that the Civil Patrols were "voluntary" and that their goal was to secure peace (AA for ICJ 1987: 21). These Civil Patrols were renamed once again under the Cerezo government as Voluntary Committees of Civil Defense (*La Hora*, 12 May 1986, 1), to emphasize the voluntary nature of the work. The army document also claims that "From its founding, the patrols were set up with the understanding that their mission would be temporary. Their function will cease when the inhabitants feel that their integrity is safe and when the Guatemalan Army judges that the general living conditions are normal" (Ejército *Las Patrullas* 1984c:

10–11). In his monthly press conference in February 1986, Defense Minister Hernández stated that the PACs would continue and that the president would evaluate "during the next 3 months the functioning of these patrols" in order to decide whether to continue the project. He emphasized that the patrols "were necessary to control the population" (Comité Pro-Justicia y Paz 1986: 7).

Nonetheless, there is abundant evidence that throughout the 1980s, the PACs were as voluntary as mandatory voting during the elections. For indigenous men between fifteen and sixty years of age, patrolling for twenty-four hours approximately every twenty to thirty days was obligatory, with peasants in the conflict zones who had refused to patrol accused of subversion, running the risk of their families being deprived of food and of being killed. Testimony from Civil Patrollers describes how military commissioners and army officers terrorized villagers by ordering their soldiers to kidnap, torture, and kill those who opposed participation or who refused to commit human rights violations against their own communities.

Jefes of the Civil Patrols

With only a few exceptions, the three top commanders of the Civil Patrols were not selected on the basis of leadership qualities or for their "community interests," but rather because they were trusted by the army; most were former soldiers. The military charges the guerrilla with undermining the traditional village structures; yet the *jefes'* newfound authority and abusive behavior contributes to the undermining of trust and cohesion in many indigenous communities, as one Civil Patroller complains: "The problem is there are spies everywhere. You can't trust anybody. The army has successfully made one distrustful of one's neighbors. The Civil Patrol as well: they are always ready to denounce anybody as a collaborator [with the guerrilla]" (CEIDEC, quoted in Arias 1988: 189).

The Adjunct Human Rights Ombudsman in 1991, César Alvarez Gudamuz, whose life was threatened by Civil Patrollers during one of his investigations of the killing of two peasants by a PAC in El Quiché, publicly stated that the Civil Patrols were "out of control": "We have various cases [in the office], mostly in El Quiché, where Civil Patrollers are accused of murder and many other crimes. We know the ways in which the Patrols abuse their power and impunity, acting without any control whatsoever. They are constantly violating human rights" (*La Hora*, 6 July 1991, 3; interview).

Terror and mistrust are important factors in understanding why the Civil Patrols remained; equally significant is corruption. With all PAC members contributing up to Q5 quetzales ($1) weekly to buy bullets and oil for their weapons, those who could not or would not pay were brought before the PAC *jefe*, threatened, and forced into an "agreement" to pay Q200–300 ($40–60 in 1993). Get-rich-quick stories of corruption by several PAC leaders abound, such as one who managed on the basis of such extortion to build a two-story house and buy various pickup trucks (*Noticias de Guatemala*, 1, no. 3 (February–March 1993: 11).

While the leadership for the renamed local Committees came directly from the Civil Patrols, with mayors "elected-appointed," according to Gramajo, a more long-term difficulty arose within this schema—that of "second-class mayors":

Q: How were the mayors [within the eight denominated zones of conflict] selected? Elections were held [in 1985] and the army selected them. The [mayors][8] became involved with matters of development through Civil Affairs, and government ministries responded to their demands.
Q: So, the Civil Patrols are precisely . . .
The organization of the community.
Q: With the gun?
At the beginning, with the gun. We [the army] were present [in these communities] in '83, '84, '85: there is no doubt that the military government was present. And in 1986, the Civil Patrols became in the Constitution Voluntary Committees of Civil Defense, no longer Self-Defense, and the IICs became Councils of Development (*Consejos de Desarrollo*) with the same participants.
Q: So it was just a linguistic change?
No, in reality, what changed was that guns [of the PACs] were no longer present. Some areas continue using guns, but this is due to political ineptitude. But we have a problem now and I hope we can repair it. When the 1985 elections were being prepared, the local leadership, the real leadership, was in the Civil Patrols because the army had chosen them. When I ordered these Patrol leaders, the true leaders, to renounce their positions if they wanted to participate in politics [i.e., run for mayor], they, for reasons of team spirit, for camaraderie, for loyalty, I don't know what, refused to do so. So the first-class leaders are Patrol leaders, the second- and third-class leaders are mayors who cannot mobilize the population. That's what we're suffering with at the moment. In these elections now [in December 1990], I don't know what class of mayors there is; it would be better if those who are in the PACs become mayors and thus continue being leaders, *but within the civilian system*. Simply stated, military society was more capable than civilian society [in developing leaders]. That's all there is to it. So the issue is not whether [the PACs] are voluntary or involuntary; what it has meant is that they are getting in the way of providing good civilian leadership—which is the result of that initial mistake [of ours]. But we're only human. (interview; his emphasis)

Despite his disappointment, Gramajo pointed to the Santiago de Atitlán massacre as an example of how useful the "first-class" caliber of Civil Patrol *jefes* could be. The massacre occurred on 2 December 1990, when members of the military garrison in the town fired into a crowd of 5000 T'zutuhil villagers who were protesting army harassment, killing 13 people, including 3 children, and wounding 17. Like many communities around Lake Atitlán, Santiago had adamantly refused to allow the army to organize a Civil Patrol, and had thrown the army out of town (cf. Carmack 1988). According to Gramajo, "First-class Patrol leaders" in the town could have foreseen "villagers organizing themselves," and could have controlled such dissent "before it got out of hand": "Why did [the villagers] organize themselves? Why did they fight [the army]? Because the Patrol had not been organized. So, this is a retrocession back to the situation in 1982 when the people were defending themselves against both the army and the subversion. That's what happened there in Santiago—where the army works and the guerrilla works, and the people suffer. We are not advancing [in our strategy there]" (interview).[9] Because of the wave of national and international human rights criticisms, as well as a petition signed by 15,000 villagers, the army, in an unusual concession, relocated its garrison outside of Santiago a few weeks later.

Once the army had destroyed, reconstructed, and penetrated the geographic and cultural fabric of villages in the northwest highlands and had militarized the Civil Patrols leadership, they believed they could expect these new power brokers to step down. Notwithstanding Gramajo's confusion, it seems clear that the new indigenous leaders, many of them former soldiers or military commissioners, having been appointed by the army to lead Civil Patrols in 1982, found themselves in extraordinarily powerful positions in their villages, especially with the vacuum left by the repression. In refusing to play out the military's long-term plan of having the military-appointed, army-backed "true leaders" slide into civilian mayoral positions—democratization qua militarization—these Civil Patrol *jefes* caused the plan to backfire; in not wanting to become mayors, these Civil Patrol leaders fell out of sync with the institutionalization of civil-military cogovernance with regard to security (as occurred with the convergence of the IICs and the Councils of Development). Once again, the contradictions of a democratization born of counterinsurgency are exposed: once a surveillance apparatus is established in which former soldiers and former guerrillas without uniforms and without pay, under the controlled supervision of (and often fear of) Civil Affairs officers, become power brokers in corruption and elimination, they may be reluctant to slide into the designated civilian mayoral slots necessary to maintain the military's strategic shift to low-profile status for international consumption.

Patrolling as a Form of Self-Defense

While we know some Patrollers can develop an unquestioning loyalty to the army, it cannot all be so easily dismissed as brainwashing by the army. Some Civil Patrol leaders do take a harder line against resisters than even the army does, revealing that some do revel in the control and abuse of fellow villagers. For example, the human rights group, CERJ (Council of Ethnic Communities for the Rights of the Marginal and Oppressed: All Are Equal, *Runujel Junam*) in El Quiché formed by several hundred indigenous peasants in July 1988 to demand the immediate abolition of the PACs, has sharpened village conflicts. The army's reaction was predictable: it encouraged the more loyal Patrollers to threaten dissidents, and if the dissidents refused to patrol, to kill them (Stoll 1993: 142). By 1991, 25 of CERJ's 6000 members had been forcibly disappeared or killed. CERJ sent a letter to the President of the Supreme Court, describing the forms of intimidation used by patrol leaders:

On November 22, 1988, we [the undersigned] were obligated to attend a meeting which took place in the municipal town hall of Patzité, Quiché, under orders of the *comandante* of the Civil Patrol, today a "VOLUNTARY" committee. This violates Article 5 of the Constitution of the Republic. The comandante of this Patrol is Sr. Miguel Us Soc, who, among other things during the meeting at which neighbors of 7 communities were present and who were also obligated to attend, told us the following: That very soon the civil patrols of the communities present [at the meeting] were going to be reorganized . . . with the principal objective to change the name [of the Patrols] such that they will no longer be voluntary but obligatory, and those who denied their services to them would be considered guerrillas. He also told us that he would distribute military shoes, pants, arms, radio-communication equipment, and other goods which were necessary, and he intimidated us, and practically threatened us in respect to the denunciation we had made to the Human Rights Ombudsman. . . . Mr. President, we are making this denunciation because we fear for our lives. (Statement of CERJ sent to the media, 23 November 1988)

After one demonstration of CERJ to denounce forced military recruitment in Santa Cruz del Quiché in May 1991, at which G-2 agents and military commissioners infiltrated the crowd, CERJ President Amílcar Méndez Urízar presented a complaint to the Secretary of the Departmental Government of El Quiché, who replied, "Here comes Méndez and all those Indian sons of bitches who we're going to kill." Amílcar Méndez, elected a congressional deputy in 1995, continues to receive threatening phone calls.[10]

There have also been denunciations of abuses by the PACs themselves. For example, three union members in Chichicastenango were "captured by a Patrol" and disappeared. They then reappeared, after having been captured by "elements of the Comité de Defensa Civil and the Military Commissioner" and taken to "Military Zone 14 in Sololá where they were investigated and found innocent of charges and returned to the Civil Defense Committee of Panimaché I of Chichicastenango, whose members let them return to their homes" (*El Gráfico*, 19 and 23 August 1988: 79, 65, respectively). Similarly, a large group of peasants from El Quiché denounced accusations of subversion and threats of death by Patrols to the Human Rights Commission. "Many of them are under pressure by commanders of the Patrols, who the peasants accused of enriching themselves in the shadow of those in power who give them arms and the investiture which the army offers them." Several peasants explained that when they announced that they wanted to quit the Patrols, "military elements" carried off their documents and accused them of being collaborators with the guerrillas, and demanded they leave their village of Chiníque (*El Gráfico*, 10 August 1988:

6). For the army, these scenarios of "Indians killing Indians" have been useful for human rights violations-distancing purposes.

Yet in seeking answers to the question What explains the continuation of patrols ten years after the violence? ethnographic accounts of Civil Patrols provide a more nuanced picture: they reveal a logic of ambivalent and qualified support for the Patrols as a localized way out of the violence and as a means of self-defense, with many rural people fearing a return of violence to their village. So, to play it safe, until the army had given the word that Patrols would come to an end, many continued to patrol. Moreover, they wanted to leave on good terms with the army to ensure that (1) they can get their guns back and (2) current confrontations will not haunt them in future violence. Stoll has reported that in 1989, with four EGP columns still operating in Ixil country, nearly everyone resented being forced to patrol but they were afraid to stop. Why? "Because the guerrillas would be free to contact the population again and the army would return to kidnap suspected infiltrators" (1993: 142). Most Ixils, he writes, "are best understood as determined neutralists" (132).

Yet one of the other aspects these studies make clear is the growth of a strong sense of localized sovereignty within these communities. They take the army and its emphasis on indigenous participation at its word: with the guns and training, Civil Patrols have provided the villages with their own means of self-defense. As Kobrak explains, "Ríos Montt's plan to make active participants in the war was certainly brutal, but more welcome to many villagers than becoming passive victims" (1994: 5). He argues that unlike the earlier forms of oppression that enriched others, the Civil Patrols were locally organized and locally obligated in the name of local security, with many rural Indians viewing PACs as less an attack on community than as a way to strengthen village sovereignty, as less a submission to their oppressor than as an escape from both sides of the violence. "A Civil Patrol leader explained that there is a national law, the constitution, which makes Civil Patrols voluntary, but that [his community] has a local law, decided [upon] by the villagers themselves. The whole village must patrol, he said, in order to prove their loyalty to the government" (3). Some villagers, moreover, consider patrolling as a way to remember the violence and honor its victims: "To abandon them disrespects the dead; [it] endangers villagers in the here and now by sowing dissension and allowing the violence" to return (6).

Most wanted an orderly end to the Patrols: one that did not cause dissension or violence, and one that respected consensus. "Few PAC critics exercise their individual right to withdraw. They prefer a community decision" (7). Thus, "support" is equivocal, reflecting within this context of violence and terror the syncretic use of army discourse against "subversion," and at least formally following the rules of the game as dictated by the army as a way of avoiding further violence.

What this picture fails to take into account, however, is the central role PACs play in the army's logic of localized statism: by initially linking food with locally organized and locally obligated patrolling — the Beans with the Bullets — and then mobilizing that population into either "new soldiers of the locale" or Civil Patrols of Self-Defense, the military created a network in the highlands of *centrally controlled but seemingly localized security*. This has provided an illusion of village sovereignty while ensuring national control by the High Command. This equation of local security efforts with loyalty to the army-state has ensured a coherent intelligence-gathering mechanism under the rubric of "participation" and "integration." Whether the army's project has created its own dynamics of dissent, providing unintended spaces for localized cultures of reciprocity and sovereignties, is uncertain. But what it did manage to do was divide the indigenous population against itself, co-opting the guerrilla structure of Patrols to use against both the guerrillas and the indigenous communities, while at the same time augmenting their own institution with desperately needed soldiers and providing themselves with roadworkers for increased military access to remote areas. In sum, the Army continues to provide what its Plan intended: "development within a context of rational and effective security."

Military's Response to Civil Patrols Protest

The military has responded in a variety of ways to the increasing human rights denunciations made by *patrulleros*. The following is a good example of the psychological warfare tactic utilized by the Army Public Relations Office (DIDE), which turns a human rights denunciation around on the "denouncer" — in this case, a PAC member — focusing on him as the guilty party and discrediting his claims, rather than on the issue at hand, clandestine cemeteries: On 27 February 1988, Pedro Xirún Guarcas, a peasant, reported to the human rights group of the relatives of the disappeared, the Group of Mutual Support, the existence of a clandestine cemetery of twenty-three bodies at Chijtinamit, Chichicastenango, El Quiché. He said his two sons had enlisted with the guerrilla in the region, and had later, with the amnesty, served in the PAC. One night they went out on patrol and never returned. According to medical reports, all twenty-three men had had their throats cut. On 14 March 1988, Guarcas denounced that he and four of his relatives had received death threats from the *jefe* of the Civil Defense Patrol in Chijtinamit. On 18 March 1988, Defense Minister Gramajo labeled anyone who denounced the existence of clandestine graves as "subversive": "The dead were all buried by subversives and that's why clandestine cemeteries now exist. It is very odd that there are people who know exactly where these graves are located. They know where they buried their dead and now they're trying to make it look as if they were victims of PAC" (Comité Pro-Justicia y Paz, March 1988: 5).

During this same period, relatives of the disappeared were ordered by the army to sign blank sheets of paper that were filled in as letters to the Human Rights Ombudsman, stating that "people are being punished who have fought against those collaborating with a subversion that has brought us so much harm. . . . Now that there is peace, the defenders of our community are being blamed, victimized and imprisoned. . . . We urge you not to proceed against those who have defended us from the grip of communism. . . . We would like to inform you that from now on, we will be willing to take whatever measures necessary to prevent these cases from proceeding. Yours Sincerely: ——." As one officer from the Santo Tomás Chichicastenango military base said to the gathered Civil Patrol commanders on 8 March 1988 to exhort them to sign these blank "petitions": "And if some reporter turns up in your district, you don't have to say anything; that's what we've got the Civil Patrols for, and now that we're living in a democracy, nobody's got the right to ask questions in your community." Then they handed out blank sheets of paper and each Civil Patrol commander signed them (Comité Pro-Justicia y Paz, March 1988: 4–6).

Another tactic used by former Defense Minister Gramajo was to write a 13 November 1990 letter to the head of CERJ, Amílcar Méndez: "Countryman, . . . Your work and the recognition you now receive [internationally] confirm that Guatemala has and deserves a better future." Despite this hail-fellow-well-met attitude, Gramajo's opinion of CERJ was that it was a *grupo de fachada* (guerrilla front group) interested only in making human rights a political issue:

Q: Those *patrulleros* who reject patrolling and have organized themselves into CERJ, what do you think of them?
Well, the CERJ, in my opinion, is a skeleton [of an organization]. It has a *jefe* and staff, but it has no masses, and if there is an isolated incident, they grab hold of it (*lo agarran*). And Amílcar [the *jefe*] is not alone, nor is CERJ large. Nonetheless, what is curious is that CERJ only works against the PAC; it doesn't work for a general agenda of human rights.
Q: That's to say that if CERJ worked for human rights in general, that would be seen as better or worse?
It would be seen as something permanent. That's to say, human rights means many things, but he [Amílcar Méndez] only works against what is apparently forced patrolling. Patrols, depending on what term one wants to use [angrily] because it says in the constitution there already exist Voluntary Committees of Patrols in 1986, and since there is the term "voluntary," his only work then is to seek out wherever patrolling is *in*voluntary, right? But if he were attending to all the abuses and not just where [the Patrols] are involuntary, then it would be a more efficient human rights organization. In other words, he's using politics [to resolve] a philosophical matter. (interview)

Assuming that Gramajo was more fully informed about CERJ than he let on, he chose to ignore that CERJ was concerned "not only with dismantling the Civil Patrols but also forced labor and forced [military] recruitment . . . with fighting for the right to life, to culture, rejecting paternalism and discrimination, and for the right to live as one chooses without any coercion or imposition or repression on the part of the State or anybody" (Méndez, interview; CERJ member, "Contra la patrullas civiles" *Otra Guatemala,* January 1989: 12).

Additionally, former President Cerezo has stated that "hard line officers tell me that Amílcar Méndez is a man compromised by the guerrilla. In other words, he is a *militante guerrillero* not a human rights militant, like some are.[11] And nothing will happen to him *because this is the decision that has been made: that nothing will happen to him*" (1991 interview). If this is the case (despite all the death threats and attempts on Méndez's life), it clearly demonstrates that military intelligence has the ability and the will to protect what they view as Opponents of the State from disappearance and death *when they so choose.*

By 1992, however, ten years after the creation of the Civil Patrols, the military began to recognize how useful the formal renaming and, in some cases, the disbanding of some Civil Patrols would be internationally. A Foreign Relations Ministry bulletin announced that "Some 2000 peasants from ten rural communities in Dolores, El Petén, dissolved the PAC to convert themselves into Peace and Development Communities. . . . These ex-patrollers decided to turn in their guns to form committees of peace by which they hope to contribute to solving the diverse problems and developing their own communities. The departmental governor and other government authorities were present" (14 February 1994). In other cases, the military has allowed for the formal disbanding of some PACs in areas where the guerrilla is no longer operating. But most of these nonpatrolling villages have been new, small resettlements set up by "reeducated" farmers moving out of the older model villages in Ixil country. "Instead of refusing to patrol, the new villages could simply fail to begin doing so in the kind of unobtrusive manner preferred by peasants" (Stoll 1993: 296). By mid-1992, the army was displaying a more pragmatic attitude toward the new era of human rights, even in the Ixil country: Ixils would have to patrol only as long as the guerrillas operated in the vicinity—that is, as *emergencia.* It accepted, at least publicly, the Human Rights Ombudsman's demand that Patrols were intended to be voluntary, despite the anti-Patrol and anti-forced recruitment protests of the indigenous human rights groups, CONAVIGUA (National Coordinating Committee of Guatemalan Widows) and CERJ—something the military was none too happy about: "Conscientious objection must be accepted in Guatemala," Rosalina Tuyuc, leader of CONAVIGUA announced in 1993 (*Boston Globe,* 19 August). These confrontational human rights tactics often clashed with the more staunchly pro-Patrol and severely army-loyal PAC leaders. But internal surveillance is intended to control a population by that very population, saving the army the trouble of using its own troops "before the situation gets out of hand" (Gramajo interview).

This pitting of villager against villager ensures enmity before solidarity, contributing to the destruction of the indigenous social fabric. Thus, while the army is responsible for forming and overseeing the Patrols, it also distances itself from the new Peace and Development Committees that, unlike the army, are being found guilty of human rights abuses by the courts.[12]

Civil Patrols as Committees of Peace and Development and the World Bank

In 1993, 1276 Committees of Peace and Development consisting of 92,971 unarmed adult men "emerged," according to the army (Ejército 1994). This same year, the Social Investment Fund (FIS), set up under the direction of the World Bank to help alleviate poverty in the rural areas and to "increase human capital through social investment," developed an agenda of prioritized projects that sounded surprisingly similar to the army's list of development schemes in the Poles of Development in 1983–84: latrines, school construction, health clinics, and road construction. Even more surprising was the comment by the director of FIS, Pablo Schneider, that FIS would most likely be funding Peace and Development Committees (Comités de Paz y Desarrollo) — the newly converted Civil Defense Patrols. Moreover, FONAPAZ (Fondo Nacional para la Paz) would be funding the Peace and Development Committees to promote peace and "demobilization," according to director Danilo Cruz, although exactly how this would contribute to demobilization was not spelled out (Center for Democratic Education Research 1994: 4, 6). With the Civil Patrols one of the linchpins in the army's long-term strategy for the management of security in the highlands throughout the 1980s, and with much evidence that many *patrulleros* have committed grievous human rights violations, the funding of these patrols — and, indirectly, the Defense Ministry — by the World Bank in the early 1990s ironically brings to a closure the army's decade-long attempt to see to it that their development-qua-security project be consolidated, financed, and hence legitimized, even if indirectly, by the global economic community.

Final Comments

Civil Patrols, together with Civil Affairs, have been the army's centerpiece of a permanent counterinsurgency strategy in the highlands. Local civil patrol chiefs, appointed by the local army commander and inculcated into the army's Beans and Bullets strategy, signaled the continuation of a network of militarized informants, even if the Civil Patrols were diminished or eventually disbanded as occurred in 1996 (see Chapter 12). *Jefes* of these Patrols, "the first-class leaders able to mobilize," have seriously undermined trust within many indigenous communities. But Lieutenant Colonel-political scientist Cruz Salazar is quite clear about the original purpose of combining these PACs with the Poles of Development as a necessary part of the 30/70 percent strategy—a purpose that remains a key and integral part of *el proyecto político-militar*.

Ríos Montt intervened with a total change of tactics: Beans and Guns is nothing less than the mobilization of the peasants into the Patrols of Self-Defense. These PACs— for all the criticisms one could make of them—have in reality been very effective in combating insurgency. First, because this mobilization implied that it denied necessary information to the guerrilla, and second, it denied the logistical support, transport and so forth, to the guerrilla. And at the same time, it passed on more information and more support to the Army. From a tactical point of view, the PACs are extraordinary, fantastic! What I am insisting upon is very important because this structure now [in 1986] is precisely *without conflict* because of this tactic. To adopt the Patrols, which is a very strong and effective military instrument by which to neutralize and weaken the insurgency, allowed the Army to go on and create the Poles of Development. The first goal of the Poles is that they run parallel to the PACs in collaboration with the Army to satisfy needs the peasant couldn't satisfy before. They are creating new villages, giving basic facilities, such as water, electricity, and roads. Thus the peasant begins to see that although he was under tremendous pressure by the military, he begins to see a change. Thus, it is a very interesting tactic: *you demand and you give*. You cannot have the Poles without the PACs: they go together, or you continue [to fight the war]. Without the Poles, the patrols would find only pressure and no satisfaction.... [However], even though the PACs and Poles are very effective in fighting the guerrilla, there is an authoritative pressure on the peasant which is indisputable. And this must end or be very much eased up. This means that if there is a Pole of Development, the Army has control over the population; it has control over the entire community. One is subjected to a military regime as though one is on a large military base and the peasant is thus totally subject to the will of those who run the Pole. This must disappear. One must indoctrinate, make the peasant *consent* to playing a role in helping the government and the Army, but feel free from all pressure. This is necessary. This is why one opts for a "mixed" solution [of civil-military co-governance].
Q: To control . . . ?
To control the civilians. *It is necessary.* (interview; his emphasis)

Chapter 5
Civil Affairs

Psychological Warfare, Social Intelligence, and the Sanctioned Mayan

> Civil Affairs in operational military terms refers to the conjuncture of activities of the army participating with civil authorities and the general population to facilitate military operations against the declared or concealed enemy in order to prevent and resolve the problems derived from underdevelopment and actions of terrorist groups.
> — Civil Affairs manual *Forjar y libertar* (To Forge and to Liberate)

For most Guatemalan officers, the "secret weapon" and strength of the Guatemalan military since 1982 lies with its Civil Affairs and Local Development companies. Civil Affairs demands the participation of the local population in local development projects and security apparatuses, including the Civil Patrols in the 1980s, and the alias-PACs, Committees of Peace and Development in the 1990s. Unlike the older U.S.-sponsored strategy of Civic Action, in which military units worked to improve the military's image on a piecemeal basis, Civil Affairs entails a more permanent involvement by the military in the organization of local action "to promote and improve standards of living and development for the population" (Letona 1989: 26). These are referred to in military parlance as the "soft aspects of war," to be used in order to "integrate" local efforts with national strategy. At the core of the Civil Affairs strategy is the concept of "minimum force." "We are no longer going to kill [the subversives]," Gramajo told me:

We will isolate them, punish them, be more sophisticated in fighting them. We're going to say to *el pueblo* "Look, if you want to be in agreement with us, then put down those weapons and come do orthodox politics." . . . This [manual of Civil Affairs] which is being revised so that we are within the government (*estamos dentro del gobierno*) is of enormous sophistication [for the Army]. Here it speaks about, and this is one of the most important parts in reading about matters of war, "minimum force." We are not renouncing the use of force. If we have to use it, we use it. Much more sophisticated in order to get the job done [he whispers]. . . . So, as soldiers, we use force but not with our eyes closed as the warrior or insurgent. We kill with our eyes open, conscious, knowing what we are doing. We aren't assassinating anyone; what we are doing is lamentably exercising the force of arms to be able to succeed in favor of the nation. . . . But remember, we have three objectives in this military strategy: (1) to bring the population down from the mountains (*descender la población*) (2) recuperate those who have been indoctrinated with foreign ideas, and (3) neutralize the armed insurgents. (interview)

Minimum force entails the "penetration" of the rural population by special forces units — *especialistas* — to serve as "buffers in small-scale confrontations (*choques*) out there." He adds,

The Army with guns is here [on one side] and *el pueblo* is on the other side. So, the Army without guns locate themselves *within el pueblo*, and *el pueblo* speaks with the Army without guns, [thinking], "They cannot harm me. On the contrary, they help me to develop, they give me medical assistance, education, everything. If the army has to grab (*agarrar*) some people, it is [already located] there with them; they don't harm them [though] because they don't carry guns. [But] if I carry a gun, if I'm an insurgent, then I'm not normal and they *will* harm me." (interview)

Civil Affairs, established in June 1982, built on the Operación Ixil plan. In May 1981, Navy Captain Juan Cifuentes presented a series of proposals to the Army Chief of Staff, General Benedicto Lucas García. This document, published in the army's *Revista Militar* in September 1982 as "Operation Ixil: An Appraisal of Civil Affairs in the Ixil Area," speaks of the need to adopt "an intensive, profound and carefully studied psychological campaign to rescue the Ixil mentality." Several proposals are set forth. The first is the 100 percent proposal for the army to "put all its efforts into Civil Affairs Units to complete its assigned mission [of] intensifying the ladinization of the Ixil population until it disappears (*esta desaparezca*) as a cultural subgroup foreign to the national way of being (*extraño al modo de ser nacional*)" (Cifuentes 1982: 38). By "*ladinización*," this documents continues, "one must understand it to mean *castellanizar*, to pressure the population to use Spanish language and culture, to suppress the distinctive *traje*, indigenous dress and other exterior displays of differentiating oneself from the group. Given that the constitutional concepts are in the official language of Spanish, these measures will facilitate communication. Without these differentiating characteristics, the Ixils would stop thinking as they do and accept all the abstractions that constitute nationality, patriotism, etc." (46). However, Cifuentes points out, there are several "disadvantages" to this approach: "No. 1: For the last 400 years, the Ixils, more than other ethnic groups, have resisted *la castellanizacion*.[1] Efforts can be useless in changing their thinking and cosmogonic concepts even when they don't have the externally differentiating characteristics." Put simply, they may seem to be one of us, but they aren't; ladinization will make it even more difficult to know how differently they think, and "will augment [already existing] resentment of the Ixil toward the imposition [of the ladino] — a resentment that will fall right into the hands of the enemy [i.e., the guerrilla]" (46–47). This is what had already begun to occur during the sporadic but highly repressive 100 percent strategy of the Lucas García "operations." The second proposal was to have the Civil Affairs Units follow a policy based on "respecting the Ixil identity, customs and language, giving them the opportunity to contribute, together with the army, to the defense of their communities. . . . Knowing the history of the Ixiles, this would be the only way to convince them to form part of the great Guatemalan nation with a pluralist society, more or less as in Switzerland. . . . Another [advantage] would be to neutralize the strategy of the enemy, utilizing their own procedures [for defense] but with many more resources." The disadvantage here, Cifuentes reminds the reader, is that "there exists the possibility that if they organize themselves into self-defense patrols and are given arms, they could go into the mountain [to fight] with the guerrilla" (47). Thus one can go just so far in respecting the Ixil as an equal. This document reveals the Army's extraordinary fear of difference toward and lack of control over the Indian. At the same time, this Article was one of the first to recognize why the *indígena* feels "distrustful of all that has come from the ladinos who they associate unconsciously with the Spaniards and their descendants who have caused them so much suffering. . . . [The guerrilla] offers them a dignity" in contrast to the "governments that have treated them like a subgroup, retarded and brutalized, by ignorance and the consumption of alcohol" (37, 28).

Cifuentes's final proposal to Lucas García was to focus all government efforts on improving living conditions for the indigenous population (in many ways, a re-thinking of the 1976 CRN-civic action model). The advantages here were "the physical incorporation of this territory within a Civil Affairs plan . . . offering work to the ixil population" with these projects. It would not, however, "resolve the problem in a definitive form. . . . Knowing the Ixil nature, all of the process would be difficult [to achieve] as they would not collaborate. [Such a plan] wouldn't work [especially] if one had to reach the point of demagogery" (48). In short, without combining military and political actions — repressive force and ladinization through Civil Affairs-centered counterinsurgency campaigns — development or security alone would be insufficient. Cifuentes recommended Proposal 2: Civil Affairs with an intense ideological campaign in the Ixil language developed through Psychological Operations (OPSIC).

It is unclear how Benedicto Lucas García responded to these proposals, but Civil Affairs Units were subsequently created during the pacification campaign in June 1982. The Ríos Montt military government established two Sections: the Office of Civil Affairs of the National Defense Staff (D-5), which, according to the 1987 Civil Affairs manual *Forjar y libertar*, "functions as advisor to the Army General Staff in all fields related to the political, economic, social and psychological aspects of military operations, such as the planning, programming, coordination, and supervision of policies of Civilian Affairs at the national level," and the Section of Civil Affairs and Community Development (labeled S-5 in 1983), which "functions as advisor to the Military Commander of each Military Zone in reference to the political, economic, social and psychological aspects of military operations . . . at the jurisdictional level of the military commanders" (Ejército 1987a: 9). In addition, each commander supervises the activities of the military commissioners with regard to intelligence matters as well as to the "application of the army's recruitment plans" (12). In the 1982–83 campaign, eleven Civil Affairs companies were assigned to as many garrisons in the most conflictive zones. Much of the task of implementing the military's new 30/70 percent strategy rested with D-5 and S-5 working in unison; they transformed guerrilla irregulars (FIL) into army soldiers and Civil Patrollers, oversaw all settlements of the displaced in the most conflictive areas in the western highlands, "reeducated" the internally displaced and refugees, directed the psychological warfare and propaganda programs (PSYOPS) targeting the civilian population, all the while gathering intelligence information in situ.[2] By 1983, all activities in the model villages, the Poles of Development, and the Civil Patrols were under Civil Affairs control and surveillance. In effect, Civil Affairs companies were put in charge of all civil-military actions of the State at the local level, as CRN director Colonel Grotewold explains:

Given its experience with small civic action projects in the highlands in the 1960s and 1970s, the only organization that had any knowledge of the villages in the highlands [in 1982] was the army. It is only in Guatemala that a special Company of Civic [*sic*] Affairs is integrated within each infantry battalion stationed at the Poles of Development. They are trained in social promotion projects and they must speak the language of the area where they are located.
Q: Do many of these soldiers come from these very villages that were destroyed and restructured into the Poles?
Yes, and they return there [as members of] the Company. (interview)

During this same period, a new category of subofficer, Sergeant-Major Specialist (*suboficial, especialista sargento-mayor*) was also being created to meet the command needs of these special companies. They are "*suboficiales* who are very well prepared to command small units," Colonel Roberto Letona Hora explained (1990 interview). These *especialistas* enter as soldiers for thirty months and advance to a higher salary and special training to become *soldados profesionales* (professional soldiers). They are trained both at the School of Civil Affairs and in a special colony without rank learning to speak indigenous dialects "like the Kaibils" at the School of the Kaibils in El Petén. They are also given two training sessions a year with Fort Bragg in North Carolina: "The Army won't admit this, but it goes on," according to an anonymous intelligence source (interview). But while the Kaibils are Special Forces elite Army units, these *especialistas* are "irregular forces" that "penetrate" local populations with psychological warfare and surveillance. Civil Affairs units with *especialistas* trained in these methods don't exist anywhere else in the world, according to several Civil Affairs *jefes* interviewed.[3] In fact, since 1989, the Guatemalan military has served as the permanent seat for the Civil Affairs subcommittee of the annual American Armies Conference, with militaries throughout Latin America attending meetings once a year in Guatemala on the subject.

Basic Objectives of Civil Affairs Operations

According to the 1987 manual, the five basic objectives of Civil Affairs operations are (1) "to reinforce actions of the army; (2) to obtain the backing of the civilian population in the fight against terrorism; (3) to strengthen the [lasting] effects of military operations by making the destruction of the enemy more blunt and definitive; (4) to limit the rise of armed terrorist bands and of their units of support [within the population]; and (5) to gain the participation of the population to achieve the improvement of their living conditions by way of plans and programs of reconstruction" (Ejército 1987a: 17). The thirty-six-page manual, with one mention of "human rights," which the military commander is in charge of making certain are observed (11), is primarily devoted to mechanisms for physical, psychological, and social control for "preventing terrorist actions," directing military psychological operations, collecting information for social and military intelligence, and organizing Civil Patrols and reservists in each community. From the national to the village level, Civil Affairs units work to "detect and eliminate potential conflict" in four major ways:

1. [Assist in] local development and coordination with civilian authorities on projects of civic education, health, agriculture, and artesanry. Levels of governing are scrutinized to strengthen the military's capacity "to detect conflicts [caused] by the poor performance of those involved in public administration and for the coordination of aid required by communities for their development" (24).
2. The collection of information "to produce social and military intelligence with the goal of preventing actions that could degenerate into conflict" (20–21). Part of such intelligence gathering has come from children in indigenous communities temporarily separated from their mothers by S-5 officers who are checking, for example, on CERJ members organizing against Civil Patrols. The children are shown toys and given sweets while being asked about what their father does, if he makes trips, what time he goes to bed and gets up, if he gets up during the night [to leave the house] ("Contra las patrullas civiles" 1989: 13).
3. The S-5 work with military reserve units to require "all citizens to lend

their military service to the nation for its defense and its maintenance of public order and internal peace" (27). Its "compliance with the functions of the military commissioners, especially [in supplying] social and military intelligence and army recruitment," is critical (28). This involves the training of reserve units and control of military commissioners, appointed in even the smallest hamlets, with special attention given to gathering social and military intelligence and to the recruitment of soldiers.

4. Voluntary Civil Defense Committees (formerly Civil Patrols): S-5 units are responsible for (a) promoting patrol participation, (b) organizing the actual committees/patrols by identifying leaders and by controlling their locations, records, and archives, (c) military and civics training, including "individual combat, basic arms, measures of active defense," (d) "employing the cooperation of the committees as they gather intelligence data as active civil defense in the prevention of sabotage and the establishment of units of production [by terrorists]," and (e) "demobilizing committees or individual members for transgressions of laws, age, or lack of such needed services. . . . These committees were born out of the need to provide citizen protection, and because of that, the Army assisted in helping them organize, in giving them training and handing out some weapons."

Under the subheading "General Objectives," the manual states that "Civil Affairs have a special projection in all stages of conflict":

1. as "preventive measures to orient the population toward a positive, supportive attitude toward the government, the Army, and a rejection of terrorist instigations: Civil Affairs operations [can be] oriented toward the prevention of terrorist penetration" and maintenance of security boundaries necessary (*el marco de seguridad necesario*) to prevent the population from "reverting back to terrorist actions once military forces have withdrawn" (14, 19) — that is, pre-emptively eliminating potential opponents.

2. "during the conflict to prevent the interference of civilian authorities and the population in military operations, such as taking measures to save civilians from possible harm, and deprive terrorist groups from resources they need for sustenance and operations" (15, 18).

3. "after the conflict to procure the voluntary participation of the population in works of reconstruction and in activities for the improvement of the socio-economic conditions of the population" (14–15). This post-conflict stage reflects the army's perception that "the process of development is always seen as demanding a certain degree of security to achieve its goals — *security that the army is obligated to provide often at the cost of the well-being of the citizenry*" (20; emphasis added).

As Navy Captain Mazariegos wrote "It would be illogical for a government concerned with development not to attend to the danger represented by distorting ideological tendencies that can infiltrate themselves into the minds of citizens and provoke antagonisms and pressures. Or, the reverse, [it would be illogical for a government] concerned with security to abandon actions of development to satisfy the basic elements of the population" (1990: 55). One of the principal objectives of Civil Affairs as tactical preventive measures is, as Gramajo states, the participation of the populace in helping the army "deny to the enemy possibilities for repenetration" (interview). For Civil Affairs, this task, according to the manual, involves developing "favorable conditions to improve the image of the Army within the population" (20) — a clear recognition by the army of the hatred, or at least its lack of legitimacy among much of the rural population. In order to prevent an insurgency from taking root again, Civil Affairs acknowledges that the army must continue to involve the civilian population in its schema — whether the population wants to or not. As Civil Affairs chief Colonel García stated, "When one employs a military methodology, military units which go directly to attend to the origin of possible problems, it is preventive labor. This benefits security enormously." In response to the question as to whether civilians have a different concept of development than have military officers, Colonel García thought for a moment and then said, "I believe there is no basic difference in terms of the concept of development. This is beneficial for the country. Perhaps, though, [a difference] lies in the form in which [the civilians] *apply* [development]. Because our concept is eminently practical. And it is designed to be applied, above all, during circumstances that are not normal and that is when it shows itself to be very efficient" (interview). This response is an admission that there is nothing "civilian" or even civic about Civil Affairs; that its very methodology assumes warlike conditions or at least potential conflict. Moreover, by assuming such conditions, and in constantly identifying and preventing "possible conflict," there is no possibility that such conditions will cease to exist. In fact, Civil Affairs is seen as a central and permanent feature of the military's strategy:

The Army is a permanent institution that has more than one hundred years of being in force and has a real presence in all the territory. For this reason, Civil Affairs tries to utilize the organizational capacity of the Army to cover all places, to arrive [at these places] and try to make contact with all groups, no matter how small, to identify the leadership no matter how weak, and to provoke a dynamic action that allows us to leave [without fear of conflict reappearing].
Q: So this work of the army, this Civil Affairs, it is permanent?
Permanent. No question [about it].

The participation of the Army in development activities is based on mandates listed at the back of the Civil Affairs manual as "Legal Foundations" that include Articles 244 and 249 of the Constitution and Articles 1 and 22 of Decree-Law 26-86, Constitutive Law of the Army.[4] Yet curiously, as Lieutenant Colonel Cruz Salazar points out, these Articles "do not specify what the military says they do: to intervene in national development. The fact is, legally sustained or not, the intention of the military's political project has been to make permanent military intervention and penetration into the very social fabric of the country" (1987: 1) — without appearing to do so. There has also been a jurisdictional conflict as to whether counterinsurgency civil action is outside the public administration, and thus outside civil jurisdictional boundaries, or whether it is so deeply immersed within it — controlling what resources are provided, keeping tabs on which department is handling which project — that it becomes, in practice, the public administration of the State (2). This jurisdictional conflict is similar to the dissonance between the Army's Constitutive Law of apolitical obedience and the 1982 Junta's 14 Points, detailing the military's political restructuring of the State; it is also exemplified by the discord between the Ministry of Development and the Defense Minister in 1987 touched on in the last chapter. All three instances underline the intentions of *el proyecto político-militar*: to penetrate and reorder the local, municipal, and national life of the nation.

Civil Affairs and Psychological Operations

One of the most significant activities of the S-5 units, according to the manual, is psychological warfare operations and propaganda. Units "investigate and pursue forces of ideological penetration . . . by way of psychological operations to identify their vulnerability, analyze their probable courses of action, measure the effect of their propaganda and implement policies to counter their effects" (Ejército, 1987a: 11). This technique, Gramajo explains, together with a series of amnesties promulgated during 1982, "were the most efficient ways we combatted terrorism" (interview). As already mentioned, the Lucas García regime discourse was based on a violent and primitive anticommunism, while the Ríos Montt regime referred to plans for security and development and offered to respect human and indigenous rights. Since 1982, the propaganda has sought ways as to how best to reincorporate "the Indian" into the mental universe of *el proyecto político-militar* and how best to counter denunciations of human rights violations nationally and internationally. The military's propaganda has rested on two ideas: the army was fighting the war, however reluctantly, with the support of the people (e.g., Civil Patrols), and the guerrillas were authors of the massacres (Aguilera Peralta 1983: 94). "We used propaganda [on the indigenous population]," Gramajo recounts, "saying, 'The Army can help you, so let's not fight. Why do you want to fight the government if the government wants to work *with* you? We are Guatemalans. Why are we fighting one another?' In other words, to insert ideas of peace, ideas about civic culture — the color of the flag, the national anthem — into the minds of the population" (interview). S-5 units are charged with "creating and developing emotions, attitudes and conduct that favor the fulfillment of the army's institutional mission." There are three "target audiences": the population in general, the enemy of "terrorist bands," and the Army's own personnel.[5] Civil education programs seek "to cement and form a positive civic attitude" in children, youths, and adults to "value their patriotic feelings [and their] concept of nationality." One colonel spoke of the need to "discipline individuals in a society so they will do things willingly, so it is not necessary to order them to do so; that way, they are convinced that their attitude and actions must be the best possible . . . Discipline is an attitude of conscience to do things voluntarily" (Gordillo, interview). At the reeducation centers of the Acamal model village, for example, indoctrination sessions were held throughout the 1980s, at which the population was forced to listen to military marches on a record player or watch films about the horrors of life in the Soviet Union (Wilson 1991: 47; Arias 1989: 209). As one "S-5 professor Corzantes" admitted, "my job was to brainwash the people (*lavarle el cerebro a la gente*). My work consisted first in erasing the cassette that the subversion had recorded onto the people, and later record onto them a new cassette" (Arias 1988: 207). Following the Operación Ixil strategy, "an intensive, profound and carefully studied psychological campaign to rescue the Ixil mentality" and "ladinize" it, villagers were expected to listen for hours to "ideological talks" (*pláticas ideológicas*) by these S-5 teachers, to sing the "Hymn of the Civil Patrols" in Spanish, and to participate in organizing "Queen of the Patrols" festivals during traditional days of celebration. In 1987–88, with two new military offensives drawing more of the displaced down from the mountains, many of the young boys spent one to three months at military posts receiving *pláticas ideológicas* each morning to counter "Marxist indoctrination" (*Crónica*, 22 September 1988: 14, 17). Civil Affairs units continue to wage psychological propaganda operations of disinformation (OPSIC) by imputing blame on the guerrilla for the past destruction. Loudspeakers from helicopters and Civil Affairs patrols emphasize hardship for families, amnesty, and rewards for weapon turn-ins (reportedly Q100 for pistols and Q200 for rifles). Leaflets dropped from airplanes and helicopters characterize the URNG as terrorists preying on peasants (see Figure 12). A radio OPSIC propaganda spot run every hour or so the week of President Cerezo's inauguration also fixed the blame for violence:

[ladino voice] Two years ago, with the destruction of the indigenous villages by the subversive, the Indians encountered in the Army of Guatemala a brave and loyal ally in the return to their place of origin [Mayan drums and flutes]. For their security, the Civil Patrols of Self-Defense were organized. For the reconstruction of their villages, the Inter-Institutional Coordinators functioned, and for their interconnection, the Army Corps of Engineers carried out their work, constructing highways and bridges as paths of rural development [marimba music, ladina voice]. Today, two years later, new horizons have been opened in the country. The Army of Guatemala has fulfilled its obligation to you. (author's taping, January 1986)

Figure 12. Army leaflet dropped from airplane in highlands, 1987:
"21 Massacred in Itzapa, Chimaltenango. How many more of you
will be victims? Join the Voluntary Committees of Civil Defense.
The Army Supports You."

Army graffiti painted on highway billboards, at roadsides, and on walls at
town entrances relay this message of the people and military working together against the subversion: "The People, the Army and Cooperatives for
Peace and Development in Chichicastenango. Indian Auxiliary," and "Welcome to Quiché. The Land of Brave Men Where the People and the Army
Have Said 'NO' to the Communist Subversion." (Army graffiti can also be
turned into a form of protest, echoing the complaints of the poor: "No
Bread, Not Even One Tortilla for the Guerrillas" was painted on the side of

an abandoned building on the road to Chichicastenango. The last three words remained whitewashed throughout the 1980s.) On television, the military recommended that those going on vacation should drive carefully, ran paid advertisements in the media celebrating Mother's Day, and announced its donations to charities for handicapped children (many of them maimed by the military's very bombings). The slogan of this psychological campaign was "The Army Trusts in their People and the People Trust in Their Army," Gramajo explains. "We are creating a consciousness within *el pueblo* with these purely psychological operations. We are experts at this, you see" (interview). While many officers interviewed pay lip service to the thesis that insurgency has its roots in the terrible misery of most Guatemalans and use Marxist terms such as "classes," "lumpen," and "historical materialism"[6] to describe those roots, they also confiscate revolutionary slogans for their own counterinsurgency purposes: "United, the army and people will never be defeated." Gramajo repeated the 1960s slogan in his interviews several times, "If you're not part of the solution, you're part of the problem." If nothing else, one cannot say that this army does not learn from its enemies.

Creation Mythmaking and the Sanctioned Mayan

Attempting to evoke an illusion of re-creating the universe, officers speak of a "natal" democracy, and of their development plan in the highlands as "a policy of a new man, a new country, a new Guatemala" (Peckenham 1983: 21). This modest sense of Creation is also found in the military literature on the "new model villages." One photograph of a village in the *Revista cultural del Ejército* (Cultural Magazine of the Army) is captioned, "It appears to be a Christmas nativity and in some ways it is. Tzalbal in the corner of El Quiché at the hour of dawn, awakens from a dream refreshed to repeat another quiet day with renewed energy for its new cornplot which, in time, will become its daily bread. Tzalbal was officially inaugurated by Chief of State Oscar Humberto Mejía Víctores the 30 of April 1984." (This same village had a large sign at its entrance in the 1980s that described it as "a village reborn.") Another photograph, entitled "Reminder of the Subversion," shows a roofless hut and is captioned, "Due to blood and fire, these homes remain stripped of their roofs, of their implements, and their vitality. Mute fragments. Ashes for a new Phoenix, in the new [model village] ACAMAL" (Ejército 1985a: 35, 22). It is a "kind of reorganized truth" that appears to simplify, purify, and make things innocent of intent or contradiction (Graziano 1992: 8). As Barthes enjoins, "History evaporates. It is a kind of ideal servant: it prepares all things, brings them, lays them out, the master arrives, it silently disappears: all that is left for one to do is to enjoy this beautiful object without wondering where it comes from. Or even better: it can only come from eternity: since the beginning of time" (1972: 151). But it is more than Creation Mythmaking; it is also a birthing discourse, with numerous references to the military as though a parent. "As the only institution giving birth to democracy," the Army is "the only one that has been pushing to bring this baby into the light. The other institutions are irresponsible or immature" (*Crónica* interview with Gramajo, 19 May 1988: 22). Gramajo refers to the Pacification campaign as "his baby." General Ríos Montt, too, has stated, "The democratic baby was very rapidly taken out of its incubator, and that is why we have [the problems] we have [today]" (*Crónica*, 26 January 1989: 8).[7] This transsexual birthing discourse reveals just how much the military sees itself as both Creator (Mother to the Fatherland) and Parent-Guardian and Protector (Father to the Motherland), and thus retains full birth right to the Nation in terms of its past and its future. These comments reveal the military's deep identification with the Nation-State, and a recognition that "its baby," democracy, is indeed born of counterinsurgency.

Such re-creational and guardian discourse should also alert us to the military's view of the indigenous community as a child needing to be disciplined, "ladinoized," entrepreneurized — that is, "forged" to fit the "new" modern Guatemalan state, as Gramajo makes clear. In his explanation why the Civil Affairs manual is entitled *To Forge and to Liberate*, he states, "To forge, you understand, refers to what a blacksmith does to make horseshoes. So we must forge *el pueblo* to force it to study, forge to excel. That is, we in Civil Affairs don't give away anything [free]; *el pueblo* must earn everything [it receives]. There is no paternalism [involved]. But when they forge themselves, they do so by themselves, they are going to be free, they are going to have an education, they are going to have economic resources, but they will not be given anything free. Civil Affairs will induce them, will show them the way to forge themselves" (interview). Part of this forging, it is believed, is accomplished by appropriating Mayan symbols to "rescue the Indians' mentality until they feel part of the nation" (Cifuentes 1982: 27–28). Civil Affairs and the National Plan of Security and Development materials were in fact "mayanified": "The symbol of Civil Affairs is a red arrow — *una flecha roja* — which became the Thesis of National Stability. An arrow and two stars: the upright arrow, the most primitive weapon of the Maya, represents advancement, and the stars represent the development and security of the country, hand-in-hand." Each of the 14 *Puntos*, too, "is delineated by Mayan numbers to make the Plan more national. There were some very pretty posters made of the Plan with these Mayan numbers," Gramajo boasted (interview). Similarly, the Kekchí term for warrior, *Kaibil*, is used to refer to the special forces of the army. Many Task Forces participating in the massacre campaigns and offensives were given Mayan names (see Figure 7). In the *Cultural Magazine of the Army*, the National Committee for Reconstruction appropriated the Quiché Indian hero Tecún Umán and *Popul Vuh* (the major religious text of the Quichés when fighting the Spaniards in the sixteenth century) as its own philosophy: "That you rise up everyone, that you call to everyone; that there is not a group, nor two among us. Everyone forward and no one stays behind" (Ejército 1985a: 6). Finally, in referring to the Thesis of National Stability, which will be discussed in a later chapter, Gramajo drew upon the military's presumptions of Mayan religious practices to present it as a kind of "exorcism of its wrongdoings (*males*). It is taking the worm out, as the shamans (*brujos*) do to cure you. They take an egg, passing it over your entire body, chanting. Once they are finished, they break the egg and it is dried, meaning they have extracted the evil. *This* [he holds up a copy of the Thesis of National Stability] *is the army's egg*! We are stating our evils, we are now satisfied, we no longer have these problems [of human rights]. The people outside of Guatemala have to see that this Thesis is the dried egg [for the army]" (interview; his emphasis). Absolving the army of all its sins, the Mayanified Thesis represents a catharsis of the army's wrongdoing, a distancing from the past as well as from responsibility for the future.

Clearly, such appropriations of Mayan custom and language do not serve to promote Indian identity and culture; instead, they stand as a form of Sanctioned Mayan prototype constructed and continually reconstituted through the military's optic, deprived of memory, and mute to the recent "subversive" past. These symbols nourish the distant, mythic heroics of war the military first draws on to fight a counterinsurgency campaign that brutally ravages indigenous highland communities. They then provide the rituals by which this same military purges itself of the stain of massacre to regain its professional status. All the while, the army attempts to reshape the contents of an "appropriate memory" of the "subversive" Mayan past. This in itself is an admission that memory is a potential resource for political action. But the evoking of a new world with "new traditions" and the inclusion of Indians in the Council of State is of vital importance for the military if it is to establish acceptable boundaries of "politically correct" Mayanism and an imagined community-nation. The irony is that Mayans represent a nationhood and yet are the ones most marginalized from it; moreover, the "evil" the Mayan shaman supposedly "exorcised" from the army was exercised precisely on that population: " 'I sinned; I saved' seems to be a phrase of the dramatic persona of the State played by the terrifying gangster now turned law-abiding professional" (AVANCSO 1988a: 49). The prototype of the Sanctioned Mayan that is being created here is emptied of agency and history and is best illustrated by the army's Indian "eponymous mascot of the Poles of Development" (*mascota epónima de los Polos de desarrollo*) found on the back covers of two of its *Cultural Magazines of the Army*, published by the Department of Information and Dissemination (DIDE) between 1984 and 1985 as propaganda on the Poles of Development. (*Eponymous* means to give one's "name to anything, said especially of the mythical personages from whose names the names of places or peoples are reputed to be derived" [Oxford English Dictionary].) This light-skinned human mascot in indigenous dress and Honor Guard spats is given the diminutive

Figure 13. Polín Polainas, eponymous mascot of the Poles of Development, *Revista Cultural del Ejército,* January–June 1985, back cover.

name "Little Pole Leggings" (*Polín Polainas*) and presented as "omnidimensional, omnipresent, it doesn't matter his origin or his attire. Yesterday from Quiché, today from Sololá, Polín Polainas, candid and courteous, coming to plow the Guatemalan fields, leaving in his wake his exemplary studied love, and inspiring the portent of peace, development and accord, like the supreme yearnings for a national unity" (Ejército 1985a, 1984b; see Figure 13). As Roland Barthes warns, "Myth is speech stolen and restored. Only speech which is restored is no longer quite that which was stolen: when it was brought back, it was not put back exactly in its place. It is this brief act of larceny, this moment taken for a surreptitious faking, which gives mythical speech its benumbed look" (1972: 125). In such a mythical world, sophistries abound: "areas of conflict" and "places with subversive presence" (*lugares con presencia subversiva*) magically become "areas of harmony" (*áreas de concordia*) and "areas where there are health clinics, schools, teachers and other authorities which cannot be qualified as areas of conflict" (Gramajo interview, *Crónica*, 22 December 1988: 17–18); mandatory Civil Patrols of Self-Defense are renamed Voluntary Committees of Civil Defense and then Committees of Peace and Development without any operational change; a village is destroyed to be "reborn" as a "model village" with a new name within a Pole of Development; "innocent laws," such as the amnesty decree, create an image of benevolence while they protect the army's impunity; "innocent errors" (*errores inocentes*) are supposed to excuse human rights violations as mere "excesses" or "deficiencies." Ideological heresy is invented in order to root it out, using the tactic of guilt reversal: massacring villagers in order to save them from subversion, or denouncing the victim or accuser of the army's brutality as guilty of subversion rather than addressing the accusation. There are also linguistic formulations that fall in between: what were thought to be opposites are merged into curious, hyphenated forms, such as forced-voluntary (*forzovoluntario*), coercive-consensus, violence-peace, and civil-militarized. "Things," Barthes writes, "lose the memory that they once were made" (1972: 132).

1987 and 1988 "Offensives" and Psychological Warfare

Psychological warfare of disinformation has also been waged on a national level, with each side — the army and the guerrillas — manipulating their own version of events. On 21 September 1987, for example, one month after the signing of the Esquipulas II accords and as the first government-guerrilla/ military Dialogue began in Madrid, the Army began a vigorous year-end Ofensiva '87 involving 4500 soldiers "to confront and pursue the guerrilla until destroyed" and Civil Affairs to relocate displaced villagers and provide logistical support with the CNR and BANVI (Banco Nacional de Vivienda), for local development. As Gramajo states, "In the first place, the strategy was not to kill, you see; the strategy was to recuperate people and insert peace (*meter paz*)" (interview). Between September 1987 and April 1988, "we brought out [of the mountains] almost 5000 [displaced persons] who [the guerrilla] had in the north of El Quiché."[8] Despite this image of peace and goodwill, according to the URNG, "400 bombs of different weights and potency were dropped in the Ixcán just in the two months of October and November of 1987" (quoted in Cruz Salazar 1988a), together with heavy army presence. "In 1981," one returning Nebaj resident related, "2000 soldiers came in an offensive wave; I'm incapable of telling you how many there were, [but] the soldiers were always around. They came every 2 months, every 3 months, every 5 months until in 1986, they stopped coming. . . . In September 1987, [though], is when it was very difficult because with all the soldiers and [Civil] Patrollers, one could no longer remain in one's house. An adult could put up with it, but the little ones? Many women went down to the riverbanks to live in the bushes; sometimes it would rain, sometimes they would give birth down there; many were crying from hunger" (AVANCSO 1990: 25). This year-end offensive was followed by a second one at the beginning of 1988 — Fortaleza '88 — which, according to Gramajo in a December 1990 interview, "is not over yet." But because the army does not generally report counterinsurgent actions against the guerrilla, it was an intensification of an undeclared war, with heavy casualties on both sides. Gramajo insisted in a 1988 interview that, contrary to the URNG's claim of controlling 50,000 square miles with 3500 armed combatants, there were no longer "areas of conflict" in Guatemala, only "places with a subversive presence" of "small terrorist bands" without any influence over either the population or geography. The Guatemalan weekly, *Crónica*, reported that "the only real fact that is tangible and real is the inventory of those killed in this hidden war" ("Versiones de una guerra oculta," *Crónica*, 22 December 1988: 17). But even here, the body count varied depending on the source: the URNG estimated 1984 army soldiers dead and wounded, while the army reported 60 officers, specialists, and troops dead and 291 wounded. When I questioned Gramajo about these offensives, he claimed the guerrilla admitted to the greater effectiveness of the 1987–88 campaigns because the army remained in the mountains six or seven months. "Before, whenever the guerrilla felt pressured [by the army], he would hide for a month and then reemerge. Now he can't do that because the army will not withdraw, never" (interview). The evidence "strongly suggests that the offensives during the second and third year of the Cerezo regime were vigorous and destructive, and that the army was not taking the ceasefire seriously" (Gramajo, interview by Cruz Salazar 1988: 3). ORPA commander, Gaspar Ilom, stated that in the last three months of 1988, the URNG had detected a campaign of psychological warfare by the army to cover up the increasing number of disappearances and assassinations, including massacres, during an intensification of the counterguerrilla offensive. Such psychological warfare, he argued (which included, as in the 1982–83 campaign, soldiers dressed as guerrillas) was intended to discredit the URNG with the population by blaming them for such repressive actions as well as to demoralize the guerrilla forces themselves. Gramajo denied this, saying that the guerrillas committed the massacres to continue their battle internationally, given their military failures in the mountains. He argued that 1989 would see an intense battle diplomatically in which "the dogma of the URNG" would be debated against "military orthodoxy" (Cruz Salazar 1988a; *Central America Report*, 30 June 1989: 194). Despite Gramajo's denials of psychological warfare tactics, these assertions by the URNG fit neatly into the ascribed responsibilities of the Civil Affairs Units. During the 1988 offensive, for example, Colonel Vargas, one of the Civil Affairs field officers in Nebaj (one of the most devastated areas during the early 1980s campaigns), spoke of the army's dedication to "permanent persecution" by means of large and constant ("24-hour") dragnets in the mountains, "fixing rebel units into determinate positions in order to annihilate them. . . . By taking away their social base, we can asphyxiate and be done with them in the Ixil Triangle." After many hard years of living in the mountains and jungle, the displaced were being drawn out of hiding. As in the 1982–83 campaigns, "recuperate the displaced" continued to be the strategy "because without the help of the social base, the subversion cannot function or live. It is a very new stage in the war with people coming down [out of the mountains] all the time." As in 1982, the army utilized the captured to draw others down. "When a group arrives, they rest and are fed, then we ask them if they have more relatives in the mountains. We ask them to bring them down and we offer them transport by helicopter," Lieutenant Alburez Camey, another Civil Affairs officer stated. "This process of having them lure their own people down is much more efficient because the displaced know the camps well and where to go and how to infiltrate themselves [into the guerrilla]" (Robinson 1988).[9] According to Alburez, bombings were conducted at least three times a week by military planes in the areas where the [guerrilla] camps were thought to be located. Officers tape-recorded former guerrillas assuring them of the good intentions of the army, and played these tapes over the loudspeaker as the helicopters flew overhead.[10]

Similarly, refugees returning from Mexico encounter a military presence at the government's "re-orientation" centers: "The Special Commission to Attend to the Repatriated and Displaced — CEARD — began their activities in the Ixil region in February 1988, and opened their doors to house the refugees by the end of May, [where] there is a constant presence of soldiers and civilian-dressed military personnel (*militares vestidos de civil*)." In February 1987, when the Catholic Church of Las Verapaces offered protection to 100 refugees, the commander of the Military Zone, together with G-2 and G-5 personnel dressed in civilian clothing, asked the frightened refugees, "How many people are still out there [hiding]?" and "Where are they?" Even in 1989, when many officers were arguing that the Poles of Development and Civil Patrols were "finished," Civil Affairs units were so ubiquitous in the Ixil Triangle that one indigenous resident was moved to remark, "Here one simply doesn't see or feel that there is [at present] a civilian government in Guatemala" (AVANCSO 1990: 27–29).

Curiously, Gramajo made the argument in 1990 that the guerrillas no longer had the population's support, that they were now mere "terrorists": "They are no longer guerrillas who live among the population, like Robin Hood, because no village will have them. No, now they are terrorists: they jump on their motorbikes to go to the South Coast, do their dirty work blowing up electrical towers or building a highway barricade, and return to Guatemala City. . . . But our strategy has been very costly for them; they have been reduced in numbers" (interview). National Defense Chief of Staff, General Manuel Antonio Callejas y Callejas also stated, "We [the army] continue to consider the guerrilla a simple nuisance in military operations, although we do worry that they are still controlling the peasants. For this reason, we [in Civil Affairs] are working to liberate the peasants" (*Crónica*, 7 January 1988: 18). One could ask, as did *Crónica* in its column "Questions," if the guerrillas were only a "nuisance of only a few bands" with no support among the population, why then spend so much money and effort trying to eliminate them?

But by 1987, Gramajo soon realized that he needed yet another kind of intelligence to complement psychological operations and broaden the reach of the Civil Affairs Units even further into daily local village and rural life.

Social Intelligence

Social intelligence is an approach that reveals the army's rethinking of its tactical low-profile and "minimum force" responses to local resistance. It is so full of nuances that it is best described by a long and detailed discussion with the two generals who have had the most to do with its development and implementation: Generals Héctor Gramajo and Sergio Camargo Muralles. In explaining social intelligence, Gramajo reveals the broad and permanent reach of the army in the highlands:

Social intelligence is the form in which the army serves the government. That is, if there is an institution that goes to all corners of Guatemala, it is the army. The Ministry of Development cannot know how many latrines are needed in all the *aldeas* because they never go there, and if they go, it's only every [few months]. It's just not done [by them].[11] So, in that village, the teacher doesn't speak the dialect of the place in which there is no drinking water and where the mayor is corrupt. These social indicators are something the army can obtain. And then these are passed directly on to the president so that the presidency, with this information by way of the ministries, can correct them. And if they don't correct the problem, then it's their problem because we are no longer correcting anything because we are not the government. This is social intelligence: social facts which the government does not know about unless the army passes them on. . . . For example, recently there appeared an article in Guatemalan newspapers about a priest in Chiquimula who complained because the army was conducting a census of how many parishioners went to mass, asking them "Are you a Catholic?" "Were you baptized?" "Were you married by the church?" "Do you attend Mass?" "Do you contribute to the church? Yes or no?"
Q: An army questionnaire, then?
Yes. And the Church became jealous and wanted to make a big deal out of it. I told them, "Don't worry, *señores*, we have no argument with you. We are an institution that is very much up-to-date (*somos una institución muy actualizada*)." These are studies of the social reality of Guatemala, and we have the right to know the social reality of Guatemala in order to be able to maintain the peace.

Q: But why would you want to know how many Catholics there are in Guatemala?
This is precisely [what] social intelligence [is about] because if I am going to encounter the possibility of a religious struggle in Guatemala, the Army is responsible for preventing such a thing from happening. Thus, to what extent is religious fundamentalism going to throw itself into fighting the evangelicals, and how would they, in turn, react? Where does the problem lie? These are data the Army needs in order to prevent such a thing from happening, even though there is no problem because no one is a Catholic [in Guatemala]; everyone is only halfway Catholics . . . So that in this case when they speak of a religious war now for [1990 presidential candidate Jorge] Serrano, we know that it won't happen because people won't be mobilized [around this issue]. *That* is social intelligence.

[Another example is to ask the question] "How high are wages?" [whispers] The commander of a [military] zone says, "*Mi general*, we're going to have trouble on the South Coast. Sugar refinery A pays Q12 an hour while sugar refinery B pays only Q6 an hour. Everyone is going to work for A, but because B has land in the east, they bring in their own workers who are obligated to work for them [at that wage]." So what is the job of the commander of this zone? He speaks with the *dueño* (owner) of B, telling him, "Raise your wages! [pounds the table] because if there is a meeting or a demonstration of the workers, I won't defend the refinery." *That* is social intelligence.
Q: In other words, to calculate the social conditions . . .
That can create fiction. [He draws a map.] Here we have a river and a village, and here we have a *finca* of an INTA functionary.[12] Here is the main highway, the Transversal del Norte. From here to here is 100 kilometers. Along this little road arrive corn, fish, and Alka-Seltzer from Mexico to this village by the human animal (*el lomo humano*) — people carrying these things on their backs. So, this little village is very important from this side, which is El Petén. The [Cerezo] government sent tractors, trucks, and everything for road building, and everyone in the village was happy. The road begins like this and then suddenly swerves to serve only the *finca*. So then what happened? The villagers burned the [road-building] machinery [in response]. If we had had social intelligence, what would we have done (because this actually did happen)? Should we burn the village? Or give the tractors to the village? What does the army do? Well then, this is social intelligence, it's not military intelligence (see Figure 14).
Q: What analysis would have led you to conclude to burn the village?
This [action] would tell the [military] zone commander that subversives had burned the machinery. But they aren't subversives, only villagers abandoned by this public functionary who used the resources of the State [to build] his road rather than theirs. That is social intelligence. Another example is when the doctor of a village doesn't arrive and the village has no medical attention. Then, Civil Affairs has to report to the [military] zone commander, "We don't have a doctor." The commander then tells the Defense Minister, "There is no doctor." He, in turn, asks the Health Minister, "What happened to the doctor in such-and-such a zone?" The Health Minister [says,] "Look, the doctor is on vacation, send a replacement . . ."
Q: But you yourself have said that the army doesn't meddle in such issues . . .
Of the *government*. We only say that to the President.
Q: But you complained of there being no doctor.
We say this to [President] Cerezo. [The question should be,] What's wrong with Cerezo [in not doing anything about it]?
Q: If I understand correctly, if the social conditions in the future cause "frictions," as you say, this means that . . .
The army won't be there again with its eyes closed [repeats]. [It is] a social intelligence which knows the *causes* [of the friction].

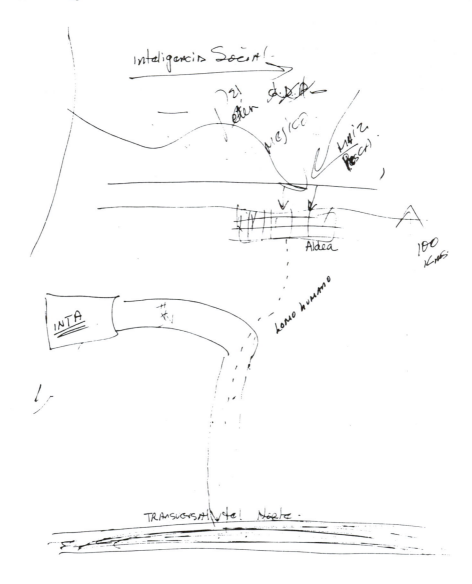

Figure 14. General Gramajo's sketch: social intelligence-gathering.

Q: Closed eyes refers to the 1980–81 strategy [of Lucas García] that asked . . . Are you with me or against me?
Q: Does that indicate an absence of strategy or a culmination of strategy?
No, no, an *absence* of strategy [by Lucas]. Brute force, nothing more.
Q: To kill everyone?
Simply brute force.

Q: But, as I understand, it was blind, it was brutal, but in the army's mind, it was necessary?
It depends on how far the problem got out of hand. If it did get out of hand, then yes [it was necessary]. . . . In contrast, military intelligence asks, Who is the enemy? Where is the enemy? What is the enemy doing? We have now defined who the enemy is and who the population is. We now differentiate [between the two]. Social intelligence is [directed] toward the population; military intelligence is [directed] toward the enemy. And if the government were to use all the information from social intelligence — wheeow! [his hands make a sweeping gesture] *Tremendo*! (interview; his emphasis)

In the early 1990s, as Military Zone Commander at Quezaltenango, General Camargo came up with the idea of recruiting university-educated Mayan women from that indigenous city to serve as *promotores especialistas* — nurses, social workers, and psychological operatives (*operadoras psicológicas*) as well as military recruitment teams. He explains, in a 1994 interview, how these women enter a village alongside a Civil Affairs unit to "converse" with people, especially the women, to gather social intelligence for the army:

Those who work in psychological operations determine the levels of penetration that *el mensaje contrario* (counterinformation) has [on the village]. For example, everyone says that the army only serves the rich (*los ricos*) that the army is the force of the rich (*es la fuerza de los ricos*). These female *operadoras* see how much the locals believe this and think of ways to counter it by propaganda and by actions to change people's minds.
Q: So these units enter villages, asking questions and calculating the level of penetration?
In some cases perhaps, but it's not so much from asking as it crops up in the conversation, and that has to do with the unit's ability to get people to talk. The thing is not so much to enter to ask questions as it is to establish communication. Once that gets going, then we can talk about everything, and in doing so, we can ascertain attitudes. One chats. Perhaps the first visit doesn't succeed in totally penetrating [what is going on in the village]. Perhaps we aren't able to go beyond the cordialities, or things don't go well. But we don't lose hope; we just go to another village. They will eventually come to see that we are doing the same thing everywhere in the area. (interview)

With each Unit providing information about each village, a general analysis is made of each area, and Civil Affairs Units, in turn, begin to respond to the population's expectations "with small things. Once you fulfill small expectations, you can begin to impose development, because in the end, what interests us is that development is provided, making the population less susceptible to the subversion and drug trafficking. So it doesn't matter who provides it, or what it is, just so it is provided. . . . We want our weapon to be civil affairs, not guns or bullets," Camargo concluded (interview).
Social intelligence in fact penetrates much more fully into daily social activities of the population than does military intelligence to understand the conditions under which dissent emerges — not to correct these discontents — as the army views "the solving of the problem" by way of higher

wages or better living conditions not their concern — but to catch out any potential dissent before it occurs, or if it does occur, to keep these discontents within acceptable, controllable boundaries. As we will see in a later chapter, this policy dovetails with the army's definition of "Opponents of the State." Social intelligence is the best of both worlds: to define one's task as the control of "security issues," which includes taking "preventive measures" to control and possibly eliminate potential or real Opponents of the State, and to pursue the "appropriate" economic and political trajectory — that is, to be precisely in control of what politics *is*—while absolving the army of any inept decisions that might be made by civilian governments in the meantime. Social intelligence is in fact the army's own preventive measure against being blamed for inept economic and political decisions, and for deflecting the populace's skepticism onto the elites.

Conclusion

Military intelligence, social intelligence, and psychological warfare provide the military with a broad range of resources with which to penetrate local village life. Civil Affairs Units are eradication squads to be used when "delinquent terrorists appear" and as prevention squads (by whatever means) when they don't, with the final objective of linking all intelligence gathering from these communities into army intelligence's computerized system. With all resources oriented to gathering "social and military intelligence" in order to "detect and counteract possible conflicts in the community" as well as to "increase the capacity of the Army to detect conflicts [caused] by the poor performance of those in public administration," a network of vigilance of both peasants and public officials has been created based on a politics of threat. Leafletting campaigns, too, create a sense of the army's omnipresence. By selectively denouncing high-profile members of the community — the parish priest, the local congressman, human rights activists — communities are divided against themselves, with some looking to the military and its representatives — Civil Affairs and Civil Patrols — for stability, law, and order. It also wages war propaganda to counter national and international criticisms against its past and present human rights violations and its interference in development projects. As the institution responsible for fraying the social fabric of local and national life for the past three decades, it is determined that the new democracy not be cut from whole new cloth without their supervision. Yet the very reason for the need for psychological warfare and social intelligence gathering is the military's implicit recognition of both their responsibility for the massacre campaign and their subsequent scurrilous image in highland communities brutally ravaged by the early 1980s campaigns. Given this legacy, gaining the hearts and erasing the minds of the Sanctioned Mayan may prove to be a more difficult task than the military bargained for.

Chapter 6
A Military View of Law and Security

> We invited the subversion to lay down their arms. We had military en-
> counters, there was a war. . . . Later, we legalized a concept of special
> powers (*fuero especial*) because the violence did not permit us to impart
> justice. And we gathered up the assassins and criminals, we judged them
> and we *shot* them, but in accordance with the law.
> — Ríos Montt, 1989 television interview[1]

> Violence [in Guatemala] is not only physical, it is also a violence of the
> law. The military violates statutes, laws, everything. If they complied with
> their own statutes, there would at least be a minimum of guarantees, but
> there are no guarantees here of any kind.
> [Not even of life?]
> Ha, of life? That is even less certain. Violence and law have been di-
> rected toward an all-out physical violence. . . . We now have a mortgaged
> justice: we don't own it and we certainly don't control it. . . . Yet the
> institutionality, the legality, the constitutionality of our society — they
> are our only hope — and I myself have lost all faith in them.
> — Guatemalan lawyer who defended Special Tribunal prisoners,
> 1984 interview

Law, like ideology, serves a belief system and interests about the proper
order of things. Within an activist state, decrees, prohibitions and obligations between the individual and the state — between "the governed and
the governors," as Colonel-lawyer Girón Tánchez repeated in interviews —
impose an exclusive worldview. Law sets categories and prescriptions that
order reality as to what the world should be and what is considered inside
and outside the law. Just as law can be used to reform institutions to provide
justice, it can just as easily be used to invent institutions that oppress. As
anthropologist E. A. Hoebel has remarked, "the law has teeth . . . that can
bite if need be" (Gluckman 1965: 181). Contrary to the notion of "choice,"
whereby a military government can take either coercive or persuasive action
(cf. Janowitz 1964), law can be used as a double-track strategy: on the one

hand, coercively to limit and absorb conflict to preserve the status quo and on the other hand, persuasively to create "a commonsense tradition" (Cain 1982: 95) to absorb or limit political conflict while presenting a rule-of-law image internationally.

The use of legal structures by military regimes in Central America is, of course, not something new. In the first half of the nineteenth century, the liberal constitutions that established the present juridical-institutional structure in Central America (and that sustain the principle of republicanism, the division of powers, and the separation of Church and State, and that often provide liberal codes of labor and welfare) in practice provided dictatorial governments with constitutional legitimacy. These heads of government asked the legislators to make constitutional reforms or to vote in transitory articles that allowed for their reelection. This created a distortion of the political system, generating strong executives and weak, "monosyllabic" legislatures (Torres-Rivas 1986: 478), with few of the Constitutions guaranteeing fundamental rights or freedoms until recently (Solórzano 1983: 43–44; cf. García Laguardia and Vázquez Martínez 1984). In all Central American countries, moreover, the absence (or tenuous existence) of structural conditions favorable to constitutional democracy is complicated by a history of paternalistic interventionism by the United States. In the past, though, a gap between the traditional ideals of liberal, just legal structures and the executive use of law always remained. Herein lies the difference between the past and the more recent forms of counterinsurgent constitutional order in Guatemala that came with the immersion of security within constitutional forms. But while militaries have long resorted to constitutionalism as a means to seek both domestic and international legitimacy, their perception of law is not so clearly understood. What is the perception of law that military regimes impose on their societies to create "proper" legal orders? Do they consider themselves above or within the law? How do they define human rights? How do they perceive the political opposition? How are law and security related?

There appear to be two concepts of law operating in Guatemala: First, the law enforcement theory, based more on the imperative positivist theory of law, which assumes a rule *by* law and not a rule *under* law (Matthews 1986: 1). Usually, by formalizing legal inquiry, "by re-classifying the problem into a supposedly doctrinal category" (Horwitz 1977: 40), one is able to defuse its political significance in the name of promoting an objective, professional, and even scientific rule of law, known as legal positivism (cf. Hart 1961). This theory legitimizes the rule of many coercive governments as being in accordance with the rule of law because their actions are *covered* by law. It is the imagery of the regularity of law that can be comfortably convened to illustrate that the government is in accordance with a legal order that it helped produce. A 1983 interview with Ríos Montt reveals this vision of law enforcement: "When the [1965] Constitution was in force, I could not search for someone in a house. So, I had to establish a legal framework so that now I can enter a house [and] be within the framework of the law" (*New York Times*, 15 July 1983).

Such legal positivism, Shklar argues, is more capable of being combined with the politics of repression (1964: 207–9), and of all the legal theories, it is a useful tool for transforming power into law. In addition, it is a theory that separates morality and ideology from law, offering the illusion of a pristine impartiality that dovetails nicely with the military's penchant for procedural exactness as well as an assertion of ideological immunity. Indeed, the very core of the military's excessively formalist legalism is its assumed moral and ideological neutrality. As General Gramajo states: "The Army is objective and not political, which allows us to understand and analyze the national reality with a pragmatic focus and an orientation toward the national interest" (CEM speech, 30 April 1987: 4).

The illusory purity (some argue sterility) of legal positivism—with its scientific nature—guarantees a nonideological position for the military, freeing them, in their minds, from an adherence to any ideological or moral point of view. "We have very clear laws that give us cutting norms. . . . We are servants, not conditionalists or arbiters of anything" (Colonel García, interview). A distinction then is made between the political and the ideological: *political* is equivalent to being "amoral and rational"; *ideological* means impassioned, moral politics with "inherent internecine splits and self-interested parties" (Colonel Gordillo, interview). The military is the former, political parties and the opposition in general the latter, with law-as-science serving as the military's immunity to "ideological contamination" (Shklar 1964: 6). The separation of morality from law in legal positivism is thus interpreted by the Guatemalan military through their optic of law enforcement, in which they place themselves above issues of morality in order to maintain national security.

Nevertheless, no apparent contradiction exists for many officers between this impartial ideal and the necessary conjuncture of law and politics qua national security, according to Colonel-lawyer Girón Tánchez, who authored most of the military government's laws between 1982 and 1986:

Q: It seems from what you've said that this juridical-political structure is a complete one. The law serves for everything, for civic actions, social norms.
You cannot separate the political from the legal. It is a conjunction of juridical norms which transcend toward the political. And for that reason, it is called a juridical-political system because it accommodates itself to all the juridical norms. But it also creates a conjunction of such norms.[2]

Positivists, moreover, as Jiménez de Arechaga points out, view law as "purely instantaneous and ahistorical, seeing only those laws in force at the present moment." This temporal view of law "allows one to identify the law with total precision" about how best to apply it practically. The *jus-naturalistas* (natural law believers), on the other hand, perceive of law as a continuum that takes into account not only the present, but the past and the future. Unlike the temporal positivists, they include a moral element in their conception of law because they consider morality to be an indispensable factor in the supremacy of a juridical order (1985: 37). Within this schema, the military are the more spontaneous legal positivists in that they demand precision, historical amnesia (with an amnesty law), and a distancing from morality in their law.

The other theory of rule of law operating in Guatemala is that of procedural justice, which views justice as nonarbitrary, with specific laws, due process, and independent courts. What is most significant is the use of this second theory by the institutionalist military strategists: to immerse security within a constitutional order that is procedurally — and even materially — concerned with a rule of law based on social and political justice. The success of *el proyecto político-militar* is due partly to the extraordinary dominance of the military itself, and the weakness of the judicial system. But partly it is due to the dichotomous way law and politics are often thought about in procedural justice: we are urged to draw a clean line between law and nonlaw, "focus[ing] on rules, [which] tend to narrow the range of legally relevant facts, thereby detaching legal thought from social [and political] reality" (Nonet et al., quoted in Mathews 1986: 2).

It should be noted that the Roman law tradition of most Latin American countries — as against the more interpretative Anglo-American law tradition — is much more explicitly structured. In general terms, behavior is stipulated so that everyone will know the rules and, the argument goes, so that everyone is equal before those rules. However, just as the Spanish saying reads, "Él que hace la ley, hace la trampa" — He who makes the law also defines the ways to cheat by it — it is clear that the military, in utilizing such a legal apparatus, do not view themselves as bound by this system of regulations. It is their view that it is a structure by which to regulate the governed while the governors act with impunity. As we shall see, by using the very structures of potentially equalizing Roman law traditions, the military abuse trust and faith in such traditions.

Let us first turn to an examination of the self-referential, self-justifying view of coercive consensus and constitutionalism held by military and civilian lawyers involved in promulgating decree-laws between 1982 and 1986, who proceeded to immerse this structure of legalized security within the 1985 Constitution. Then we will examine the relation of law to state security, officers' views of law-as-operative (with Special Tribunals and amnesty decree-laws selected as examples of operationalized law), and finally their view of the army's constitutional mandate.

The 1982–1985 Military Governments' Decree-Laws: Self-Referential, Self-Validating, and Self-Justifying Law

Consonant with the military destruction and reconstruction of indigenous life in the highlands to counter "subversion," both "the electoral system" and the very "constitutionality of the country" — points number 12 and 14 of the National Plan of Security and Development — were also to be "re-structured" in this consciously politico-military project. After the 23 March 1982 coup, with the 1965 Constitution decreed suspended, political parties banned, and the Congress dissolved (Decree-Laws 2-82 and 3-82), the new military regime acted without any legal basis. The intention of decreeing a Fundamental Statute of Government (Decree-Law 24-82) one and one-half months later (as a "species of Constitution" according to one of its authors, Colonel-lawyer Girón Tánchez), was to "juridically normalize the country" (interview). The Statute would implement a "juridical-political structure in the Nation that guarantees moving the country toward honesty, stability, legality, and security [and] a regime of constitutional legality that leads to a political plan and democratic government arising from popular elections" (Recopilador de Leyes 1982: 67–69). A twelve-month state of siege (kept alive each month with Decree-Laws 45-82, 61-82, 71-82, 76-82, etc., "as the causes of alteration of social peace and public order which gave rise to the establishment of said State of Exception" persisted) was reduced to a state of alarm in June 1983 (Decree-Law 71-83). This electoral and constitutional restructuring was implemented over a period of a year with the promulgation of Decree-Laws 30-83 (Organic Law of the Supreme Electoral Tribunal), 31-83 (Law of Citizen Registration), 32-83 (Law of Political Organizations), and 34-83 (Law of General Registration of the Population). By 1984, Decree-Laws 3-84 and 4-84 were being effected for "the election of the National Constituent Assembly," by which the country would be moved "toward the establishment of a regime of constitutional legality." The Assembly was elected, and "based on this new Constitution and electoral laws, the military government ordered [legislative and presidential] elections" by issuing an army bulletin (Gramajo, interview).

If the military moved the country from a state of siege to a country of laws, just how does this military view such lawmaking? The controlling image of law imposed by the Guatemalan military regimes in 1982 and 1983 is that of the state decree — usually a form of summary decision making. Some of those decrees, nonetheless, did reference legal norms established by the 1956 and 1965 constitutions. Even so, the preamble to the 1985 Constitution refers to "the consolidation of the regime of legality, security, justice, equality, liberty and peace" (Constituyente 1985: 1). Unlike previous constitutional preambles, it melds law with security, and suggests a view of law that is more complex than that associated with summary decision making. A key reason for this complexity is that the major legal architect of many of the decree-laws under Generals Ríos Montt and Mejía Víctores between 1982 and 1986, Manuel de Jesús Girón Tánchez, was an articulate Air Force Colonel-lawyer who had participated in the National Constituent Assembly that had drawn up the 1965 Constitution. He served as Secretary to the Chief of State under these two regimes.[3] He was, according to Gramajo, "*el hombre congreso* and *el hombre legislativo*, who drew up all the military laws, all the decrees, everything! He would think up a law, write it down, and Mejía would recommend it," serving as "the army's link to the National Constituent Assembly that at the time was drawing up the Constitution. . . . The law that says that Ríos Montt cannot be president [is because of] Girón Tánchez. The law that says that military men must wait five years before becoming presidential candidates [he then points to himself as a potential candidate] — Gramajo! [he laughs loudly] — is all because of Girón Tánchez. He was a *buen muchacho*, very well intentioned. In spite of having so much power, he could do things that were well balanced" (interview). Girón Tánchez's familiarity with Guatemalan law — and his versatility in using it, ignoring it, abolishing it, and reinventing it whenever necessary — should not be underestimated. Indeed, it was through such negotiation and pressure that counterinsurgency became constitutionalized. In speaking with him, one sees the overall vision of law is that of "regulating the hierarchy" (with the Constitution at the top), with "one law maintained and another substituted," of filling in spaces when the Constitution "disappeared" while "sacrificing human rights just a little." It was Girón Tánchez who understood the importance of law even though the military had a monopoly of force:

Why bother to promulgate a [Fundamental] Statute [in 1982] even if we have a monopoly of force? Well, because the [1965] Constitution had disappeared [and anyway] it had come to be tainted by the many previous spurious governments. At that time, Congress didn't exist and a commission of well-connected lawyers, of which I was one, wrote [the Fundamental Statute].[4] It was a species of constitution with a minimum of individual guarantees [that were] not as broad as they are now. With the disappearance of the 1965 constitution, there had to be a law that regulated the relations between the governed and the governing. (interview)

However, the final purpose to such legal finagling was not to reestablish the previous constitutional order but to "restructure" and "align" law to fit purposes of security and to create, in the end, a new kind of counterinsurgent constitutional order. Girón Tánchez explains that

Transitory Article 16 puts into force all those decree-laws emitted by the Chief of State because one could not place Congress in full charge [of the State]. It was well understood that the Chief of State [Mejía] was going to emit the [16] decree-laws and they were to be left in force. Thus, there is no disparity [between them and the Constitution]. For that reason, one says to *re*structure because it tries to give a different form to the constitutional norm. (interview)

When asked how one "harmonizes" the two parallel legal structures, the decree-laws and the new Constitution, Girón Tánchez asserts:

There was no problem [because] I was regulating the legislation together with a group of people and ministries, listening to all those beings involved with the laws because to legislate it was extremely difficult and if one was not careful, one could commit much arbitrariness, and one could also compromise much in the country. Well, the decree-laws were perfectly adapted to the Constitution.

When asked to be more explicit, he says:

The Constitution was not yet in force, but we — to prevent the Constitution from being in a contrary juridical position to the laws — were promulgating, studying the Constitution and we attended to it. (interview)

"Regulating the Constitution" meant that Transitory Article 16, which approved all previous decrees emitted between 23 March 1982 and 14 January 1986, was ratified by the new Congress under pressure from the military government. One congressman admitted before a congressional investigation committee that, at a secret meeting, some of his colleagues were pressured and paid by powerful ruling groups to emit and modify laws favorable to them.[5] But the traditional legislative procedures proved too slow for the military project. Girón Tánchez proclaimed that the decree-laws that established the Supreme Electoral Tribunal and the National Constituent Assembly Elections[6] were emitted so that the civilian regime would be "borne of its own people" (despite admissions by officers that the creation of the Assembly and the subsequent 1985 legislative and presidential elections were the military's decision).[7] Yet his reasons as to why sixteen decree-laws were emitted so rapidly (indeed only a few days before Cerezo's inauguration) exemplify a self-referential,[8] self-validating discourse-without-a-public:

A rapidity, yes. I'll explain; it is very simple. The issue is, you know, that the legislative houses are often very slow in emitting laws, but there is no specific intent to favor anyone's interests. It was simply to delineate a series of regulations which are necessary and were lacking in Guatemalan society.
Q: You told the newspapers that "there was an oral agreement" with the new President concerning the decrees.
Vinicio Cerezo wanted to create three new ministries. What would have happened [if we had gone] through Congress? The cumbersome, boring process of having to discuss the creation of these ministries, and we didn't know, as in all such assemblies the world over — it is absolutely impossible to know how much time it would take to emit this law, not to say at the end of it all, that they don't pass it! He wanted that during his five years he would have the facility of development, and we couldn't wait four, five, six months for something as important as development. . . . If it is delayed any more, [there will be] problems with development . . . and for this reason, we didn't use the legislative faculties to pass the laws. (interview)

The appointment of the Supreme Court Justice also serves as an example of self-referential lawmaking, with "the High Command respect[ing] the juridical framework which had been established [with] the Fundamental Statute that [in turn] provided juridical security. Only a few modifications were made in regard to who decided the appointment of the Supreme Court Justice: the decision was made by the Army itself as to who was to govern [the courts]" (Andrade Díaz-Durán 1988: 7). Another of the "few modifications" was the dismissal by Decree-Law 38-84 of 3 May 1984 by Head of State General Mejía Víctores of then-president of the Supreme Court, Ricardo Sagastume Vidaurre, who had denounced "the absolute dependence of the judicial organism and administration of justice regarding the de facto power. . . . My legal action against the abuse of some military, police and government officials' authority is the cause for my dismissal" (Sagastume, 1986 interview; Comité Pro-Justicia y Paz 1984: 23 n. 5). In the same decree-law, a new Supreme Court Justice was appointed by the Mejía government. When asked what the relationship was between the Constitution and these sixteen decree-laws, former Foreign Minister Andrade stated that the civilian legislative bodies in the past had legalized actions of military de facto governments: "Decree-laws are not part of the Constitution. [Yet] what happened was that the [National Assembly] constituents legalized the decree-laws of the military governments. This is not new in Guatemalan constitutional law. It occurred in 1975–76 to legalize the actions of de facto governments. This has to occur; otherwise, there would be a juridical limbo" (1991 interview). Although several lawyers argued that these decree-laws of the de facto government were not incorporated into the Constitution "and other laws of the Republic," and thus could be changed and amended, others were not so sanguine. The latter group spoke of the extraordinary ambiguities as "lacunae and errors of the new [1985] Constitution" and the "pseudo-juridicality of the de facto military government."[9] There was "no coherency or neutrality"; rather, "the Constitution was shaped by a series of mutual concessions between the army and the dominant class" (Sarti Castañeda 1986: 27). The "original sin" of this constituent process was its illegitimacy, with the military government ordering the elections and obligating it to take juridical actions (Linares Morales 1985: 5).

Similarly, former Foreign Minister Andrade's confusing his acting in the name of the public with the participation of the public is illustrative. As part of the "political reordering" of the country begun after March 1982, he explained,

The Supreme Electoral Tribunal was able to initiate laws in order to make the process go smoothly. One tried to simplify things, to do things not only rhetorically but in deed to fulfill the objectives that had been established by the Army which were in response to the clamor of the people, the clamor of the nation. It was only a little while after the [coup] that the Army Chief of Staff, together with the Supreme Electoral Tribunal, by way of an Army bulletin, affixed the calendar dates of the elections. The people of Guatemala would be convened for elections for the National Assembly in 1984 and for Presidential elections in 1985. It was a reiteration of [our] solemn and public agreement. (1988: 9)[10]

In a 1991 interview, he added,

The Supreme Electoral Tribunal modified some of the laws that had been approved before, and suspended others, precisely to make the whole process of consulting the public more agile. The purification [process of the elections] would, in turn, forge *el pueblo*. (interview)

This lack of (and indeed contempt for) full public dialogue regarding the Constitution typified the National Constituent Assembly process in general. There were no opportunities or mechanisms by which to submit revisions or voice protest to the articles either before or after the legislative process. For example, some 200 Constitutional articles of a total of 303 were not revealed to the public until they were published in the official gazette on 3 June 1985. Although there were few "social subjects" in the political arena to speak of during this repressive period (Gutiérrez 1990: 10), one group of relatives of the disappeared that arose in 1984, the Group of Mutual Support, who asked that the legal category of "political prisoner" be included in the new Constitution, was thrown out of the Assembly. The only two kinds of "citizenry" given voice were the dominant economic sector and the military. When political parties did try to organize, they were seen as "disruptive" to the "democratic project." Although elections were meant to create immediate public consensus, Andrade describes his and the military government's "preoccupation" with the proliferation of political party committees ("more than 30") after the 8 August 1983 coup in causing "delays" and as "a species of political instance in interminable dialogues with a massive participation of representatives. Despite the positive publicity [that we gained] from these dialogues, they also were a way of setting back *el proyecto* which the de facto governments, the provisional governments, [had planned]; these committees were defining it as a process of negotiation and of consultation with everyone. [Given] this impulse, there was always the possibility and doubt [within the military government] that if [the project] did not continue along an orderly and precise line with an impulse toward a democratic project, there could be a certain cause and effect in setting back the popular consultation" (1988: 4, 5).

Expediency and control of the political discourse were the major concerns at the time. In fact, the army was so preoccupied with structuring and managing the kinds of dissent that might arise from expectations created by *el proyecto*, that they attempted, according to one member of the original 1982 junta, to create new political parties:

There was an attempt on our part to have new parties created, but we committed the mistake of allowing the traditional parties, with their hegemony and monopoly over political effectiveness, of keeping their own mastheads and symbols. It was like competing with Coca-Cola! (Colonel Gordillo, interview)

Given this extremely hurried and self-referential legal discourse-sans-public that sought legislative approval post hoc of its decrees, we can begin to understand the army's self-perception of being the only institution with "a capacity to dictate law to those lacking in it" (General Juan Leonel Bolaños Chávez, interview; Ejército 1987b: 2).

Law and State Security

Once we had discussed the ways in which the 1982–85 military governments had "harmonized" security needs in comparison to the 1985 Constitution, I asked Colonel Girón Tánchez, "If one begins with this norm of legality and security, where does one locate state security within this legal structure?" He answered that

It was immersed within the Fundamental Statute of Government. That is why it was emitted! For the juridical security of the inhabitants, for the security which pertains to slowly fulfilling political rights." In the new Constitution, however, he went on to point out, "*It is within, it is immersed within, the new Constitution. . . .* It is an attempt to create an alignment of a state of law with security. (interview; his emphasis)

We shall later discuss the implications of such immersion for the military's vision of State security. For now, we need to understand that once this "alignment" was complete, two things occurred: One consequence of immersing security within the Constitution was that rights were made subject to obligations to the State; another is that the Army's obligatory role as Guarantor of the State was constitutionally mandated with counterinsurgency operations within the law and those considered to be subversives, by definition, outside the law.

Conception of "Rights"

Juridical norms, based on nineteenth- and twentieth-century natural law, have usually contained a double characteristic: they are imperative and attributive, duty imposing and power conferring (Tapper 1973: 249; cf. Linares Morales 1985). From this perspective, juridical norms impose duties and concede rights that must be respected both by the governors and the governed. The Guatemalan military's vision of rights, in contrast, is an imperative positivistic theory of legal obligation in which law is separated from both morality and politics. Obedience is demanded of the governed in the guise of obligations and duties, while the governors stand at once within, above and (occasionally) outside the law in order to preserve it. As Colonel Gordillo declared: "The citizen does not have only rights, but also obligations. Above all, he must comply with these obligations because everyone has the right to discuss, to speak, and thousands upon thousands of rights; but obligations, one doesn't make enough of *them*" (interview; his emphasis).

Within this legal scheme only one-half of the juridical norms of rights within a nineteenth-century image of rule of law are fulfilled, while the twentieth-century principle of consent (i.e., the socially approved use of force as the distinguishing element of law), upon which the philosophy of human rights is based, is blatantly ignored. Similarly, despite the 1985 Constitution's preamble, which urges full respect for "Human Rights within a stable, permanent, and popular institutional order, where the governed and the governors act with absolute loyalty to the law" (Constituyente 1985: 2), rules and rights for governors and the governed, through the military lens of law, are clearly made distinct. No mention is made of the governors conceding rights, only of demanding obedience and having the "rational power . . . to make [their] force felt" (Gramajo, interview). The only "equality" within this perception of law is that of *obligation*: the governors are obliged to force compliance from the governed to protect public order; the governed are obliged to comply with this forced obedience.

Within this Hobbesian universe of law-sans-public, of a coercive consensus,[11] human rights are defined as socially and legally bounded norms of conformity for security purposes. They become "securitized": continuously subject to qualification or denial whenever they are deemed to be in conflict with security interests of the State. Rights and duties coalesce into what Girón Tánchez and Andrade Díaz-Durán both termed "juridical security" when referring to human rights. Securitized law — that is, state security interests with no separation made between the political and juridical — represents not only State power but State mission (Damaška 1986: 52): that of forcing obedience, compliance, and sanctions against those the State deems must not escape from its boundaries.

The notion of boundaries is very important to this view of rights. When Girón Tánchez was asked about his oft-used phrase "within a legal boundary" (*dentro de un marco legal*) he replied:

One uses this phrase in both a juridical and a literal sense. A legal standard is a conjunction of norms of the greatest hierarchy — in this case, the Constitution. It is the *marco legal* within which all juridical and political activities occur. Within this boundary, one cannot escape; one cannot move outside of it precisely because it is a boundary, isn't that so? It is a boundary.
Q: For that reason, one speaks of both legality and security, with security meaning one may not transgress those boundaries?
Clearly, one may not go outside it and that is juridical security; it is one of those essential pacts. You can be certain that no one will escape from the boundaries the Constitution establishes. Perhaps one leaves the boundaries. There lies the sanction, the sanction of penal order, the penal sanction for civil disorder. Well, [in that case] you're finished (interview)

Non-securitized and inherent rights not subject to the power of the State do not exist within the military's definition of the term in Guatemala.

"Operative Laws" and Constitutional Mandate

General Gramajo has stated repeatedly that the army—the institution that planned and executed the *apertura*—"is continuing our [military] actions, our operative pressure, because the Constitution mandates this. The Army of Guatemala is participating actively in strengthening the democratic system [and] is pledged to maintain all military action as a basis for national stability. And we are pledged to maintain the constitutional order as a principal factor by which to achieve that national stability" (Ejército, 1987: 16, 21).[12] Here Gramajo is referring to the Constitutive Law of the Army, which repeats Article 244 of the Constitution. (Girón Tánchez confessed in an interview that the reason this law was repromulgated was to keep it from being repealed by Congress.) What precisely does this "constitutional mandate" entail if the Constitution consigns the army as "the depository of the coercive force of the state," as one Civil Affairs colonel on the National Defense General Staff stated (interview), which allows for power to be exercised by whatever [counterinsurgent] maneuver necessary? How does the military think of law in relation to "military operations"? Denying any contradiction between fighting an insurgency while establishing a democracy, 1988 Army Public Relations Chief Colonel Luis Arturo Isaacs Rodríguez explained that the military is "complying with the operative laws against the delinquent subversives and against common delinquency" (interview). Civil Affairs Colonel García shrugged, "We [the army] are what give laws their force" (interview). A final example comes from the director of the Committee on National Reconstruction, who considered the concentration of refugees in Poles of Development to be decreed by law "because the security of the country depended on it" (Colonel Grotewold, interview). Law, in this instance, is operative, providing the military legal entitlement to force compliance, even to the point of physical injury or death, making law part and parcel of the operations that provide security and peace. The salience of law here is what one can *do* with it, how it can be used to carry out "operations" against opponents and how power can be consolidated in its name without releasing one iota of control.

Thus, within this mental universe, the perception of the rule of law is based on a Hobbesian vision of the world in which law is important only when it is literally or even potentially disobeyed. Emphasis is on the law as sanction rather than as a system of rules. Rights are perceived as having no abstract or inherent quality attached to them: they do not inhere (as subject) to an individual by virtue of being, but are provided as something thrown (as object) before the individual and accorded by the State only conditionally (Damaška 1986: 52).

Nor does the military separate the demand for rights from the potential consequences of those rights being used actively: it is well understood that an authentic provision of rights would necessarily challenge the status quo, especially with regard to the army's longstanding impunity. Determined to force compliance with the norms that "the public" has institutionalized, it is not enough for the military to will the governed to obey; the public must face the prospect of sanctions being imposed through legalized force. A formalist dogmatism of law is created in which "a hierarchy of sanctioned rules, sanctioned norms or the command of the sovereign spring from a determined . . . striving for objectivity [as] . . . virtues of the highest order. But they are the virtues of technicians and of strategists, not of those who must make social choices for themselves" (Shklar 1964: 214).

The Military's View of Opponents as Outside the Boundaries of Law

Officers interviewed are clear to distinguish the violence of the State as necessary and inherent to the legal order, and violence exercised by groups on the margins of both the State and the law as illegitimate. To operate "within the law" accomplishes a separation, at least rhetorically, between the legal coercion of the State-as-sovereign and the space outside the law occupied by the enemy:

The subversives are outside the law, they are the delinquents and when they work outside of it, then they are a recognized entity. They are outside of the law and we are within the Constitution: Article 245 prohibits any armed groups not regulated by the laws of the Republic. We are within the democratic framework and within the laws of such a framework. (Colonel Isaacs, interview)

Similarly, in the document *Operación Ixil*, Cifuentes states . . . "The enemy can act arbitrarily, as he is outside the law" (*fuera de la ley*) (1982: 39). In 1989, General Gramajo published the Thesis of National Stability, which proclaimed, "Opponents of the State will try to participate in the legal arena with attitudes and proposals that favor illegality" (1989: 51–52).

This us-versus-them attitude reinforces the idea that unjustifiable violence only occurs outside State structures; violence by the State to defend itself is mandated, and thus justifiable. Defensive, preventive measures are collapsed into offensive, strategic ones, and the more effective the security apparatus is in defining the boundaries of "legal" action, the more reasonable it will appear in defining and isolating those unwilling to conform as "outside the law" and as "enemies of the state." Groups active in denouncing human rights abuses are, in turn, denounced by the army as *grupos de fachada* outside the boundaries of "lawful" dissent. The assumption is that all denunciations of human rights violations are part of the international campaign against the State of Guatemala.[13] It is curious that the military believes itself capable of recognizing illegality, given that, for the most part, its commanders have neither legal training nor legal advisors to whom they turn for advice. Yet the military alone is deemed capable of recognizing illegal subversion and dissent. For the military, then, law is defined not by the realm of measurable juridical procedures and boundaries. Rather, it is placed squarely in the world of uncontemplated, imputed criminality of the remote future in which individuals are guilty *of what they have not yet done*, and need to be punished for what they might do in the distant future.[14] Many innocent victims, who were merely suspected or imputed to be involved with the guerrilla by military commanders have been kidnapped, tortured, and killed by army intelligence *patrullas* "as they had no information to share" (G-2 operative, interview). Moreover, one might not know where the boundary of penal sanction lies in this uncertain mental universe, as one prominent Guatemalan journalist pointed out during the tumultuous years when the counterinsurgency structures were being established in the highlands and the Army authorized journalists to write strictly on the basis of Army bulletins and not to mention the word "guerrilla," only "subversive," "terrorist," or "delinquent gang" (Beltranena 1992: 153): "One doesn't know from one day to the next whether one can publish anything about the counterinsurgency campaigns or the Poles of Development or Civil Patrols without taking great risks because the rules change all the time. What is permitted today may be a terrible mistake tomorrow" (1984 interview).

If accidental acts are to be treated as premeditated ones, then individuals can never be sure when they are in danger of being outside the legal boundaries, and "finished." Such a preemptive strategy not only sets in motion a paranoia in which everyone is suspect; it also provides officers with a basis for justifying killing. Ultimately, one must conclude, this theory of punishment has more to do with the provision of a legal facade for elimination tactics than with concern for protecting human rights within constitutional and juridical boundaries. While military officers point to the ability of subversive groups to be both outside the law (as subversive) and within it (to infiltrate and institutionalize themselves in order to subvert the legal process "with a legal face"),[15] the military itself manages to be within, above, and sometimes outside the law.

Within and Above the Law: The Army as Both Intra- and Supra-Constitutional

Seeing itself as the only institution capable of "adjusting" and "harmonizing" the legal system to meet security needs, and of bearing the burden of the State and of Law (given their obligation and mission to provide juridical security), the Guatemalan military views itself as the supra- and intraconstitutional guardian — simultaneously above and within the law. An example of this thinking is the 25 October 1986 decision by the Military War Tribunal (Auditoría de Guerra based within the Ministry of Defense's Office) concerning the military occupation of the national university (USAC) campus in September 1985, when much of the physical plant was destroyed. The university rector at the time presented a formal complaint to the Public Ministry asking for material damages to be repaired. The Auditoría decided that this occupation was no illegal act because "the laws which were in force at this time obliged the government to combat delinquency in order to maintain public order" (ACEN-SIAG, 30 October 1986, 72, p. 4). Similarly, at a press conference in March 1986, Defense Minister Hernández said that the Army was "calm" concerning the possible repeal of amnesty Decree-Law 8-86 (one of the sixteen passed just before President Cerezo was inaugurated in January 1986) because all the army's activities had been based on a "strict adherence to the law" (*La Hora*, 21 March 1986: 3). In answer to the question as to whether the military would cede to the repeal of the same amnesty decree-law, then National Defense Chief of Staff General Gramajo equated law with institutionality: "[Congress] should [repeal the law]. We are not bothered by anything. On the contrary, we are proud of having pacified Guatemala. So that it doesn't matter to us in what capacity the law is applied: we know we work institutionally" (ACEN-SIAG, 8 July 1986, 64, p. 8).

A final example is that of the capture and detention of five suspected guerrillas by the army in March 1986. Three were assigned to a *tribunal de paz correspondiente* (a local civilian court) even though they were detained at a military base. Defense Minister Hernández denied the illegality of such actions because "the corresponding judge knows of the detained and will bring the case through the court." He suggested that the army would lobby Congress for longer sentences for subversives and for separate places of detention to prevent the prisoners from giving "lectures on subversion and raising the spirits of the most recluse" ("Cinco guerrilleros consignados a tribunales," *La Hora*, 21 March 1987: 3). The military, in other words, sees nothing amiss with mixing military law with civilian tribunals, or having the civilian Congress legalize military de facto government actions and decree-laws: they all form part of the "mixed solution" of the *proyecto político-militar* in which the sanction that "pacifies" matters more than the rule that is "applied." Whether decree-laws are immersed within the Constitution or the Constitution is adapted to the decree-laws, political violence becomes concentrated in law for the army's purposes.

Although its central image of law is the state decree that is wholly divorced from contractarian notions of law, the military in Guatemala is not above using the constitutional forms and language at hand to "harmonize" and "regulate" the agenda and implant it within the new constitutional order. For example, while the position of Human Rights Ombudsman was created to investigate human rights violations, Article 30 of the 1985 Constitution limits the Ombudsman's access to information regarding national security. Yet the situation can also be reversed with law "getting in the way" of security needs, raising the question of when do State security needs override law? Because legislative procedures may delay and even constrain military activities, officers admit they must occasionally go outside the law "temporarily" to combat subversion. *Operación Ixil*, a key document outlining counterinsurgency, illustrates how operating "within the law" has its limits. Concerning "Juridical Matters," it states:

The juridical regime is in crisis but it is far superior to follow the laws of war which pertain [to this situation]; one must not forget that the laws of Guatemala continue in force unaltered. The enemy can act arbitrarily, but he is outside the law. We have all the structure of the Law which assists us and thus — even in a situation almost of war in which we live — we must attach ourselves to the law *up to where* it permits us to fulfill the mission. (Cifuentes 1982: 39; emphasis added)

The goal of "pacifying and re-establishing law and order" assumes that one can step outside the law long enough to "pacify" and then reenter without having committed any arbitrary or illegal acts because one is "in a situation of almost war." Captain Mazariegos, director of CEM in 1990, discusses "the limits of the law" within the context of army operations:

We know up to where the limit of the law is and we try as much as possible for all our actions to be within the law. But one has to also remember that military actions are responses to military confrontations, and we cannot aspire to 100 percent respect for human rights! The subversives are dressed as civilians and many times, they place themselves within the population. So, in such a response, we could commit 10 percent or 20 percent of error but this is not intentional. It is just within the same military action.
Q: So, are you saying that in order to maintain security, the military must, from time to time, go outside the law to maintain the law?
That's it exactly. We might go outside the law *unconsciously* to maintain security, but we do not break the law. (interview)

When I also asked Colonel García if there were cases when the law was an obstacle to national security and the Army had to step outside the law to maintain it, his response was one of self-defense: the army had to fight a war under the conditions of illegality set by the guerrilla:

Under ideal circumstances, there should not be a moment when one acts outside the framework of the Law. And this doesn't happen, although perhaps at times it does occur very crudely when one has to confront someone in combat who assaults you. *But it was not us*, the military in this country, *not us who started this war*. This [war] came from an external aggression. They were persons who were trained professionally to subvert the order in this country and in the Army. In accordance with its function, as its constitutional mandate, [the Army] fought [these guerrillas] on their terrain and under the conditions they offered. What happened was that our organization proved to be more efficient, more efficacious. (interview; his emphasis)

In contrast, General Gramajo stated that if the law had been violated during his tenure as Defense Minister, "it would have been done deliberately by official order of the [Commander-in-] Chief [Cerezo]. [But] to violate the law means that you are not institutionalizing the country" (interview). The difference between Gramajo and García or Mazariegos is informative: for the former, it is a question of institutional correctness; for the others it is an issue of necessity. But these responses may be two sides of the same coin. As one military journalist wrote, "While the army in practice guarantees justice, the application of the same will be real within the courts: if there is no peace, which is the climate of justice, the court by itself will not be able to bring peace. Never will the action of security interfere with the action of justice, if it is not interfering with security through legalistic formula" (Troy, quoted in Comité Pro-Justicia y Paz 1984: 23).

At the army's behest, laws of war have come to supersede rule of law whenever it is deemed necessary to fight subversion in order to protect the security of the state. For a retired military lawyer, involved in legal affairs of the army since the 1950s, State security is, by definition, supra-law:

> In the year of Watergate, when my American friends were considering whether Nixon had broken the law, I asked how it was that they believed that a country can be solid, structured, and powerful if it didn't have a system of [State] security? The security of the State is above all else, and the President must be in violation [of the law] for that security so that we can all be secure. How can you criticize the security of your country? . . . The security of the State is above the law, and [if need be], you can change the law to adjust it to State security. Reagan can change treaties with Gorbachev, but national security stands above all law. I don't believe that I have ever, in my thirty-five years of legal experience [here in Guatemala], come across a case in which one could say: "Here the law supersedes national security." It could be that the state of national security itself is violating rights, but one must see whether the person [whose rights are being violated] is doing something against the security of the State. One must always protect [the State]. It is a very difficult matter to control. (Colonel Diéguez Pilón, interview)

The Military's Mission: To Maintain the State's and the Military's Institutionality

With multiple decree-laws maintaining a continuous state of siege in 1982 and a state of alarm in 1983 that severely restricted or suspended all individual and collective rights,[16] the military's mission of defining and protecting the entity and supremacy of the state became at times so intertwined that these states of exception "in which human rights are sacrificed a little" become indistinguishable from the state itself, as this exchange with Colonel Girón Tánchez, the author of these decree-laws, indicates.

Q: How does one relate the juridical structure to the need for security?
Ah, yes, well, we began fundamentally with something that was already established.

We recognized that the State had to be maintained—its organization, its institutionality—all had to be maintained. If at some moment in life we lacked the state we would probably fall into some Marxist-Leninist postulates which attempt in one given moment in the revolution of Marxism-Leninism to suppress the State. We thus decided that the state was an entity which had to be kept in force and its institutionality maintained. If, for example, we were to establish, let's say, the state of siege, the state of alarm and the state of war and all these states which aim for the security of the State and its inhabitants, then we would be worried about running the risk that the State — that is to say, the government—would disappear, and we would fall into a state of anarchy. This state of anarchy then would run counter to the logical consequence for the security of its inhabitants.

Q: So, how can one maintain this security which you say is necessary?

Security is maintained through the expertise process of considering these states of alarm, states of siege which infringe upon and reduce in some form the human rights of persons. Human rights are sacrificed a little but it is for a question of superior order in order to maintain the integrity of the country's institutionality.

Q: But there seems to be a tension here between national security and legality. How can such a state be maintained within juridical norms?

Yes, the juridical norms give you the opportunity of a framework by which to establish such norms of exception. . . . And clearly all these norms are legal. Why? Because they are contained in the law, because of their complete positivity—that is, it is a norm to be obeyed.

This exchange exemplifies the final "harmonization" of the traditional and special forms of law within the Guatemalan state. In a 1988 speech, Andrade was at pains to point out that with the change of regime in 1983, "the state of alarm and state of siege [that had been put into place under Ríos Montt] were lifted and this was very important, because in [such states], liberties of the citizen and of the press were restricted [and] subjected to certain censure and that, in some way, limited the free political game" (1988: 7; interview). In other words, while the Ríos Montt regime was an Emergency State with a declared state of siege and state of alarm, the Cerezo regime became a counterinsurgent constitutionalized state with a regularly extended but undeclared emergency for a "war situation" to limit the political damage of security operations.

Girón Tánchez's final remarks further clarify the complete identification of the army with the State:

Do you know why we [the military] created the juridical-political structure? *Somebody* had to emit the laws, *somebody* had to establish a regime of legality in the country. [he laughs] Because who else could have created it but us? Who else in the structure? They had to depend upon us. If we had not created it, *nobody* could have [He laughs again]. Clearly, I feel civilians are not qualified. [They] lack the feel for organization and order and discipline. Do you believe that in a modern state the army in some form does not participate in politics? It is inevitable. The essence of the politics of the army revolves around the fact that the army doesn't vote. But within the general politics of the State, as regards the entity of the State itself, the Army is obviously actively participating in politics. It is impossible [for us] *not* to participate

Q: Particularly here in Central America, I imagine the army needs more subtle kind of political participation.

Exactly. [he whispers] This is politics. And international politics definitely have much to do with this. And the army is going to participate. It is obvious.

Q: In order to maintain security?

Of course, this is part of the fundamental politics of the country! (interview; his emphasis)

"The Law Is Harsh but It Is the Law": Operationalized Justice—Special Tribunals

There is no situation in which [the] ideological habits of legalism are more obvious] than in political trials," Judith Shklar wrote in 1964 (143). This is certainly the case for the Special Tribunals (Tribunales de Fuero Especial [TFE]) in Guatemala. In 1982, 15 people were sentenced to death by these special Tribunals, and shot; another 14 were sentenced to prison. With the transfer of 400 cases to the Supreme Court, an estimated 112 people were released, many of whom were later assassinated. Born "out of the inefficiency of the common courts," the Special Tribunals were decreed by Ríos Montt (Decree-Laws 46-82, 111-82) to provide "rapid justice" and to "cleanse the courts" of the guerrilla, "even if it means a diminishing of rights," according to Colonel-lawyer Girón Tánchez, one of the Tribunals' authors. They were "the personal invention of Ríos Montt. He came to me [saying] 'Let's have tribunals which really make justice in this quasi-secret form" (1986 interview; Girón Tánchez 1983: 10) — quasi-secret in that the names of the judges were not made known to the public, nor were lawyers able to meet with the prisoners or provide them due process. Many were told to "serve" their papers to an office in the Public Ministry, and wait for the verdict.

Although Gramajo claims the Special Tribunals "didn't do very much: they only killed about four or five by firing squad," 15 is the number given by other officers, including Ríos Montt (interview). According to one Guatemalan lawyer who attempted to defend several Special Tribunal prisoners, however, "none of the 15 was authentically proven to be a terrorist as set forth in the Penal Code. And if you think I lie, then let the proceedings of every one of those executed be revealed [to the public]" (Alonso 1986: 12;[17] 1984–86 interviews with four TFE lawyers). But with the transference of an estimated four hundred cases to the Supreme Court, the traditional forms of law became immersed with those born of counterinsurgency, as one lawyer explains:

I want to say one thing: when the Secret Tribunals were created, the Law we believed in was never appropriated because the Secret Tribunals were indeed that — clandestine: there was no oral debate or defense, there was no meeting with one's client. . . . The executive and legislative functions had been subsumed under the executive. When I submitted the habeas corpus, I saw the differences: on one side,

...Court in all its majesty, all the organisms of justice, and on the other side, the Secret Tribunals, which were not part of the Supreme Court. Thus, we were in the presence of two judicial organisms: one which acts publicly and the other which acts in the shade, clandestinely. Different, you see? *Two* different powers. With the transfer of 400 cases of the Secret Tribunals to the Supreme Court, the juridical barbarity becomes synonymous with the Supreme Court—creating an even graver situation. (1984 interview)

It is precisely this appropriation and "adjustment" of the traditional le[gal] apparatuses for national security purposes in Guatemala that is so sign[ifi] cant because it abuses trust in the rule of law, and undermines prospects f[or] democratic restructuring and non-exclusive participation.

In 1990, I asked former President-General Ríos Montt what happened [to] the 112 TFE prisoners he claimed were released. "They were later assass[i] nated [by the army] on the street, in their homes, in the countryside, be[-] cause they were dangerous." He said the Tribunals also served to purg[e] elements of the police and military under Lucas García: "Those who do no[t] fulfill their duty and follow the law must be eliminated, gotten rid of. So[,] they were sanctioned and there was no discrimination: policemen, officers[,] and soldiers alike who had done wicked things—PUM! [He mimics shoot- ing a gun against his head.]" (interview). But according to other sources, only police officers and five EMP *especialistas* (two of whom were soldiers) were executed; military officers were exiled, put on unassigned status at partial salary (*disponible*), or cashiered. Apparently, police officers were forced to watch the firing-squad executions in the cemetery as a lesson against corruption (anonymous, 1990 interview).

Point 7 of the National Plan speaks of the need to "restructure the judi- cial organism with the participation of the [Guatemalan] Bar Association to accommodate it to the ruling situation and achieve its ethical, moral, and juridical ends." When asked who the judges for the Special Tribunals were, Colonel Girón Tánchez spoke of them as "judges of law, men capable of dictating solutions which involve death as the penalty" (interview). Ríos Montt has said the judges were both civilian and military (interview),[18] while Gramajo has claimed they were all civilian: "The names of the judges were not to be published, although they are in the archives. The military govern- ment knew the names."[19]

When General Mejía became Chief of State on 8 August 1983, the first thing he told Colonel Girón Tánchez was, "Look, do me a favor, repeal the law of the Special Tribunals," and four days later the Special Tribunals were dissolved with Decree-Law 93-83. "But some of those objects (*objectos*) in- dicted had already been condemned to death and shot. There was no repair- ing that. But the TFE were born dead" (interview). Why were they dis- solved? International criticism had become too damaging to maintain the Tribunals: "It was truly painful to listen to the comments abroad about their functioning, which were no more, no less, secret tribunals," Andrade explains (1988: 7–8).[20] Gramajo agrees: "The bad luck was that one week before [the TFE prisoners] were shot, the Pope asked for their clemency, and it wasn't granted. And one week after they were shot, the Pope arrived in Guatemala" (interview). As Ríos Montt summed it up, "If [justice] is not rapid, then it loses its effectiveness, and confidence in the law is lost. Normally, the legal process just goes on and on and on" (interview).

Amnesty Decree-Laws: Counterinsurgency and Legalized Impunity

The multiple amnesty Decree-Laws 33-82, 34-82, 27-83, 43-83, and 89-83 were useful to the military in two ways. First, amnesty was used as bait to draw the "lawless" guerrillas out of hiding to either turn them into informants and soldiers or eliminate them. Ríos Montt stated at the time that the first amnesty decree-law "gives us the juridical framework for killing. Anyone who refuses to surrender will be shot" (Black et al. 1984: 126). Second, amnesty was useful for pardoning Fuerzas de Seguridad del Estado (State Security forces) for acting in self-defense (along with the support of the population in the Civil Patrols) against the illegal and violent aggression. Amnesty is the most unequivocal admission by the military of guilt for egregious human rights violations: it fully anticipated that its troops would and did commit massive criminal acts in carrying out the Pacification campaign, and thus serves as an obstacle to justice.

By 1985, the army proclaimed that an "extensive, permanent and generous" amnesty had facilitated "a national conciliation"—that is, that amnesty-as-bait had succeeded in destroying much of the guerrilla network of support (Ejército, 1985a: 13). Another amnesty decree-law was passed by the Mejía Víctores regime only a few days before the inauguration of President Cerezo in January 1986. In approving Transitory Article 16, the National Constituent Assembly juridically validated amnesty for all those responsible for grave human rights violations. But, just to be certain, the military government passed its own decree-law, which specifically states:

Article 1. General amnesty is provided to all persons responsible for or involved in committing political and related common crimes during the period 23 March 1982 to 14 January 1986. As such, no penal action of any kind may be begun or continued against authors and accomplices of such crimes, nor against those who covered up these referred-to crimes, nor against those who intervened in whatever way in its repression or persecution.

Its author, Colonel-lawyer Girón Tánchez, explains why this particular decree-law was viewed as necessary:

We have [up to this time] been using amnesty in only one sense: in order to benefit those military men who fought the guerrilla. For them specifically. But now a general amnesty has been established [that covers] the period between 23 March 1982 and

14 January 1986, which is directed as much at the guerrillas as at these military men. They all totally accept responsibility for their violent acts. *Yes, they have committed political and common crimes and for this reason, they are all responsible.* But what is the goal of amnesty? To promote peace and tranquility, a concordance between peoples in conflict. Naturally, one cannot succeed with a partial amnesty dedicated absolutely to one sector; thus it is a total amnesty for everyone. *And in the future, then, whatever happens, happens, and it will not be something of our doing.* (interview; his emphasis)

Law, in this instance, is operationalized as a distancing from responsibility for human rights violations, yet serves as a clear admission that the armed forces and, in the military's eyes, the guerrillas are guilty of such abuses. This approach tries to "sanitize" the memory of a society for past crimes committed, while using the law to provide impunity from future crimes and potential future reprisals. In brief, it covers the military on all fronts. In preempting any investigation of human rights violations, protecting the military from future "vendettas" against its past, present, and future violence, law serves as an obstacle to justice. The papal-style edict that "they are all political criminals but they are all excused" makes the military the final arbiter of who is to be absolved of criminal activity. In defending the amnesty decree-law, General Mejía Víctores referred matter-of-factly to the long-term impunity the military has enjoyed since 1963: "[It was passed] in order to protect the members of the Army by extending a previously existing amnesty law passed by President Peralta Azurdia [1963–66]. I thought it convenient to protect my men" (*La Hora*, 13 March 1987; interview).[21] (This attitude is in marked contrast to the rapid sentencing of Civil Patrol members, such as two *patrulleros* found guilty for allegedly killing two neighbors in San Pedro Carchá 6 months after the promulgation of the 1986 amnesty decree-law [*La Hora*, 14 May 1986].)

President Cerezo also played his part: he not only promised not to indict those responsible for crimes committed against tens of thousands of Guatemalans, but he also refused to revoke the 1986 amnesty decree-law: "It is not good to judge the military while pardoning the guerrillas," he argued (*La Hora*, 25 September 1986: 3). Invoking the rule of law throughout his term, President Cerezo sidestepped executive action in repealing the law, which was requested repeatedly by the Guatemalan Congress. (Similarly, although he promised to set up a commission to investigate the fate of the disappeared, he also claimed that the 1467 habeas corpus petitions filed with the Supreme Court on 30 May 1986 by the Group of Mutual Support precluded independent presidential action.) In contrast, one top Christian Democratic congressional deputy referred to the amnesty law as "pure casuism" (1988 interview). With the signing of the Esquipulas II accords, which sought "national reconciliation to establish the basis for a firm and long-lasting peace," Central American countries were asked to promulgate laws conceding amnesty to those who participated as either "authors or accomplices" in "linked political and common crimes committed against the political order of their respective States" ("Congreso de la República Decreto 32-88," *Diario de Centroamérica* 8 July 1988).

With a new military offensive in full swing in 1987–88, Defense Minister Gramajo took advantage of this opportunity and sent officers to successfully pressure Congress for two more amnesty decree-laws: number 71-87 for six months and number 32-88 in July 1988,[22] despite strong criticisms of "incongruencies" between these new decree-laws and the Constitution and penal code.[23] In November 1987, Defense Minister Gramajo claimed that 2000 had taken advantage of Decree-Law 71-87 (*Diario de Centroamérica*, 26 November 1987); Guatemalan anthropologists witnessed the internally displaced relocated under the governmental program in March 1987 being forced to sign the amnesty as "the military authorities assumed they had been transgressors of the law (that is, subversives), without taking into account that, juridically, amnesty is a right one can choose" (AVANCSO 1990: 29–30); and in May 1988, the press reported peasants in the mountains "accepting protection of the army."[24] As the president of Congress's Comisión de Gobernación, Licenciado Ramiro Leal Espinoza stated to the press at the time, "The basis for amnesty must be forgive and forget (*el perdón y el olvido*)" (*La Hora*, 30 May 1988).

Dysfunctionalized Law: Investigations Without Convictions

During the late 1980s, many judges, prosecutors, witnesses, and victims suffered serious threats and assassinations from both criminal offenders and local and military authorities, causing some to resign and courts to be temporarily closed (Tomuschat 1992: 61; WOLA 1992: 34–38). But with human rights pressures building in the 1990s for investigations of political assassinations and disappearances, and indictments of those very few military and police officers found responsible, an alternative procedural technique used by Army Intelligence has been to announce an investigation that then leads nowhere, with the investigation blocked by the Chief of Police or the Head of Intelligence or the Defense Minister. In those rare instances when the government has announced arrests and criminal proceedings in cases of human rights abuse, punishment has rarely been meted out. For example, in 1991 four police officers were convicted of the murder of a homeless teenager, but the conviction was overturned on technical grounds (WOLA Reports 1989 and 1992; Amnesty International 1992: 4).[25]

The new tactic is to admit that "abuses" and "excesses" occur, as General Gramajo and other officers have done, to allow for particular cases to be brought to the courts, where police and military officers are released for lack of evidence (or fear of reprisals), or sentenced and overturned on technical grounds. As of 1992, "nine soldiers and one low-ranking officer had been convicted for carrying out murders, but no high-ranking officer has been convicted for ordering one" (WOLA 1992: 3). As of December 1996, this situation had not changed. The response of military officers to the issue of abuse is to blame the court system: judges and lawyers are "incompetent" and "corrupt": "It's just that the judicial system doesn't function. It should have its own police because the corrupt, venal, and inept judge will always say, 'It isn't my fault, it is the fault of the police.' So the executive government is to blame, not the judicial branch. . . . But the army has done everything possible to combat terrorism within the law" (Gramajo, interview). Such techniques use investigations to deflect criticism: we the army have tried but takes a while to learn how to live within a democracy; we have tried and would have succeeded but for the ineptness of the courts. Criticism of the courts, though, is withheld when a ruling is made in favor of the army's political project.

Ríos Montt as Presidential Candidate and the Courts

In August 1990, the Electoral Council (Tribunal Electoral) decided that Ríos Montt, ousted in August 1983, could not run for president because the Constitution does not allow (1) the reelection of past presidents or (2) a run for elected office by anyone who has participated in a coup. Several parties then petitioned the Constitutional Court (Corte de Constitucionalidad) to make a recommendation that would echo the Electoral Council's decision, which they did in late August. In early September, close to the deadline for presidential candidates to register, Ríos Montt requested a temporary injunction (*amparo provisional*) from the Supreme Court, stating that the government did not have the right to keep him from running for office. He made this argument on two grounds:

1. As to the bar against a second run for president (the first time had been in 1974), the Human Rights Charter states that the only permissible restrictions for running for office are age and education. Thus, he was being denied his human right to participate as he saw fit.
2. In terms of his participation in the 1982 coup, Ríos Montt went to a judge in Jutiapa (outside of Guatemala City) and asked him to give him amnesty under the Esquipulas II provision that states that all who had participated in the war would be declared free of political crimes. The judge granted amnesty to Ríos Montt, who then claimed he was as clean of all political crimes as *una palomilla* (a white dove), as one Guatemalan intellectual remarked (interview). In response to Ríos Montt's public announcement, the Supreme Court provided him with a temporary injunction, arguing it needed more time to think this case through before the elections; at the last minute, they agreed with the earlier denials.

Once the Supreme Court had ruled negatively, Ríos Montt appealed again to the Corte de Constitucionalidad. Because they had already made a recommendation against him, Ríos Montt wanted all the judges to be excused from deciding on his case, and requested a new slate of judges. There weren't enough judges to fill the slots, however. Hence, "there was a real constitutional crisis because neither the Constitution nor the Corte de Constitucionalidad could address the issue because this situation had never been imagined," said one U.S. lawyer working in Guatemala (interview).

Meanwhile, there was also a political crisis due to Ríos Montt's loquaciousness: when he was granted the amnesty, his statement became front page news: "If a *guerrillero* can someday be president, why can't I?" When he was given the temporary injunction, he waved the paper in front of a large crowd in the plaza that Sunday, proclaiming it was permanent and that he would be a presidential candidate. Given that this constitutional-political crisis was so close to the elections, it was proposed that two sets of ballots be printed—one with and one without Ríos Montt's name or, given the great expense and the consequent disorder, one with his name crossed out. Ríos advised people to vote for him anyway, and if he didn't win, he would declare fraud.

For the institutionalist officers, there was real concern: Ríos Montt represented the traditional careerist officers in the Army and had much backing from the extreme-rightwing landowners and industrialists (CACIF, and especially UNAGRO). His candidacy would have seriously disrupted the military project. By his own account, Gramajo, back in 1987, appointed officers for promotion (with a few exceptions) who were Flecha to gird the Thesis against just such events. In the end, the Supreme Court decided against permitting Ríos Montt to run for president in 1990. Gramajo exclaimed, "Thank God the Court functioned in the end! Otherwise, Ríos Montt would have been the winner! This case represents Guatemala entering into the concept of *legality*—a small step on the moon, but a leap for Guatemalan humanity!" (interview). Ríos Montt and his wife were denied the right to run for president once again in the 1995 elections.

Conclusions

The immersion of State security "operative laws" within the 1985 Constitution permits the military to claim a constitutional mandate to control "enemies of the state" as they see fit, to operationalize citizens' "rights" as "obligations," and to define human rights as forms of "juridical security." Law in this mental universe is part of the "technics of domination" (Sumner 1982: 122), as the line of demarcation between those who can act with impunity and those who cannot. Rather than a vision of law that enhances rights, it is one that establishes boundaries "from which one cannot escape." It is a legal universe that says: We make the rules for you while we follow only the ones that suit our purposes. The result is to make repression part of the legal fabric of State power such that states of exception are no longer necessary. This undeclared-exception governance was illustrated in April 1987 when the army threatened local residents who failed to respect the 7 P.M. curfew in Santiago Atitlán and Sololá (areas the army had selectively bombed that month), with kidnapping, disappearance, and assassination. The Mexico-exiled Guatemalan Human Rights Commission stated, "These actions are occurring without a state of siege or curfew and under a state of law" (*El Gráfico*, 2 June 1987). In this counterinsurgent constitutionalism, "operations" may be simultaneously within, outside, and above the law without any sense of contradiction, for justice in Guatemala "will not interfere with security."

Chapter 7
Army Intelligence

G-2 is *un escuadrón de la muerte* [a death squad]. It is a death squad that exists only to kill.

— a G-2 operative

There may be democracy [in Guatemala], but it is army intelligence that controls and directs it.

— National Police detective

A Project to Merge Intelligence with a Democratic Apertura

This chapter is about the doctrinal and operational aspects of army institutions dedicated to espionage, abduction, torture, and assassination in clandestine cells on military bases, in subbasements of the National Police headquarters, and (when these were sealed off) in private houses. As the self-proclaimed "granddaddy" of military intelligence, former Defense Minister Gramajo has admitted, "The G-2 gathers an enormous amount of information [but] the army isn't to blame for all the violations. Some are carried out by Intelligence for personal reasons or drugs. Assassination [in Guatemala] is a means of resolving conflict. We still have some bad habits. It depends on the *Jefe* (Chief of Intelligence) whether or not G-2 is given autonomy [to act on the basis of this information], and there have been a variety of *Jefes*. . . . There are officers who work in *Operaciones*, in *Inteligencia*, and in *Administración*, and according to who the *Jefe* is, the criteria change [for each sector]. Sometimes the criterion is that [the officers] are intelligent, and at times it is that they are [merely] obedient — just hired thugs. But what I'm saying to you is that G-2 influences a great many decisions about opponents [of the State]" (interview).[1]

From a variety of sources, a sketch of the powerful Medusa-headed and clandestine intelligence bureaucracy within the Guatemalan State emerges.

Intelligence basically consists of three entities: Army intelligence, which was hierarchized in the 1980s as D-2 (Directorate of Intelligence) under the National Defense Chief of Staff), followed by S-2 (Section Intelligence Chiefs at each military zone), and finally G-2 (Group Patrols at the battalion, platoon, squadron, and company levels). But because Army intelligence is still referred to as G-2, or simply La Dos, this shorthand will be used where appropriate. G-2 has over 2000 agents nationwide, including 100 fulltime military officers in the three branches Gramajo mentions above. Until 1998 it operated out of the twin towers of the National Palace. Additionally, there is the Presidential General Staff (Estado Mayor Presidencial, EMP), of which only the Office of Presidential Security operates directly out of the office of the president; the other employees reside in the Presidential Annex. "Thirty percent of EMP employees are army intelligence officers who hold the key positions," while the rest are civilian staff divided into the economic, human rights, social, and political sections (Gramajo, interview). Since 1982, a third arm of intelligence, the military's Directorate of Information and Dissemination, or DIDE, directly under the Defense Minister, has worked closely with the Civil Affairs (S-5) companies and Civil Patrols in gathering intelligence. Their tasks include psychological operations and other "soft aspects" of the counterinsurgency war, such as working with NGOs in the highlands and providing journalists with army public relations literature. Usually, at least the three top positions of DIDE, if not all, are held by army intelligence officers with close connections to the School of Intelligence.

While part of the 1982 *proyecto militar* established a formal, constitutional *aperturismo* to suit security concerns, another task outlined in the National Plan for Security and Development was to provide "a centralized direction to the antisubversive effort . . . improv[ing] internal security bodies in accord with the situation" (Ejército 1982a: 1). This entailed the co-optation and coordination of the most powerful, clandestine "parallel government" in Guatemala, G-2, and the purging of the Estado Mayor Presidencial — two parts of the hub responsible for the majority of the political abductions and assassinations in Guatemala since 1954. One of the major tasks of the Army General Staff after the 1982 coup and throughout the 1980s was to bring these two parts of army intelligence under control by "working with them and not against them" (Gramajo, interview). This task has been accomplished by (1) outfitting military intelligence with the latest equipment and training by Argentine, Colombian, Taiwanese, Chilean, and Israeli military intelligence (with many of these exchanges begun in 1977); (2) reestablishing in 1983, if not earlier, unofficial covert assistance and training by the CIA, the U.S. Army, the U.S. Defense Intelligence Agency (DIA), and the U.S. Drug Enforcement Administration (DEA) — aid that "may have been coming in after 1975, but was stopped (at the request of the British) when the U.S. didn't honor the purchase of equipment for the invasion of Belize"

(Sereseres, interview); (3) training and *ideologizando* intelligence officers in newer forms of psychological warfare in Guatemala, the United States, and Taiwan; and (4) instituting a military unity and professionalism in an attempt to break the oligarchic stranglehold over much of army intelligence. In turn, G-2 officers, appointed to the EMP by a series of National Defense Chiefs of Staff, have become the principal means for the military to exert a high degree of influence over civilian presidents since the late 1980s.

Notwithstanding these adjustments, the intentions of *el proyecto* have not been to "purge" the G-2 of its heinous deeds, but to reconfigure its bureaucracy and to perfect its clandestine functioning by "co-opting" and "professionalizing" its officers and operatives and continuing to computerize its archives for the purposes of improving the management, control, and elimination of Opponents of the State (*Opositores del Estado*) — a project, we will see, civilian presidents of the 1980s and 1990s were very much privy to and complicitous in. Part I of this chapter describes the subculture and operations of army intelligence. Part II outlines the history of G-2 and its parallel presidential office known over the years as La Regional and Archivos between 1954 and 1982. Part III illustrates how the Ríos Montt and Mejía Víctores regimes utilized G-2 to fight the insurgency while trying to make the paramilitary forces less autonomous from the Army General Staff's control. Finally, Part IV covers the relationship between G-2 and the Cerezo regime, during which time Gramajo tried to co-opt G-2 hardline officers with CIA funding and to redesign its methodology with CIA trainers. In response, certain hardliners within G-2 increased the number of the more public human rights violations to at once discredit and test then Defense Minister Gramajo and, by extension, President Cerezo, to see how far they would go to support and protect G-2's autonomy and impunity. At least two coup attempts headed by former G-2 officers were also staged during this period. This chapter ends with a brief discussion of the uses of terror and killing as manifestations of G-2/Defense Ministry/EMP infighting, the rise of paramilitarism within the G-2-dominated EMP under the Serrano regime, and the "civilianization" of intelligence under President Ramiro de León Carpio.

I. Army Intelligence: The Operations and Subculture of G-2

Army Intelligence is a special branch in which most are career officers. "Anyone can choose [to work in] it, but it's better if the most brilliant officers do," explained Gramajo (interview). Once the intelligence bureaucratic procedures of authorization for operations were reestablished under Ríos Montt and hierarchized under Mejía Víctores (as D-2, S-2 and G-2), both the D-2 control center (with its computer file lists of Opponents of the State on the fourth floor of the National Palace) and El Archivo or the EMP (commanded by intelligence officers with copies of these files in the Presidential Annex), began to provide daily military, economic, and political analysis to the Army General Staff, Defense Minister, and President. This analysis might be based, for example, on information from a local commander who speaks with the S-2 garrison chief about a particular individual. He, in turn, will have G-1 consult its archives, checking its information gathered by other intelligence officers, operatives, and National Police informants among others. Faced with a teachers' strike, for instance, the name and address of the head of the union, his or her birthplace, information on members of the person's family, their past political and union activities (and those of relatives), and how the strike is proceeding, would all be part of the "analysis." This last piece of information is often gleaned from police and G-2 union infiltrators and gang members (who would also be paid by G-2 to initiate violent actions in demonstrations against the police) (National Police detective, interview). If the information indicates that this person is actually or potentially responsible for certain "illegal acts," the Army General Staff would make its recommendation, with three basic options: "disappear them, eliminate them in public, or simply invite them to leave the country" (Colonel D'jalma Domínguez, quoted in Nairn and Simon 1986: 15). G-2 files thereafter indicate when this person died, without saying who was responsible. When asked whether written orders to eliminate individuals are part of the *archivos*, Gramajo laughed heartily and replied, "I don't think there are *archivos* like that!" (interview).

Nonetheless, procedures are followed: orders are given by senior officers to surveil and/or eliminate, with information gathered and then compared to the intelligence file. One army first sergeant who entered the service during the regime of Kjell Laugerud and left his position to work as a G-2 *investigador* under the regimes of Lucas García, Ríos Montt, and Mejía Víctores and during the first two years of Vinicio Cerezo (1978–87), explained in an interview how the G-2 functions. G-2 agents work with six to eight others without rank and with equal salary in a *patrulla* under the command of a major or captain:

An order to kidnap an individual comes down from the High Command, signed by the military zone commander to "capture or investigate this individual who they have been informed of being engaged in certain activities."[2] If our *comisionsita* (assignment) is to first investigate, we go out in civilian clothes and with money to buy information. We go, say, to a village bar. We offer to buy someone a beer with the line "We don't know the town. Do you happen to know a person called so-and-so in your neighborhood? He told me he wanted to do such-and-such and he's never gotten back to me. What does he do for a living?" And this person may respond, "Well, they say he's a *guerrillero*." You tell them then that you are "also a *guerrillero*, but don't worry, nothing's going to happen to you." You ask if this guy's with his family the whole time and if he was away, where he was living during his absence. You then compare this information [with the *archivo*]. You may also go as a salesman buying or selling roosters or pigs, or whatever, door-to-door [to see who's at home]. This is done at the most within a week's time [as surreptitiously as possible] because the person might get suspicious and escape. And if it turns out that this person doesn't really exist, that he hasn't been living here, it is because he has been with the *guerrilla*. Then the order is given to *limpiar*, or abduct and eliminate him.

An "abduction" entails a *patrulla* of a minimum of four and up to eight *elementos*: four means

we grab a car and go. But if we know that the person is well armed and will resist, then we grab two cars and go as a *patrulla* of eight. The cars must be large with six or eight cylinders in case we are pursued. You arrive at the house very rapidly, you have men at the windows, at all the doors, so he has no possible escape. And if he doesn't resist, then the orders are to bring him back to headquarters alive.

There are usually a number of people who witness the abduction, but "because you are dressed in civilian clothes, they will say we were criminals, *guerrilleros*, or the Army. But who dares to say: 'The Army abducted him,' or 'It was G-2'? No one." *Desconocidos* (unknown assailants) becomes the safe substitute term for G-2. The victim is then taken to the G-2 section of the garrison, where he is tortured either by the same or a different *patrulla* in a *calabozo* (secret cell) for information.[3] The victim is tortured and either turned into an *oreja* (G-2 informer) or killed.

This G-2 *investigador* recounts how most of his colleagues don't live past the age of forty or forty-five years of age "because we know too much. The saying with G-2 is *aquí se hace, aquí se dice, y aquí se queda* (here is where one does [such work], here is where one speaks about such work, and here is where one remains), and when one is no longer serviceable to this Section, your own *compañeros* will be the ones who kill you." One intelligence colonel remarked that this secret brotherhood (*cofradía*) is part of the general subculture of the Escuela Politécnica training: "An officer asks himself, 'If I have information that needs to be kept secret, then I do so. A colonel over here is stealing cars, a general over there is stealing timber, another one is killing. These officers are shifted around in their posts but *todos lo saben* (everyone knows what's going on), and the cases never get resolved. It's a question of adapting to *la fibra*," the subculture of the Escuela based on intense loyalty, discipline, and keeping secrets.

Given the "delicate nature" of G-2 activities, General Gramajo believed he needed to reassert hierarchy and "professionalize" intelligence. Gramajo explains:

We returned things to normal by providing intermediate [S-2] *jefes*, keeping [information] at each level, and not leaving one's circle of responsibilities. Because if you allow for . . . a captain or a major who knows he is in danger by the delicate nature of the matter (*el tema delicado*), and can in one stroke speak with the President, then they will have a certain amount of independence. (interview)

What passes as "normal" is an aberration born of strategic planning: it is not about stopping the killing but about restoring the hierarchy to be able to neutralize or eliminate perceived Opponents more efficiently and intelligently.

When asked whether those in G-2 can earn more money than regular officers can, he replied,

Openly, no, but they have resources for moving around. The G-2 specialist, an officer of security, has a pass to enter hotels, he has credit to move about, to rent cars, to pay clients. They have a better standard of living [than regular officers], and there also is the opportunity to improve one's lifestyle even more. From time to time, there are some who return [to careerist concerns, i.e., making money on the side legally and illegally] and there is a problem [with this].

In fact, as one G-2 specialist relates, "As a *sección especialista*, we were told that we had to earn more than the soldiers because we were different. We didn't use uniforms, we didn't have to pay for hotels or cars or bus fare or anything" (interview). In 1985, the salaries of these *especialistas* doubled from Q250/month ($41) to Q500/month ($83), with most of these checks issued either through INDE, the governmental Instituto Nacional de Electrificación, or INGUAT, Instituto Guatemalteco de Turismo. But to Gramajo the training G-2 officers and specialists receive— "They have to have their courses [to be qualified]," he emphasized—and the fact that they must be able to move around in all places, since "the Intelligence organism has to have its investigation" capacities, justifies this divide among them.

Problems with G-2 personnel persist, though, indicating that this professionalization Gramajo refers to doesn't undermine officers' threat mentality or stop the killing by G-2 *patrullas*. Colonel Luis Francisco Ortega Menaldo represents this new G-2 "professional": he served as a captain in Arana's G-2 (and married Arana's daughter); he was made G-2 Deputy Chief by Gramajo in 1986 and served as G-2 chief during the latter part of the Cerezo regime. He worked with Defense Minister Gramajo and Chief of the National Defense Staff Callejas y Callejas in reorganizing G-2, working as "Gramajo's personal intelligence man." He is seen as primarily responsible for providing Gramajo the intelligence about the 1988–89 coups, and for bringing the Mobile Military Police into antinarcotics work with the DEA. As Chief of the Presidential General Staff under President Serrano, he was the most powerful man in Guatemala, traveling to all military bases in 1991 to speak to officers about the necessity for dialogue with the guerrilla. Despite his avowed professionalization, however, Ortega Menaldo's threat mentality persisted. He wondered out loud, for example, at a meeting in 1991 why a particular Social Democratic politician, Luis Zurita, had left the country for exile in Canada, given that his Social Democratic colleague Dinora Pérez (a former PSD congressional candidate who had been assassinated a few weeks earlier by the G-2, according to one intelligence source), was "dead and could no longer talk."[4] Impunity for murders by La Dos since 1954 has bred such thinking.

II. History/Background

Since 1954, army intelligence has been the principal obstacle for (the handful of) civilian presidents in Guatemala to gain oversight and control over the decision making powers of the armed forces. It thus has been referred to as the unelected, parallel government of Guatemala (cf. Nairn and Simon 1986). The official-yet-clandestine organizational precedent for the sole purpose of tracking, controlling, and eliminating both armed and unarmed opposition was a presidential coordinating committee for high-level security meetings set up by the CIA with Castillo Armas after the U.S.-financed 1954 coup, and included the defense minister, heads of the police forces, and the President himself. A black list of 70,000 suspects, compiled by thousands of *comisionados militares* appointed for the primary duty of "identifying and apprehending" suspected communists (i.e., supporters of the Arévalo-Arbenz regimes) (Sereseres 1978: 185) was used and constantly supplemented for targeted assassinations well into the 1970s (McClintock 1985: 32–34; Black 1985: 31). During the time of President Ydígoras (1958–63) and after the Cuban Revolution, files began to be systematically kept on opponents: "Papers began to arrive [in army intelligence headquarters] on Nicaraguans who were collaborating with Guatemalans to depose Ydígoras, or on Guatemalans who went to El Salvador and later to Nicaragua to depose Somoza. So we began to keep a file on *oponentes castristas* [Castroites]. And thus began the vigilance and all that against the opponents—in this case, they were defined as communists, the number one item on the U.S. agenda, not on the Guatemalan agenda. But the U.S. advisors we had gave us the money to set all this up" (Gramajo, interview).

It was under the government of Colonel Enrique Peralta Azurdia (1963–66) that a central coordination communications and intelligence hub was officially established linking the National Police, the Detective Corps, the Treasury Guard, local army commands, and the presidential staff at the National Palace and placing them under the specific guidance of U.S. advisors (McClintock 1985: 70–74). In August 1964, Peralta also created a Presidential Intelligence Agency, based in the Casa Presidencial, under which a Centro Regional de Telecommunicaciones (or La Regional) operated using a VHF-FM intracity frequency to link the National Police, Treasury Guard, Detective Corps, Government Ministry, the Presidential House, and the Military Communications Center. La Regional, with money from U.S. advisors, also served as a depository for information on activists for purposes of political abduction and assassination.

By June 1965, in reaction to urban guerrilla assaults, a special counter guerrilla rapid deployment force (Comando Seis) had been created within the National Police to deal with "emergencies," its special training provided by the U.S. Public Safety Program. It was reportedly the most brutal of the police's specialty squads (McClintock 1985: 80–83). One of the changes made in intelligence with the inauguration of civilian President Méndez Montenegro (1966–70) was to shift the Presidential Intelligence Agency (which had controlled La Regional) next door to the Presidential Guard Annex within the National Palace complex under the control of the Defense Ministry and the Army General Staff, and to change its name to the Guatemalan National Security Service (Servicio de Seguridad Nacional de Guatemala). It remained the nerve center for coordinating counterterror assassination operations by security forces, as well as for staying in touch with the U.S. Southern Command, Honduras, and El Salvador. Under the subsequent military regimes, "unofficial" paramilitary groups, first used in the 1966 counterinsurgent Plan Zacapa campaign (Sereseres 1978: 188–89), became the instruments by which to spread terror and violence throughout Guatemala. The police forces as well as G-2 reported directly to the Defense Ministry; the office of the Attorney General (Ministro de Gobernacion), upon which they administratively depended, had neither the power nor the control over either official or unofficial security forces. Thus, La Regional, operating through its own Policía Regional, whether controlled by the presidential office or the Army General Staff, has been associated since at least 1966 — a period when forced disappearance began to be utilized as regular policy[5] — with government death squads and thousands upon thousands of killings. With the 1970 election of the MLN-military coalition government of Colonel Arana Osorio, who had "much authority as he had just won the *foquista* war" in Zacapa, stated one intelligence colonel, La Regional served as a security command center, to coordinate "a covert program of selective assassination" (McClintock 1985: 170). Under his administration, political violence by "special commandos," of the military and a Fourth Corps unit of the National Police "acted under government control but outside the judicial process" (Sereseres 1978: 189) to abduct, torture during interrogation, and extrajudicially execute thousands within a "very efficient policy of terror" (Rosada Granados 1992: 3). According to one EMP chief, this was the beginning of an epoch of "good intragroup relations and the most successful in combating urban insurgency" (Colonel Otto Pérez Molina, *Crónica*, 20 August 1993: 19–22). Under General Kjell Laugerud, La Regional continued to be used for elimination purposes.

Throughout this period (since 1954), security remained under the control of the Army General Staff and tightly connected to the extreme-right *latifundistas* of the private sector: "With the rise of the insurgency in 1960, this alliance drew even closer together, such that between 1970 and 1978, they were almost one and the same. In those days, there was a knot so tight that you couldn't distinguish between the military hierarchy, the political leaders and the government officials" (Gramajo in Schirmer 1991: 13).

Executive involvement in political repression reached new heights during President-General Lucas García's regime (1978–82) in close coordination with Colonel Montalván Batres, Chief of the newly established Estado Mayor

Presidencial (EMP), Interior Minister Donaldo Alvarez Ruíz, and G-2 Army Colonel Germán Chupina in charge of the National Police. Meetings of this group, referred to as CRIO (Centro de Reunión de Información y Operaciones), were held to draw up hit lists for its Comandante Especial to carry out death squad killings out of the large Guardia Presidencial annex one block from the rear of the National Palace. Gramajo recounts:

There would be a meeting, at which [President] Lucas would sit with the Interior Minister, the Chief of Police, the Chief of G-2, the Chief of the Office of Presidential Security, the Chief of the Treasury Guard, and the Chief of Migration. That's what was called CRIO.
Q: A meeting for what purpose?
To make policy regarding security. I don't know, analysis for coordination.
Q: To draw up a list of people to kill?
Perhaps. Lucas would give his direct orders [to kill], and Alvarez was very important in this activity. (interview)

The Presidential Office under Lucas and Montalván "did everything" regarding control of intelligence and army and police operations, working in tandem with the security forces and lower-level G-2 officers in planning and providing the manpower to carry out assassinations of leaders of the popular movement and of political parties,[6] and thousands of others accused of forming part of the revolutionary movement. Although several officers, including Gramajo, state unequivocally that Lucas was directly "in control" of the EMP, ordering the political killings, they nonetheless emphasize that "the civilians like Donaldo Alvarez" and the death squads were responsible for carrying out "the politically motivated assassinations in [Guatemala] City. The armed forces were certainly part of the operations in the highlands, with Lucas personally overseeing tactical maneuvers, but the army did not have a monopoly on the use of force [in the city]." The armed forces, they insist, are blamed only "because Lucas was a general" (interviews).[7] In fact, this shift away from the Army General Staff to the Presidential Office and security forces, it is argued, was "to be able to assassinate without having to depend upon the army," as one source close to military intelligence put it (interview). The modus operandi of CRIO under Lucas was to use the police for low-level killings. Because of a Presidential order in early 1981 that all Army garrisons in the city were to develop a procedure to speed up troop deployment to certain locations, the Presidential Office also controlled G-2 garrison chiefs who, in turn, controlled troops for CRIO's rapid deployment force operations in the city in 1981–82. Requests were thus made for G-2 *confidenciales* from army outposts to come into the city for higher level targets of assassination. Surveillance would often be conducted by one unit and murder assigned to another (G-2 operative, interview; McClintock 1985: 172–77; Amnesty International 1981) (see Figure 15).

Hence, with Colonel Montalván Batres the key player under Lucas, the

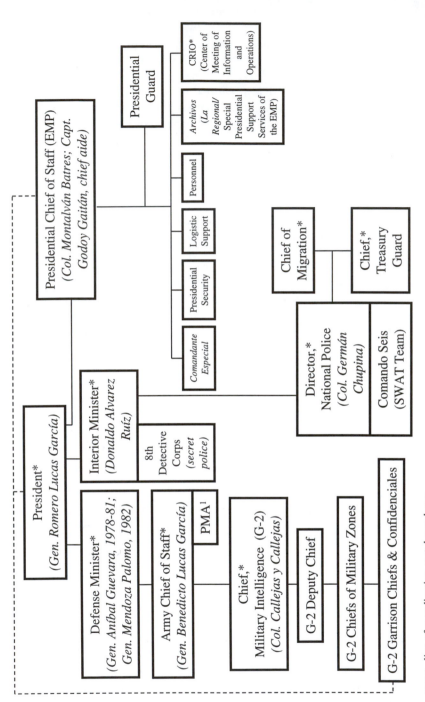

Figure 15. Military intelligence structures during General Lucas García regime, 1978–82.

---- line of coordination, not dependency
* members of CRIO
[1] Officers disagreed as to whether the PMA was under the control of Chupina

President*
(Gen. Romero Lucas García)

Presidential Chief of Staff (EMP)*
(Col. Montalván Batres; Capt. Godoy Gaitán, chief aide)

Presidential Guard

Comandante Especial

Presidential Security

Logistic Support

Personnel

Archivos (La Regional/ Special Presidential Support Services of the EMP)

CRIO* (Center of Meeting of Information and Operations)

Interior Minister*
(Donaldo Alvarez Ruiz)

8th Detective Corps (secret police)

Director,* National Police
(Col. Germán Chupina)

Comando Seis (SWAT Team)

Chief of Migration*

Chief,* Treasury Guard

Defense Minister*
(Gen. Anibal Guevara, 1978-81; Gen. Mendoza Palomo, 1982)

Army Chief of Staff*
(Gen. Benedicto Lucas García)

PMA[1]

Chief,* Military Intelligence (G-2)
(Col. Callejas y Callejas)

G-2 Deputy Chief

G-2 Chiefs of Military Zones

G-2 Garrison Chiefs & Confidenciales

Presidential Office "had control of every intelligence effort in the country and intelligence operations within the city." The exception was the MLN. In 1978 Lucas fired the MLN's Finance Minister and the MLN lost the elections; it responded by blowing up 29 Mobile Military Police — what Gramajo refers to as "MLN terrorism against the Army." The tight MLN-Army alliance would be permanently damaged (interview, Schirmer 1991: 13) (see Figures 16 and 17).

Faced with an "urban side to an insurgency" during a partial cutoff of military aid from what the *luquistas* referred to as the "Jimmy Castro" administration in 1977, one former G-2 administration officer relates:

We turned to countries such as Argentina and Uruguay which had had large problems with subversion [in the mid-to late 1970s], and we turned to Colombia for military intelligence. With these countries' aid, we developed our own countersubversive intelligence, and we saw a total turnaround in [our] concepts of managing [guerrilla] war intelligence. (Major Díaz López, interview)

According to Gramajo, "Those who trained us a lot in intelligence were the Argentines" (interview).[8] Part of this new "management" included the monitoring of water and electricity usage of suspect houses in Guatemala City since at least 1980 by an Israeli computer system located within the EMP in the annex behind the National Palace.[9] This system was teamed with a sophisticated Argentine computer network analysis developed during the "dirty war." It could zero in on buildings with high electricity and water bills or overnight electrical or water surges, where it was assumed clandestine meetings were taking place or an illegal printing press was in operation, and provide addresses. Aided by this technology, army troops were mobilized quickly "to encircle whole zones to search houses, especially in zones 15, 14, 6, and 5, to carry out arrests and everything . . . just by a call over the [police] radio or a key word [on the telephone]" (Gramajo, interview). Six months of "infiltration, including of groups in Washington," of using informants and collaborators and then surveillance, of capture and torture of suspected key figures (*personajes*) and uncovering guerrilla cells (*focos*), such as several Jesuit priests considered "responsible for the national EGP," meant that some thirty guerrilla (primarily ORPA) safe houses and arms caches in Guatemala City were raided in the summer of 1981, effectively destroying an extensive guerrilla urban network (G-2 colonel, interview). In one case, an urban guerrilla cell was operating out of the same rooming house where one colonel lived, and they would pass and greet each other daily; in another, a sports coach within the Escuela Politécnica "turned out to be a *jefe* of an EGP urban commando," according to two G-2 officers (interview).

It is obvious that military intelligence is one of the most important protagonists in the internal armed confrontation with the guerrilla; our efforts meant a loss of

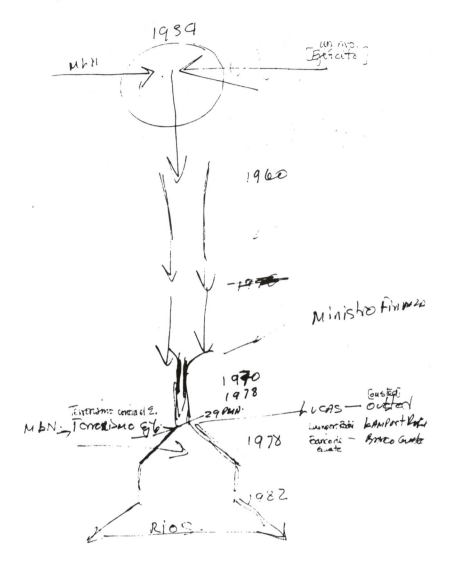

Figure 16. General Gramajo's sketch: MLN–Army relations, 1954–82.

important structures for the guerrilla first at the urban level and later in the high-lands. Because of our efforts, we knew which was the Ho Chi Minh Front, the Indo-china Region, the Saigon Region — all of that terminology was part of their organiza-tional structure, and all of it was anonymous. With infiltrators, informants, and the capture of important people, we learned how to decipher messages and discover caches. These Jesuits, like Pellecer, did not believe [in God]; they were an ideological movement. (G-2 colonel, interview)[10]

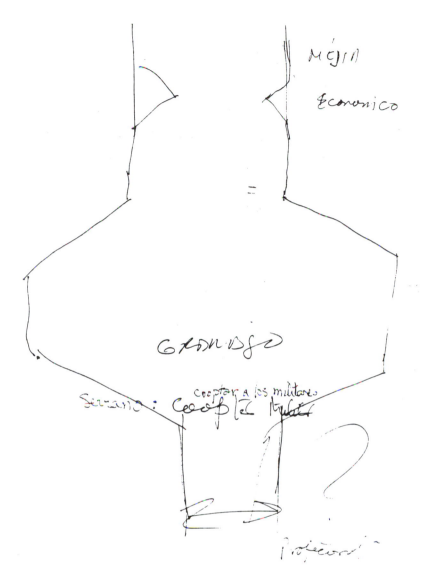

Figure 17. General Gramajo's sketch continued: MLN-Army relations, 1983–90.

These summer raids in 1981 allowed the G-2 to track the insurgency back to Chimaltenango by September. Xibalbá, a Kaibil unit led by Lieutenant Héctor Mauricio López Bonilla (one of the *oficiales jóvenes* of the 1982 coup), simulated, infiltrated, and "neutralized" a 28-man EGP unit of the Augusto César Sandino Front in the area. López Bonilla apparently "persuaded" several *guerrilleros* to collaborate on arms caches throughout the *altiplano*—what he refers to as tactical smarts (interviews). "But the infiltration lasted only 8 hours, at which time, all 28 EGP *guerrilleros* were eliminated" (anonymous officer, interview). Army Chief of Staff General Benedicto Lucas initiated the counterinsurgency campaign in Chimaltenango on 1 October 1981. By the second half of 1981, "with the discovery of the arms caches and the social uprising in the *barrios*," CRIO began to coordinate all intelligence and security forces for more flexible and efficient counterinsurgency operations both in the city and the highlands (Gramajo 1995: 163).

Under the direct orders of President Lucas, the Presidential Office had control over every intelligence effort in the country, including troops via G-2 garrison chiefs (without the garrison commanders or the G-2 chiefs of military zones). These garrison chiefs were able to bypass the hierarchy of the army "to organize the coup d'état against themselves, betraying the president" (Gramajo, interview w/o attribution). Thus, while this system was effective in destroying the guerrilla infrastructure in the city and managed to claim an estimated 35,000 victims throughout the country, it (together with the naked corruption) ironically hastened the deterioration of G-2 discipline and military procedures, which, in turn, helped the 1982 coup leaders (many of whom were G-2 subordinates) topple the Lucas regime.

III. Army Intelligence and *El Proyecto Político-Militar*

Under the Ríos Montt regime, there was an attempt to rein in the corruption of the Lucas regime in which at least "110 officers [were] involved" (Sereseres, interview). In addition, the operational autonomy of the G-2 and paramilitary forces of La Regional (Office of Special Presidential Services/CRIO) and the National Police all needed to be brought under control. Because G-2 officers who had staged the coup moved up into the upper ranks of government, "leaving novices to run Army intelligence," Colonel Gramajo, newly appointed Army Deputy Chief of Staff and Army Inspector General, stepped into this vacuum as "de facto G-2 chief between the 1982 and 1983 coups" (interview). For Gramajo the autonomy of the Intelligence sector was "the first real problem we *jefes* of the National Plan had to face: because of G-2's [extremist] views, we had to control this sector. We reorganized the security forces but this was hidden, secret, and not very effective. . . . The Guatemalan army was changing very slowly" (interview). In fact, intelligence changed little between 1982 and 1986. Some of Lucas's inner circle were exiled as military attachés; others were made *disponible* (unassigned with partial salary). Army hierarchy and discipline were reasserted by decreeing a new Organic Law of the Military dealing with promotion, retirement, and the need to step down from one's position if one assumed public office. "That way, one is able institutionally to control people who are internally disruptive" (Sereseres, interview).

By the end of the first month, the Eighth Detective Corps (Octavo Cuerpo de Detectives), formerly the *judiciales*, or simply the secret police, of the National Police, infamous for torturous interrogations and killings and referred to by the junta as "the main factor of repression," was investigated. Many detectives were accused of criminal activity and forced to resign. The Corps was disbanded and replaced with the DIT, (Departamento de Investigaciones Técnicas), which within a year was again being purged of several high-ranking officers (Keefe 1984: 202). The secret Special Tribunals set up 1 July 1982, were justified by several civilian and military sources, including Ríos Montt, as an attempt not only to control "the subversives" but also to "clean the house" (*limpiar la casa*) of corruption (interview). Five "psychopathic *especialistas*" from La Regional (two of whom were soldiers) who had preyed on the well-to-do were convicted of "violent immoral abuse" and executed by firing squad on the first anniversary of the coup with other Special Tribunal prisoners at the main cemetery in Guatemala City (intelligence analyst, interview; Gramajo 1995: 204). Some of the junior officers who staged the 1982 coup were later sent abroad "to maintain the army's institutionality" (Gramajo, interview).

With the Army General Staff working out a new counterinsurgency strategy, all security forces became tightly coordinated through G-2 garrison chiefs and G-2 officers in charge of police forces to conduct more flexible (rapid response) and efficient antisubversive operations in the city as well as in the highlands. A Special Operations Brigade (BROE), trained by reportedly two hundred Israeli military experts (ACEN-SIAG, 30 April 1984: 15), and armed with $750,000 worth of police arms and equipment (Barry et al. 1983: 73), was to serve as both a SWAT (special weapons attack team) in the city and to work with lightly armed rapid-strike forces in the countryside. Commanded by an army major, the BROE was tightly connected with the counterinsurgency plans of the Army General Staff. Additionally, the Mobile Military Police (Policía Militar Ambulante, PMA), reportedly under the command of National Police chief Colonel Chupina, after the coup was placed under the command of the founder of the special forces–trained Kaibils, Colonel Nuíla Hub, to serve as a kamikaze militarized police strike force also under the direction of the Army General Staff. By 1983, its size was estimated to be 3000 officers and men. Both the BROE and PMA effectively duplicated CRIO's rapid reaction force under Lucas, yet exemplified the new Army General Staff's tightly coordinated web of intelligence gathering and operations against "opponents" both in the city and in the countryside.[11] Gramajo's "returning things to normal" meant better coordination and control of G-2 and police operations dedicated to surveillance, abduction, and killing, with security forces operating under serial states of siege

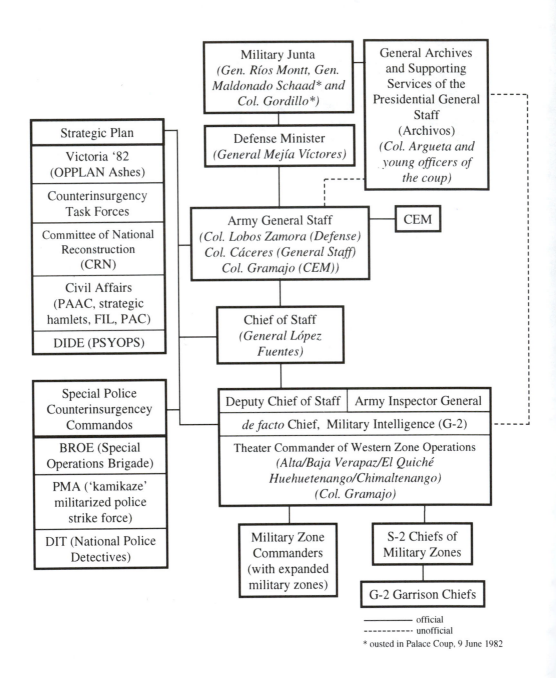

Figure 18. Army structures after March 1982 coup.

and alarm with the power of arrest, and of holding victims without bringing charges or permitting writs of habeas corpus to be filed on their behalf. It was a web from which very few escaped with their lives (see Figure 18).

"CRIO was an army-controlled organism," stated a former G-2 administrator, "which acted efficiently against subversion and common delinquency. Seeing a problem in whatever part of [Guatemala] City, CRIO mobilized police or military units and they quickly eliminated the problem" (Major Díaz López, interview).

The difference under Ríos Montt was that, instead of La Regional, the Army General Staff was in control of the newly technologized and professionalized paramilitary and military forces. Professionalization of this context meant that bodies would no longer be dumped on the streets. There would be "no more dead bodies on the roadsides" announced Ríos Montt in his television address the first week of April (McClintock 1985: 230). One eleven-year G-2 veteran, transferred after two to six months (as are many G-2 *especialistas*) to yet another army garrison for protection after a spate of assassinations (while his commanding officer would "lie to the victims' families telling them that I had been either jailed or killed") describes what the change of the High Command meant in terms of G-2's operations:

"With Ríos Montt, they changed our name from G-2 to S-2. Then the High Command gave us the order to no longer assassinate people in plain view, or leave the bodies on the streets. Rather, they had to be killed at a military base without alarming people. And, we had to bury the bodies precisely without people taking notice. Whereas, under Lucas, we would leave four here, another four there. Up to twenty. Along one fifteen-kilometer stretch of the highway, between towns, you would find twenty cadavers." There is no doubt, he added, that "G-2 is *un escuadrón de la muerte* (a death squad) . . . that only exists to kill." (interview)

After the March 1982 coup, the name of La Regional was changed to General Archives and Supporting Services of the Presidential General Staff, Archivos Generales y Servicios Apoyados del Estado Mayor Presidencial — AGSAEMP — EMP for short. Archive and computer files would continue to be kept on students, political activists and leaders, human rights activists, journalists, trade unionists, among others. Under the directorship of G-2 Colonel Victor Manuel Argueta Villalta,[12] the leaders of the 1982 young officers' coup, worked, irregularly, with the Army General Staff and G-2, directing its intelligence toward "affairs of State" and political "opponents of the government," and, in general, creating frictions with the more senior officers (Gramajo, interview).

Additionally, as part of the army's Department of Culture and Public Relations (Decree-Law 78-82) and psychological warfare strategy, a new Directorate of Information and Dissemination of the Army (DIDE) was established to disseminate material on the army's counterinsurgency war by way of pamphlets and its own television and radio stations. Directly under the supervision of the Army General Staff at the time (later moved under the Defense Ministry), DIDE worked closely with Civil Affairs in conducting psychological warfare, collecting intelligence, and "doing analysis on Opponents of the State" (Gramajo, interview).

In 1983 Ríos Montt was replaced by the *ultraderechista* General Mejía Víctores (who had served as Ríos's Defense Minister), who, when asked in a 1990 interview, "When will subversion end?" responded, "When there are no longer any communists" (interview). Mejía "tried to bring the MLN and the Army back together between 1983 and 1986" (Gramajo, interview) by reincarnating CRIO's weekly meetings of G-2 and Army General Staff personnel for elimination purposes, but the MLN-Army intelligence network gap was apparently beyond repair (see Figure 16). Nevertheless "the killings continued, the same tactics used" under Mejía (G-2 operative, interview), including orders from G-2 to the Chief of the National Police Detectives to "cleanse" two leaders of the Group of Mutual Support. Their investigation of disappeared relatives was "getting too close," explained the *especialista*. "I am an *elemento* of the government and I am seen abducting someone, and a GAM member later recognizes me and shouts out, 'He's the one! He's the one!' Well, that person, very prudently, very cautiously, must be eliminated.[13] The disappeared, you see, including [those relatives of] GAM, are individuals who have been assassinated and buried and they will never find the graves. That is the secret of the G-2, the *judiciales* or whatever other institution that kills people" (interview). The practices of surveillance, "investigation," abduction, torture, and assassination continue to be carried out by El Archivo and G-2 in clandestine cells on military bases, in basements and subbasements of the National Police headquarters, and when these were sealed off, in private houses. Bodies of victims have been thrown from helicopters into lakes or the sea, or buried in mass graves on the premises as well as outside of military garrisons.

Overseen by the newly titled National Defense Staff and, ultimately, General Mejía, killing Opponents of the State was meant to "prepare the environment" for the electoral *apertura* in 1984 and 1985. By May 1985, officers in charge of the communications center, GUATEL (National Telecommunications Center) and INDE (National Institute of Electrification) were replaced with civilians as a demilitarization on a public level took place, although officers still hold many of the second and third deputy positions. At this time, General Gramajo was one of Mejía's top advisers, along with EMP chief and special forces Colonel Pablo Nuíla,[14] Foreign Minister Andrade, and Colonel-lawyer Girón Tánchez. While Andrade was traveling to Costa Rica to persuade political exiles to return to Guatemala to participate in the upcoming legislative elections and to the United Nations to try to change the army's image internationally, and Girón Tánchez was writing decree-laws to immerse counterinsurgency structures within the state, Gramajo served unofficially as Mejía's "liaison man" with "the U.S. Army and the U.S. Embassy," continuing the G-2's longstanding collaboration with AID, the CIA, DIA, and MILGroup in the U.S. Embassy (Gramajo, interview). Although there was "little training [of officers], only map grants" (Sereseres, interview) between 1977 and 1982,[15] an estimated $35 million in indirect or covert military aid flowed to Guatemala (cf. Schoultz 1987; McClintock 1985). Another $30 million of CIA covert assistance also became available to the Guatemalan military after 1983, and especially after 1985. As one source close to army intelligence explained, "The CIA has been working in Guatemala all along, so this kind of intervention is not that unusual" (1990 interview).

With the election of President Cerezo in 1986, Gramajo's efforts, first as Chief of the National Defense Staff and then as Defense Minister in late 1986, to co-opt, centralize, and professionalize G-2 were expanded with the support of President Cerezo, "who was like a baby with intelligence matters. . . . As Chief of the National Defense Staff, it was my duty to control La Dos. I told [Cerezo], 'I am going to support Intelligence, penetrate Intelligence.'" He proceeded to select his inner circle on the basis of fraternal relations, personal loyalties, and experience in *luquista* G-2 and *aranista* La Regional offices — a tactic he also used in having Cerezo appoint rightwing General Jaime Hernández Defense Minister (who was then ready to retire) for the first six months of his regime to neutralize the *mano dura* (hardline) faction of the army panicked by Cerezo's presidency. He chose *luquista* G-2 *Jefe* (1980–82) Colonel Manuel Callejas y Callejas to be Deputy Chief of the National Defense Staff (to whom the G-2 chief must report directly),[16] Colonel Ortega Menaldo (who also served as a captain in Arana's La Regional) to be deputy G-2 chief (and later G-2 chief), and Captain Edgar Augusto Godoy Gaitán, La Regional Montalván's chief aide, to be director of the Estado Mayor Presidencial. As a veteran G-2 officer who had "brought psychological warfare to Guatemala," the necessity for intelligence was for him without question: "I realized that we had to continue the intelligence effort [under the civilian regime]. It was very risky, but we had to do it" (Gramajo, interview) — "risky" in the sense that while he was perfectly aware that G-2 had served for forty years as the violent answer to any form of dissent in Guatemala, Gramajo chose to reform the institution from within, selecting officers from the G-2 *cofradía* who were deeply implicated in G-2's most violent and repressive episodes. From his own perspective, he believed that in order to make changes within G-2, he had to co-opt the more extremist members of G-2 to support *el proyecto político-militar* and thereby strengthen his own position as Defense Minister:

I mean, they are powerful and we have to use that power. . . . They all knew what they had to do and I told them, "We are going to change everything." So we began by giving a course with the theme to penetrate, not eliminate, but you cannot stop thinking about your work: penetrate, discredit, buy off, but don't kill because this, in the end, doesn't pay. As in Cuba, they send some to Siberia, eliminating some but killing fewer exiles with the exception of those who abandon the country for political persecution. . . . And if they kill, they kill with justice, isn't that so? In Cuba, there are no *desaparecidos*.

By quietly observing Cuban tactics and intelligence "in action" in the field in the Angolan war with the assistance of the South African military between 1982 and 1990,[17] Gramajo and his collaborators were slowly training the G-2 in counterinsurgency/countersubversion analysis and operations, utilizing "minimum force" or more selective persuasion and elimination tactics "so they [the international community] cannot say then that you are using force" (interview). "Reform" in this context means continued abduction, imprisonment, and torturous interrogation in secret cells in order to create a network of informants released back into society; those who do not cooperate are killed (a practice utilized with former *guerrilleros* and Civil Patrollers in the highlands after the 1981–83 massacre campaigns). The difference between this approach and that of the past, as former President Cerezo explained it, is that "we have the thesis that a guy who knows a person who is involved with the *guerrilla* must be watched, must be taken prisoner, or phoned to speak to in order to convince him to cooperate with us, or stop cooperating with the guerrilla, while another local [G-2] officer can believe that it is much easier to just eliminate [that person]" (interview). Interrogation sessions shifted to depend more on psychological measures (e.g., threats against family) and cooperation (show us where your *compañeros* and safe houses are) to elicit as much information as possible. And if victims are killed, they are killed for refusing to stop cooperating with the guerrilla. They were warned, they refused, and thus were "killed with justice." Gramajo chose to maintain the military hierarchy, even giving some "hardline" officers representation in order to keep them from mobilizing against the project's agenda, while he slowly attempted to change the balance of forces within G-2.

Gramajo and the CIA

The trump card that Gramajo could play that marked him as autonomous from the G-2 but dependent on the United States, was his "good relations with the CIA," whom he turned to as part of this "penetration" of La Dos. Gramajo called upon the CIA station chiefs throughout the 1980s[18] to help "reorient the methodology of the G-2. The CIA brought in people for intelligence training" for "more modernized intelligence methods and analysis," Gramajo explains. "We wanted a more professional intelligence effort that would not harm the country's international image" (interview). This was nothing new; covert technical assistance and aid had been provided since 1983, if not continuously throughout the 1960s and 1970s. It included computers, communications gear, and special firearms, as well as collaborative use of CIA-owned helicopters flown out of La Aurora airport and from a separate U.S. air facility (Nairn 1995a). Gramajo's "friends at the CIA" also provided "something like $50,000, a great amount of money just for special PSYOPS equipment, [such as] movie projectors" for S-5 matters (interview).[19] As we have seen, the salaries of G-2 *especialistas* doubled from Q250/month to Q500/month during this period. "I said I wanted efficiency and quick movements from them [G-2 *especialistas*]," Gramajo explains. "So, I provided good cars for investigations. I didn't want them to do bad things for lack of funds [i.e., killing for hire]. This was a way to co-opt them. So, the G-2 personnel began to say how Gramajo was very interested in intelligence with all this training. I did not treat them poorly because they are very useful" (interview).

Additionally, "civil materiel assistance" for the counterinsurgency war was flown in by what Gramajo referred to alternatively as "an American NGO," "the collaborators," the "air commandos," the "Phantom Division" ("a group of retired CIA officers living mostly in the Washington area"),[20] and "my friends at the CIA," supplying the Guatemalan army with medical equipment and aid, compasses, walkie-talkies, and Vietnam-era metal jeep parts for the army's munitions factory, among other things (interview). As one lower-level G-2 *especialista* stated ruefully, "Only the big shots went to the CIA (*A la CIA iban solo gente grande*)" (interview). This request from the CIA was par for the course, given its long and apparently uninterrupted history of aid, training, and direct intervention in Guatemala. When asked to briefly describe the structures of intelligence in Guatemala for the last thirty years, one D-2 director stated, "It's quite simple and I won't deny it: between the 1960s and 1990s, we had a structure from the CIA. The money, the resources, the training, and the relations were all from and through the CIA. Later in the 1990s, this was supplemented with the DEA. This was the case because our intelligence, in the end, has had to serve the interests of the U.S." (Navy Captain Julio Alberto Yon Rivera, 1996 interview).

Exemplary of this close G-2–CIA relationship stands a modern glass-and-concrete structure with an antennae-bedecked roof: a fully equipped intelligence school, inaugurated in 1987, at a tightly guarded, high-walled compound next to the runway at La Aurora Military Base in Guatemala City. "It is an installed capacity with all the technology [necessary] for [the G-2's] education," Gramajo boasts. In the fountained entrance are two plaques, he continues, "with the name of Gramajo and another saying that the resources for the school came from the CIA" (interview).[21] In return, the G-2 "saved" the Gramajo-Cerezo project from coup attempts staged primarily by *ultraderechista* G-2 officers and civilians who expected Gramajo to support the first coup against Cerezo.

As Defense Minister in early 1987, Gramajo also used Q20,000 of his Q30,000 discretionary funds to "make from them [the G-2] my own group, or not my own group, but at the least, I was [working] with them. [I was] very accessible and supportive of them [as Defense Minister]. Quite a lot of support, more buildings, more equipment, more of everything. Other elite groups are the paratroopers and the Kaibils. I also supported them. So that no one can say that the elite groups are not any good . . . I presented them with medals; we glorified them in speeches" to begin to create a new culture. "They were the first to understand the new attitude." Other officers were "very radical in their views. . . . We put two in jail, and another left the country, and the terrorist acts of throwing hand grenades into marketplaces stopped" (interview w/o attribution). Since at least 1988, some of the more hardline officers have been sent to Taiwan's two-month courses in political warfare: "It is the ideal place to train Guatemalan officers. While the old man Chiang [Kai-chek] kept saying that the mainland was bad, now they are our brothers! Now Taiwan speaks of democracy, freedoms, and political party organizing" (Gramajo, interview).[22]

Yet another aspect of this reinstitutionalization for a reformed and "more professional" intelligence service included training *suboficiales*, who previously were drafted into G-2 at a low salary and allowed to seek extra income moonlighting for *latifundistas* and businessmen. Recently, with the *ascenso de los cabos* (promotion of the corporals) these *sargentos mayores especialistas* have played a central role in implementing the G-2's and EMP's "reforms"; they have also since become publicly implicated in human rights violations (see note 28).

While concerned with co-opting the G-2 hardliners into the *proyecto político-militar*, Gramajo was at the same time grooming and promoting his own "loyalists" to implement the new G-2 methodology and approach: "I was preoccupied with being a mentor to certain key people within Intelligence . . . knowing that the efficiency of leadership is to maintain a presence without being present. The majority of them worked for me directly because they were part of my staff. Officers selected from the ranks worked with me two years as aides in charge of my security, my comfort. They accompanied me to work, to my sports workout, everywhere. A type of on-the-job training. Now, all of them work either in Intelligence or in academia." Officers of Gramajo's *promoción* and the Flecha special forces platoon commanded by Gramajo in 1966 were often promoted over more hardline officers.[23]

However, these calculated risks at reforming the G-2 to a great extent failed in Gramajo's estimation:

Some members [of G-2] remain autonomous; they have retained their own personal style. So when there were [human rights] cases, one didn't react like this [he hits his fists together]; nor did one close up shop. One had to be a little flexible, treat them with [incentives]. They were *derechistas* who needed to refine themselves and who were not supporting *el proceso*. Our strategy was precisely to take advantage of them, provide them with more academic horizons, and now they are the ones who support *el proceso*. They saved us from two *golpes de estado* (coups d'état). They were the ones who discovered everything.

Nevertheless, with the dissolution of CRIO and the "kicking out of some of the Mano Blanca (White Hand) death squad types" (intelligence source, interview), Gramajo's order for troops to ignore the taunts of human rights groups (as for example at the 30 June 1987 Army Day parade when members of GAM spit upon troops, yelling "*asesinos!*") raised the ire of *derechista* officers, including the Retired Officers Association. They demanded of Defense Minister Gramajo that "something be done!" But the "Cuban methodology" countersubversion course given to G-2 officers at the Center for Military Studies with the assistance of the CIA in early 1987 was the last straw: a group of colonels and majors staged a mini-revolt. This led to the expulsion of many of these officers from the army by Gramajo, who by reputation was unable to tolerate opposition. One of these officers was Major Díaz López, a G-2 administration officer who would become one of the leaders of the 1988 and 1989 coup attempts: "When Cerezo entered [the presidency], he destroyed CRIO! That was one of the things that made the army angry because they [the Christian Democrats] gave full rein to the subversion. Nevertheless, little by little, there arose such a dangerous situation for them: both common and subversive delinquency make people very angry. And SIPROCI—not a paramilitary organism but a coordinating organism—was created" (interview). We first need to examine the other part of the intelligence web; SIPROCI will be discussed in the next chapter.

The EMP and El Archivo

The Presidential General Staff, Estado Mayor Presidencial (EMP), which includes El Archivo or the Department of Presidential Security (DSP) under the direction of the EMP Chief, began to serve as "an independent place to handle affairs of state" after the March 1982 coup, but most especially during the civilian presidencies of Cerezo and Serrano (Gramajo, interview). While Gramajo was "reforming" the G-2, he and Cerezo set out to establish a civil-military *coyuntura* (joint effort) to more faithfully reflect the concerns of *el proyecto politico-militar*, especially the need to prepare the armed forces for political battles ahead over human rights. Because of his "fascination" with intelligence, Cerezo wanted to be kept informed by the G-2, and the EMP was set up for him by G-2 in the Casa Presidencial to serve as "the eyes and ears of the President." He had access to copies of all G-2's intelligence files and kept in touch with Gramajo about individual human rights cases.

The EMP is divided into five sections (see Figure 19): Analysis, International Intelligence, Technical Intelligence, Counterintelligence, and the Department of Presidential Security (DSP) within which operates a Comandante Especial. Only the DSP operates directly out of the Casa Presidencial; the others work from the Presidential Annex. Thirty percent of the 530-member staff at the EMP are army intelligence (G-2) *especialistas* who hold "the key positions. The major part of the structure of control within the

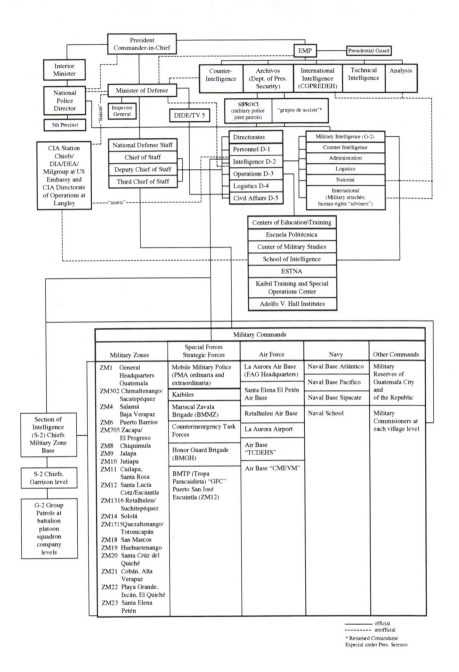

Figure 19. Structure of military and civilian intelligence during Cerezo-Gramajo Cúpula, 1986–90.

EMP is military," Gramajo admitted (interview). The other 70 percent include 300 civilians within the EMP. To estimate the number of agents operating outside "the plant," multiply this 300 by "almost 4" (*Crónica*, 20 August 1993: 19–22) or "up to 8," according to one intelligence source, for a total of between 1200 and 2400 agents. "These are mostly civilian agents drawing from the presidential funds but with no power to make arrests" (Gramajo, interview). Replicating the hierarchical structure of an S-2/G-2 unit with its investigative sections, EMP *especialistas* work their gang networks of informants (*orejas*) in the city for information on the social movements in the barrios and infiltrate or "penetrate" human rights groups, such as the Human Rights Ombudsman's Office, the Catholic Church's Human Rights Office, and unions for information regarding strikes and demonstrations (National Police detective, interview).

Like La Dos, the EMP abducts, interrogates, and sometimes kills its victims. This task is assigned to the Comandante Especial with its "well-prepared" *sargentos mayores especiales*, who command "policelike" *patrullas* with special firearms and fast cars, as Major Díaz López explained in 1988:

The government has a civilian paramilitary organism with the capacity to intercept communications, such as local and long-distance telephone calls. It has included some actions of eliminating persons. It is an apparatus that the Christian Democrats created with the technical support from Germany and Venezuela. Two people are directors [of this apparatus]: Oscar Díaz Urquizú who got into a problem recently which has not been resolved,[24] and the other man goes by the name of Ramírez. When they tell people that in the next few days they are going to eliminate [individuals], they know there is the possibility they will do so, because [these] groups exist to limit the organized [movement] for the Christian Democratic Party, and they will act at whatever cost to do so.
Q: This civilian organism, what is it called?
It doesn't have a name. They don't call it anything but the Organism of Civilian Intelligence. But it is clandestine, which is to say we know about it only because there are testimonies [of its activities]. (interview)

Inteligencia Técnica conducts telephone, electronic, and agent surveillance as well as maintains files on passport registration and usage, drivers' licenses, car registrations, and tax files. It is in charge of investigations of government bureaucrats, politicians, journalists, trade unionists, human rights activists, student activists, and even military officers and EMP employees, such as chauffeurs, maids, and cooks. According to one source, many of the chauffeurs of the diplomatic corps are policemen (who were former soldiers), who each evening recount the day's events to a telephone number at El Archivo or the Guardia de Honor (the EMP Chief is also Chief of the Honor Guard). As such, El Archivo/DSP serves as a database on primarily political "opponents of the state." Thus, while G-2 followed "the guerrilla," the EMP was in charge of investigations of trade unionists, all political activists, and even military officers; both parts of the map have proved useful in charting the military's course in political and human rights waters. Under the civilian regimes of Cerezo and Serrano, the EMP had three "circles of control" under observation: the persons closest to the President, his cabinet and their aides, and politicians. It thus offered the presidents access to an enormous amount of public and private information about their political allies and enemies. "Working breakfasts, extramarital affairs, private conversations" are all part of the dossier "provided to the President. . . . The eyes and ears of the EMP aren't going to close" (*Crónica* 20 August 1993: 19). Because EMP analysts are the military's principal vehicle to maintain a high degree of influence over the president's view of and decisions about security issues, the position of the EMP Chief has become one of the most powerful as he controls the agenda of the president. In fact, several institutionalist officers who have served in that position, and have played public roles that identified them too closely with the civilian president, have found their careers ended at the rank of colonel, and have even received death threats from *derechista* G-2 officers. As one G-2 officer explained, "*Comandantes* don't like the *protagonismo* within the government that the EMP Chief enjoys. He has relations with the press, embassies, international organisms, and at times he must provide an opinion. This rubs the high-ranking *comandantes* the wrong way, envious that he is giving his opinions which possibly they think they should themselves be doing." At this point in the telephone conversation, the line was cut off, and on redial, the officer laughed, "Now they don't like what *I'm* saying over the telephone!" (interview).

In contrast to that of Technical Intelligence, the principal task of International Intelligence has been to deflect and neutralize domestic and international human rights criticism against the army, and together with the Analysis section, to research and analyze the economic, political, military, and social "factors of power." Gramajo explains that when "politically oriented NGOs" of human rights arrived in Guatemala, it was the army's strategy for Cerezo's Presidential Human Rights Commission (COPREDEH) in the EMP to deal with them. During the Cerezo regime, the strategy of the armed forces was "not to acknowledge provocation from human rights groups" such as GAM. "We were very draconian in sustaining the heat but we never talked about topics like the truth commission or trials for officers. It was the president's problem because he was a politician, and besides, he was chief of the armed forces." (President Cerezo, in turn, stated that he was not able to fulfill his role, given that he held no more than 30 percent of the power with no control over the armed forces as agreed upon in the 1985 accord made with the military before he assumed the presidency.)

COPREDEH would also "write a position paper on every topic [of human rights]. But remember," Gramajo reminds the listener, "COPREDEH had input from the armed forces, especially for the official position, especially to coordinate military efforts like providing logistics to Guatemalan representatives [going] to New York or to Geneva, to all of them. The Defense Minister signs [the position paper], the President, too. There are official positions for many things." As Defense Minister, Gramajo saw his task as "helping to develop [this] official position. So, to do this, I worked with the Interior and the Foreign Affairs Ministers. I worked with all of them to provide procedures to gain an official position [on human rights]. For instance, in Geneva, we were very sophisticated. The opposition said something about a case in Sololá and nobody was prepared for that, and they [our representatives] faxed us [a request for information] at 1 A.M. so we could start working on it. I had people to do that in Guatemala City but I myself would be up for that, and the very next day at 10 A.M. they would have an official position" (interview w/o attribution). COPREDEH worked hand-in-glove with the International Affairs Division of Military Intelligence to "counter" human rights criticisms.

One civilian who served as "a political advisor to the military on human rights" at COPREDEH explains: "What we do is educate officers to avoid speaking on the basis of the military's traditional scheme [of anticommunism]. . . . the position of advisor (*avisador*) is currently being created: they are people who reside in Geneva, Washington, the United Nations, to follow what human rights organizations are doing and what reports they are putting out. Here we are constantly revising our counterattacks. There is a lot of interesting work in capturing the strategies of [human rights] people in the international arena, what they are trying to accomplish, and to prevent this from damaging Guatemala" (interview).

Since 1989, COPREDEH has written all governmental human rights reports. The civilian regime, Gramajo would tell a retired officer in 1988, "has allowed the army to carry out much broader and more intensified operations because the legitimacy of the government, in contrast to the illegitimacy of the previous military governments, doesn't allow the insurgency to mobilize public opinion [against us] internationally—something which proved to be an obstacle [before] in fighting the guerrillas" (Cruz Salazar 1988a).

In this capacity then, the EMP serves as one of the spokes in the intelligence wheel, with all information coming to the President and/or the Defense Minister. Gramajo claims he did not "officially" have control of or full access to the EMP, which he knew was observing him and monitoring his telephone calls. He, in turn, "made friends and penetrated [the EMP]—that is normal espionage—so that I could know what they were thinking about at the presidential intelligence level. I assured them of my loyalty; I did not supervise or interfere with these guys. But I also realized I might be blocked by them. So I made a deal with them: you [EMP] work on the political things—we don't want to work on radicals, human rights activists, students, and so on—while the G-2 follows the insurgency" (interview). Nonetheless, this division of labor is rather disingenuous for two reasons:

(1) the armed forces consider many if not most of the political and human rights groups to be *grupos de fachada* for the guerrillas; and (2) the EMP competed with G-2 and DIDE to present the best and most complete biographical profiles and analyses of "political things" to the Defense Minister and the President. Gramajo explains,

G-2 worked for me, but it is connected with the EMP. They do and do not cooperate with each other. . . . Anything G-2 told the President, they would tell me, but only after they had told him. The G-2 would say, "Listen, the president wants to see me on Tuesday evening," and I would say, "Go ahead." So, on Wednesday, he would tell me that the president had directed him to do such and such. "Okay," I would say. But G-2 better not try to go around me! (interview w/o attribution)

Defense Minister Gramajo was very much in control with his flow charts and his cross-check procedures (see Figure 18):

If I wanted an update on the teachers' strike, I would ask the EMP and the DIDE (which was doing that kind of intelligence to find out the real thing without the EMP's influence). If I wanted an update on the ORPA situation, I would ask G-2, and then I would draw my conclusion. But I introduced DIDE and used it as my cross-check on EMP. [In this way], G-2 realized they didn't have a monopoly on me, so they had to improve their findings. I always told them, "Don't gather intelligence from the newspapers, please. Do intelligence gathering [on your own] because you have to separate the truth from the intelligence and you don't do that by reading the papers." They had to improve because they were competing with DIDE [for my attention]. (interview w/o attribution)

This intragroup coordination within the intelligence sector charted by Gramajo beginning in 1982 was intended to gain as much sophisticated intelligence on everything going on within the borders of Guatemala and beyond: affairs of state, political opponents of the government, and the insurgency. Thus, although admittedly antagonistic at times, relations between the G-2 and the Presidential Office "have always, always been close" one G-2 officer stated (interview). This does not mean there have not been turf battles within Intelligence that did not express themselves as human rights violations.

In the 1990s, under President Serrano (considered *ultraderechista*, by institutionalist officers), the EMP under the guidance of Colonel Ortega Menaldo was transformed into a bureaucratic entity unto itself, taking on many more surveillance tasks and repressive operations, including opening an office in the main post office to monitor letters addressed to political activists and politicians. When Ortega Menaldo moved from being Gramajo's "right-hand man" as G-2 Chief in the late 1980s ("He was very loyal to me, detecting the 1988 coup attempt") to being EMP Chief in January 1991 under the Serrano regime, he reportedly took along with him thirty G-2 officers with whom he had worked (most of them had been captains under Lucas). The EMP didn't report to G-2, and there was "a renewed decentralization of intelligence, each group with its own files and networks, completely distinct" (anonymous intelligence source, interview). Reporting only to President Serrano, Ortega Menaldo became "the most powerful man in Guatemala." El Archivo, with its own Comandante Especial for death squad killings, was reconstituted from the days of Ríos Montt and Mejía Víctores. With the self-coup of 25 May 1993, both Serrano and Ortega Menaldo were ousted, leaving an institutional vacuum. Appointed President Ramiro deLeón Carpio decided to dissolve Archivos in 1993. But far from getting rid of this head of the Medusa, like their predecessors had failed to get rid of the Special Tribunal sentences — it merely transferred the files to G-2's Directorate of Intelligence of the National Defense Staff (*Dirección de Inteligencia del Estado Mayor de la Defensa Nacional*). Both former President Serrano and EMP Chief Otto Pérez Molina under President deLeón Carpio have since stated paradoxically that it was not opportune to make the dossiers public "because the data contained therein are irrelevant" (*Crónica*, 20 August 1993: 22). The "civilian" Secretariat of Strategic Affairs (Secretaría de Asuntos Estratégicos) set up in 1995 and headed by economist José María Argueta, former ESTNA director, includes the Service of Civilian Intelligence and the Crisis Committee (Comité de Crisis), within the Casa Presidencial. This does not mean, however, the demise of La Dos; officers, such as military attaché General Roberto Letona Hora, make it clear that G-2 activities will continue while "we will not interfere with civilian intelligence" (1995 interview). In another interview, two intelligence colonels refer to G-2 as following the intelligence model used in Germany and the United States: "I've visited German intelligence headquarters, and when [their officers] are working for the government, they are separated from their military responsibilities; U.S. army intelligence officers are often 'loaned out' to the FBI and CIA. The civilian Ministry of Government in Guatemala has in the same way given some of its work directly to G-2, regarding investigations of kidnapping, for example" (interview).

G-2 and the Police

Corruption and incompetence remain widespread within the National Police, military officers readily point out in interviews. For these reasons, they explain, the DIT (Department of Technical Investigations) was dissolved in February 1986, and 100 detectives fired because of "multiple abuses of power" (they were not prosecuted, though, because of the amnesty law) (*Central America Report*, 7 February 1986: 35–36). They often fail to mention that the others cashiered from the DIT were merely reincorporated into the uniformed squads of the newly established DIC, Department of Criminal Investigations. Nor do they mention that most of the directors of the National Police over the past forty years have been military intelligence officers who work directly with G-2. In February 1988, for example, during the "white van" murders of students, the National Police director, who had twenty-five years of military intelligence service and was a close associate of Cerezo, Colonel Julio Enrique Caballeros Seigné, admitted he was "working jointly with army intelligence to solve the kidnapping and deaths" (*El Grá-fico*, 19 February 1988).[25] Even when competent police investigative units, trained by U.S. police officers and FBI agents through the U.S. Criminal In-vestigations Training Assistance Program (ICITAP), had been established, G-2 officers continued to serve as National Police and DIC directors—and continued to thwart politically sensitive investigations of abductions and killings. This ensures institutionalized impunity of the armed forces, includ-ing abuses by the police. One ICITAP-trained National Police detective states,

The G-2 always show up at a crime scene. They have a [police] radio. They are always there. You can recognize which of them is G-2 because they always carry either a .45 mm or a .9 mm [pistol]. They often wear sunglasses and dress in tennis clothes, but you can pick out their weapon under their belts. And they usually arrive on a bicycle or a motorbike.
Q: Is it possible they were responsible for these crimes?
It is more than just possible. Since the G-2 use only two calibers of weapon—a .45 or .9 mm—there is a lot of speculation within the National Police about this. Publicly, the spokesperson says we are not related to the army and that we are in charge of criminal investigations in Guatemala. But there are always two investigations going on simultaneously: that of the police and that of the G-2 watching the police. (1992 interview)

Politically sensitive investigations of killings of high-ranking figures, such as that of Danilo Barillas Rodríguez, leader of the Christian Democratic Party and close friend of President Cerezo[26] in front of his home on 1 Au-gust 1989, are usually blocked. A "special report" (in contrast to an "official report" for common crimes) is written for the unit's immediate police chief. This particular report contained the fact that two G-2 *especialistas* who had arrived by motorbike were already taking photos of the body before the police investigative unit arrived. It was determined that the caliber of the weapon was a .45 mm, and so forth. The detectives' *jefe* turned the report over to his boss until it reached the director, who then shared it with G-2, which had already filed its own internal report. "And that is where the investigation stops completely. In almost all cases of political killings, no instructions [to pursue our investigation] are forthcoming, and the case is effectively closed. We are first told to be extremely careful [in our investiga-tion] because it is a political killing and then we are told to do absolutely nothing. Do not question the neighbors. Do not try to find witnesses. Do nothing. Then we hear that the National Police spokesman has changed the terms of the case for the press, referring to it as 'common delinquency or robbery.' Then we know it is a dead case. Out of fear, one does not dare to challenge such orders" (interview).

In one interview Gramajo asserts that "military resources" are used in criminal, but not political, investigations. When asked to differentiate between the two, he states that a common criminal is "someone who robs a bank. We investigate that. A congressional deputy is killed, so it must be determined which it is [a criminal or political crime]. That is where the army doesn't get involved, only the police — except the police aren't very careful about this." He laments that given police and judicial incompetence, it is unfortunately necessary for the armed forces to intervene in investigative police work: "A well-organized country has a system in which the police prevent crime, the judge punishes the crime and the military have nothing to do with criminal investigation. But since the knowhow doesn't exist, then lamentably [the military] must do so. But this is not so bad given that the military institution is the most developed. The inefficiency of the judges obligates the military to get involved" (interview). In short, army intelligence does conduct its own criminal and political investigations.

Commenting on the first civilian police chief appointed for the first time in forty years, Gramajo is more forthright about the need for the police to work with the military: "On 31 May 1985, six months before [the inauguration in] January 1986, we threw everyone out of government. So much so that we left the National Police to a policeman and everything fell apart. He became so corrupt, losing proceedings and everything . . . that we had to replace him with a military officer [Colonel Caballeros]. That was our fault in leaving the functioning of the police [to the police] during this period" (interview). In another interview, he states, "It's going to take fifteen to twenty years for the new [civilian police] chief to stop relying on the military or on people with military backgrounds [e.g., retired officers who served as police chiefs] to investigate and prevent crimes."[27] Hence, Presidents' warnings since 1986 that the incompetent police would be taken over by the armed forces is a slight understatement (e.g., "President de León Carpio Called out Troops Against a Crime Wave," *Boston Globe*, 8 December 1995).

G-2 and Human Rights Violations as Internecine Battles of Intelligence

In interviews, both Gramajo and Cerezo have admitted that G-2 is responsible for "most of the killings" in Guatemala. Yet how much in control of G-2 did Gramajo deign to be? One source close to army intelligence stated that Gramajo "didn't want to know how, who, or where. He would be angry about the killings, but he did nothing about them. It was a way of protecting himself. And if the Defense Minister didn't know, the President knew even less" (anonymous source, interview). Yet, in order to "co-opt" G-2, Gramajo had to constantly prove his loyalty to the army and G-2 hardliners. Often, as he has admitted, this meant "not closing up shop" but "working with" and compromising with the demands of the old guard *ultras* of army intelligence. This last section illustrates the limits to which the institutionalist High Command was either able to willing to go in "reforming" G-2. The G-2 "hardliners," Gramajo describes in this anecdote, "tested" him:

After becoming Defense Minister, a hardline officer at a very low level of the intelligence shop kidnapped a university student who had left Guatemala for exile in Mexico. But because of the new [political] environment, she had returned but she was not exactly (as they say) "out of business" — half legal, half illegal [as a *guerrilla*]. And so, without any orders, without any authorization, and against the regulations we had set up, they capture her. But I realized it was a test to see how the new Defense Minister would act in those situations. Cerezo called me and asked what was happening. I told him, and he said, "Okay, I'll wait for your reaction." I called Callejas and he claimed, "We don't know what happened; we know nothing. We will look into it and maybe we will come up with something." I said it does not matter if she is a leftist because we want the leftists to comply with the law. As long as they don't carry guns, we have no problem. Meanwhile, the student's father and older brother come to talk to me. I told them I didn't know exactly what was happening, and I called [G-2] right then and there: the guy who answered was ambivalent, but because the family was right there, I needed some credibility, so I told them to release her immediately. That night she was released. I confessed [to the family] that these things are happening over which I have no control, but they are not acting on my orders and I will not permit this.

Later, Gramajo added that this "hardline officer," among "only a handful," was "known for abductions," and thus sent to the School of the Americas "to learn something about democracy" (interview w/o attribution).

Gramajo didn't need to "investigate" to "discover" who had carried out this abduction because he already knew G-2 to be responsible for "most of the killings," and he knew precisely the "hardline officer" responsible for this particular abduction because "there were only a handful"; for "credibility reasons" in front of the victim's family, it was a matter of calling and demanding her release. In other words, when there is pressure and the will to retain one's credibility as Defense Minister, individuals abducted and being tortured by security forces can be "found" and released. There is also the lackadaisical tone to Callejas's claim of ignorance: *mano dura* elements of G-2 knew full well they would not be prosecuted *even if they killed the victim*, given Gramajo and Cerezo's co-optation project ("One had to be a little flexible, treat them with [incentives]").

Such "testing" provides a glimpse into the murky and byzantine power struggles within the traditionally extreme rightwing world of G-2 — what some Guatemalan analysts refer to as "symbolic killings." They are manifestations of a political opportunism by one *línea* to use violence to undermine the human rights image of an image-dependent regime, to gain concessions from the other *línea*, and in so doing, to attempt to reestablish traditional internal G-2 power relations of the ultra *cofradía*. Without a doubt this opportunism is useful to both the "100 percenters" and the "30/70 percenters" — the latter, as we have seen, who also have their own agenda of necessary killing and psychological warfare techniques for inter-national image- and mythmaking. Nevertheless, a number of these killings fit a pattern of "publicness," or intentionally "overt operations," which have been used by the "more intransigent" *línea* of G-2 to embarrass and under-cut the institutionalist officers who are considered to be working for "the other side." While the exposure of brutalized corpses in the past under military governments was intended to sow terror among activists (the tor-tured corpses of two members of GAM in 1985 left by G-2 by roadsides during the Mejía regime), these "operations" are often public assassinations of high-profile members of society that have the double advantage of warn-ing the civilian regime not to overstep its bounds, while testing and/or publicly discrediting a fellow officer (e.g., a Defense Minister or an EMP chief). The severest penalty, though, is for this officer to "lose" his career (i.e., forced early retirement). The normal course of events in Guatemala has been that senior officer(s) who order an abduction and killing, even if they are named in court papers as intellectual authors of a major "public assassination," such as the Myrna Mack killing, have never been indicted.[28]

The interpretation that neither Gramajo nor Cerezo utilized the channels to stop the killings because they didn't control particular elements of G-2 ("Things take time and it is not easy," explained Gramajo) cannot account, however, for those crimes that Cerezo and Gramajo *did* know about, could possibly have prevented or stopped, or could have prosecuted those officers responsible. Instead, many crimes were covered up or became part of the psychological disinformation campaigns that denounced the victim[29] rather than dealt with the denunciations in order "to defend the State of Guate-mala." As Chief of the National Defense Staff, Gramajo stated it was his "duty to control La Dos"; he has since assumed full responsibility for viola-tions incurred during his tenure as Defense Minister (interview without attribution).

The Intelligence Oversight Board Report

The 1996 Intelligence Oversight Board (IOB) investigating CIA activities in Guatemala between 1984 and 1995 confirms not only that the CIA main-tained a "close liaison relationship" with the Guatemalan security services, especially G-2 and the EMP, but that the Directorate for Operations (DO) at CIA headquarters was also aware that CIA assets and liaison contacts were "credibly alleged to have ordered, planned or participated in serious hu-man rights violations, such as assassination, extrajudicial execution, torture or kidnapping while they were assets" and to have covered up the crimes.[30] In fact, "egregious violations continued," with "some of the stations' closest contacts in the security services remain[ing] a part of the problem" (IOB Report 1996: 20). Not only are we told that the DO "intentionally withheld" such information from Congressional Oversight Committees (3, 20) but we are also informed that CIA station officers were contemptuous of having to supply Congress with semiannual human rights reports (27). While the CIA "endeavored to improve [G-2's] behavior" and attitudes "by stressing the importance of human rights" in courses at the intelligence school, the IOB admits "the [Guatemalan] army acted with total impunity" in the 1980s; even in the 1990s, "senior officers are still rarely charged for their roles in ordering or covering up such crimes" (19). CIA station officers, too, "continued to view the communist insurgents . . . as the primary enemy," and the Guatemalan government and security services as "partners in the fight against this common foe" (20). Hence CIA Station Chiefs in Guatemala and the DO in Washington have operated on the assumption for at least ten years, if not since 1966, when G-2 was established, that thousands upon thousands of Guatemalans and several Americans would continue to be tortured, disappeared, and assassinated by their own "assets," while they were claiming in their reports to Congress to be "supporting the transition to and strengthening of civilian democratic government, encouraging respect for human rights and the rule of law . . . fighting the communist insurgency and, in recent years, advancing the peace process." In brief, by underwriting the Guatemalan intelligence services—to the tune of $3.5 million in fiscal year 1989 alone—the CIA has been sanctioning the G-2's murderous impunity, and thus is itself deeply complicitous in establishing a violent democracy.

Conclusion

But for the control of G-2 by President Lucas García by way of La Regional/CRIO between 1978 and 1982, military intelligence has been the focus of state power since 1966. Dedicated to surveillance, "investigation," abduction, torture, and assassination, the web of army intelligence has penetrated all sectors of civilian and military life in all departments of Guatemala for the purposes of improving the management and modality of killing thousands upon thousands suspected of being either Opponents of the State or collaborators of those opponents, as well as for personal and drug-trafficking reasons. G-2 has served as the army's death squad for four decades. With the 1982 coup, *el proyecto politico-militar* put into place a much broader intelligence net based on psychological and technologized special warfare techniques, first for wider "sweeps" of *aniquilamiento y recuperación* (annihilation and recuperation) of the "displaced" and later for more selective killing for the purposes of statecrafting—something General Lucas and his Regional/ CRIO chief Colonel Montalván could only dream about. Within this context, "professionalization" refers to the increasing technical sophistication of the entire intelligence apparatus from D-2/S-2/G-2 to EMP to DIDE to neutralize, buy off, and/or eliminate Opponents of the State, while waging political war to deflect international criticism. Such professionalization, though, was not intended to protect the lives of the one hundred Guatemalans killed each month during the Cerezo regime. As one leader of a trade union decimated by the repression noted the week Cerezo was inaugurated, "Maybe they will be better equipped to torture us" (1986 interview).

The tactic of gradual penetration and reform of *ultra-derechista* G-2 officers, moreover, resulted in the inability and/or unwillingness of either Gramajo or Cerezo to control rampant human rights violations. Later Gramajo was to admit that his intentions were to "rehabilitate the handful" of the most hardline and corrupt officers, some of whom "could not be rehabilitated" (interview). This strategy of co-opting the G-2 had the consequence of failing the country by not actively combating impunity and stopping the killing. One can only conclude that Gramajo, with his long career as the "granddaddy of G-2," and the CIA, with its complicitous legacy of pouring millions of U.S. tax dollars into training, equipping, and housing intelligence activities, are directly responsible for allowing abductions, tortures, and killings to continue rather than shutting down the operations altogether during the Cerezo regime — lavishing goodies as an incentive to professionalize but not to democratize. Put simply, what Gramajo and the CIA knew about the G-2 and the inexorability of these human rights violations and when they knew it is not even in question.

This chapter has dealt with the belief that it was necessary to "return things to normal": to co-opt army intelligence, to bring the EMP and police forces under control after the Lucas regime, and to "professionalize" the methods and tactics of institutions devoted to violence. The majority of officers in Guatemala hold the belief that it is still necessary and "normal" to *limpiar* selectively in order to maintain the State. The next chapter describes the politico-military project vis-à-vis human rights and the presidency during the Cerezo regime. It argues that the expansion of the Estado Mayor Presidencial helped to militarize the presidency.

Chapter 8
The Regime of Vinicio Cerezo

The Christian Democratic Party-Army Pact and the Militarization of the Presidency

> In Guatemala, no civilian is interested in the state. When a politician suddenly finds himself in power, he doesn't know [what to do], he has no aides, no people with public administration experience who know how to help him exercise power. And it is then that the politicians come to realize that the military are very efficient. . . . Within this scheme of ours, the President is responsible for everything. I informed Cerezo of all the activities of Intelligence when I was Defense Minister so that he would take the blame, not me! . . . With a presidential order, SIPROCI [the System of Civilian Protection] was established, and the army was allowed to conduct criminal investigations without being outside the boundaries of the law.
>
> —former Defense Minister Gramajo

> With SIPROCI, the President began to coordinate the actions of all the organisms of security—including those of G-2. Naturally, I can say that I was one of the few Presidents who was coordinating actions [he chuckles] of the Central de Inteligencia of the army, and I don't think there are many who have gotten to know the place physically [as I have] [he chuckles again].
>
> —former President Cerezo[1]

An analysis of a civil-military equation of power must also consider the civilian president's attitudes toward the military, the opposition, and intelligence operations. It also must evaluate the extent to which the president is able to command military obedience regarding intelligence and police operations, military promotions, military participation in the cabinet, and military accountability in the judicial system as the formal commander in chief of the armed forces. Stepan's measure of military accountability comes in the form of two questions: "Do the military accept that the president, subject to appropriate legislative approval, is the sole legitimate source of commands concerning the use of military force? Or do they believe they have a right to discretionary obedience and the right to take major initiatives in the area of domestic order?" (1988: 111–12). As we have seen in earlier chapters, rather than seek a transitional democratic model based on a separation between civilian and military spheres in which military involvement in politics is reduced and the armed forces are relegated to the barracks, the Christian Democrats in Guatemala — faced with a political climate in which few of the functioning (and, by definition, these would be extreme rightwing) political elites were open to any kind of idea of *apertura*— had decided by the mid-1970s to collaborate with the "less intransigent *línea*" within the military. This *línea* would themselves come to recognize by the early 1980s that their own institutional survival depended on such a civilian-military formula. While the electoral solution of unequal "co-governance" by civilians and military would prove politically useful for both sides, it completely begged the question of civilian control over the military.

Background of the Guatemalan Christian Democratic Party

The Guatemalan Christian Democratic Party (Partido Democracia Cristiana Guatemalteca) (PDCG) had its origins in a university group belonging to the Acción Católica Universitaria, a movement led by Jesuit priests. During the 1944–54 democratic period, this group maintained open opposition to government policies by publishing the anticommunist magazine *Acción Social Cristiana*. It could be characterized as "in defense of the Church, Catholic ethics and its relation to the agrarian bourgeoisie."[2] The Guatemalan Christian Democratic Party was founded after the CIA coup in 1954 by René de León Schlotter (Minister of Development in the Cerezo government), and Roberto Carpio Nicolle (Vice-President in the Cerezo government), among others, and sought to present itself as the "third alternative" to the polarities of *arbencistas* (of the left) and *liberacionistas* (of the extreme right). It has since been characterized by two themes: its anticommunism and its willingness to politically collaborate with the army. In the 1950s, it maintained close ties with the coffee oligarchy and other political parties functioning at this time, principally the National Liberation Movement (also founded with the 1954 coup). In 1964, internal splits appeared in the party in response to the calling of constituent assembly elections by President-Colonel Enrique Peralta Azurdia (1963–66). The bloc refusing to cooperate with the elections was headed by de León Schlotter together with a newly formed conservative Social Christian Student Front at the University of San Carlos, among whom included Vinicio Cerezo, Raquel Blandón (Cerezo's future wife), Alfonso Cabrera (Foreign Minister under Cerezo), and Fernando Andrade Díaz-Durán (Foreign Affairs Minister under Mejía Víctores and UN Ambassador under Cerezo). Under the influence of the Alliance for Progress and with the rupture of relations with the church, the ideological position of the party between 1963 and 1974 shifted from anticommunist liberal to anticommunist developmentalist. Once again it represented itself as the third alternative to the polarities of capitalism and socialism, with PDCG agrarian reform the instrument by which to activate industrial development. It was during the 1970s that debates waged within the PDCG about the extent to which the party should deal with the socioeconomic situation, despite its ideological promotion of *pluralismo político* to gain union support. Members of the National Confederation of Workers (CNT) questioned the PDCG's central and solitary interest in winning elections at the expense of taking a critical stance on the socio-economic situation and supporting the popular sector. Many left the party at this time, and because of this reduction in its popular ranks, the party began to more fervently seek political connections with the military and the commercial-industrial elite. With the 1974 elections, the PDCG sought out military candidates who had not been openly involved in the repression. All three Christian Democratic candidates in the 1970s were army officers: in 1970 Colonel Jorge Lucas Caballeros, in 1974 General Ríos Montt, and in 1978 General Peralta Méndez (whose slogan was "Contra la imposición, Peralta Méndez es la oposición").

As Secretary-General of the Christian Democratic Party in 1975, Vinicio Cerezo wrote a pamphlet entitled "The Army as Alternative," which argued that in order for the Christian Democratic party to govern, it had to come to some kind of agreement with one of the two real powers in Guatemala.[3] President Cerezo explains in a 1991 interview with the author that the "thesis" in his 1975 pamphlet never intended to send the military to their barracks, but rather was very much committed to making them equal partners in a democratic project, thus gaining the presidency for the party. To do so, the Christian Democrats were willing to first underplay and then entirely drop their most radical claim of the 1970s — agrarian reform — in order to win a short-term goal in the 1980s. Cerezo first sketches the political geography of 1975, a landscape naked of all but four parties:

I wrote a document some years ago about the need for the Christian Democratic Party to make in some way an agreement with the army in order to begin the process of democratic change in the country. That document spoke only of the Christian Democratic Party because it was written from a historical party perspective. In other words, it was written after 1974 when we had had an electoral fraud [with the election of the military/oligarch candidate General Kjell Laugerud] and there were only four political parties [functioning in the country] — three of them were part of the military hierarchy that controlled the political situation, were directed by the military hierarchy, or functioned in agreement with them. And I speak of the "military hierarchy" because it wasn't the army as such, but a group of military officers who made the decisions as to who would be the successor in power. The only party that existed as legally registered as a party in the democratic opposition were the Christian Democrats, although other *tendencias* [ideological groups] existed that functioned in agreement with us, such as the Social Democratic Party (PRA) and political groups on the left not identified as parties, such as the United Revolutionary Front (FUR) and a section of the Revolutionary Party (PR). But there was a [larger] thesis in this document [of mine]. I am explaining to you the historical perspective because I was not speaking in practice of *one party and one army* [in the document] but of the need for the democratic parties and the army to reach an agreement in order to transform the authoritarian structures and push forward the democratic process. (interview; his emphasis)

Cerezo goes on to point out in the article that, given the authoritarian tradition of government in Guatemala, the only way democracy could begin to function would be by way of the traditional structures — a view that places electoralism at the center of democratic transition:

The thesis arose from a very concrete reality. Democracy is a system which arises and lives from the participation of the people in [making] political decisions by way of diverse types of organizations. But as we have lived [in Guatemala] under generally repressive authoritarian governments which have not opened [political] spaces for the organization of the people, the only concrete declaration initially of democracy are the political parties, which many times find they must meet within the refuge of unions, cooperatives, and peasant organizations. They cannot openly declare themselves in any other way. The subsequent repression between 1974 and 1982 not only demonstrated that this was true [for political parties] but for popular organizations as well. And thus in Latin America — as in all the countries of the world — democracy begins to function within the traditional structures of power which include the economic oligarchs, the army, and the political parties that emerge in order to put democracy on the electoral course. You know, it is after the coups d'état [in Guatemala] that political parties have arisen to participate in the elections. But it is [only] within democracy that popular organizations are going to be created that will make their own attempts at democracy much later on, and after many years.

Cerezo argues that for many decades the army had been serving the economic oligarchs as a way to maintain authoritarianism. It was in the 1970s, however, that a group of military officers, in agreement with a very traditional sector of the oligarchy, decided to utilize political parties for their own interests,

but in practice, it was the same old game: the only difference was that military men inserted themselves into powerful positions, and instead of using economic power, they used military power as a key to opening the door to the economic oligarchy.

In order for any democratic process to occur in Guatemala, he continues, democratic political parties had to ask themselves,

How can we consolidate a democratic process without [including] one of these factors of power? We can't co-opt the economic factor because it would be the main one to be [adversely] affected by the democratic process, but we could convince the army to make themselves independent to function as an institution in favor of the democratic process and not in favor of the maintenance of an authoritarian society. And that was basically my thesis [in the 1975 pamphlet].

It was also in the 1970s that the Christian Democratic Party began to raise the issue of the economic oligarchy's exploitation of the army with a certain group of officers. Cerezo emphasizes:

They began to take note of the fact that they were wielding a lot of power, and yet remained the instruments of a sector that was receiving the benefits of that power, and not sharing in it. Moreover, everyone was blaming the army for all the evil in Guatemala—including the guerrilla!—for the simple reason that the guerrilla is another political army, another group of militarized politicians who had to become an army. In order to polarize [Guatemalan society], they have to attack the army, while the evils of Guatemalan society derive first and foremost from the economic and social structure. The army is the instrument that appears in front, but they are *not* the principal cause of [the way] things are. (his emphasis)

Although the PDCG politicians "went to the army telling them these things," Cerezo makes it clear he does not take credit for this change in attitude. There were officers who had been thinking along these lines already and it was these officers who began "a process of reflection." "We know," Cerezo points out, "from history that ideas take a long time to ripen." We also know that the army, for their own strategic and institutional reasons, came to the same conclusion at the beginning of the 1980s: the need for a democratic transition. As Cerezo remarks,

"They recognized that there was no political space in the country—a situation that was leading to polarization and eventual total war. And a total war waged by one institution against the people could only produce its [the army's] own destruction." Moreover, because the army is composed of an emerging middle class, Cerezo recognized that it was at the time and still is "susceptible to listening to the possibilities of a new role for the army in society."

The Ríos Montt candidacy in 1974 is illustrative of the PDCG's planned collaboration with the army. As Cerezo puts it:

The candidacy of Ríos Montt at that time was planned by the Christian Democratic Party as an action by which to strengthen our reformist thesis. His candidacy didn't arise just by accident. When the candidacy was proposed to him, he was high up in the army [as a general], but he had been relegated to Washington by the military hierarchy that selected the presidential candidates. And Montt maintained at this time—something which I think he still maintains, although from a totally different ideological perspective now—that the army has an institutional role that entails strengthening the constitution, and so forth. That was his thesis, and for this reason, he was sent off to Washington [in exile]. And we, together with the Social Democrats, searched for someone [like himself] among the military leaders who could strengthen that thesis [of institutionality].

The 1974 program of the Christian Democratic Party was called "The Road Toward Peace" (El Camino hácia la Paz), with Ríos Montt's own campaign entitled the "National Salvation." His candidacy was clearly a testing of the political waters by the Christian Democrats, but it was not until 1982 that the "thesis" could be implemented and Ríos Montt could finally take office. The difference between 1974 and 1982, however, despite the similar slogan-eering by Ríos Montt, was *the absence of reformist intentions*. By that time, the Christian Democrats had shed their educational, health, and agrarian reforms to be considered reliable collaborators with this new, more moderate, or at least "less intransigent," sector of the army from Cerezo's perspective.

This shift by the Christian Democrats was also opportune for the American New Right, ascendant under the Reagan Administration. After the 1978 presidential elections, and throughout the brutal repression of the Lucas García regime (in which some 300 PDCG activists were killed), the Christian Democrats, unlike the equally decimated PRA and FUR, which formed a Democratic Front Against the Repression (FDCR), still refused to take a clear oppositional stand. Instead, the PDCG intensified its relations with the U.S. government with two goals in mind: to convert itself into a revised party with a hierarchal executive structure before a potential *golpe de estado* occurred and to strengthen its legal-political space for the 1982 elections.

In May 1984, meetings took place at the American Enterprise Institute in Washington among members of the Committee of Santa Fe,[4] Latin American Christian Democratic leaders, and representatives from the West German Konrad Adenauer Foundation[5] to discuss cooperative links of the New Right in the United States with the more right-leaning Latin American Christian Democratic parties, formulate a common agenda as to how to counter the insurgency movements, and promote collaborative projects in Guatemala and El Salvador to counter Sandinista Nicaragua (ACEN-SIAG, 18 January 1986: 14). One of the main ideas that emerged from these meetings in Guatemala and Washington was to seek a convergence between the armed forces and the Christian Democratic parties of Central America: it was to be a convergence of counterinsurgency with constitutional legitimacy—the army's "mixed solution" and the Christian Democrats' "*concertación*" (Gaspar 1985: 13–14), or what other Guatemalans have cynically called *continuismo*. In July 1986 President Cerezo announced a "new military doctrine that will attempt to end the traditional separation of the Army with respect to the civilian administration. We want to integrate the Army into a national, fundamental objective which is the consolidation of democracy. It will be a crucial theme which can be very important in the development of armies in Central America. . . . This is to say that the military is being integrated into the administration like a political institution, not apart from it, which exercises power in conjunction with the civilian government" (*La*

Hora, 17 July 1986: 3). But has this *coyuntura* entailed civilian oversight and military accountability?

Civil-Military Discussions Begin, 1982–1983

Two months before the August 1983 *relevo* against Ríos Montt, the Christian Democratic leadership publicly demanded a fixed date for the National Constituent Assembly elections, and the army took up the initiative to set such a date. However, as we know from chapter 2, Ríos Montt announced to his commanders that he had decided "to change priorities," placing economic issues above the political ones and delaying the elections. The new strategy would take him "at least seven years." On 8 August 1983, Ríos Montt was "relieved" of his position, and replaced by Mejía Víctores, whose presence assured the return to a constitutional process. Meanwhile, the Christian Democratic Party prepared itself for the 1985 legislative and presidential elections: its political literature at the time emphasizing that it was a party that had not been compromised by the repression. More importantly, it was to be seen as a party that apart from admitting to the possibility of co-governing harmoniously with the military, could serve as a mediator with the infamously belligerent private sector.

It was during this time that the Christian Democrats initiated talks with the private sector as well as the army. Once the army had begun to "open the political spaces" in August 1983, discussions began as to the need for a new relationship between civilians and the military, and the roles each one of the institutions had to play. Cerezo recalls that

we entered the discussion around the [writing of the] new Constitution, and a dialogue ensued among the private enterprise sector, the political parties and the army who participated in the selection of the Constituent Assembly. There thus arose an interesting discussion. First, [we dealt with] the historical necessity and the gaining of consciousness by the military that their role had been *hipertrofiado* (excessive). The first issue was, how are the politicians and military officers going to relate to one another, right? Secondly, in discussing the role of the army in society, we noted the excessiveness of the army was because security had been converted into the national objective *por Excelencia*. They began to question the famous doctrine of national security as an ideological thesis, replacing it with a Thesis of National Stability in which security is perceived of as a prerequisite for stability, and not the reverse — stability for security. This apparently is a word game but historically it will be crucial. The third kind of discussion we had with the leaders of the army was that if the army was an institution at the service of stability, it had to submit to the laws, beginning with its own laws. This implied the elaboration of a forced retirement law, for example, to which Gramajo himself was subject. (interview)

As we shall see, the Cerezo regime set out to institutionalize *el proyecto político-militar* to serve the collaborative scheme for the twenty-year transition.

No Great Expectations: The Cerezo-Military Agreement

Those military and civilians who set out in 1982 to selectively recompose the state without disturbing the fundamental economic and social structures, considered that the 1986 civilian regime (presided over by whomever won the elections) was never intended to be transformative, only "eminently transitional," as the Thesis of National Stability states:

The period initiated in 1986 will not be reflected in the future in dramatic changes in the economic, social or political order. This period is more significant as one of transition as it is creating the basis for the future mediation of Guatemala, principally in the political order and social relations . . . so that the conjunction of all this . . . will be more similar to those of a modern Western civilization, more institutionalized, more pragmatic and at the least more just. (Gramajo 1989: 15)

As evidenced by his 1975 pamphlet as a young Christian Democratic congressional deputy, this view was very well understood and agreed upon by Cerezo. It was reconfirmed in his meeting with the military government's top officers, a meeting at which he was reminded "not to pursue a path of governance of great achievements or to even try to resolve the national problems of a structural nature that afflict the nation."[6] Gramajo has stated that at a five-hour briefing on 17 January 1986, after having studied the July 1966 "pact" the armed forces had made with civilian president-elect Julio César Méndez Montenegro,

we briefed President [Cerezo] on the state of the nation and outlined our strategy to deal with it. We outlined a set of regulations similar to the code of conduct that outlined the [pacification] operations. "We are no longer an anticommunist but a prodemocratic armed forces. For the purpose of facing the insurgency, it is the same [strategy]. Cerezo approved of our strategy and [agreed to] remain within" our plans. (interview without attribution)

As a consequence, in his inaugural speech, Cerezo made reference to the "house" of Guatemala being disorganized and stated that the Christian Democrats had arrived to organize it and correct past abuses and misbehavior of past authoritarian governments. (Gramajo thought "the speech was a good political piece, full of rhetoric and sophisms" [1991a: 26].)

But Cerezo went further. In speaking of the army's Annual Plans of Action that were presented at the presidential cabinet meetings, he made it clear that these outlines of the army's objectives were "no longer apart from but were made an element of the Government's Annual Plan of Action" in his Presidential Memorandums, a bureaucratic measure Cerezo introduced. It is within these Presidential Memorandums that one finds, as Cerezo comments, "security as part and parcel of the Government's Plan of Action, and not as the primordial objective [as under National Security Doctrine. . . .

These plans by the army eventually became the Thesis of National Stability, and it was formulated under *my* regime," he states proudly. The Center for Strategic Studies for National Stability, about which Cerezo also speaks proudly, where he has attended several conferences, was also drawn up in one of the two Presidential Memorandums that document these cabinet meetings (see chapter 10): "We believed we had to institutionalize this [civil-military relationship]."

According to Gramajo, Cerezo fully accepted the strategy of military fundamentalism of "pure professionals," saying that only through an "alliance of professionals" would Guatemala move forward as a democracy, with Cerezo presenting himself as "the professional politician" (1991: 28). Neither Cerezo's nor Gramajo's definition of "professionalism," however, entails apoliticization of the army. Cerezo believes the army should be politically active:

One must accept that the army forms part of the cabinet, of the strategy of governance, and so they are also participating politically! [This is] something I think is correct because if the army is co-responsible for the policy of government, they must also have the right to voice their opinion about it. We can no longer have the traditional attitude of some governments historically in Latin America that says: "You [the army] have all the responsibility but you don't have the right to politics." That cannot be the case any longer. It would be equal to my obliging all political parties to respect the governing party and not scheme as to how to depose that party from power [in the next elections]. You see, they [the army] must also be part of the power [structure]. From there, coparticipation in all [governmental] decisions is fundamental in order to create a national character.

This collaborative mood was so strong that Gramajo enjoined by saying that "The Chief of Staff, the President, and the Defense Minister are the High Command where military policies are formulated; the army is commanded by this trio" (interview). With security then the prerogative of this collaborative *proyecto*, politics-as-the-continuation-of-war became institutionalized during the Cerezo regime.

The PDCG Strategy of Advance and Retreat

As the first civilian president in thirty years, Cerezo saw a great deal of social mobilization in his inaugural year: demonstrations, walkouts, strikes, and protest marches. The PDCG's economic policies caused major animosity because they represented the contradiction of wanting the support of workers and the popular sector while putting into place a neoliberal model. According to Gramajo, Cerezo often said, "This is the [PDCG] strategy. This year we have to open the pressure valves in order to sense how high the pressure is, and release most of it" (1991a: 3). The PDCG served as the "shock absorber,"[7] the release of pent-up frustration and anger after so many years of poverty and repression, presenting itself as a populist alternative while it was unwilling and often incapable of actually delivering on its promises: "They want a trade union immediately. I'm a good politician, but I can't create miracles. We must go step by step, and they must wait. The same with human rights" (Christian Science Monitor Television interview transcript of Cerezo, 26 September 1988: 7–8). The Christian Democratic thesis, stated Cerezo,

was to push as far as possible because you would always have to retreat a little. This happened with everything [during my presidency]. Thus, [we had] an absolute *apertura* with the unions and because of this, we had many problems. We had 1700 demonstrations [during my presidency]! [he laughs]
Q: You're referring to strikes by workers?
No, the teachers' strike that lasted two months was something quite incredible, almost without a coup. It was a marvel of coordination. Actually, it was terrible for us, and it cost us the elections. But from the point of view of the management of strikes, never in the history of the country have there been so many strikes with so little violent consequence. But the system of [citizen] protection [SIPROCI] arose to deal with this possibility, and to combat common criminality. Because what happens in almost all the democratic processes is that with the rise of unions, common crime multiplies, for many reasons.

Cerezo's thesis of "advance and retreat" implies that there are limits to an *apertura* and that one must always be prepared to compromise (which was after all, the original PDCG thesis of the mid-1970s), although he denied that any agreement was reached as to exactly where limits lay. He said the PDCG was "finding the path in accordance with the circumstances, but there were no limits." No limits were necessary, one could argue, because the party's own reformist project was devoid of any transformative intentions, such as wage increases, human rights protections, or land titling. Given the PDCG's history of collaboration in the 1960s and 1970s, the agreement not to include or to consider any substantial reform should not be surprising. It was simply not in the Christian Democrats' own political interests at the time.

What is most striking about the PDCG strategy, however, is that even while the administration was praising the significant rise in union activities, oppositional activities were connected without hesitation with common criminal and even guerrilla elements. This convergence of criminal/subversive categories collapses security "needs" with traditional criminal procedures and "normalizes" State repression. As two editorials in *La Hora* averred six months into Cerezo's presidency, "To show that nothing has changed with the installation of a civilian regime, President Cerezo declared with respect to critics of the government that 'the criticisms are expressed by radical groups on the left. Those who criticize belong to the guerrilla. . . . To be a guerrilla is a crime' " (9, 12 July 1986). These declarations could have come from the mouths of military officers. Similarly, Cerezo's public campaign regarding human rights violations—about which he asserted, "in Guatemala, there are no massacres, but rather a wave of common violence and criminality" (*La Hora*, 13 June 1989)—could be interpreted as a conscious retreat to play by the rules in order to see how far one could advance with the armed forces (especially the G-2, which Gramajo was courting at this time with training and equipment). It was similar to the collaborative political path the party carved out for itself in the 1970s, in which antisubversive operations were deemed necessary, and popular mobilization beneficial but only within certain boundaries. Cerezo's Cabinet Ministers also were active in downplaying violence as common delinquency: National Police Director G-2 Colonel Caballeros attributed the violence to "alcoholism and traffic accidents"; Interior Minister Rodil asserted that "whenever a dictatorship ends, common crime goes up throughout the country" because "common criminals know that a democratic government has to stick to a series of legal procedures which make delinquents think they have more space in which to act" (*La Palabra*, 13 June 1986). In answering questions before Congress regarding the mistreatment of GAM members by the police during their sit-in at the National Palace on 26 September 1986, Rodil (accompanied by National and Treasury Police directors) asserted that the security forces "were within legal boundaries." He reminded the deputies that those who offended or insulted the executive head or heads of other parts of the State could be jailed for two to three years, or suffer another such sanction against disobedience, in accordance with the Penal Code (ACEN-SIAG 30 October 1986, 72: 7). During the squatter invasions in January 1986 (in the days of Cerezo's inauguration), the Christian Democratic Party Secretary, Demetrio Moliviatis Viena, stated that "the government cannot permit these [land] invasions because it would be accepting disorder and chaos within the State." This statement implies that disorder and chaos occur only outside the institutional framework. Another Christian Democratic government official said on a popular radio talk show in Guatemala City that the squatters were destroying the green areas of the city and "should only congregate in the central square to voice dissent" (personal taping, 17 January 1986). Bodies of several leaders of the squatters movement ended up in the garbage dump the week following the inauguration, once the foreign journalists had left the country.

The PDCG thinking parallels, then, the counterinsurgency language and logic of the armed forces. It is also strikingly similar to that of the hardline businessman (a CACIF representative) and newspaper publisher José Rubén Zamora: "The problem with the unions [is that they are] political arms of the guerrillas, and they slow down the private sector. We know this by their publications, denunciations and demonstrations" (Smyth, *The Progressive*, 26 March 1992: 28). With violence explained at once as political opposition and as nonpolitical common delinquency, the PDCG served as a public relations camouflage in "normalizing" (one might say in the "homo-ciding" of) political assassinations and thus undercutting human rights pressures during the first years of this collaborative *proyecto político-militar*. What was most unusual, though, was President Cerezo's access to intelligence operations and files, and his establishment of SIPROCI from within the Presidential General Staff.

The Christian Democratic Militarization of the Presidency: SIPROCI and Access to Intelligence

From the last chapter, we know that the Presidential General Staff was expanded under the Cerezo regime. After the failure of the new government's "Emergency Plan" for dealing with growing violence, the System of Citizen Protection (SIPROCI) was established and functioned out of the office of the Archivo between May 1988 and 1991. It integrated 26,000 agents from the units of military intelligence, Civil Patrols, National Police, Treasury Guard, Mobile Military Police, General Office of Immigration, Office of Administrative Control of the Presidency, and the Department of Presidential Security (DSP) and included special military commanders who all depended, at least formally, on the President directly. With security to be "part and parcel of the Government's Plan of Action," President Cerezo claims that he himself not only established SIPROCI (approving directives presented to him by the Defense Minister and Interior Minister regarding its functioning) but also coordinated all its actions:

There in the Presidential Residence there is an Office of Presidential Security but the system of presidential security forms only part of SIPROCI. Everybody believes that it is one thing; what it does have is coordination of the vital information for the teams of security and intelligence. And it has a [process of] coordination of the groups of action (*los grupos de acción*), when they are necessary. As such, the President of the Republic began to coordinate the actions of all the organisms of security — including those of G-2. I can say that I was one of the few presidents who was coordinating actions [he chuckles] in the Central de Inteligencia of the army, and I don't think there are many who have even gotten to know [the place] physically [he chuckles again proudly].

Q: Does this mean that you were receiving files of intelligence, saying, "I want to see this case file and that case file?"

I arrived [at the Central] and demanded, "get me that one [file] and that one." They would bring the documents to me and explain them to me, and everything. Things that I think they have never done before, not even with Ríos Montt!

Q: How is it that they came to accept this?

Because we were in *la línea* [i.e., because we were in agreement about *el proceso* and because I was hierarchically commander-in-chief]. . . .

Q: But as I've understood it, G-2 believes it needs to have its own separate security apparatus.

Yes. It *is* incredible [that this occurred], and it was a very important advance. Because, look, how should I explain this? SIPROCI didn't have an office. *It functioned out of the Presidency of the Republic.*

Q: If, as you say, this strategy is more centralized — neither a policy of the State nor decisions of individual commanders — from "tactical agility" to a "centralized doctrine," does this mean that the actions of G-2 have become more controllable, and SIPROCI is part of this new scheme?

Yes, let me explain. SIPROCI is an idea of civil coordination. It was my idea. It's not true that it's a subversive thesis as is claimed outside Guatemala. That's absolutely false. Rather, in the beginning it was the army that resisted this action, and we [in the executive] had to almost impose the system of civil protection, or civilian protection. [They resisted] because this implied that *all the organisms of security of the State, including G-2, were to be subject to the president.* So, they [cooperated] because G-2, even though it respects the president and serves as an instrument of political security to protect him, at the same time, the decision [not to comply] would cost them the independence of action for the antisubversive actions. Coordination was established by way of an agreement with Gramajo and the Chief of Staff, Callejas. (his emphasis)

The G-2 opened an office in the Casa Presidencial, where Cerezo would be briefed on intelligence. In a later interview, Gramajo confirms Cerezo's access to intelligence files but paints a picture of a reluctant president who was forced by the High Command to know what was going on, even though publicly Cerezo claimed he didn't know. Gramajo's own concern for plausible deniability is also striking: "*Within this scheme of ours, the President is responsible for everything. I informed Cerezo of all the activities of Intelligence when I was Minister [of Defense] so that he would take the blame, not me!*" [He laughs; his emphasis.] Later, I ask him,

Q: Earlier, you told me that you told Cerezo of all your activities as Minister of Defense.
Yes, because he is Commander-in-Chief.
Q: And you said you did so "so that he would take the blame, not you."
No, no, no, yes, of course, he has the authority and thus he has the responsibility. If I keep information from him, then I have the responsibility. If I give him all the information, and he gives me an order, then I fulfill his orders.
Q: I am asking because many of the human rights reports state that Cerezo didn't know what was going on.
This is what they assume. But my insurance is this: during my tenure [as Minister of Defense], my insurance is that my *jefe* knew everything. If there is something that has been omitted or committed, it's not my responsibility, then, it's his.
Q: For example, activities of Intelligence regarding human rights violations?
Yes, that and drugs and military operations.
Q: He knows everything?
He knows everything. Human rights [issues] as well because we are not hiding anything.
Q: What were the relations between the ministry and the presidency?
Professional. That is, to recognize that he is the Commander-in-Chief, although he didn't want this [recognition] from the beginning as it made it very easy for him to say, "I am not going to have the power [to do anything]." Only 30 percent [of power], didn't he say? We didn't allow him this [he bangs the table]. We told him, "You are the Commander-in-Chief and the Army is directed by the Commander-in-Chief, the Minister and the General Staff."
Q: Was there a discussion about this?
Yes, from the beginning. [I told him], "I have no problem in providing you with the intimacies of the Army because you are the Commander-in-Chief."

Q: And he received archives of the Intelligence [Service]?
Everything that he asked for, he got, including things that he didn't want to know about![8] (interview; his emphasis)

Gramajo goes on to explain that one of the major purposes of the civilian presidential office is to

take the heat, especially with regard to human rights issues. This was not dumped on [Cerezo], understand; he agreed to handle the political angle because he was a politician and he liked political things. That way, the military didn't have to talk about topics like the truth commission or trials for officers. That was the President's problem because he was a politician, and besides that, he was the Chief of the Armed Forces.

Nevertheless, by his own admission, Gramajo

got involved in that [Ursuline nun Diana] Ortiz case. Because nobody cared about the government. When something nice happened, the government would take credit for it, but when it was something bad or risky, nobody would stand up and address the problem. Cerezo was not around, and no one in his government would address problems like the Ortiz case, so I jumped in to [publicly] defend Cerezo. It was a political move on my part. I did it for the State of Guatemala. It was the only time. (interview without attribution)

Despite this attempt to make the president more responsible for dealing with and absorbing human rights pressures internationally, architects of the *proyecto* have been perfectly cognizant of the need to continue to serve as tutor of police and security forces and, by extension, guarantor of the State. Gramajo, for example, states that although reluctant to get involved in police activities, SIPROCI was created by the military to prevent crime:

The strategy and the mechanism for applying [the Thesis] is to make [political] spaces. If the military filled those spaces, then it was because we had to do so. If we don't, who will? The military had much to do with the prevention of crime. Now it doesn't. So, who is preventing crime? Since the police are incapable [of doing so], the military returned to create SIPROCI. The [low] degree of efficiency of the police obligated the military to interfere. And so, I told this to the President, and with a presidential order, a presidential *acuerdo*, within the boundaries of the law, the Army was allowed to conduct criminal investigations, and SIPROCI was formed. (interview)

One National Police detective stated that the Fifth Precinct of the National Police had been delegated to serve "SIPROCI's needs," and was always "the most aggressive in its 'cleansing operations' (*operaciones de limpieza*), often torturing and killing 'street delinquents' and students" (interview).[9] Under the Serrano government, the military-police patrols, renamed the Hunapú Task Force, "cleansed" street gangs and demonstrating students and unionists in Guatemala City. In December 1995 as well, President de León Carpio called out *patrullas conjuntas* (joint patrols) to "combat delinquency."

Not only was Cerezo "fascinated" by intelligence, but in an interview, he identifies with G-2, speaking in the plural "we" (and of unionists as "they"), making the convergence of civilian and military intelligence at least linguistically, if not semantically, complete:

We know a lot. There are very many people who function in teachers' and labor organizations whose names I could give you who serve as contacts for the guerrillas. They are *perfectly* identified, but they are important leaders in the system, and thus it is better not to [here he stops himself in mid-sentence]. . . . No, on the contrary, they are watched. When I met with the unionists I told them, "Please don't be disingenuous nor believe that we are disingenuous. Military intelligence in Guatemala is well-informed, and you all should know not to get mixed up in [he stops himself again], do what you feel you must but within the legal scheme. But if you involve yourself with the guerrilla, you involve yourself with war!"

While Cerezo proudly presents the history of SIPROCI as a political advance for the presidency in gaining access to intelligence files and operations, it did not signify civilian oversight or control; it didn't even indicate reform. The military intelligence network was not overhauled or dismantled, but was duplicated within the Estado Mayor Presidencial. With Cerezo having access to intelligence files, being briefed on intelligence operations, and perhaps even ordering intelligence operations, it is possible he was far more complicitous in the cycle of violence during his regime than human rights groups ever imagined. And while Gramajo grants Cerezo the courtesy of being reluctant to gain such access, Cerezo himself boasts of such access today. Given the extraordinary scarcity of information about G-2 during these many years of military governance, it might be argued that the access granted to Cerezo may, at the least, set a precedent for future civilian presidents. But to interpret this opening as anything other than the army's intent to confuse responsibility with blame without granting the President power would be naïve. This intentional obfuscation echoes Colonel-lawyer Girón Tánchez's remark with regard to amnesty laws being enacted "for everyone so that in the future, whatever happens, happens, and it will not be something we [the armed forces] can be blamed for." The armed forces' intent to withdraw from politics so as not to be blamed for poor political judgment as well as for human rights violations is one of the more salient features of *el proyecto*. While the PDCG has focused on its penetration of the military intelligence apparatus, the army has focused on consolidating a co-governing yet not co-responsible partnership that says "We will co-govern with you but the armed forces will no longer take the rap."

What can we conclude from these admissions by Gramajo and Cerezo? Gramajo realized the need to make the President responsible (directly or indirectly) for human rights violations that he knew were bound to occur, and to consider himself, the Defense Minister, and the National Defense Staff to be "just following the President's orders." With Cerezo's access to intelligence files and operations, one can no longer say that it was strictly a military-coordinated state: the Cerezo regime was at the least a direct collaborator in the project, raising the issue of not only compliance but also complicity in the militarization of the presidency (in contrast to the utterly marginalized civilian regime of Méndez Montenegro). It appears to be a case of both sides using the other for their own political needs — a collaborative project in the full sense of the term. This agreed-upon elimination-from-the-agenda of all those actions "outside the law" has resulted in a perfidious, legalized order of security in which there is an *institutionalized* lack of coherence between the democratic language of human rights and the reality of guaranteeing those rights.

How "Useful" Was the Cerezo Regime for the Army?

If the military project decided upon a "mixed solution" of civil-military governance in order to institutionalize its own version of a democratic transition, it is important to understand officers' perspectives as to what they believe they need in order to achieve their objectives, and to what degree the Cerezo regime "worked" for them. "We got two years out of his five," Gramajo believes,

because there was no leadership by which to mobilize the people who wanted more understanding and less polarization. The leadership remained within the party and didn't reach the national level. Guatemala has a new generation of politicians who right now are not showing very good results because they are very, very cheap politicians [he laughs], while this generation of the army is becoming more professional. What we need are more responsible politicians who are more concerned with statist issues than with issues internal to the party after the political campaigns. We need statists (*estadistas*) not just politicians. We did no campaigning for either Cabrera [the PDCG candidate] or for Serrano [the winner in the 1990 presidential elections], and the defeat of the Christian Democrats means [at least] that our strategy of autonomy worked. (interview)

Although Gramajo has since written critically about the Christian Democrats' ability to be an oppositional party, offering no cohesive plan by which to administer the government or exercise real power, he is also sympathetic to the realities of governing Guatemala during this period:

I believe that the Christian Democrats had a strategy to govern when they first came to power but they were overwhelmed by events: the air accident [of the Venezuelan father of Christian Democracy, Dr. Aristides Calvani]; the intense political struggle over economic policy, and the strong, coordinated opposition from powerful economic groups; the talks with the insurgents in Madrid; the two coup attempts; the complexities of local politics, especially the PDCG's attempt to strengthen their allies in the labor movement; the arrogance and overconfidence of PDCG leaders after the April 1988 elections, and above all, the unceasing political campaigning from the very outset until the end of the administration [in 1990]. These cumulative events wore down the president's image and discredited the party. They made it impossible to maintain a steady course in the early stages of Guatemala's experience with democracy. (1991b: 42–43)

After the first coup attempt in May 1988, Cerezo's party associates in government reportedly failed to show up for work, traveled abroad, or wasted time, using the excuse that another coup was imminent. "The government almost ceased to function [and] to [Ministry of] Defense analysts, it appeared that the President had either abandoned his initial plans and strategies, having perhaps changed his priorities, or simply reacted to the issues of the moment."[10] In short, by the end of Cerezo's tenure, he had completely lost touch with reality; his cabinet was composed mostly of "personal friends and second-class politicians and bureaucrats" (Gramajo 1991b: 41). Although Cerezo had initially drawn functionaries from many sectors (other political parties, the private sector, universities, the army) to fill governmental positions, by the end, several progressive civilians were complaining that Cerezo and the PDCG had not learned the lesson of the Arbenz government [in 1944]: its success had stemmed from the creation of a coalition government, not a one-party regime. The Cerezo regime was also faulted for "presidential centralism"; it had no unified criteria for policy, it often displayed an incongruency between the direction of government and the ministries, and the Presidential Memorandums served more as individual initiatives than coordinated efforts. Moreover, an expensive lifestyle tainted by corruption and scandal targeted Cerezo himself as a "vulnerability of the State," according to military officers, including Gramajo—a charge that underscores the important international legitimacy card Cerezo was supposed to have played. Class resentment, too, was articulated with the question raised by several civilian and military informants: "What if I told you that this is Cerezo's first real job?" The most consistent criticism came from domestic and international human rights groups, which faulted the government for an unwillingness to investigate grave human rights violations, and for the appointment of his most intimate friends to the Human Rights Commission to ensure disappearances were *not* investigated.

Yet, again, we need to remember that Cerezo was not *meant* to serve as anything other than a "holding pattern" for an *apertura* in a slightly altered yet bounded legal and political order called democracy. We need to also remember that Gramajo "wouldn't have had a chance to become Defense Minister if it had been during the period when military officers were 'elected-but-appointed' (*electos pero mandados*) because I wasn't part of *la camarilla* (the inner circle). Let's just say it was a conjuncture of history that gave us the opportunity to make a new strategy because we had regained [the army's] hierarchy" (interview).

This *concertación*, or co-governance, was viewed by the PDCG and the institutionalist faction of the army (as well as the Committee of Santa Fe) as the only solution to a cumulative erosion of political authority and an incapacity to govern. Thus, rather than interpret Cerezo's role as window dressing for the army, we should view the years 1986–90 as a collaborative project in which the Christian Democrats were not forced to participate, but *chose* to do so, after having prepared the political groundwork for more than a decade. Gramajo speaks angrily about "civilians principally from the official party who, to justify their ineptitude, still want to make others believe that the military doesn't allow them to do many things. This is nothing more than an excuse for justifying their [own] ineptitude or their lack of will" (interview).

Given Gramajo's dissatisfaction with much of the Cerezo administration and concerns with the viability of a co-governance with the *ultraderechista* 1990 president-elect, Jorge Serrano (despite Gramajo's long-term friendship with him),[11] I asked the former Defense Minister what the High Command's profile was of a future good candidate who would meet the army's needs.

We now have moderates in government, and there is risk that the conservatives will win because the moderates are inept. While we no longer have to contend with extremism, such as communism, we have to put up with the extremism of inefficiency and ineptitude. Let's imagine that Ríos Montt is allowed to run,[12] or that another candidate appears along the lines of the Cristiani formula of El Salvador. I believe it's going to be difficult to find a Cristiani in Guatemala but we can play out the formula: a moderate who the ultrarightists put forward but who accepts *el pueblo* and accepts the U.S. because [he counts on his upheld fingers] he (1) has refined manners, (2) is efficient, and (3) speaks English. . . . When I speak of Cristiani, I am speaking of the people who support Ríos Montt who must find a civilian from the economic fraternity: pleasant, upper-class, educated, charismatic, who speaks English without an accent. The Cristiani factor in Guatemala implies concern for security issues,[13] the economy, administrative efficiency, social affairs, and access to international matters. In other words, someone who both the political and the economic powers would accept.
Q: Are you saying that Ríos Montt is a kind of Cristiani?
Yes, but militarized! The difficulty is that those who would be president represent only their own interests, not those of the nation. No, you see, the key [for us] is for the moderates to continue [in government. The problem is], however, that the moderates are inept and the conservatives are efficient — so we need an efficient but moderate [candidate]!
Q: A civilian?
By preference because as things stand now, a military [candidate] is always associated with the conservatives. So, a lot of time will have to pass before a military [candidate] can be identified with other groups and not with the conservatives. (interview)

The *Factor Cristiani* underscores the vision of pro-Thesis officers whose double political optic includes an analysis not only of domestic political acceptance but also Washington's.

Cerezo's Three Stages of Transition for the Military

In 1991, I asked Cerezo whether the Thesis of National Stability had prevailed in the army after Gramajo's retirement:

Yes, it continues to prevail (*vigente*) even though it is *sotto voce*, and there is a discussion in the army about leadership because the people who succeeded Gramajo have discussed this issue with him. In other words, he didn't invent this tendency [to believe in *el proceso*] — it was already underway — but he did form a part of the leadership around it. And those officers who spoke up for it in the early 1980s [under Lucas García] were sent out of the country or dismissed, and as they say in Venezuela, a military [officer] without a uniform is like a traffic cop without the right to give tickets [he laughs]. (1991 interview)

Cerezo then goes on to outline his own thesis of the three stages the army must pass through in the "historical process of democratic consolidation," which might be seen as the ultimate goal of the PDCG project:

The first stage is that in which the army ceases to be an instrument of the economic oligarchs who want to maintain the status quo and who oppose [any kind of] change. The second stage is that in which the army considers itself part of the institutionality and not the only institution — as the soul of the nation, and not as the most important institution of the nation — around which everything must revolve, and they have advanced to this stage. And the third stage is when the army converts itself into an instrument of the institutionality, it is at the orders of the institutionality.

We are currently at the second stage. This is precisely where the discussion is at the moment between civilians and the military: either the national objective [of stability for security's sake] above all else or stability and economic development, with security as only one element. The Thesis of National Stability is in fact about institutional stability for economic development: it assumes that without economic development there is no security, and without security, there is no economic development. If we consolidate that [stage], the next stage is only a matter of years, *if* the politicians maintain a clear perspective during this process and do not want to make the army an instrument at the service of their own interests.

Despite his criticisms of the Cerezo regime, Gramajo did give Cerezo a historical role: he may not be appreciated at this point in time, but maybe ten years down the road, he, together with Gramajo himself, will be considered to have played an important role in the transition process.

Conclusions

The argument that the Cerezo regime was mere window dressing for the army's rhetorical commitment to democracy is mistaken: the Christian Democrats actively collaborated with an army that is very much committed to a military-civilian electoralism bounded by security constraints. Since 1986, it has been a collaborative project in the full sense of the term, with each side plying their own "thesis." The gamble is that by accepting the game of those in power, one is able in the long term to beat them at their own game. But as one PDCG congressional deputy commented dryly about *el proyecto político-militar*, "One doesn't know when one is being absorbed and when one is absorbing."

While Stepan's measurements of presidential inroads into military prerogatives (a civilian role in intelligence and police, and military promotions, etc.) are useful guides, it is too easy to assume in the Guatemalan case a democratic commitment on the part of civilians who are seen as totally stymied by the military. While it is true that the Cerezo government had to enter the presidential office with massive and heinous human rights violations of the most recent previous three military governments left pending, and with the understanding that the civilian regime was "merely transitional," with human rights continuing as business-as-usual, what is one to make of a president who articulates his identification with the need to fight "delinquents/subversives," displays excitement with intelligence access ("We know a lot"), and proudly proclaims he is the author of the police-army Citizen Protection patrols that have been documented committing kidnapping, torture, and killings? These declarations and admissions expose naked strategic interests of a political party, and the inadequacy of measures of accountability and oversight of the civilian president himself.

With democratic rhetoric far surpassing their ability and willingness to act, the Christian Democrats committed the fatal error of moral bankruptcy. The PDCG's checkered history of compromise and collaboration caused one Guatemalan lawyer and member of the Human Rights Commission, to question the nature of such PDCG *concertación*: "The question is, up to what point of *concertación* between the Christian Democrats and the Army can one go before one no longer has democracy? Up to what point does one compromise? The danger lies with the civilians — those without uniforms — who are reinforcing the very same commandments of the Army!" (1988 interview). Within this "national strategy," civilian rule is eclipsed by the entirely *undiminished* military role in the regulation of political life in Guatemala: it is a military institution strong enough to make civilian rule count while ensuring that it remains irrelevant.

Chapter 9
Contradictions of the Politico-Military Project

Officers of the Mountain and the 1988 and 1989 Coup Attempts

> The right wing believes that the government is manipulating the army, and the left wing believes that the army is manipulating the government!
> — Guatemalan social scientist

> One cannot envision a total democracy without limits. It is very difficult to reconcile democracy with guerrilla warfare. And we prefer to have a controlled civilian [president]....I don't mean controlled-manipulated, you understand, but I would prefer that he be to some degree controlled by the Army such that what is happening — taking us headlong toward a socialized system, taking us into chaos — won't happen.
> — Officer of the Mountain former Major Díaz López

Successful or not, coups d'état, *golpes de estado*, because of their subversive character often provide outsiders a rare glimpse into the subterranean world of internal ideological debates and deep divisions within secretive and guarded institutions. While appearing to be monolithic, perfected, and in some ways invincible, the two major coup attempts (and two minor ones during this same period) staged by Guatemalan officers calling themselves the Oficiales de la Montaña (Officers of the Mountain) on 11 May 1988 and 9 May 1989, revealed serious fissures and distrust within the armed forces, underscoring the vulnerability of a politico-military project riddled with internal contradictions of a democracy born of counterinsurgency. Because these fissures came from within the one institution that was assumed to have accommodated itself to the political change — indeed, it was the one institution that had *effected* the political change — these coups represented the worst threats confronted by a project already fraught with difficulties.

To understand how these coups came about, we must ask whether the project propelled by the Christian Democratic government and Army High Command was viewed by the majority of officers as effective from the politico-military standpoint, and whether it coincided or collided with their ideological sentiments. Within the framework of such civil-military perceptions, did the officers view the politico-military project as changing direction (i.e., becoming too reformist) or did they have long-standing disagreements with the original project of 1982? One should keep in mind that the higher ranks in Guatemala have tended, since the 1970s, to be more reformist, while the lower ranks have been traditionally more rigid and conservative in their beliefs, and thus more subject to psychological campaigns of impending chaos and doom (as occurred among young German troops late in World War II). These younger officers also tend to have more visceral reactions to the guerrilla and to "communism" in general — reactions the extreme right-wing *latifundistas* have traditionally cultivated and depended upon to protect their interests. This attitudinal difference by rank does not, however, hold for military intelligence officers; most are likely to be more "extremist," according to retired Lieutenant-Colonel Cruz Salazar, among others (1988 interview). While the High Command was perfectly aware of such ideological vulnerabilities within its ranks, and set about to wage its own indoctrination campaign for "freedom" rather than "democracy" (the latter being too closely identified with Christian Democracy), it seriously underestimated the extent to which such a campaign for its officers was necessary.

Within the armed forces, the 1988–89 coups represented three fundamental disagreements, over (1) the handling of the counterinsurgency war, with the institutionalists intensifying and systematizing the massacre operations into campaigns and combining them with the "soft aspects" of war (Civil Affairs, model villages, etc.), (2) the advisability of providing any political space to popular organizations and movements, and if so, how bounded that space should be, and (3) the necessity to modernize the state (e.g., through tax reform). Although considered militarily unsuccessful and technical or dry (or as some refer to them, "white") coups — that is, without a change of government or head of state — their cumulative effect achieved, in the end, the retrenchment of policy and the closing of political space, and the regaining of "a controlled Presidency." Given the prohibitive costs of coups or even of attempted coups, the threat of coup attempts or even just rumors of threats of coups, may be the wave of the future, especially if they accomplish the concessions these coup attempts did.

For the most part, the Cerezo regime and the Army High Command kept to the framework originally established after the March 1982 coup: a formal electoral democracy in which the army would continue exerting a major share of power as a means of defeating the insurgency and protecting against their resurgence, and in which the civilian government would not pursue a transformative agenda of structural reform but present itself as "eminently transitional." The politico-military project succeeded in reducing the immediate guerrilla threat and in slightly co-opting elements of the popular movement with the promise of social and economic programs. The PDCG kept its promise of not investigating military involvement in past violence or corruption and rejected meaningful land reform. Hence the honeymoon between the private sector represented principally by CACIF (confederation of industrial, commercial, and agricultural interests) and the PDCG lasted for about one-and-a-half years after the elections. But when the PDCG did move to restructure the tax system — for example, "to create by satellite a Catastro Nacional (National Registry) of rural and subsistence property for new taxation," an intelligence source revealed in interview, and also an income tax increase of 5 to 7 percent ("Not a drastic increase by any other standard," Cerezo's Finance Minister, Rodolfo Paiz, stated in interview, "but by Guatemalan standards, it was tremendous") — without properly preparing the political ground, the most economically radical group of all, the national association of cotton and sugar *latifundistas*, UNAGRO, backed by CACIF, began to speak about "the communists" in government. In addition to these reforms, Defense Minister Gramajo prohibited the army from guarding private property or accepting food and lodging from *finqueros* as compensation for "killing the union leader organizing his workers" (interview). Nor were licenses for arms permitted. UNAGRO reacted "in a way they have many times before: to cry for help to the army to solve their problems," one institutionalist officer complained. "But if we do not fight tax reform *now*," countered one prominent member of UNAGRO in an interview, "the next will be agrarian reform!"

If one looks back to the civilian regime of Méndez Montenegro in 1966 and asks who the Officers of the Mountain were who staged the numerous coup attempts at that time, it was also the traditionalist UNAGRO, according to Gramajo: "The Oficiales de la Montaña made their appearance on 19 July 1966. Julio César Méndez Montenegro was president for sixteen days when a letter appeared in the newspaper *La Hora* signed by the Officers of the Mountain, accusing him of being a communist. He had wanted to impose taxes and he couldn't: the military wouldn't support him, and the then Finance Minister Fuentes Mohr was replaced. And the Officers of the Mountain were forgotten about. It was a campaign that equated military officers with anticommunism, antitax, and all of that. Later, when [President] Cerezo began to impose taxes and went to Madrid to speak with the subversion, the Officers of the Mountain made their appearance once again. So, who are they? I went back to look at who they were twenty years ago: they were UNAGRO. Now who are they? They are UNAGRO. Once again from UNAGRO is Anzueto Vielman, Mario David García, and Danilo Roca.[1] Their method of broadcasting their *comunicados* was [the newspaper] *Prensa Libre* — *puro conservatismo*. So it was them and not military officers [who are the Oficiales de la Montaña] today, but they wanted to influence our officers by speaking about the fight against communism and the fight for our dead brothers and all that. So, they were never officers from the mountain, they are civilians from the city" (interview).

When the PDCG tax reform was not quashed through political channels, UNAGRO sought support from a small but loquacious group of active, discharged, and retired hardline officers who had their own gripes with the armed forces. With a promise of Q5 million,[2] mostly from UNAGRO, and the cooperation of a group of journalists contributing to destabilization efforts, an unsuccessful coup was staged on 11 May 1988. A split within CACIF, however, hindered the *golpistas*' efforts. On the one hand stood the *ultraderechistas latifundistas* (especially the *azucaceros* (sugar growers) who several institutionalist officers and civilian advisers described as "*muy duros*"), including "the old activists of the rightwing: Sisniega Otero, Danilo Roca, and Edgar Heinemann who still manipulate the anticommunist rhetoric and coup actions because they claim that the guerrilla and unionist both work against their profit margin on the *finca*," one Guatemalan analyst remarked cynically (interview). "They work together with the new resentful ones [*los resentidos*] — retired Lieutenant Colonel D'jalma Domínguez[3] and Mario David García." On the other hand, the industrial and commercial leaders — clothing and fish merchants and bankers, many with degrees in business administration — did not go along with the coup because "they see the economy and their factories falling apart and although they are also very conservative, see themselves by way of *el proyecto* winning in the elections" (civilian intelligence analyst, interview). Although this sector contributed money to the first coup because of peer pressure, they were "all the while crossing their fingers that it wouldn't be successful" (officer, interview). This latter group refused to have anything to do with the second major coup on 9 May 1989, now viewed as mainly an internal army *intento* (coup attempt). At the armed forces' Forum on Counterinsurgency in Guatemala City on 17 April 1987 (which President Cerezo cautioned Gramajo against holding), Gramajo warned the UNAGRO *latifundistas* "to cease organizing a coup, cease this conspiracy because we know you are involved and all you will accomplish is to create fissures. You won't bring down the government!" One of the bankers in attendance admitted that "It's the doing of those of UNAGRO. We, the financiers, cannot say no [to them]" (Gramajo, interview). While the PDCG might be blamed for not preparing the political ground for a tax increase, the UNAGRO *golpistas* discovered, to their surprise, there was less support for destabilizing the new regime, especially from the Defense Minister's office, even though the continuing boycott by the economic sector to pay any taxes created a fiscal crisis for everyone, including the military.[4] "The coup attempt took place because the oligarchs had lost their dominance in Guatemala. But the *intento* was insufficient to change the tax law; nevertheless, they continue to refuse to pay," Gramajo stated (interview).

Who Are the Oficiales de la Montaña?

Although Gramajo calls the Officers of the Mountain "civilians in the city," he also admits that many of UNAGRO's fears are echoed by a "cross section" of military officers.[5] They are officers who fought in the 1981–83 counter-insurgency war and believed scorched-earth tactics and repression were the only ways to defend Guatemala against *subversivos y delincuentes-terroristas.* Together with ultrareactionary *latifundistas*, these officers continued to carry around the mental furniture of the 100 percent solution of total war and the traditional model of authoritarian rule. Angered by the government's lack of support for the contras in the 1980s, by the serious lobbying for the first dialogue with the guerrilla in October 1987 in Madrid, and by the arrival of Rigoberta Menchú and RUOG members in Guatemala in March 1988 (after eight years of exile), the Cerezo regime was viewed suspiciously by one of the Oficiales' *comunicados* as "green on the outside and red on the inside, bringing forth a Marxist state." Another states, "The Christian Democratic Party seeks to provoke a general insurrection that would permit the URNG to cut out the political stages and take power immediately" (see Appendix 2). These officers were deeply worried at the time about a PDCG-initiated union movement that "they now cannot control, running a great risk because it is escaping control. At any given moment, thousands could close the streets in the capital against the National Police. If the situation deteriorates too much, if the strike is truly strong, I believe the only way to prevent civil war is for the armed forces to take power. Because once it begins, it is impossible to stop" (Díaz López, interview).[6] In short, one must wage war in order to prevent war. Additionally, by way of Civil Patrols and Councils of Development in the highlands, they saw the PDCG undercutting the MLN power base: "In the 1988 municipal elections, the peasant was given a sack of corn, a machete, and a vote for the PDCG. These Councils and Patrols have been converted to perpetuate the party in power. If the army had manipulated the 6 million illiterate peasants [that way], it is certain that this president would not be Cerezo. It would have been a rat (*un raton*), that the Army wanted." But the real danger, Díaz López continues, "lies with the 7900 rural social *promotores* who are *guerrilla militantes* who have an enormous capacity to organize the masses into an enormous army at the service of the subversive!"

Not surprisingly, many of the Oficiales' demands paralleled UNAGRO's interests in destabilizing the Cerezo regime: "We in the army felt threatened by the presence of many Marxists in the [Cerezo] government. We were clearly aware that the actions of this government were working toward the establishment of a socialist regime. The economic crisis is [itself] the product of a strategy of the Marxists to destroy the middle class and to develop the struggle of classes. And they can only do this if there is a rich minority and a poor minority, but the middle class was large in Guatemala in the beginning of 1970 and this was an obstacle for them." Also like UNAGRO, they believed that by "limiting [economic burdens]," such as taxes, "eliminating privileges," being "antimonopolist," especially against U.S. corporations, and "totally eliminating state intervention into the economy," they would have a better solution than the Christian Democrats: "The idea is to destroy, sell, and put into private hands — national and foreign (depending on who offers better services to the Guatemalan people) — the telephones, the railroads, the electric company, and so forth." The state would also be made smaller, eliminating at least seven "unnecessary ministries." Private enterprise was to be encouraged without letting the state bureaucracy grow. Nor would the Oficiales be "deceived" by agrarian reform: "We look at the agrarian reform in El Salvador which didn't work at all." They believed in promoting agro-industry "because the peasant doesn't necessarily need a plot of land, only well-being in the peasant areas in order to develop them. For example, we could promote agricultural production, say vegetables. But I'm not just talking about production for consumption but for export as well. This would generate a series of peripheral industries. Guatemala has only focused on industrial development" (Díaz López and Vielman, interview).

But it was the belief that the High Command was no longer the representative of the army but had been converted into a representative of the party and the government that set many officers' teeth on edge. President Cerezo succeeded in "capturing" General Gramajo, they argue, when the two were both in Washington (when Gramajo was with the military delegation there), and later when Gramajo was head of the Cuartel General in 1984:

There exists a clear connection between the Army Command and the Christian Democratic Party. They are complicitous in obeying a global strategy to neutralize the Army. We hope that the army serves as a brake on the errors and wrongs we have seen developing in this government. Nevertheless, when [the High Command] was converted into an instrument of the [PDCG], this produced real anger [among officers] and marked a division in the army. On the one side, the military High Command that is creating sovereignty economically speaking, and on the other, the officers who were fighting in the mountains.
Q: So you think that the High Command is part of this process of socialism?
Yes, I believe so. Look, I think that the High Command perhaps doesn't go along completely with the principle of socialism, but I believe that the High Command is participating in a project that it doesn't understand. That is to say, General Gramajo doesn't really know what he is doing. For personal ambition, for wanting to project himself out into national politics, he has embraced a political cause that he doesn't understand. And because he doesn't understand it, he's not taking into account that the problem is *not* Christian Democratic philosophy but the *usage* that the Communist Party is making of it within the Christian Democratic Party.
Q: Are you saying that the Christian Democrats are ignorant of what is happening as well?
Well, I believe that the highest directors [of the party] know precisely what is happening and the evidence of such a party nexus between the PDCG and the communists is clear to someone [like myself] with access to military intelligence. (Díaz López, interview)

He goes on to explain. "There is a coterie of officers who are very much influenced by the political parties of the right wing, and I won't deny that some officers have three or four friends in these parties. *We know each other because it is the same army intelligence we have been sharing for years*"[7] (see Figures 16, 17). Given this long-standing "party nexus" and sharing of intelligence between the "*ultra*" *línea* of G-2 and the *ultra* political parties, one could make the same argument of manipulation by the extreme right. In addition, the Army High Command—in this case Gramajo—is given no credit for having ideas or political influence of his own; as a gullible officer, he is merely swayed by PDCG/communist talk. This same logic, ironically, is applied by the High Command to explain the reason for the coup attempts: gullible officers are swayed and bribed by extreme rightwing UNAGRO *latifundistas*. Both *lineas* further apply this same logic to the indigenous peasant, who is assumed to fall prey to "foreign ideologies."

Distrust and suspicion are turned into scathing diatribes against the president and Defense Minister in the Oficiales' clandestine comuniqués: President Cerezo and sixty members of his government are "drug traffickers" and "subversives," the Minister of Defense Alejandro "without balls," Gramajo a "communist." To counter such attacks and because "there were always dissenting voices" within the institution, Gramajo speaks of organizing "retreat seminars" for the commanders (including "the leader of the hardline officers, Colonel Lima") four times a year beginning in 1986. But the giveaway that the Oficiales were a significantly influential dissenting force within the Guatemalan military comes from Gramajo's own 1988 address to the graduating cadets of the *Escuela Politécnica*, when he refers to the "three enemies: the internal enemy—that maladapted, frustrated, nihilist officer for whom nothing is going well; the greedy officer who allies himself with the small group of manipulators"; and finally, the Marxist-Leninist subversive with whom he doubted there could be a dialogue for the Peace Accords (1988b). Although they agreed with many of the *latifundistas'* fears, many middle-ranking, *mano dura* officers during the scorched-earth operations voiced their gripes with the reinforcement of the military's "disciplinary system of hierarchy, obedience and nondeliberance," for example, following orders and not voicing one's political opinion ("We couldn't express ourselves openly," one *golpista* complained) after the 1982 coup. As we saw in an earlier chapter, these new directives led to several mini-rebellions during the 1982–83 massacre campaign, causing one commander to step down and Gramajo having to rescue two others. Reportedly, a demonstration at the CEM during this same time period by middle-ranking officers protesting Gramajo's promotions, led to the dismissal of a number of officers. One Oficiales' *comunicado* states that "the damage done to the army by the subversion is less than that caused by Gramajo" in not promoting or in discharging officers between 1986 and 1988. Captain Rodolfo Muñoz Pilona complained, "That should give you some idea of the fact that if you didn't align yourself behind the directives of what they call 'loyalty,' then you left" (*Crónica*, 25 August 1988: 17–18). Angered as well by the dialogue held with the URNG in Madrid in October 1987, twenty-five *mano dura* officers were elected from different military zones throughout the country to visit each military zone "to convince other officers that the army was not in agreement with it" (Díaz López, interview). And, just five months before the May 1988 coup, according to an army bulletin, three high-ranking members of the Army National Defense Staff in the northeastern military zone of El Quiché were dismissed from their posts and transferred elsewhere for having "failed in the offensive of the year" to dislodge the guerrilla (by way of Task Force Kaibil Balam) (DIDE, 1 January 1988) (see Figure 17). One of these Task Force officers, Colonel Jaime Rabanales Reyes, commander of Santa Cruz del Quiché military zone publicly voiced his disagreement with this first dialogue that had "created strong disagreements within the armed forces." These officers also expressed their "disgust" with the interference of the Ministry of Development in civic tasks in the countryside — considered to be the exclusive jurisdiction of the military (*El Nuevo Diario*, 30 January 1988).

With the 1987–88 offensives underway, criticisms of how the counterinsurgency war was being fought abound in *comunicados*[8] that speak of more officers dying in the fighting in these offensives "than have been killed by the guerrilla," due to the High Command's corruption and disregard. As one leader of the *intentos* stated,

Our troops were fighting, spending ten to fifteen days without receiving food, eating fruits and vegetables they could find in the mountains. Many soldiers and officers have died because they have not received medical attention because they could not be flown out as there were no helicopters. We don't accept that our bosses get rich ("buy luxury helicopters for their fat asses") while our soldiers don't eat or we watch them die. Three months ago, there was an officer wounded in the lung in the Ixcán who was flown to the hospital at Playa Grande base. But the hospital had no anesthesia and the doctor had to operate without it. It is not possible that the Army is fighting [under these conditions]! But this is the difference: the people who know the war and the people who only see it from afar who have not suffered in it. (Díaz López, interview)

These Oficiales perceive of "a real division" in the army: on the one side, the High Command, which had economic dominion, and the intermediate-level officers who had "been at war since they left the military academy twenty-five to twenty-eight years ago. But the war has had different levels of intensity. And the worst levels of the war have been between 1979 and the present. The officers who fought with major intensity in 1979–83 are now colonels and majors, and from there on down to lieutenants, second lieutenants, and captains. These are the people who have had to fight in this war, who saw their soldiers dying, officers who were away from their families sometimes for one year." They target Defense Minister Gramajo as doing "all his course work at schools in the U.S." and as being the "son-of-a-bitch Minister of National Defeat." Díaz López states that it was among these middle-level officers that it was decided as "necessary to execute a military action that would put an end to this problem. The general idea of the movement was to provoke a profound change in the structure of the country—not just to try and change the faces, but to try and change the structures of the country." Oficiales believed that with the institutionalists' semantic shift from an "anticommunist army to a prodemocratic army, we would become softer," Gramajo explained impatiently. "They failed to understand that the issue was to continue fighting the war but by broader means" (interview). More significantly, they clearly failed to understand that *el proyecto político-militar* did not diminish but rather enhanced the military's hegemony.

Other Events Leading Up to 11 May 1988

In early March 1988, the Episcopal Conference of Guatemalan Bishops published its annual pastoral letter entitled "Clamor for Land," which tepidly called for "agrarian redistribution," prompting letters of outrage in the press from conservative business and agricultural sectors. After two large labor demonstrations in January of that year, President Cerezo agreed to meet representatives of the newly formed Labor and Popular Action Union (UASP) (six labor union coalitions) on 8 March. A *pacto* was signed on new minimum wage increases of Q50 ($20) a month, price controls on basic commodities, a moderate electricity rate increase, and the promise to form an Executive Advisory Commission for Human Rights to investigate political crimes committed over the past fifteen years. This *pacto* was considered the most significant act of the twenty-five-month-old government. On 5 April 1988, the first *comunicado* of the Officers of the Mountain was circulated in Guatemala, which called for the denunciation and overthrow of the government and the military High Command "for treachery against the nation and the democratic institutions." On 14 April, another *comunicado* was distributed, announcing the reactivation of the death squad Movimiento Anticomunista Nacional Organizado, or La Mano Blanca (White Hand) because of the pending 18 April arrival of a four-member RUOG (United Representation of Guatemalan Opposition) delegation to Guatemala. This *comunicado* further accused Cerezo of being "partisan to the establishment of a communist dictatorship" in Guatemala (*El Nuevo Diario*, 19 April 1988). A list of 300 persons marked as "communists" by the death squads was distributed. The results of the municipal elections in which the Christian Democrats won a majority further increased the despair and panic of the extreme right wing.

The month of May began with a Workers Day parade, the first public appearance of the Committee of Peasant Unity (CUC) (which had gained legal recognition from the Christian Democratic government)[9] and the finalization of the March accord. On 5 May, Congress discussed a possible extension of the amnesty law (Decree 71-87) for another six months. That same morning, the Group of Mutual Support (GAM) staged a demonstration in Santa Cruz del Quiché, demanding authorization to identify bodies discovered in a mass grave in the region. And although the government reiterated its stance that it would not undertake negotiations with the guerrilla, there was discussion that the Commission of National Reconciliation would meet with the URNG guerrilla leadership while attending a conference in Costa Rica (*Crónica*, 26 May 1988: 11). On 10 May, Mario Sandoval Alarcón, the father of the Movimiento Liberación Nacionalista, the ultraconservative death-squad-spawning party of 1954, announced that "if the government doesn't accept what is happening and doesn't adopt the necessary corrective measures, the situation could get much more difficult in the short-term" (*El Gráfico*, 10 May 1988).[10] Even though every active duty officer involved in the conspiracy "was warned by the National Defense Staff that the government knew about a coup plot," and was forced to sign a statement acknowledging the High Command's warning (Gramajo, interview), the *intento* was launched on 11 May 1988.

First Coup Attempt

At 1 A.M. on 11 May 1988, Lieutenant Colonel Padilla Morales, the forty-two-year-old commander of the First Infantry Battalion at the Retalhuleu (Reu) military base, ordered his troops to board the private commercial trucks waiting at the gates of the compound for Guatemala City, 150 kilometers away.[11] They were ordered to tie the red handkerchiefs they found in the trucks around their necks. Padilla, like other young commanders at three other military zones (Jutiapa, Chiquimula, Zacapa) and the Tactical Wing of the Air Force, was given instructions to surround the National Palace and suppress any resistance by the Presidential Guard. An investigation by base commander Colonel Méndez López a few minutes later revealed that the entire battalion, of 336 troops, five superior officers, and 11 subordinate officers, was gone. Méndez then called the Army High Command. Defense Minister Gramajo telephoned Colonel Perussina (one of his loyal Flecha officers) to intercept and detain the troops marching toward the capital. He managed to detain Padilla at about 2:30 A.M. "But the very first thing I did was phone Colonel Lima, commander of the Chiquimula base and leader of the *mano dura* officers." Gramajo asked him how the troops were. " 'Fine,' he says to me. 'The troops are in the barracks with a canteen full of water' — meaning they are afraid to move. So I said, 'Don't you dare move or you'll be in trouble' " (interview). Lima, though, did move his troops that morning, only to be blocked by the Mariscal Zavala troops on the outskirts of Guatemala City, while unknown armed units temporarily occupied GUATEL (Empresa Guatemalteca de Telecomunicaciones) and Radio Nacional. (He would later tell Gramajo that he drove into the city in civilian attire at 9 A.M. to see that there were "no uprisings, nothing" and realized the coup was a mistake [interview].) The third set of troops left their base at 2:30 A.M. by order of Colonel Gustavo Adolfo Cifuentes Dardón, the forty-three-year-old Second Commander of the military zone of Jutiapa, 80 kilometers southeast of the capital. Unlike Reu's commander, Jutiapa base commander Colonel Luis Getellá Solórzano said he did not discover the mobilization until 8 A.M. The Jutiapa troops had positioned their artillery equipment on one of the main highways into the capital. But because G-2 had telephoned an informant's house in Jutiapa to ascertain that the military base was empty, the troops had been stopped by the Honor Guard and two armored vehicles at 6:30 A.M. They were persuaded to take off their red scarves and return to base. Later, Major Díaz López would explain this action by the fact that "many of the civilians [going to work] stopped and talked to the soldiers," trying to persuade them not to stage a coup. "The troops didn't want a bloody confrontation within the army, and with civilians standing in front of the artillery tanks, the commander didn't want to cause civilian casualties." Once they discovered the High Command was opposed to their movement, most of the officers and troops had no inclination to disobey; they claimed that was the first talk they had heard of any coup. There were also some protest actions in the military zones of Suchitepéquez and El Quiché, which maintained telephone contact with General Gramajo (*Inforpress Centroamericana*, 12 May 1988: 14). A little over eight hours later, at 9:30 A.M., all was back to normal. "There was not even a single shot, no loss of discipline or much less any disrespect toward a superior officer," one officer recounted (Iglesias and Varley 1989: 3). Laid out principally by a group of civilians and retired or discharged officers, the failed plan had relied on the assumption that Gramajo would lead the troops and command the movement against Cerezo. The Reu troops were to go to the National Palace and accept Gramajo's orders to oust Cerezo, with Chiquimula protecting Reu's flank, while Jutiapa was to bomb the Honor Guard from the hills. Meanwhile, the civilians would instigate uprisings in the whole city against the National Palace and the President to prevent the movement of troops loyal to Cerezo. "They really thought the High Command couldn't sustain itself against such pressure," Gramajo stated. "They have no respect for the armed forces" (interview). Major Díaz López later admitted there had been "some errors of coordination: [for one], we couldn't count on the commanders who have been made generals and make good salaries" and who remained loyal to President Cerezo and Defense Minister Gramajo. "They organized an action to neutralize us by not participating in the coup, and in the end, the movement could do nothing. We expected more action in the interior of the country" (interview).

Earlier, at 7:30 A.M., General Gramajo had provided Cerezo and his Cabinet with the names of five civilians to stand trial. "Trembling, the Attorney General, sitting at the table, said it was not possible to indict them as there were not enough facts." Instead, they agreed to treat the coup attempt as an act of military insubordination and to work within the military tribunal system. "As always, the civilians behind everything are clean and the military officers suffer [for their actions]." At 10:15 A.M., General Gramajo, in camouflage uniform and accompanied by eleven high military commanders mainly from the capital, held a press conference at which, in a conciliatory tone, he stated that "speculations, disinformation and some unscrupulous[12] persons in the end were able to penetrate some officers of the army, and because of this, there were some acts of indiscipline in two military zones today at dawn. The officers involved were tricked into believing that the orders to mobilize were in support of the government." He admitted that the purpose of the movement was to take the National Palace and effect a coup. Nevertheless, this was the intent of "only a small group of malcontents." Without giving names, he went on to insist that "these events have been encouraged and provoked by radical [rightwing] civilians, enemies of the democratic system and the government which the Guatemalan people have elected." Such civilians had not only participated in the coup but had lent their private commercial trucks and financial resources to help it succeed. He warned that "these groups would no longer be permitted to continue with these types of activities" and would be subject to judicial investigation along with the responsible army officers. He further stated that Officers of the Mountain didn't exist, only "civilians of the city" (Iglesias and Varley 1989: 5), with reference to retired military officers who had been out of the country and had lost touch with the national reality and the Army. If Gramajo minimized the coup, Cerezo spoke of it as a "reasonable insurrection." At a luncheon speech to the Guatemalan Rotary Club, he characterized the movement of troops as a "natural" expression of dissatisfaction by one of the many sectors in a political democracy: "The army officers are also human and in an act of indiscipline expressed their discontentment with some of the government's actions. It is only logical for them to express their dissatisfaction. Now that we live in a democratic environment, all the sectors have demonstrated against different governmental acts. Workers, peasants, public employees, even judges have demonstrated. The only ones left were members of the army who are also human. They are people who should be heard. I think one has to be flexible and consider the officers' grievances as we have done in the case of other sectors" (Iglesias and Varley 1989: 10). This moderating approach by Gramajo and Cerezo may be understood in two ways. First, knowing that the strategy of the rebels was to maximize the coup attempt with the backing of most of the owners of the media (newspapers, radio, and television), Cerezo admitted to the *Miami Herald* that "We sought to minimize the seriousness of the rebellion because we knew that part of the plan of the rebels was to maximize it. They counted on other officers joining them if the action appeared to be successful" (13 May 1991). Second, if we remember that the strategy of the Christian Democrats was collaboration, ultramoderation, and self-constraint, this particular stance should come as no surprise.

Over the next few days, six active-duty army officers were arrested on charges of rebellion and their cases referred for prosecution to the Auditoría de Guerra (a military tribunal). Colonel Cifuentes Dardón and Lieutenant Colonel Padilla Morales were arrested at their respective zones, and they, in turn, implicated two former army officers, Major Díaz López and Lieutenant Estrada Portillo, as well as a number of high-profile civilians, in the attempted coup. It appeared as though the army was going to prosecute the officers; however, the crime of sedition, typically applied in such situations, was reduced to a charge of a simple lack of military discipline and punished by minor arrests and temporary suspensions of active service without pay (Cruz Salazar 1988b). In separate statements both officers claimed to have been tricked into participating in a coordinated movement against the government: Lieutenant Colonel Padilla claimed to have received a series of telephone calls from "friends in arms"[13] who told him and like-minded officers that "Operation Save Guatemala" would be for the benefit of the Guatemalan people. He admitted knowing that the purpose of the movement being planned was to overthrow the Cerezo government and install a new one. He also admitted having several meetings with a former army intelligence officer, Major Gustavo Adolfo Díaz López, to coordinate the coup, at which he learned that a number of civilians were involved. They included Gustavo Anzueto Vielman, Dr. Mario Castejón, Mario David García, Nicolás Buonafina, and Danilo Roca.[14] According to the plan, Castejón would be president and Colonel Lima, Army Chief of Staff.

It appears that few lower-ranking officers and none of the soldiers were told that the purpose of the mobilization was to overthrow the government until after it had been stopped. (According to Iglesias and Varley, one lieutenant testified that when he was ordered to prepare his company, he thought it was a secret inspection to determine the company's readiness. It was only on the road that he first heard they were moving on the capital in an attempted coup [1989].) This seems to confirm Gramajo's public statement of officers being tricked into mobilization. Yet the question remains as to why these officers were so willing to believe that a coup was underway. Are we to believe that the civilian "brains" managed to persuade some rather gullible officers to carry out the coup while they remained behind the scenes? Or were the civilians, as they were to argue later in court, innocent targets of the army's search for scapegoats? In short, was this merely a case of some 600 innocent troops and officers being organized by a handful of officers and civilians, or did this represent significant dissatisfaction within the officer corps?

At the end of May 1988, Gramajo made several changes in base commanders, admitting later that he did take advantage of the coup attempt to rotate, discharge, retire, or "exile" certain hardline officers. For his part, Colonel Getellá (the only West Point graduate on active duty in the Guatemalan army, a former Chimaltenango Military Zone Commander in the 1982 Iximché Task Force campaign, and a protagonist in the 1983 *relevo* of Ríos Montt) was relieved of his command for failure to discover and prevent the mobilization of his zone, and sent to a base in El Quiché; Colonel Guillermo Vargas, commander of the zone of Zacapa, and Colonel Edgar Solís of the Air Force's Tactical Group, were relieved of their command for "an omission" in the fulfillment of duties, although none of the three commanders was assigned to a military tribunal. Colonel Nuíla Hub, founder and chief of the Kaibil Special Forces in the 1970s, chief of the Military Police in 1982, EMP Chief under Mejía (1983–84), and later director of the Center for Military Studies, was sent to Ecuador as military attaché. Colonel Byron Lima, founder in 1980 of the Kamikaze Counterinsurgency Tactical Unit of CRIO, Agrupamiento Táctico leader under the Chacacaj Task Force commander in Huehuetenango in late June 1982, Playa Grande base commander in El Quiché in 1982–83, and Chiquimula military base commander, was sent to Peru to serve as military attaché, "where he could have no influence." Gramajo explains his strategy: "If I had ousted Lima, the leader of the hardline officers, he would have become a civilian and a hero — a free civilian moving around the country where he would have gathered forces with the economic power groups and had even more power. So, I ignored him. Six months later, he sent me a message thanking me, asking my permission to visit Cuba!" (interview). Officers of lesser rank, including Díaz López and Vielman García, were "jailed, stripped of their rank or sentenced." The High Command distinguished between "temporary dismissals" from nine months to one year for two colonels and two captains, and "definitive dismissals" of possibly nine officers (*Inforpress Centroamericana*, 16 June 1988: 13).

The Civilians

Because civilians (including former army officers) could not be prosecuted in a military court under Guatemalan law, the civilians named by the military defendants were forwarded to a civilian court and a civilian judge was appointed to the case. The civilians to be investigated included Gustavo Anzueto Vielman, Dr. Mario Castejón, Mario David García, Nicolas Buonafina, and Danilo Roca, as well as three former officers, Major Gustavo Díaz López, Captain Vielman García, and Lieutenant Estrada Portillo. On 18 May, as Judge Ana Maria Orozco entered a formal order acknowledging receipt of the case and commencing the investigation, the residence of the foreign correspondent for the Soviet newspaper *Tass* was bombed.[15] (*Comunicado* 9 later claimed credit for "expelling the Russian Agency *Tass*.") Later that same day, one of the civilians accused of planning the coup, Díaz

López, appeared on the television news show *Aquí el Mundo*, owned and directed by Mario David García, who had called on viewers to wear red handkerchiefs in support of the uprising. Díaz López charged that the Christian Democratic government had a plan to move the country, step by step, into socialism, evidenced by the arrival of Cuban charter flights and those of Nicaraguan Aeronica, the establishment of *Tass* and *Prensa Latina* offices, the increasing resources and firepower of the National Police by Government Minister Rodil Peralta to sideline the army, and trips by the First Lady to Cuba. He also accused Cerezo of making secret trips to Nicaragua, speaking with Cuban and Soviet diplomats during his trips to Mexico and Costa Rica, and sending a representative to the Esquipulas I meetings. He accused the Christian Democrats of "penetrat[ing]" and destabilizing the Guatemalan army. As an example, he said that on 11 April 1986, Minister of Defense Gramajo swore loyalty to the powers of the State. To Díaz López, this meant the submission of the army to the interests of the Christian Democratic Party. For his part, Estrada Portillo declared to the press that Christian Democracy was "a green vehicle that transports red passengers," an instrument out to destroy the army (*Inforpress Centroamericana*, 16 June 1988: 13). MLN congressional deputy Juan Carlos Simons demanded Gramajo investigate Díaz López's charges of the Guatemala-Cuba plan "to communize" Guatemala politically and not militarily (*La Hora*, 18 May 1988). On 19 May, the government suspended Channel 3's frequency, just as the five civilians were preparing an *Aquí el Mundo* group appearance.

Based on Padilla's and Cifuentes's statements, Judge Orozco ordered the arrest of Díaz López and Estrada Portillo on 27 May, and despite numerous requests (for Military Police guards for their safety, for an appeal to stop the investigation and two requests to be released on bail), the two remained detained until mid-June while the judge continued her investigation. Three death threats against the judge,[16] the bombing of the offices of the Guatemalan newspaper *La Época* on 10 June,[17] and the promise by magistrates in the Appeals Court to decide in the defendants' favor in order not to receive threats meant the men were released only a few days before the new amnesty law was approved by Congress. Although the civilians were not allowed to leave the country, they were not jailed in a detention center as long as they promised to appear before the court if they were called over the course of one month. Meanwhile, they became heroes in the press (*Inforpress Centroamericana*, 16 June 1988: 14).

Concessions

Although it was an unsuccessful, "technical coup," the Cerezo government responded to the *intento* with a major retrenchment in its efforts to open the country politically and reform it economically: the *pacto* was tossed aside for a neoliberal economic plan (*Crónica*, 26 May 1988: 12); on 23 May (the same day that Congress approved the amnesty bill), Cerezo announced that Government Minister Rodil Peralta would step down, as would Minister of Foreign Relations Alfonso Cabrera. National Police Chief G-2 Colonel Julio Caballeros would be sent abroad to spend a year at the Inter-American Defense College in Washington. There also appeared to be an acquiescence to traditional G-2 methods, with a significant rise in disappearances, particularly in the countryside. *La Época* reported on 27 May that disgruntled factions of the army presented the government with a list of twenty-five demands sometime after the aborted coup of 11 May. These included: cancellation of the government's dialogue with the guerrillas; the requirement that every exile or refugee returning to Guatemala request and receive amnesty; cancellation of the planned agrarian reforms; limits on the growth of labor unions and of *campesino* and human rights organizations; the resignation of Minister Gramajo; and the cancellation of any relations with the socialist bloc. "We are reliably informed," stated Colonel Nuíla, "that [President] Cerezo — after 11 May — met with the commanders of military bases throughout the country who asked for a more 'anticommunist' attitude, excluding dialogue with the guerrilla and involving a change of policy toward Nicaragua and the closure of news agencies Soviet *Tass* and the Cuban *Prensa Latina*" (Comité Pro-Justicia y Paz, August 1988: 9). Gramajo, however, is adamant that the *golpistas* did not make any demands or that the *intento* had any effect: the result, he argues, was "the same because they didn't exercise any pressure, because they had been thrown out of the army. How is someone in jail going to exert pressure for concessions?" (interview). More significant for him was the fact that the coup did not alter the tax reforms.

Nonetheless, while the formal system of government remained, there was a sense of resignation and despair. As Cerezo's Public Relations Secretary, Claudia Arenas, stated to the author in August 1988, "Undoubtedly, the *intento* had a political effect; it marked a new stage of government. There were problems and many high expectations, but everyone has lost their patience. In order to continue to support *el proceso*, we are obliged to seek a new equilibrium" (interview).

Amnesty

On 23 June 1988, the Guatemalan Congress approved a new political amnesty law, which took effect on 9 July. The new law extended the 180-day decree emitted in November 1987 as a result of the Esquipulas agreement of Central American presidents. Like the previous decree, the new amnesty referred to "political and related common crimes against the internal political order, public order and social tranquility." Ironically, the first to benefit from the new amnesty were those who were against the Esquipulas I meetings altogether: the three military officers implicated in the May coup attempt (who had been jailed following the uprising) who became perhaps Guatemala's first recognized political prisoners, as well as the seven civilians (including two former Army officers, three of whom had been released for lack of evidence by the court). The previous amnesty had expired on 5 May, and the government was facing pressure at the time from the right wing not to accept guerrilla dialogue proposals. Less than a week later, with a weakened administration, Cerezo was forced to approve of a new general amnesty that included the coup organizers who said they were defending Guatemala against "the communist threat" (*Central America Report*, 15 July 1988: 211). Gramajo speaks of his disappointment when the government did not utilize its full legal powers to prosecute the *golpista* officers:

Q: So why did you [in the government] give amnesty to the *golpistas* of the first coup attempt?

We didn't give them amnesty. Listen carefully. The first *intento* began at 1 A.M. and by 7:30, I was speaking with Cerezo. I told him, "We must take prisoners, institute legal proceedings, and make an example of them." But the Procurador General [Attorney General of the Public Ministry], whose name was Palencia, began to tremble [from fear] because he had to institute proceedings [against the *golpistas*]. As the *Procurador*, he had never done anything like this before, and after a little while, he began to cry. Claudia Arenas was braver than Mario Palencia. So, when I saw that there was not going to be any way of getting the legal aspect moving, I told the President, "Mr. President, I am going to treat this like a matter of military indiscipline, and we're going to deal with it within military proceedings. It's not necessary to involve the Attorney General because he's such a coward." I was *very* angry. "But," I said, "because we're going to keep a low profile within the Army, you are not going to sponsor demonstrations or popular reaction in support of your government against the *golpistas*. We are going to deal with this within [our own institutional framework], but you are not to mobilize your people meanwhile."

Q: Without giving it any importance politically?

Yes, that's right. So, first we dealt with the various officers administratively: a month in detention, later court-martial without honors, everything. But there were some, like three or four [officers], who, because they had stolen a weapon or had pushed their way through a door or driven a stolen car and gotten into an accident, remain as prisoners. I believe the government was only interested in ingratiating itself with these officers. They granted them *all* a general amnesty—both the guerrillas and the *golpistas*—once again, for there was already Amnesty Decree 8-86 which they renovated in '88.

Q: This amnesty [of '88] also included Rigoberta Menchú and Rolando Castillo [of the RUOG mission]?

Yes, all of them.

Q: So, you [in the Army] were indeed angry about this?

We weren't exactly angry except that the normal procedures needed to be followed. It was one of the major frustrations I've had. People write about human rights and yet they don't know that it isn't the soldier or the Ministry [of Defense] or the police, but that it is the system, it is the judges, the secretaries, the accusers, the attorney general [who don't follow the law].

Q: But who exactly was responsible for this amnesty?
[Supreme Court Justice] Vázquez [Martínez].
Q: But wasn't he under a lot of pressure from Cerezo?
I believe so. (interview)

Thus, what must have seemed a great opportunity to utilize the civilian legal apparatus to indict the *golpistas*, and thus distance this decision from the High Command, was, in his opinion, lost. Rumors circulating in the 4legal and political spheres in Guatemala at this time were that the government was pressuring the Attorney General to prosecute the case against the civilians aggressively, with the prosecutors ordered to submit a list of fifty questions. Yet these questions were said to be "narrow, repetitive and self-incriminating, formulated not to produce any further information" or incite any destabilizing actions (Iglesias and Varley 1989: 22).

Gramajo has since written that he promised himself and "my fellow officers that there would not be another coup. I worked hard at this. In the Army, I gave lectures, proffered advice, wrote warning letters to individuals, ordered transfers, organized seminars and took many administrative and educational measures to ensure that the Army remained loyal to democracy. Special attention was given to the garrison and zone commanders and to the members of the intelligence service. I also spoke at universities, private clubs, labor union halls, diplomatic receptions and meetings of the economic associations and chambers. I addressed all of Guatemala, except the politicians. I wanted to avoid 'being penetrated by politicians' and I wanted to persuade the army officers that there was no chance that the Defense Minister would make an alliance with politicians. I even avoided the Christian Democrats who were in power. By acting coolly and professionally, the Army was unable to assess the despair of the politicians, their inefficiencies and their general attitudes which ultimately would invite another coup attempt. History will have to judge if I made a mistake" (1991b: 39–40). Despite these efforts, cashiered *golpista* officers cynically viewed these mini-conferences as ways for Gramajo "to convince us [Officers of the Mountain] that the PDCG isn't taking us headlong into communism" (López Díaz, interview). The deal struck on 20 May 1988 with Colt in the United States for 25,000 rifles "to improve our weapons . . . is a game to buy us off" (*Comunicado 6,* 22 May 1988). Another coup attempt was staged on 9 May 1989, two days before the anniversary of the first *intento.*

Events Before the 9 May 1989 Coup Attempt

By February 1989, there were announcements of at least four death squads operating in Guatemala: Jaguar Justiciero, Los Comandos Urbanos Revolucionarios, El Frente Contra la Delincuencia, and El Movimiento Armado Centroamericano (*El Gráfico,* 7 February 1989). In April, a large prison riot at El Pavón broke out, exposing the government's incompetence at a time of crisis.[18] Navy Captain Héctor Romeo García Reyes either was fired or suddenly resigned as director of the National Police, saying he did not wish to be part of the "politicization" of the National Police for the benefit of the Christian Democratic presidential candidate. A spate of unclaimed bombings and threats against opposition leaders occurred: a grenade was thrown at the house of Dr. Mario Castejón (who had charged corruption on the part of government officials), bullets were fired into the bedroom of former Christian Democratic presidential candidate retired General Ricardo Peralta Méndez's home, and the daughter of Danilo Roca was beaten and threatened "because of her father's writings" (*Crónica*, 19 May 1989: 11; *Inforpress Centroamericana*, 5 May 1988: 133). Interviews with guerrilla leaders also began to be published in the Guatemalan dailies during this period, raising the ire of officers.[19]

This tense climate, together with the call to mark the anniversary of the first coup attempt and Cerezo's State of the Nation address, in which he announced his twelve-year neoliberal economic development plan entitled Jaguar 2002 in the same month that the PDCG Secretary General, Alfonso Cabrera, announced his candidacy for president, sparked the second *intentona*. Rumors began to circulate within the military that the Christian Democrats — and Gramajo — planned to be in power for another twelve years.

The Coup Attempt of 9 May 1989

The High Command knew another major coup was being planned; "we just didn't know when. So instead of overreacting, which would have made them heroes and would have damaged the institution, I told G-2, 'Don't follow the officers; don't tape their calls.' It was a calculated risk. But I did play with them: sending them all to a soccer game in Cuba 'for a holiday,' and when they arrived, they thought they had been exiled. But nothing happened. When they returned, G-2 called them one by one to say 'Listen, we know what you are doing. If you continue, you will be punished'" (Gramajo, interview). Two days before the first anniversary of the 1988 uprising in the military's ranks, dissident — reputedly primarily Air Force — officers met with civilians in a house located in an upper-class neighborhood (*Crónica*, 19 May 1989: 12). More programmatic and more actively planned by military officers Colonel Ramón Quinteros and former Major Díaz López, this coup attempt against *both* Cerezo and Gramajo this time reflected the lessons learned from the first major *intento*: the necessity for air support as well as the backing of military bases in the capital. At 5 A.M. on 9 May 1989, Colonel Oscar Méndez Tobias went to the general army barracks, and then together with Colonel Raúl Dehesa Oliva, left the house in the wealthy neighborhood with 150 soldiers to take possession of Radio Nacional and Channel 5 (the army's television station), GUATEL (the main public communications agency), and the post office, and to block roads to the Atlantic and Pacific coasts. One hour earlier, Díaz López, Castellanos Góngora (with his civilian brother), Colonel Ramón Quinteros, with the support of the second commander of the elite Air Tactical Group, and Colonel Julio Padilla Gálvez and his seventy-five troops, had taken up positions around Defense Minister Gramajo's residence, Casa Crema. These three officers surprised the guards and reached the second floor. When Gramajo saw that the situation had gotten out of control, he sent his wife and children away in a car, but they were stopped by soldiers and held hostage. "Quinteros, Castellanos, and Díaz López tried to pressure me. Quinteros communicated by radio with me and said, 'We have your family; we want to speak with you.' I only answered, 'Let them go free!' He responded, 'Let us speak with you.' " But Gramajo refused, stalling for time.[20] Two days earlier, Gramajo had changed the Honor Guard second commander for one loyal to him to counter the battalion commander. During the hostage taking of Gramajo's family, these two commanders had a disagreement that allowed the troops of Mariscal Zavala to move against the *golpistas*. "They were short of people, and others were not obeying them. So, I did not answer their demand for me to surrender." When Quinteros replied that he would kill his Personal Chief of Staff if Gramajo did not speak with him, "I said bring [Quinteros] in to talk with me, and as soon as they closed the door, I captured them" (interview). The *golpistas* had also taken the house of the Chief of the National Defense Staff, General Callejas y Callejas, who had telephoned Gramajo at 3 A.M., warning him of the coup. Meanwhile, Air Force Captain Jesus Adalberto de la Peña Corado had boarded an AT-37B plane while Colonel Carlos Mazariegos Ramírez (dismissed from the army for his participation in the first coup) took off in a Sikorsky combat helicopter to provide air support overhead. Apparently, there was no bombing of the Defense Minister's residence only because of the heavy cloud cover at dawn. Officers in the Casa Crema intercepted a message of the *golpistas*: "Release the bomb!" "I can't, you can't see anything from up here!" "So what? Calculate where the house is, even if you make a mess of it!" The pilot didn't comply with this order (*Crónica* 19 May 1989: 13). Immediately, forces loyal to Gramajo in the city responded with armored troops from the Mariscal Zavala base, under the command of General Mendoza, placing combat vehicles (such as M-5 tanks) in positions to intimidate the smaller *tacuazines* (transport vehicles) surrounding the Defense Minister's home, while ground-to-air missiles from the Mariscal Zavala base targeted and undercut the plane and helicopter flying overhead. The Honor Guard, under the command of General Marroquín, rushed to the Air Force base at the airport and controlled it "at the point of a gun," while others repossessed GUATEL, Radio Nacional, and National Police Headquarters, forcing the *golpistas* to take off their scarves. Eyewitnesses tell of private citizens on their way to work, once again pleading with the rebel soldiers in tanks at the entrances to the city, to lay down their arms and not stage a coup. In the interim, the recently discharged Chief of National Police led a column of soldiers to handcuff and gag the new Christian Democrat police director, Mario Cifuentes, who was later released.

As the estimated 960 dissident and 6000 local forces menaced each other, negotiations began. With both Gramajo and Callejas effectively neutralized, Vice Minister of National Defense, Colonel Arturo de la Cruz, demanded Colonel Quinteros give up. By 10 A.M., the rebellion was over, with no bloodshed reported. An hour later, President Cerezo held a press conference with Interior Minister Valle Valdizán and Defense Minister Gramajo (in the standard brown army uniform, not battle fatigues he wore after the first coup) at his side. He declared that it had indeed been a coup attempt, that it had failed, that there were no demands for anyone to step down, and that the Army was taking "rapid and necessary measures to control these people." Gramajo then spoke, saying that there were three groups of officers who participated in the coup: "Those who were dismissed one year ago, five high-ranking officers who were displaced, and four active-duty high-ranking officers."[21] All but two of the officers (who fled) had been arrested and would be tried. This time Gramajo qualified the coup not simply as "indiscipline"; the government press bulletin spoke of "an attempt to subvert the constitutional order." Most significantly, Gramajo revealed that the economic activities of Colonel Juan Adenolfo Gálvez del Cid and his private airplane company were being investigated, countering an established military tradition not to publicly denounce fellow officers to civilians (*Crónica*, 12 May 1989: 12–13). In contrast to the announcements made by Cerezo after the first coup attempt as to the civilians involved, the president denied that there were any civilians involved,[22] evidently seeking to avoid the civilian court investigation that had been converted into antigovernment protests in the press and on television in 1988. And in contrast to the first coup, social groups and politicians fervently announced their support of the constitutionality of the country with a demonstration of some 25,000 in front of the National Palace the next day. Congress passed a resolution "repudiating whatever action that alters the established order and supports the regime of legality and the electoral system as the only means for legitimate change." Only the ultra-right-wing parties refused to support the resolution, with FUN (Frente de Unidad Nacional) demanding Cerezo step down to avoid a coup (*Inforpress Centroamericana*, 11 May 1989: 14).

The Military Tribunal, the Sentencing, and the Release of the Oficiales de la Montaña

In the end, of the thirteen officers formally accused of sedition and rebellion (the charge of kidnapping was dropped) and another eight under arrest, eleven army officers were convicted and sentenced on 29 November

1989 for their participation in the attempted coup of 9 May 1989. Similar to the May 1988 failed coup, sources spoke of many more people directly implicated — perhaps fifty to two hundred — including security personnel and civilians (such as National Police officers who aided their former chief when he captured and tied up his civilian successor). Two industrialists had been detained at the airport during the coup and were later released (*Inforpress Centroamericana*, 19 May 1989: 147). The conciliatory tone toward the disgruntled officers of 1988 was replaced with a firm determination for harsher judgments.[23] The three lawyers defending the officers, the most vocal of whom was Licenciado José Carlos Acevedo, argued that the Military Code of 1878 was unconstitutional, as it had never been ratified by a constitution since its decree. They demanded that the cases be transferred to the civilian courts, as all instances of justice should depend on the Judicial Organism and not on the executive or, more specifically, on the Military Tribunal or Ministry of Defense. The Human Rights Ombudsman at the time, eighty-one-year-old Gonzalo Menéndez de la Riva, whose only act up to this point had been to fight the 40 percent rate increase of the electric company, agreed that the military code was unconstitutional (*Prensa Libre*, 16 June 1989). In response, Minister Gramajo stated that the Auditoría was only dependent administratively on the Ministry, while judicially it was part of the Supreme Court in transferring cases to the Court of Appeals. The *golpistas'* lawyers further claimed that their clients had been cross-examined in their absence and mistreated — a claim that the Human Rights Ombudsman investigated and found no evidence of. Finally, arguing that the supposed *golpe de estado* was only a product of the imagination of Cerezo and Gramajo, they pleaded that their clients wanted only to be heard. In his statement to the press (and this time *golpistas* were held incommunicado from the press), Licenciado Acevedo used Cerezo's acceptance after the first coup attempt that army officers needed to protest like any other sector:

The military officers have manifested their nonconformity in strictly military terms. You see that doctors of IGSS are on strike and that their own lawyers present their *amparos* in the courts. The military follows its own orthodoxy: one does not explain that there was an attempt to enter the defense minister's house; the officers only wanted to speak with him and explain their protest. They did not want to provoke any political effect, much less break the constitutional order, retaining Gramajo in his official residency. . . . The intent of my [four] clients was precisely to save the Constitution and rescue the dignity of the country and the army. (*Crónica*, 19 May 1989: 14)

Despite the lawyers' arguments, the Auditoría (composed entirely of senior officers) handed down sentences of ten-years imprisonment each to five defendants, two years to two others, and absolved four more for lack of evidence. The surprisingly long prison terms were seen as a message from Defense Minister Gramajo as well as the future Defense Minister Bolaños (who acted as head of the tribunal) that future coup attempts by junior officers would not be tolerated. Once the sentences had been handed down, the government accused the officers' lawyers of unprofessionalism, contending that they were interested less in defending their clients than in destabilizing the political situation. Gramajo also revealed that various civilians were known to have financed and directed the coup, but they could not be arrested due to a lack of evidence. Nevertheless, on 2 February 1990, the sentences of the seven convicted officers — five colonels, a captain, and a lieutenant — were suspended and they were abruptly released from custody by a civilian Court of Appeals. Gramajo comments angrily:

This is the law: if the sentence is more than ten years, it is incommutable. However, if it is between five to ten years, one can reduce the sentence for good behavior. If the sentence is zero-to-five years, one can just pay a fine, with the judge setting the fine at anywhere between Q1 to Q1 million each day, as he likes. The military court gave ten years to eleven of the officers; to other officers it gave less; there were twenty-two in all. So they had to serve because the sentence was incommutable. The civil Court of Appeals, however, gave them four years, so they were released but are to this day still considered guilty. Convicted but free because they paid their fines. But they have a criminal record, and cannot leave the country for four years, cannot be elected, and can no longer serve as officers.
Q: Does this reflect badly on the Army?
Why? It reflects very badly on the civil courts, not on the Army!
Q: How, though, will these coup attempts affect the prestige of the Army?
I believe that with the exit of a total of 60 officers — 60 out of some 2000 officers is a small number — is nothing compared to the 60 or so who left on 13 November [1960] out of some 300 officers. We are all right in terms of percentages.[24] In the future they are going to say the Army is now professional precisely because it will be easier [for us] to adjust to pressures from interest groups or to participate in the reduction of the [armed] forces. All of this [we will be able to deal with] more tranquilly and not react violently or crazy for the preservation of our institution which has been our normal response. (interview)

"Calculated Risks" and Calculated Gains by the High Command

One criticism lodged against Gramajo after the numerous coup attempts was that he had not established an apparatus or mechanism that sufficiently "ideologized" middle- and lower-ranking officers with the fundamental thesis of *el proyecto* — that is, that a democratic transition did not mean an end to but an expansion of military action and power. Many officers were confused by this "mixed solution," and thus susceptible to *comunicados* castigating the defense minister and playing on visceral fears of communist subversion in the government *cúpula* — thereby divorcing the High Command even further from the ranks. Many of these officers were "participating within a system even though they rejected it," explained Colonel Cruz Salazar (interview). In speaking of "calculated risks" in moving too quickly with the military's plans to establish a democratic transition while continuing to "fight the subversion," Gramajo acknowledges this lack of ideological preparation. And while he adamantly rejects the Officers of the Mountain's assertions of the strong differences between those of the command and those in subordinate positions, his admission that all his press releases at the time were geared to the soldier confirm his concerns for the influence such *comunicados* were having on many of his officers:

All of us are officers who have been in the mountains fighting — because twenty years ago they said to [President] Julio César Méndez, "Come out here, communist, come out against us; we are here in the mountains fighting communism." Well, it's exactly the same today: those officers who are in the mountains were those who were in combat because those in the city weren't. But, as I said to the officers, "Look, no one is going to believe that [there is a split between the combat troops and the noncombat officers] because I'm not a general by correspondence. I earned my rank of general in the mountains; I have my experience. You, too, will be generals, but not right now; wait a while." So that every time I spoke to the press, some of my message was for the *pueblo* but most of it was for the officers. (interview)

The degree of risk was also connected to Gramajo's attempt to co-opt G-2 because most of those directly involved in the *intentos* were army intelligence officers.[25] At one point in our conversation, Gramajo states that he "suspected" G-2 was responsible for the three bombings at the home of the Soviet *Tass* correspondent, the offices of the Cuban *Prensa Latina*, and the center-left Guatemalan weekly *La Epoca*. At the same time, it was "his" G-2 officers who "discovered everything about the coup attempts, confronted the troops at the hour of the coup and tried to reason with the *golpistas*. They are the vanguard! So it was this elite that stopped the coup attempts. It was they who supported *el proceso*, they who saved it from two coups!" (interview). A National Police officer who served as an occasional informer for the G-2 stated, "Another example of infiltration is during the coup attempts: the Public Ministry has many informers and they sent all their informers out, the Presidential Honor Guard's G-2 had its informers out, and the President mobilized all his forces against the coup attempts" (interview). Gramajo was also working closely with the CIA and the DIA to "keep tabs on potential coup plotters."[26] Gramajo's "calculated risks" not to have G-2 "follow officers or tape telephone calls" in order "not to provoke them" was very much dependent on such outside intelligence sources, at least after the first *intento*. Gramajo states that the DIA officer at the U.S. Embassy, Colonel George Hooker, did not know of the first coup beforehand, "because if he had known, I would have known" (interview). If so much "intelligence" was on the front lines to detect and then avert a coup attempt, why was military intelligence so lax in allowing the coup to happen the first time round, and allowing the officers to enter the Defense Minister's residence in the May 1989 coup attempt? The way in which Gramajo was surprised and unprepared for the taking of his family as hostages points to either a failure of military intelligence at least on his and Callejas's part, or perhaps an unexpected split in loyalties among the ranks of intelligence officers themselves. The "surprise" may have been intended to publicly demonstrate to officers and troops alike how little control Gramajo had over G-2, to publicly embarrass him by taking him and his family hostage, and to emphasize the general weakening of his position as Defense Minister.

But there were also substantial, calculated gains to be made from the *intentos*. One cynical interpretation offered by several Guatemalan analysts is that the army itself staged the second coup attempt as a convenient excuse to accomplish several things:

1. the coup attempt allowed the army to partially reorganize its base commanders and purge its extreme rightwing elements;
2. the coup also allowed G-2 to purge the leftist elements of the press and increase the political violence dramatically after the coup; and finally,
3. the coup gained sympathy for the army in Washington, making Gramajo the soft-line savior of Cerezo's government.

I presented Gramajo with this analysis, divided into these three areas, and asked his opinion.

Well, the *intento* did provide us — although let me make it clear that it was *not* deliberated, it was not the reason for the coup — the opportunity to accomplish number 1. Yes, I am responsible for taking advantage of this opportunity to get rid of certain officers. Regarding number 2, [attacks against the press] was a revengeful reaction of the extreme right.

Q: But there are some who believe that it wasn't in fact civilians, that it was G-2.

I suspected that at the time. Yes, it could have been, *but I did not order those attacks*! As regards number 3, yes, we took full advantage of this support, *but we didn't stage the coup in order to receive such support*. But yes, it was more argument for military aid; it was much easier to get aid [after the attempt], that's certainly true. The Defense Minister was welcomed by [the U.S.] Congress after the coup attempts, whereas before it was more difficult, that's true.

Q: What an opportunity for you!

Yes, it was. But it was a problem when the Washington press, in an article, used the term "feudal" to describe "the feudal *latifundistas*." In a meeting with the *golpistas* in 1988, there was an agreement with UNAGRO. They told me, "Don't use the term 'feudal!' " And I responded, "Then don't you stage any more coups!" Because they were calling me a communist, they were saying "Gramajo is a communist," and in one of their communiqués, instead of Minister of National Defense, they wrote "Minister of National Defeat (*Ministro de Derrota Nacional*)!" (interview; his emphasis)

U.S. military aid to Guatemala jumped from $5.5 million to $9.4 million in 1988 and remained at that level in 1989, at a time when aid to all other Central American countries, including El Salvador, fell. According to Elliot Abrams, the United States made it clear to the *golpistas* in 1988 that if Cerezo were overthrown "we will cut you off without a penny. You will be pariahs [again]" (Lundberg in Rosenthal 1992: 111).

After these *intentos*, regular retreat seminars and conferences were held for all commanding officers about the Thesis of National Stability. The High

Command recognized its error in assuming that after decades of antiguer-rilla training there would not be resistance. Moreover, "the war has not ended!" complained Navy Captain Mazariegos, head of the Center for Military Studies, in 1990. "That is our major problem. There are still ambushes and dead soldiers. Here in the capital we can see it a little more calmly, but those in the areas where there are still *delincuentes-subversivos*, their mentality is a little resistant. So when officers hear of the Thesis, they are confused: they think it means eliminating military action. On the contrary, military action can be made *stronger* to support the Thesis" (interview; his emphasis).

Gramajo has admitted that he took "calculated risks" in moving too quickly with his scheme of liberalization and professionalization, although he blames the Christian Democrats for being sloppy with their 1987 tax attempt, as well as for their reluctance to indict either the 1988 or 1989 *golpistas*. In a *Crónica* interview in late May 1988, Gramajo recognized as a personal defeat the ability of the conspirators to succeed in mobilizing officers; many lower-ranking officers who lived daily with the "antisubversive conflict" had not been able to comprehend this as an institutional issue. "Perhaps I have been too optimistic in believing that Guatemala already possessed a modern army." Cerezo echoes this perception:

The position of Gramajo was *so institutional and so much in favor of the plan* we were executing that there was a little pendular movement backward. Naturally, [Defense Ministers] Hernández [and] Gramajo and the officers of this period were very involved in and convinced of the Thesis, that the army had to return to their basic [institutional] role [in society], that it allowed me to remove the army from many places, but perhaps we moved too quickly, for this naturally provoked some reaction, among them the coup attempts. The two coup attempts were a reaction from the traditional sector of the army because they were not so much against the system [of civil government] as against what they perceived to be the army making too many concessions to the civilian sector. . . . They saw the army as allowing us, myself, and the party, to do too much. (interview; his emphasis)

The one clear lesson to be drawn from the coups, according to some military analysts, is that a process of consciousness-raising about the weaknesses and advantages of democracy for the army is vital. "Only the practice of democracy will show the way for political comprehension," opined Cruz Salazar (interview).

Convergence of Thinking Between the Two *Lineas*

Despite these differences between the two sides, however, much convergence in the thinking between the Officers of the Mountain and the Gramajo *línea* exists. Both are extraordinarily (and not surprisingly) nationalistic; both believe in the necessity to maintain a civilian presidency — but the differences lie in how far and how much a civilian president should be allowed to maneuver. Both believe in the necessity to control the opposition and provide a certain amount of political space — but the difference lies in how much control, how much space, and how early and how quickly one responds to perceived "disequilibrium." For example, the Gramajo *línea* has been interested in sustaining a good international image and attempting to shift the strategy from military to political reform, and shifting the burden and visible responsibility for "demonstration control" from the army to the police; the Officers of the Mountain are tormented by the guerrilla publicly accusing the army, and have demanded immediate paramilitary responses to popular demonstrations. Gramajo himself has endorsed a "professionalized" form of selective militarism. There is also some similarity between the two sides in recognizing the need to remain independent from the oligarchic pull — yet given the Officers of the Mountain's close connections with MLN/UNAGRO civilians, especially during the first *intentona*, it is difficult to understand the nature of the independence these officers purport to desire. Gramajo, on the other hand, remains adamantly opposed to allowing the *ultras* to control the army, and is mindful of the institutional hazards as well as oligarchic disdain for "uneducated, lower-class" military officers:

In Guatemala, there is a minority who want me to flunk out of Harvard [Kennedy School of Government] because they cannot conceive of a peasant from the western highlands who is also a military officer gaining academic credentials like themselves who were born with "good [upper-class] names" — such as Rodil, Beltranena, etc. This makes them uncomfortable, so they say things like "We heard that Gramajo isn't studying," because that's what they want to believe. And now, [rightwing, private] Francisco Marroquín University in Guatemala has called up all the *golpistas* and offered to enroll them! (interview)

What Gramajo understands — and what the radical rightwing officers and particular members of the oligarchy fail to comprehend — is that the Cerezo-led faction of the Christian Democratic Party was in perfect agreement with this flexible, bounded *apertura* in which intelligence is still free to selectively repress and if it deems necessary, eliminate elements of the opposition. And while those on the left argue that Cerezo was controlled by Gramajo, and the hardliners on the right argue that Gramajo was controlled by Cerezo, as we have seen in Chapter 8, there was much collusion on the part of both.

Conclusion

While the military appears to be monolithic and invincible, the two coup attempts staged by Guatemalan officers calling themselves the Oficiales de la Montaña, on 11 May 1988 with UNAGRO/MLN *ultra* civilians and on 9 May 1989 primarily as an internal coup, reveal serious fissures and distrust within the armed forces, underscoring the vulnerability of a politico-military project premised on a democratic *apertura* born of counterinsurgency. These *intentonas* represent a last-ditch effort by a group of military and civilian radical right wingers, used to sharing "the same intelligence," to reestablish their controls over the economy, the army (particularly G-2), and social forces. They are, as one advisor close to the institutionalists stated, "playing their last hand and they know it" (interview). Many, too, are a confused and disgruntled "cross section" of officers trained in the brutal tactics of counterinsurgency of the 1960s and 1970s, who find it difficult to take seriously politicians running government. For them, to speak of a democratic transition is to speak of a change that is given by military authoritarianism to a civilian government. As *golpista* Captain Rodolfo Muñoz Pilona stated, "We have not learned to live in a democracy, but in a Christian Democracy. They want Guatemalans to live as the political party wants them to live. And democracy is much more than this. We need a strong hand to govern and to tell us where he is taking us. With a military [man] one has the certainty what goal he is trying to achieve. When a military [man] tells you, 'Let's go north,' this effectively means that we will head north. But in the case of a politician, we don't know what he is referring to because it isn't the north on the map or the north on the compass. It is the north of politics. And this is never a fixed point" (*Crónica*, 25 August 1988: 18). One might say that the Cerezo government gave them all the excuse they needed to rebel.

Yet this suspicion of democracy and politicians can also be found among the institutionalist officers: "For much of this military generation, the majority of us who are now in prominent positions only have experience with military governments. Although the army was the major *impulsor* toward a democratic process, our experience has not prepared us for acting within a democracy. We are now trying to revise our actions within what is the democratic process" (Mazariegos, interview). As we have seen, even the institutionalist Gramajo was disappointed with "the lack of unified policy" of the Cerezo regime.

These fissures and similarities represent serious contradictions yet to be ironed out in the project of "co-governance," and while the *intentos* were considered militarily unsuccessful, they could be read as political warning signs: First, what are the implications of the fissures within the army between what Cerezo refers to as the "intransigent" officers and the "less intransigent" officers for the future of Guatemala if there are no political alternatives to *el proyecto político-militar*, especially with the signing of the Peace Accords and with no guerrilla war to fight? Second, there appears to have been a clear division between long-term combat experience in rural Guatemala and the High Command sphere of politics in Guatemala City, making hardline military commanders potentially more susceptible to anti-Thesis, antihierarchy arguments by the "*ultras*," on the one hand, and useful for the institutionalists' strategy of nonresponsibility for "selective massacres" in sensitive regions in the 1990s, on the other. Third, two political decisions created deep bitterness among many middle-level officers: in 1987, the

PDCG and High Command did not support the *contras*, and this bitterness was heightened with the first dialogue between the government and the URNG. Finally, the lack of skill with which the PDCG government presented the tax reform and in March 1988 directed the arrival of the RUOG group of Rigoberta Menchú to Guatemala (in addition to the persistent propaganda offered by the conservative press), created a strong feeling of unrest in the army, making even institutionalist officers uneasy (interviews; cf. *Crónica*, 19 May 1988).

What the *golpistas* failed to understand is that this new selective strategy of combining democracy with counterinsurgency warfare, which Díaz López saw as "very difficult" to achieve, over the long run is far more efficient and sophisticated in its maintenance of control, than the cycles of full-scale violence. War is continued under a civilian regime in such a way that the army is not held accountable for violations. As Mazariegos summed it up: "Military action can be made *stronger* [under the civilian regime in order] to support the Thesis." What the Thesis of National Stability entails for democracy and human rights is the subject of the final chapter.

Chapter 10
The Thesis of National Stability and Opponents of the State

> We had to go down this road [of pacification, of redeployment, of institutional reencounter] to arrive at the Thesis of National Stability. This strategy of co-governing we have thought about very carefully. . . . The heads of government will change, but the army [with its Thesis] will continue to be the same.
>
> — General Gramajo

As we have seen in the previous chapters, the first stage of *el proyecto político-militar* was pacification by way of massacre; the second stage was restructuring the process by way of party politics and elections. The third stage underway during the "25-year transition" is to reconstitute civilian society by way of education, persuasion, and long-term crisis management of conflict that includes selective repression and killing. One comes to particularly appreciate the extensiveness of the military's project when institutionalist officers enthuse in a number of interviews, "We are planning the State in all of its ramifications!" Several long quotes have been included in this penultimate chapter in order to give the reader the closest idea possible of this military's view of present and future dissent, and of the human rights implications for Guatemalans.

No sooner was the Cerezo regime in place and General Gramajo appointed Chief of the National Defense Staff in 1986 than discussions among institutionalist officers were underway to craft a politico-military strategy of co-governance out of the 30/70 percent Beans and Bullets campaign of massacre-and-elections. To demonstrate to the Cerezo regime that "we were prodemocratic and not anticommunist" forces, the U.S.-imposed Cold War term "national security" was replaced with "national stability" (Gramajo, interview). Similar to the 1982 Plan of National Security and Development (which arose from "Strategic Appraisals" written by army colonels at the

Sixth Command and General Staff courses at the Center for Military Studies in 1980 and by a Navy captain at the eighth such course in 1981 (see Appendix 2), it was in 1986, during one of the retreat seminars held four times a year for military zone commanders at the Military Academy, that elements of a new philosophy that came to be known as the Thesis of National Stability were drafted. In 1987, at a Forum entitled "Twenty-Seven Years of Fighting for Freedom," presented by the High Command to the business sector, Gramajo made public the institutionalists' new thinking:

> Our strategic goal has been to reverse Clausewitz's philosophy of war to state that in Guatemala, politics must be the continuation of war. Thus we are acting in such a way that peace will truly arrive by way of political activity and by way of imposing our will on our opponents by means of military victory. In the end, [given that] we are [all] Guatemalans, *we want politics to be the continuation of war, and not that war be the continuation of politics.* But this does not mean we are abandoning war. We are not forgetting or betraying the blood shed; we are fighting it from a much broader horizon within a democratic framework. . . . [W]e guard the interests of the nation as a whole, not as a party or group or institution, but through political-military action that has reciprocal actions in economic, political and social activities within the geographic boundary called Guatemala. That is, we consider everything to be integrated: we military can't do everything, we can't do something apart from the politicians or businessmen or popular organizations. We must do them all within an integrated concept of the Guatemalan State. . . . We no longer seek to be part of a strategy that continues to illegally oppose the State of Guatemala; rather [we seek] to have a responsible attitude by which to conduct orthodox politics. (1987; emphasis added)

Two years later, Gramajo's *Tesis de estabilidad nacional* was published as a formal booklet by the Army Publications Office, followed by Navy Captain Mazariegos's *El estado, su estabilidad y el desarrollo de una estrategia nacional* in 1990. The think tank, the Center for Strategic Studies for National Stability (ESTNA), was also set up during this same period.

State-integrationist to the core, the Thesis expands on the already-expansive 14 Points of the 1982 Junta — Points that surpassed the military's own oath to remain "apolitical, obedient and nondeliberative." But the Thesis goes even further by institutionalizing the intervention of the armed forces as "Guarantors and Sustainers of the State"[1] into *all* forms and manner of crises integral to the maintenance of that State. "We do interfere just a little [in order] to fill the vacuum of power. We are obligated to do so, given the low degree of efficiency in many institutions," Gramajo explained (interview). It was the first time that the armed forces had formulated their own "long-term strategy that confronts social, economic and political problems. . . . We were always trying to put out one fire after another, never being able to come out from under them. We'd never structured a national strategic plan like this before!" boasted Navy Captain Mazariegos (interview). In none of these proclamations is there any indication that military power or autonomy is being diminished, or is intended to be decreased even incrementally with the entrance of each new civilian constitutionalist regime. Instead, while the armed forces insist upon their professional, nondeliberative "low profile" in political matters, military oversight is expanded and championed. As one Guatemalan social scientist explained, the military, by way of its Thesis, "*is openly and for the first time* assuming the protagonist role in the political process" (interview; his emphasis).

The Thesis focuses on several themes: (1) a national security doctrine sui generis distinct from U.S.-imposed, cold war national security doctrine; (2) an elastic and hierarchical definition of Opponents of the State that recognizes the reasons for dissent in order to better identify and eliminate the causes of opposition and its actors "at its infancy"; (3) a consciously autonomous "military fundamentalism" that breaks from the political interests of the oligarchy; and (4) the establishment of a new Center for Strategic Studies for National Security (ESTNA) to create a qualified civilian-military elite.

The Thesis of National Stability

Insisting on a sui generis concept of security based on Guatemalan realities, the Thesis asserts that "all nations have the right to formulate their own doctrine." Written before the demise of the Soviet Union, this reformulated ideology specifically rejects the U.S.-imposed Cold War national security doctrine of the 1950s, and emphasizes instead the need for countries to develop their own approaches to national security. As explains Gramajo, the army took note of the fundamental distortions to the military institutions caused by the rigid national security doctrine implemented in Latin America:

It was a graft imposed by President Kennedy under the Alliance for Progress created as a counter to Fidel Castro in Latin America. It was a huge mistake that cost us a great deal. At one point, someone asked Kennedy about this program, and he said, "I am certain that the armies of Latin America will not only defend their countries but will help to develop them as well." In Peru, the Center for Advanced Military Studies [CAEM] was established [at this time] and they interpreted Kennedy's pronouncement as, "How are we going to defend the country to achieve development? We'll take over the government!" Take over the government in Argentina, in Brazil, in Guatemala, because they wanted to develop the country as the President of the U.S. had said to do! [he laughs cynically] But it was a countermeasure, as we know, because it affected democracy [in all of these countries] while the objective was development — but interventionistic development. . . . And given what we knew of all the problems from the dirty war in Argentina, Brazil, and Uruguay in which terrible things were committed in the name of national security — not as terrible as in Guatemala in terms of bloodiness, but for *their* standards it was tremendous — we decided to throw national security out, just throw it out. (interview)

Language was carefully formulated so as not to arouse hostile reactions either from the new civilian government or the extreme right wing, and what originally was a tactic of 30/70 percent grew into a strategy:

We analyzed [the situation]. We didn't want to fight with the politicians in government, so we decided that we wouldn't speak about National Security. Nevertheless,
the objectives of the permanence of the state and public order needed to be maintained. So we began to speak of a National Stability to be able to coexist and grow for
national fulfillment, not for national security purposes. We call it "thesis" because
we're not certain it is good; we are very modest! You know why? Because if you propose a doctrine, everyone fights about it; but if you propose a thesis, then you have to
talk it through, "thesis" invites discussion while doctrine is already set in stone.
Q: So, you thought a lot about language, didn't you?
Of course, of course! Because that is precisely the key! "Thesis" is a euphemism. We
are moving along with this *proyecto*, certain that it will continue, but we call it *tesis* in
order not to awaken any reactions from "the Establishment" [using the last two
words in English]. So, you see, we could not continue with "national security" because in the end, for us, it is just a graft. And [with doctrine], they would fight it; with
thesis, they think "eh, it could be lies" and they don't fight about it. [This was true]
during the recent coup attempts of '88 and '89, they didn't speak of the Thesis. They
spoke out against stability but very little. If I had said, Doctrine of Stability, they
would have fought against it. And in order to have the possibility of great success, we
don't want to jeopardize it by talking about it too much. The thesis is nothing
definite. Nevertheless, [the plans] *are* definite but it's called a thesis! (interview)

A key element of the Thesis, military fundamentalism, exhorts officers to
prepare justifications for military actions both toward their troops and domestic elites, as well as toward Washington and Geneva. At the same time, it
rejects its historically subordinated role vis-à-vis the *ultraderechistas latifundistas* who, for the most part, see no need to justify the use of the military for
a 100 percent solution to dissent and insurgency. Gramajo states:

You see, the military was to blame for the poverty, for the bad education, for everything. And when we went to the economic elite [for support], they told us, "No, you
with your interventionism are to blame for poverty." Even our close business associates abandoned us! They told us, "You, because of this national security thing, killed
a lot of people! They were all innocent! The only evil ones were the military!" But, he
continued, "We are no longer the redeemers for right-wing *latifundistas*. . . . We are
not concubines, we are professionals!" (quoted in Schirmer 1991: 13)

The Thesis thus serves as a "purging of guilt" for the armed forces: "We are
stating our evil and [thus] have exorcised it. We have promised ourselves we
will not feel guilty for the bad that is in the country because we are not
responsible for it. *Every Guatemalan is*" (interview; his emphasis). Military
fundamentalism might be viewed then, as one social scientist explained, as
"a species of internal consciousness of the military project in which the
Army situates itself [squarely] within our society. One of the basic principles
says, 'We [the military] are not going to fight the war for others [i.e., for
either the United States or the oligarchs]. We aren't going to support the
well-being of others. And if it is going to be a democratic scheme, then we
are going to support it within the rules of the game which we have put into
place'" (interview). We will return to military fundamentalism and the

process of *concientización* (raising awareness) of the Thesis among officers in a later section. For the moment, though, we need to examine the underlying threat mentality of this Thesis of National Stability.

Opponents of the State: How Dissent Within a Transition Should Be Managed

As we saw in Chapter 6, law remains insufficient in and of itself to establish the stability required for a democratic transition. Similarly, while the Thesis acknowledges that "the political and social contract for relations among Guatemalans is well established in the Political Constitution as a popular expression of the majority of Guatemalans, having been conceived by their representatives" and views the 1985 Constitution as "highly tolerant with pluralist concerns in contrast to the past elitist and exclusionist constitutions," it cautions that "to fulfill the objectives [of National Stability], which include the security of the society . . . over space and time, decisions of the government are insufficient [to assure state stability]" (Gramajo 1989: 4). In response, the Thesis "plans the equilibrium, cooperation, alliance, and interrelation of the factors of power to confront the antagonisms and internal and external pressures that the State is subjected to so that all government actions . . . are sustained within a solid legal scaffolding" (5) (see Figure 20). National security must be girded; so too, "must law be propped up by the actions of the institution in charge of security" to guarantee that the State is maintained while the law goes about its business. The logic is that to be able to bring about democracy, peace has to first be imposed upon the country before laws can be enforced, and these peace actions must be "within the law." But if National Security Doctrine, with its implicit negativism of conflict and threat mentality, has, according to Gramajo, been rejected and replaced with the Thesis of National Stability, we need to understand how dissent and the opposition are consequently viewed within the current *aperturista* setting. The Thesis provides one of the most comprehensive and graphic descriptions of the military's view of dissent and opposition, and the management of violence it deems necessary in order to control and eliminate ever-present Opponents of the State.

Under the section in the Thesis of National Stability, entitled "OPPONENTS OF ACTIONS OF THE STATE OF GUATEMALA OR ANTAGONISMS OF THE STATE OR VULNERABILITIES OF THE STATE," Gramajo turns an eye to the security risks the armed forces must guard against. "Opponents or Antagonists" (Oponentes o Antagonistas) are listed in six categories: (1) contraband; (2) subversion: either Marxist-Leninist[2] or extreme or radical conservatism that infiltrates diverse movements and cultural institutions to form a constant conspiracy, that perform terrorist acts, sabotage, assassinations, assaults, kidnappings, or armed conflict; (3)

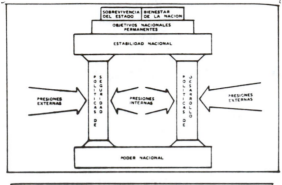

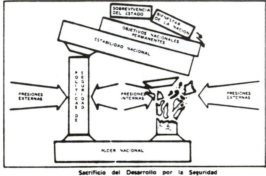

Sacrificio del Desarrollo por la Seguridad

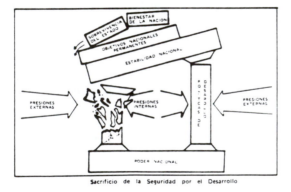

Sacrificio de la Seguridad por el Desarrollo

Figure 20. Graphics from Navy Captain Mazariegos's Thesis of National Stability. [top box] National stability and national power are held by dual columns of policies of security and development; [box 2] when development is sacrificed for security, external and internal pressures create a crisis; [box 3] similarly, when security is sacrificed for development.

strikes, violent demonstrations, and general agitation; (4) drug trafficking; (5) influence peddling; and (6) clandestine immigration and falsified papers. "Vulnerabilities" (Vulnerabilidades) are represented by five categories: (1) corruption; (2) lack of civic and general education; (3) a low level of principles, discipline, and means of forces of security; (4) external debt; (5) capital flight. "Pressures" (Presiones) are those opponents of the state "who depend upon a power to support them in their attempts to impose themselves" [on the State]. Finally, "Dominant Pressures or Threats" (Presiones Dominantes o Amenazas) are those pressures whose power attains national levels, representing an "unstable situation." The very fact that the author of the Thesis, General Gramajo, felt obliged to schematize such categories of opponents should alert us to a maintenance of the threat-of-conflict mentality, and the logic of "necessary" violations of human rights to maintain State security. Nonetheless, it is clear that Cold War justifications have been replaced by other categories, and are thus worthy of further examination.

To gain a sense of Captain Mazariegos's perception of how dissent within an *apertura* should be managed (given his booklet *El estado, su estabilidad y el desarrollo de una estrategia nacional*), I asked him to give me an example of how activities of Opponents of the State gain in intensity.

We have National Objectives: the well-being of the population (education, health, housing, minimum conditions) and the survival of the State — freedom, sovereignty, justice, all the aspects of the Constitution. Okay. But to reach this [level] of an ideal State, we have some opponents who do not want the general politics of the State to advance, and these we call Opponents. These Opponents we divide into categories [of increasing degrees of threat] depending on whether they are increasing in size or influence and thus go into the category of Vulnerabilities and Adverse Factors.
Q: For example?
OK. It depends on the degree of influence one has to be an Adverse Factor, then one passes to being a Vulnerability, then an Antagonism, until one reaches Pressure. Illiteracy begins in Guatemala as an Adverse Factor because we cannot overcome it economically or socially because we have a large number of illiterates. And this is converted into a Vulnerability when, given this type of illiteracy, it is easily taken advantage of by the population to do other things — such as things that are not against the state but that provoke certain types of problems. As an illiterate, you cannot utilize technological means for a new system of production, such as planting apples instead of corn to earn more money. So you remain poor. This is a clash (*choque*) [because illiteracy doesn't allow for modernization]. Up until then, it is still an Adverse Factor which has become a Vulnerability. But it is converted into a Pressure when it is utilized against the interests of the State.
Q: And if we continue with the same example?
As illiterates, the subversion begins to take advantage of us and utilize us well. When you talk with a peasant, the *indígena*, he does not know why he is fighting! They have told us, "Yes, you are the Army of the Rich and I am the Army of the Poor. I'm poor so I have to be in this Army." So they [the guerrillas] deceive him! *But if the indígenas aren't illiterates, then they are not deceived!* And now this becomes a Pressure, and then again a Dominant Pressure when instead of being opponents in strikes, demonstrations, and all that, they put a weapon in your hands and you are fighting. Now it

becomes a Dominant Pressure supported by another State or by another doctrine — in this case, I don't know, perhaps Marxist-Leninist with the support of Nicaragua or Cuba. OK. So we have each level with its degree [of intensity]. Dominant Pressure is when you have to apply military power because once it reaches that level, it is being supported by another State and it is armed. So, our position is that the Opponent must be eliminated at this moment, here, much lower down as Adverse Factors, Antagonisms, and Vulnerabilities. Here they can either be eliminated or overcome! OK, and it is here that the measures must be political, economic, and social to prevent them from getting to this higher level so that we don't have to use military power. So, if here [lower down] they are eliminated, it is not necessary to apply military power.

So, we have outlined what creates Opponents: particular conditions of poverty, a high degree of illiteracy, the lack of essentials, a high demographic growth, the presence of undocumented foreigners who work here . . . who create higher unemployment and yet consume scarce food products.

Q: But given this list of Opponents, if a union strikes for a higher salary, what kinds of solutions and measures would be used? Are there acceptable actions unions can take and how does one distinguish between the two?

Yes, yes, we would leave it alone as long as the union stays within the law. OK. But if this begins to become an Adverse Factor — for example, asking why there is no just wage — then it begins to be a *descontento* and becomes a Vulnerability when the workers begin to perform acts of force. Taking over a factory, for example. And this becomes an Antagonism when this passes onto the street and a fight begins with the police. This has nothing to do with the Army, but if these workers are then utilized and later create a level of travel, a level of armed bands supporting these strikes, then it becomes a Pressure. Then it becomes necessary to apply [force] to end it. Probably they [the strikers] were in the right, but it won't be resolved at this level. It needed to be dealt with earlier at the level of talks of the factory owners, workers, and the Ministry of Labor. If negotiations break down, then it is converted into a Dominant Pressure, in which it is necessary to apply military force. What we are saying [in the Thesis] is that all these Antagonisms, all these Adverse Factors, eventually become converted into Pressures, and we must resolve these problems *before* they grow in intensity. The National Police take care of the situation until it reaches the level of Pressures, then the Military Police take over, and if it reaches the level of Dominant Pressures in the mountains, then the military takes over. The Army, by way of its Mobile Military Police (PMA) that has been trained and legalized through SIPROCI, acts like the police and not like soldiers. There are many things the PMA can do under military orders; they can carry out operations and can capture victims. . . . When an Antagonism arises, *they are already there* (*presente*). And in the next stage of transition, there will be a time when the Army won't have to enter to resolve these big problems of pressures either. But these opponents must really be fought at the level of development, at the level of better salaries, at the level of talks between workers and owners so that it is more just for everyone, but not so much that it bankrupts the factory! This takes co-penetration of consciousness and education. (interview; his emphasis)[3]

In an interview with Gramajo, with the list of Opponents in front of us, I ask whether there are acceptable actions, for example, such as strikes, that unions may take in this schema:

It is when strikes and demonstrations become violent agitations, systematic opposition, to screw things up just for the sake of it (*joder por joder*) isn't that so? But "strikes" here could be placed under Vulnerability as it is caused by a Lack of Civic and General Education.

Q: How did you view the large strikes by the municipal workers [during Cerezo's presidency]?

They were created by the fact that they lack civic education, they are fighting against themselves! They weren't supporting the government. Then suddenly CACIF[4] comes forth and proclaims, "CACIF is going to defend the people! *When did CACIF ever defend the people?*" [angrily].

Q: So, there is [effectively] no political space when people go on strike? When unionists go on strike because there is repressed anger, as you say, about wages, it is assumed that this anger is being used by Opponents. Can't you distinguish between the two?

It is difficult to distinguish [between the two]. But when there is a violation of the rights of a third person (a motorist or a property owner, for example), then the strike is outside the law. . . . I understand why you [the striker] are angry, but you are outside the law. . . . There is always going to be conflict, above all in societies as primitive as Guatemala. But what we [the military] want is for these conflicts to be within certain parameters, that they don't resort to violence.[5]

Q: There seems to be a contradiction here: the Thesis states that the Army needs to understand the causes of insurgency, such as poverty, yet it must only attack the effects of such poverty.

Order must be imposed. . . . It is a good thing that there is popular expression [on the streets] but without public disorder. . . . Public disorder is [itself] an Opponent of the State. . . . The Thesis recognizes that there will be frictions, but all these forces must come together under the national interest. (interview; his emphasis)

But the military's tolerance for "popular expression [on the streets]" has been mostly rhetorical. Army intelligence uses the police for surveillance and "operations work," with demonstrations often infiltrated by police and army intelligence informers, as one National Police detective describes:

As a police officer, you are expected not only to do traditional crime investigations but to do undercover work as well: to find out who the student leaders and leaders of public employees on strike are, and to inform the police about them. The director of police, in turn, informs the army. For example, there would be rumors of strikes and the government would know about them beforehand.

Q: How did they know?

They knew from informers perhaps one or two weeks before a strike and demonstration. They would allow the unionists to go ahead and stage their strike, but they would always know about it beforehand in terms of the day and hour. . . . So that by the time the strike occurred and there were people in the street demonstrating, the strikers and demonstrators would already be infiltrated by the police and the army.

Q: How does one go about infiltrating, for example, a meeting of striking teachers?

One goes to their meeting with a friend who may in fact be a teacher, and one uses one's old student ID card. You go to these meetings over a week's period, asking your friend, "Who is that speaking?" and "Who is that guy there?" and so on. Then you get closer to these people and begin asking them questions. One comes to recognize who the leaders are. And then one informs the G-2. Then, one or two weeks later, you read in the newspaper that this or that particular person that you had identified for La Dos has been disappeared or found tortured to death. (1992 interview)

Given G-2's own political uses of violence, one can only surmise that Antagonisms such as public disorder and general agitation may be incited as a way of justifying operations to "impose order." The comment, moreover, by Captain Mazariegos that "the Opponent must be eliminated . . . much lower down" as Adverse Factors or Antagonisms such that military force need not be used, was reiterated by Gramajo in his admission of the similarities between U.S. Low-Intensity Conflict Strategy and the Thesis in managing and eliminating conflict "before it gets out of hand":

[I believe] the general approach is that the intensity of the response will depend on the intensity of the conflict. If we are able to maintain the conflict at a low level from the beginning, then our response to the conflict will also be [kept] low. So, what one must do is attack the problem in its infancy so that it doesn't increase, because once the problem increases then one must use force. So it's better to be alert early on in order to attack the problem. But the talent is to visualize the conflict in terms of how bad economic or political measures can develop into more intensive conflict, for that is when it is necessary for one to use brute force, isn't that right?

"Attacking the problem in its infancy" is to identify and eliminate any potential dissent with "minimum force" *before* it occurs. As we saw in an earlier chapter, "minimum force" is the central concept of Civil Affairs. But it is also a concept, according to Gramajo,

that must be inserted into the Guatemalan military: a soldier is better than a warrior, a warrior is brute force, a soldier is minimum force, the minimum force that I speak about in the Thesis.
Q: Minimum force but force just the same.
Ah, clearly. You can use force with just a stare, isn't that so?
Q: To control?
Clearly. If there is someone who is against the interests of Guatemala and you appear like that [he glares] and nothing more and the police appear ready to act, [he slaps his hands together] the will to act against the interests of Guatemala quickly evaporates [he chuckles]. That way they cannot say you are using force.
Q: So it's psychological warfare?
Sure, it is coercive force (*fuerza coercitiva*). One always uses force but in a much more sophisticated way [in a low voice]. You needn't kill everyone to complete the job (*cumplir su trabajo*). . . . But "more sophisticated" means "more developed," to have moral convictions, to have ethics, it is not just blind killing and massacre. (interview)

The scheme for identifying Opponents, though, is elastic, with officers including willy-nilly "those who espouse Liberation Theology as part of the international subversion" (Colonel García, interview) and "delinquent gangs" (*maras*), like those paid by political interests "to burn cars and smash windows, and burn the doors of Congress" during demonstrations, creating "general agitation" and "public disorder" (Gramajo, interview). Politicians' and military officers' lifestyles as well as businessmen's greed, too, are identified as Vulnerabilities: "What is the problem of Guatemala? It is the offensive, irresponsible, noisy lifestyle of a Cerezo, such as buying a yacht. This is a Vulnerability of the State of Guatemala, but what are we to do? It is the lack of seriousness of our political leaders, or the lack of [civic] education, or the lack of preparation [for the Presidency]. Another Vulnerability of the State is the ambition of military officers for economic power. Another is the custom of exploiting the worker. They all damage Guatemala" (officer, interview).

Within this mental universe, "innocent dissent" is an impossibility: activities that appear to be subjectively innocent and immune from "manipulation" — such as housewives protesting rising food prices or street vendors organizing for better working conditions — are viewed as low-level latent tendencies that eventually and inexorably grow into insurrectionary forces that "sometimes act with the front of common delinquency." They must therefore be "attacked" and "eliminated" in their infancy. "Preventive measures" by the Mobile Military Police following military orders have included the capture and elimination of individuals who were presumed guilty: it is an imputed criminality of the remote future that "has nothing to do with the past at all; one is punished for what one might do in the distant future" Shklar 1964: 214). A preemptive mentality so obsessed with eliminating potential subversion provides the armed forces with a post-Cold War justificatory narrative, and helps explain the continued lack of distinction between delinquent and subversive. Human rights and religious groups, for example, along with trade and student unions, peasant cooperatives, and returnee refugee communities, have borne the brunt of the military's suspicion and brutal repression, and continue to do so under the Thesis. GAM and CERJ are described by officers of all ranks and ideological persuasions without hesitation as "front groups" (*grupos de fachada* and *grupos de presión*) "financed by and speaking for the leftist political opposition and guerrilla" to discredit Guatemala. The assumption is that *denuncias* of human rights violations are *by their nature* part of the international campaign against Guatemala, and thus represent security risks or Pressures that foment public disorder; hence they are legitimately subject to attack and elimination.[6] GAM, for example, which continues to demand investigations into the thousands of the disappeared as well as of the locations of clandestine graves, is perceived as *un grupo de denuncia*, interested not in achieving justice, but only in isolating Guatemala internationally. Colonel-lawyer Girón Tánchez described GAM in 1986,

They are being manipulated because, I ask you, where do they get their money for demonstrations from? We have surmised that it is a donation from outside the country. . . . Besides this, one sees that this GAM travels frequently to Italy, travels here and there. Well, the people are of the middle class, they aren't poor, traveling like that. It is a group perfectly *usable* for whatever group that offers its support, and they, more than anything, want international support. (interview)

Other officers point to the "personal wealth" some of the leaders of these groups have amassed. For Gramajo, too, GAM is a Marxist front; but more significantly, it represents domestic and international "Pressures":

There is a lot of anger by those who were involved in and lost relatives in the struggle (*la lucha*). And there are groups who live off this anger, who capitalize on this anger, like GAM. What is their slogan? "Alive they took them away, alive we want them returned," right? No one dares to say that [their relatives] are dead, no one admits that they are dead. And yet they continue to ask after them. This is nothing more than to have a *causa* and to follow it; they are not interested in a solution. Let's say that your wife is disappeared; you declare her disappeared after five years, and you can receive her pension, you can become the owner of her house, everything. But you refuse to make this declaration because you say the slogan over and over. It's nothing more than an excuse to continue *la lucha*. . . . Now that there isn't a cold war, now that perestroika reigns, the human rights groups who base themselves on this [Marxist] ideology, are short-lived. And to survive, they are grasping at human rights violations and are not objective [in their work]. The international political situation doesn't favor them: they can't raise money in Europe any longer. . . . Central America then is the only place that's left where people suffer, and the poor in South Africa. So, they are left without work because this is normal within institutions: the primary objective of an institution is to survive. Thus, what is reported in Guatemala makes the violations appear to be on the increase even though the problem is not that great; there is simply more access to the information. And to compare 1990 with 1980 is *absurd*! (interview)

International Human Rights Pressures

Pressure might also come in the form of intervention from international human rights organizations and the U.S. Embassy, as Gramajo sarcastically and angrily describes:

[The] My Lai [massacre in Vietnam] and Lieutenant William Calley were [the U.S.] scapegoats. . . . In Vietnam, the United States fought the war outside their country; in Guatemala, we are fighting within our country. Nonetheless, the international consciousness is created by way of human rights groups who are represented in Guatemala. A society so civilized [as the United States] was so affected by [the destruction of life in] Vietnam that they created a scapegoat called Lieutenant Calley. Besides not giving her soldiers a welcome home and only five years ago building a monument to them, that society put all their pain into Calley. That same *patrón* is [now] seeking a scapegoat in Latin America, and they found him in [the Argentinian General] Videla: they imprisoned him there in Argentina but they weren't satisfied. They wanted to skin him alive! These groups are dissatisfied *all life long (toda la vida)*! International opinion, such as newspaper articles in the United States, seeks out a scapegoat, but not in their own country; [it has to be] somewhere out there. . . . [There were] *gross* violations, true enough, but the information about them was secondhand because these groups — Amnesty, Americas Watch — could not enter the country. This was even less the case for the OAS and United Nations! So everything was secondhand and biased. Now, ten years later, you have national organizations of human rights — GAM, UNSITRAGUA,[7] CERJ [he counts them on his fingers] — while Americas Watch, WOLA [Washington Office on Latin America], and Amnesty enter and leave and report on specific cases. If this had occurred during the Lucas period [1978–82], there wouldn't be enough volumes to hold the reports. Now, we still have [violations], but they have been completely diminished, so why do they cause such a sensation? Political interest, it is nothing more than political interest on the part of the human rights groups. (interview)

When asked about the killing of the American innkeeper Michael De Vine in El Petén in June 1990, during the same time period of this interview, Gramajo responded:

That's an example of what I'm talking about: a scapegoat. Look who is demanding [an investigation]: the [U.S.] Embassy. . . . We must adapt to the [political and human rights] situation. We have had to be on good behavior for ten years; we have such a bad reputation [laughs sarcastically]. We never say this openly, though, because in the circles of investigators and reporters, we would lose our friendships. Because it is a cliché as to how one thinks about the Guatemalan Army, right? There will be people who are going to say that Guatemala is *as bad as El Salvador with the priests*.

So, the military had to "equip itself" for the "onslaught" of human rights "pressures" early on.

An example of how the army "handles" such "pressures" for international purposes is in regard to a group of squatters who claimed a patch of land in the city on the day of Cerezo's inauguration. The very next day, one Army lieutenant in the DIDE office warned that

This [squatting] must be dealt with intelligently so it doesn't cause waves in the international press.
Q: How do you mean "intelligently"?
Such as paying them off and not as they have been dealt with before—you know, cleansed (*limpiado*).
Q: Why this shift in tactic?
Because we are more conscious of the international coverage now. For the loans. But we are not so certain that this [less repressive method] will in fact work. (interview)

Colonel-political scientist Cruz Salazar proclaimed later that same day in an interview that the "invasion of the land was provoked. If we wanted to investigate we would find that it was not spontaneous. . . . There are many oppositional forces we have yet to clearly identify that are not explicitly directed. . . . Fortunately, though, [this squatting] was taken care of relatively well" (interview). A few days later, after most of the hundreds of foreign journalists had left the country, twelve leaders of the squatters movement were abducted, and their tortured bodies were discovered in garbage bags at the city dump.

Within this mental universe of *delincuencia* a priori, Opponents are always present, making political militarism more and more a permanent part of governance, as "the implacable foe" never subsides. When asked why the military needs subversion, one Guatemalan intellectual remarked, "In moments of war, it is very easy to maintain an army; in moments of peace, a whole series of internal contradictions of ideological conflict arise. It is at this moment that the army most needs subversion" (interview). Minimum force for such selective, low-profile repression is the basic tenet behind military fundamentalism.

Military Fundamentalism

For this new Thesis of National Stability, with its Opponents of the State schema, to succeed, the High Command in 1986 recognized the need to put into motion a process of *concientización* (a term also used by the Christian Democrats to describe consciousness-raising about democratic culture) within the armed forces themselves. Navy Captain Mazariegos explained that a lack of "ethical education" meant a surfeit of soldiers who were unaccustomed to acting within a democracy:

We believe the Army has been key to the changes between 1981 and 1987: it created a strategic plan of war campaigns whose final objective was to unfurl the democratic process and to hand over power to the civilian authorities who were elected in pure and crystalline elections by the people. . . . At the beginning of 1985, when the democratic process began, the Center for Military Studies reopened after having been closed since 1982 due to a lack of officers having time to study because of the war, and many officers of that generation are not quite accustomed to acting within a democracy. At the beginning of the transition, the Army didn't really attend to this [lack of change of attitude]. So now we are trying to revise our actions and think within the democratic process.

One civilian advisor to the institutionalist High Command added a pithier perspective:

Some say that the formation of the military officer begins with the fact that he is governed by violence. If he is not trained with a doctrine or with values, he merely remains a *matón* (a killer), because he is trained in all the weapons to just eliminate his opponent. If he doesn't have all these values, he is, practically speaking, dehumanized, and becomes a killing machine. *El Rambo*, in short. But if he gains values and ethics from doctrines, *at least he knows why and who he is killing*. The doctrine of national security oversimplified the world: "this is my enemy, and everyone who is my enemy is a communist." Thus, [we needed] to revise the doctrine of national security and convert it into a thesis that continually asks: does [the Army] serve the national interests? It is a matter of constant revision, and [General] Gramajo had to be very careful in revising military education because at times, [the troops] remained violent and forgot this other part of their education. (Alfonso Yurrita, interview; his emphasis)

Military fundamentalism is then an educational instrument by which to implement politics-as-the-continuation-of-war thesis and create professional soldiers loyal to their institution, which serves as the "moral reserve of the nation" (Gramajo 1987: 7; interview). Military fundamentalism is not a renouncing of the use of force, as Gramajo himself makes clear, but rather a "professionalizing" of soldiering using a minimum of force—but with force all the same. If and how a military can be changed that has been intravenously fed on anticommunism since the 1950s and on counterinsurgency "irregular warfare" since the 1960s into one that accepts, minimally, the participation of civilians, and even the opposition, into political life is uncertain. But the very fact that this has become a "fundamental" issue for the military reflects how little, over the past forty years, they have even had to consider coexisting within a constitutional order established by its citizens.

As we saw in Chapter 7, writing governmental human rights reports has also become part of this new professionalism, "which is why we decorated the officers who wrote the report and argued it in Geneva. It was the educational message it conveyed within the Army: that we can fight ideas with ideas. That we don't have to be so rude but sophisticated to defend Guatemala." For Gramajo, military fundamentalism is the difference "between the warrior (*guerrero*) and the soldier (*soldado*): anybody can be a *guerrero*, learn to use a weapon, cut out the liver, and kill everyone. That's a waste of energy. Now, a soldier comes to use a weapon consciously, intelligently, and only in the interest of the nation, not for personal interest or anything like that" (interview). This fundamentalism has sought to develop "in all military men an understand[ing] that their participation consists of strengthening the system and not in resisting it, without this coming to mean a weakness on the part of the institution. In this sense, we must be the moral reserve of the nation and leaders of the civic formation of citizens when they fulfill their military service: by inculcating within them a deep respect for freedom, we also strengthen and stimulate the democratic conscience" (1987).

The attempt to isolate the military from ideological interests to develop a more accomplished professionalism does not necessarily indicate a lack of political meddling. The army's effort has been directed toward eliminating military participation in party politics while remaining directly involved in the politics of the State. A distinction is drawn by officers between ideological commitment to particular interests on the one hand and commitment as the levelheaded "Guarantors" of the State (Gramajo's "no-nonsense-generals") on the other. Retired General Peralta Méndez makes it clear that "the army doesn't play party politics; the army makes national military policy to protect the sovereignty of the state, the stability of government." A civilian Defense Minister, he insists, would "politicize" the army (identify the army with the political party in government), but a military Defense Minister must himself be "politically experienced to operate within the civilian world of politicians" (interview).

Beginning in 1986, "retreat-type seminars" were regularly held for middle- and higher-ranking officers at the Center for Military Studies, in the Military Academy, and in the training schools in different military zones.

Data from attitudinal surveys (conducted by a group of sociologists and political scientists) of officers' political thinking and behavior served to reinforce or modify terms used in what Cruz Salazar referred to as "indoctrination sessions." An example of the skillful play with language in these sessions is the substitution of "freedom" for the term "democracy," as many officers and soldiers associated the latter with Christian Democracy, and preferred not to be either supportive of or in any way related to the activities of that party. Freedom (*libertad*) on the one hand, "conjures up an image of political tolerance for the slow unfolding of actions in one's country," and on the other hand, "appears to be implicitly aligned with anti-Marxist thinking" (Gramajo, quoted in Cruz Salazar 1988a).

Gramajo, breaking the tradition of hardline defense ministers who had "exiled" reformist officers like Ríos Montt and himself to Washington, promoted officers who were supportive of the Thesis to the rank of general as yet another means (beyond the revamping of education and training) to entrench the professional ideology of the Thesis into the institution. Particular hard-line officers disenchanted with the Thesis were nonetheless appointed because of their leadership abilities and as a way to quiet *mano dura* elements; but these officers were more often than not sent abroad or later sacked.[8] The calculated risks of such a policy eventually led, as we have seen, to the coup attempts of 1988 and 1989. Yet Gramajo was confident upon his retirement in May 1990 that he had installed a hierarchically sound subsystem of ascendancy within the armed forces of Thesis-loyal officers, "whose horizons have been broadened" to ensure the *continuismo* of the politico-military project.

Dialogue as Military Fundamentalism

Waging an intensive counteroffensive while the civilian government attended initial talks with the URNG was also part of Gramajo's fundamentalist strategy. I ask him why the Army didn't want to speak directly with the URNG: "For two reasons. First, so as not to give status [to the guerrilla]: a bunch of armed men speaking with representatives of the army who are professional and organized. Second, the most important concept for Guatemala is that the army is *an institution of the State*—it is not [functioning] alone. It is important for Guatemalans to know that the army *depends on the laws* and those laws say that we are apolitical, nondeliberative, and that the State is represented by the government and the government is elected. So, if the government is going to speak with [the URNG], they can take along *un elemento militar*, a military element. *But it is the government, not the army* [that is going to speak with them.] For the democratic development of Guatemala, it is more important that *el pueblo* have the idea that one institution of the State is the Army, and not as the subversion wants them to think, that the State *is* the Army. But remember, we were present [at the talks in Madrid in

October 1987]: four politicians and four military officers. We decided then that it wasn't worth the trouble because [the URNG] was dogmatic — always the same thing over and over again: Guatemala hasn't changed in twelve years. They wanted to stop the clock at 1979. So, forget it, we decided it wasn't worth [the trouble]" (interview; his emphasis).

Deputy Chief of Staff General García Samayoa, who participated in President Serrano's Comisión de Paz, refers to the Dialogue as a general amnesty for the insurgency to "return to legality":

Q: Why did the army decide to participate in the recent Dialogue in Mexico?
Because the Dialogue is now part of the government. Ministers went, advisors went, officers went — but we were not alone. We formed one governmental commission: [we went as part of] the government. The demobilization of the terrorist delinquency is anticipated. We are not, it should be made clear, *absolutely not* negotiating away any position of the Army. This concept of Dialogue must be taken as a political instance that allows for insurgent groups to return to legality within the field of politics. Because we, within the military, are fulfilling our obligation to make them understand that they were wrong in trying to impose a totalitarian government [here in Guatemala]. But, we are not speaking of demilitarization: *that* we must apply to *them*. We must demilitarize them because they have armed themselves and they have armed civilians. A demilitarization cannot occur when there is an army perfectly well supported constitutionally and that has a historical vision of being an institution of the State. (interview)

Thus, the "flexible response" and "minimum force" espoused by the Thesis allows the army to step in to ensure or correct the perceived ineptness of the civilian-run ministries, such as when Guatemala's international human rights reputation is at stake by writing all governmental human rights reports after 1989 and presenting them before the UN Human Rights Commission in Geneva. But when the army needs to maintain a low profile to persuade its own hard-line officers of the benefits of "freedom" to continue fighting Opponents of the State, as well as to convince international opinion of the democratic intentions of the project, it can withdraw behind the civilian shield of governance. Yet when Gramajo speaks about whether the upper echelons of the Church were in agreement with the Dialogue efforts, he reveals, his low-profile public rhetoric notwithstanding, that he was very much involved in "providing the political opportunity" for the Dialogue *in order to neutralize* the guerrilla:

Yes, [Monsignor Rodolfo] Quesada [Toruño] spoke with me and I encouraged him to "Go ahead, meet with the subversion in Oslo." We [the High Command] supported these efforts, but we said nothing [in public]. . . . So, the meetings in Oslo were due to my efforts.[9] First, I sought the opportunity, and second, I provided the political opportunity. Cerezo didn't do this, *I* did. (interview)

Optimistically, retired General Peralta Méndez spoke in 1991 of a shift in language regarding Opponents of the State during the Dialogue negotiations at this time. Defense Minister Mendoza as well as President Serrano, he believed, "have not qualified the subversion as 'delinquent subversives' as much as Cerezo and even Gramajo had." I asked him why he thought this was so: "They had to accept the guerrillas' goodwill in wanting to change things in Guatemala. [Clearly], Mendoza has to speak in the language of Serrano, much as Gramajo spoke in the language of Cerezo, although neither has been entirely devoted to their President. Yet, they are government functionaries and the Defense Minister and officers must speak in the language of the government" (interview).

There does seem to have been a shift in semantic usage; but despite Peralta Méndez's optimism, it is not at all clear that this shift has necessarily been accompanied by more tolerant attitudes toward the opposition. Gramajo has admitted that it is "only a matter of semantics" when

we quit using "subversive" and replaced it with "delinquent-terrorist." We had to adapt to the international [political] environment when President Reagan railed against international terrorism of the Red Army. We thus show our international support by our vocabulary.
Q: But they are the same thing.
They are the same. But one changes oneself out of necessity. [whispers]
Q: And one uses the same tactics against both?
Yes, of course. For that reason, it is listed [here in the Thesis] in a general way. [Then he notices that terrorism is listed by itself and rethinks the category out loud.] This [terrorism] perhaps should be placed here below [points to "strikes, violent demonstrations, general agitation," to move it out of "opponents or antagonisms" down to "vulnerabilities"] because it is a consequence of this [points to "lack of civic education"], right? Yet, it represents *permanent* agitation, the desire to screw things up (*ganas de joder*) [laughs]. (interview)

This conversation highlights the opportunistic elasticity of the military's definition of the opposition. The usefulness of the Thesis, Gramajo argues, as against the "orthodox" and stodgy National Security Doctrine of the cold war, lies precisely in its "flexibility" to meet short- and long-term "needs of the state": of learning how to "gain international support from our vocabulary" but not necessarily changing threat mentality and behavior. Similarly, General García Samayoa refers in an interview to "terrorists" as "always there, with protests and strikes structured into their strategy." He first dismisses the "terrorist acts of blowing up electrical lines" as insignificant "annoyances" (*molestias*) needing to be "absorbed [by the army]" in order to maintain "tranquility for *el pueblo*." He is tolerant toward strikes, since "they occur everywhere in the world: in the U.S., in Korea, in Europe. Everywhere in the world there are protests, and they have the right to protest. To not be content with something is part of freedom; it is part of democracy to pronounce yourself in this fashion." However, when the issue of Communities in Resistance demanding land[10] comes up in the conversation, his tone changes from that of a studied tolerance to a threat mentality that assumes manipulation by "outside forces": "These poor people have been deceived and oppressed by these groups of terrorists who have not wanted to understand that that is not the way to treat civilized people. We have worked a lot with [these groups], we have told them and shown them what is the best way to take up a better life: to leave there! [T]he terrorists are using them politically. . . . The Guatemalan army has helped these populations, which the terrorists call 'in resistance' — and that is where the terrorists condemn these people. How 'in resistance'? Resistance to what? Resistance to whom? That is a mistaken concept" (interview). General Callejas y Callejas, Chief of the National Defense Staff under President Cerezo, remarked too that "it is very difficult to determine if there is some overlap between terrorism and common delinquency. Nevertheless, I believe that even when there is no concurrence, they take advantage of both of their activities to keep the country untranquil" — that is, Gramajo's *ganas de joder* (*Crónica*, August 1988: 21). Refusing to distinguish between "innocent dissent" and "manipulated dissent," officers assume that delinquency is always utilized by the terrorist; ergo, they eventually, if not initially, become one and the same, and must be dealt with by force.

ESTNA and *Los Estnicos*

In the late 1980s, institutionalist officers, primarily Gramajo, gathered a group of retired officers and civilian professionals to set up a think tank with US-AID funding called the Center for Strategic Studies for National Stability. ESTNA attempts to collapse the civil-military worlds both culturally and mentally so that they can "work together in a kind of . . . laboratory to exchange and break the traditional confrontations in Guatemala. We are trying to get rid of the hyphen between civil-military" (ESTNA Director economist José María Argueta, interview). But rather than lobbying the Guatemalan Congress on national security and military affairs (as Stepan describes the Brazilian military doing, with thirteen officers with permanent offices in the Brazilian Congress [1988: 134–35]), ESTNA has invited "key actors" to courses and conferences held at their modern conference center in the original, turreted Escuela Politécnica (which earlier housed the School of Intelligence and today includes the army's Civil Affairs offices; it also sits across the street from Casa Crema, the Defense Minister's residence).[11] The "key actors" invited to sessions have been "union, business, and parliamentarian leaders" chosen for "the capacity of leadership" — a category that did not include "nonrepresentative groups," such as GAM and CERJ, which were viewed as Marxist front groups with support from outside of Guatemala (Gramajo, interview).[12] Courses (which might last several months) have included special sessions for newly elected congressional deputies, such as the one held in November 1990 to talk about "parliamentary process" as well as the Thesis. Other sessions have involved the strategic analysis of "the role of the military in a democracy." When I asked one retired officer at ESTNA what its function is, he responded:

It is to disseminate the Thesis of National Stability. It asks nothing more of those who come to ESTNA than to listen to the opinions of others: that the unionist sees the factory owner as his enemy because the unionist is taught Marxism — the class struggle — and the factory owner is taught neoliberalism in which the worker is his enemy. Thus the unionist wants to destroy the factory and the employer wants to destroy the union. As a change, with this new attitude we are arguing that we must adopt, the unionist must know that the employer is the owner of the means of production and that he's going to fight against the owner but for a better life for himself and not to destroy the success of the factory owner. And to the employer, we are saying that he is the owner of the means of production and how much he earns is not only going to depend on how much his equipment costs but also on his labor force. With the mass communications we have today, one knows how the other [half] lives, and with workers more educated, it is more difficult to exploit them! So, one must learn to share but not just share what's left over but to share a little more in wages, which in the countryside are very bad. If they rose just slightly, the workers would have more capacity to buy, there would be more sales, and more production. And in the end, they are still the *dueños* of the money. But they fight among themselves. So, the key is to [encourage such discussions in ESTNA], and this we are doing little by little. These academic intentions of ESTNA, though, are a secret.
Q: You don't talk about them openly?
No, because the key is to create the consciousness that believes to pay a slightly higher wage is better for everyone, including for the same *dueños* because that way there is less revolt and more buying power! (Colonel Félix Armando Baeza Cortéz)

The Center for Military Studies (reopened in 1985) has worked closely with ESTNA as both a kind of socialization network and an active ideological outreach campaign for officers (although several *éstnicos*, as some of the officers who have been through the courses so identify themselves, denied this) to systematize, update, analyze, and disseminate the Thesis as a doctrinal and political management base for the military's entry into the twenty-first century.

The Military's View of Democracy

Finally, what does democracy mean for the institutionalist High Command, whose philosophy outlines a crucial role for itself in controlling Opponents of the State while stimulating the "democratic conscience" and a transition to democracy? For one, it means vulnerability. As "an instrument of political and social cohesion" on the basis of indiscriminate participation and criticism, democracy has "always caused fear" among Guatemalan officers, writes Colonel Cruz Salazar. "For us, democracy has always been subject to questions of security. . . . [W]e must shed the conceptual weight of the past . . . to grow accustomed to the government of democracy without fear" (Cruz Salazar 1982). This intimate connection of democracy with insecurity helps us to better understand both *lineas'* belief in the necessity for "preventive measures" (*medidas preventativas*) to protect the State from its own citizens. Colonel Gordillo of the 1982 junta, for one, responded when asked if one could adjust national security with democracy: "You mean, can you have security within insecurity? No, you cannot" (interview).[13]

Many officers, moreover, "confuse the very values of the military profession — obedience, discipline — with those of civilian society. They try to impose the discipline of the army on the *pueblo*. They are unable to understand the right to deliberate, the right for citizens to discuss. They just don't understand [these concepts]. So, they take them to be subversive action and disorder. And for this reason, military officers made mistakes in governing," retired General Peralta Méndez explains. Given the blind obedience of officers to authority within the structure of the army, "they have trouble translating" this training to the civilian world because it is "so counter to democratic values" (interview).

The contradictions of the "mixed solution" for the Guatemalan officer, with these fears, contradictions, and subculture of obedience, is reflected in their tightly bounded sense of political participation and the need for a disciplined civic solidarity. When Gramajo is asked, "When will you know you have arrived at democracy? When will you know this 30 percent killing effort is no longer necessary?" he replies.

Only when this society has more solidarity among the social and economic classes, and when one group recognizes the rights of another group. . . . When everyone obeys the laws, when everyone is more solidaristic with each other.
Q: But in the Opponents of the State schema, you say that everyone here is outside the law. So, you have achieved democracy when there are no longer opponents?
No, no, no, when the opponent is no longer significant.
Q: And when is that?
When he is no longer able to influence. For example, we have captured the opponent, the armed subversion with its Marxist origins. This opponent can live [in Guatemala] but when this opponent imposes actions against the government, then he is [still] significant. He becomes a threat, a pressure. But when one or two are dying a month, well then, the state continues and the government is not going to fall. There are evils that exist in society that one is never able to eliminate [entirely], but you can live with them because it's not on such a grand scale that it's going to affect the free movements of the state, right? There are street demonstrations, but they aren't important, because the market remains open, the university remains open, nothing is completely shut down, see?
Q: And meanwhile?
There is conflict.
Q: And how does one control such conflict?
OK. Within the laws of the Constitution.
Q: But we know that there are still people being disappeared and assassinated.
Because we have not yet passed this stage of transition.
Q: Thus, are you saying that during this stage [of transition] that such repression is necessary to maintain order?

Yes, of course, but within this stage of transition, the first thing we did was open up the spaces. Never before in Guatemala has there been a human rights organization; now there are five or six of them. Never in Guatemala have there been such protests and strikes.

Q: And at the same time there are . . .

Abuses? Yes, there are, because we still have some bad habits, and it is precisely a matter of education. We are involved in the strategy of participation, and [to become] very educated about civil and human rights. And [to create] a military attitude of tolerance. This Thesis will allow us to advance. (interview)

Conclusions

Repression is perceived by institutionalist officers as an endemic part of the transition for the advancement to a secure democracy. The inability or unwillingness of the military to distinguish between those demonstrators who have organic, legitimate demands and those whose actions are being manipulated by larger forces tells us two things: one concerns the fundamental issue of political freedom. To not allow political space for "innocent dissent" even for a legitimate complaint signifies that the army assumes, and feels it must always assume, complicity of its citizens in forms of "manipulated dissent." This mentalité of *delincuencia* a priori automatically views nonviolent actions as potentially violent ones, with order and peace imposed at the expense of political freedom. The Thesis's schema of Opponents of the State, moreover, dramatically exposes the crisis of credibility and representative governance in Guatemala after decades of self-serving paranoia of a predatory, murderous military-police security apparatus. We can begin to understand how the human rights record in Guatemala steadily worsened during the six years of elected civilian governance under Cerezo and Serrano (and worsened yet again under de León Carpio) to the point where killings and disappearances surpassed those in the three years previous to the transition in 1986. Joint police-military operations under strict military supervision not only guarantee military control over internal security matters but ensure human rights violations by security forces "for the next twenty to twenty-five years."

Although the Thesis purports to reject U.S.-imposed National Security Doctrine and Low-Intensity Conflict, Guatemalan institutionalist officers' hierarchized view of Opponents of the State indicates an incapacity or an unwillingness to forgo threat mentality entirely. But I do not agree with critics that it is all the same thing. For unlike the national security doctrine that dogmatically opposed giving the opposition any political space to maneuver while keeping a military directly and visibly in charge of repressive and internationally condemned measures, the Thesis of National Stability — "like the rivers, slow but deep" (Gramajo, interview) — allows the army to have it a number of ways: (1) to have a civilian regime provide an illusion of democratic normalcy, while counteroffensives continue throughout the

1980s and until 1996 to be waged against *la guerrilla* (see Figure 17), and "antagonistic" dissenters are attacked or quietly eliminated in military-ordered and -directed "police operations" before they gain in mobilization strength to become "vulnerabilities"; (2) "abuses," "bad habits," and "10–20 percent errors of judgment" are lamented while the use of force is intensified when deemed fit; (3) while claiming to be apolitical and non-deliberative, the Defense Ministry and the EMP write human rights reports to provide officers with political education; (4) Dialogue is pursued between the guerrilla and civilian sectors while the army keeps a low profile, yet lobbies vigorously behind the scenes and is adamantly unwilling to compromise in giving up its internal security apparatus; (5) civil-military discussions at ESTNA speak of democracy while participants are selectively chosen on the basis of their willingness to compromise with the Thesis.

Chapter 11
Conclusions

> This [new strategy] represents a change of mentality [on the part of the army]: how to learn to conduct an army in times of peace because we are not talking about conducting an army, we are talking about conducting a society by way of an army.
> — Guatemalan social scientist

After decades of naked military rule, the Guatemalan military have crafted a unique Counterinsurgent Constitutional State in which State violence has been reincarnated as democracy. Not intended to be transformative, but only "eminently transitional," *el proyecto político-militar*, which arose from the March 1982 coup, reconfigured the bureaucracy of the State for a "cogovernance" of military and civilians alike, leaving unchanged the structures of military autonomy and power. Counterinsurgency structures are incorporated into the very heart of the State. The genius of this politico-military project is twofold: contrary to the assumption that civilian rule entails the military's "return to the barracks," this co-governance, born of counterinsurgency, not only ensures the military's power and autonomy but institutionalizes both. To accomplish this, the military need no longer depend upon extraordinary state powers "to confront dangers to public order." Instead, it inscribes its vision of securitized rights and obligations into the traditional constitutional-electoral structures: "Human rights are sacrificed a little [as] a matter of superior orders to maintain the country's institutionality," as Colonel-lawyer Girón Tánchez remarked. The objectives to "restructure the electoral system" (Point 12) and "reestablish the constitutionality of the country as a matter of urgency so that Guatemalans may know and demand their duties and obligations within the free play of the democratic process" (Point 14) have been achieved, according to Gramajo when evaluating the 14 Points eight years later (see Appendix 2). It is these 14 Points, and not the 1985 Constitution or the Army's own Constitutive Law (which the Points far transcended), that provide the true indication of the military's intentions for *el proyecto.*

Perfectly cognizant of the substantial risks for the military institution if a military-led government repeats itself, officers are entering the twenty-first century with a self-conscious sense of autonomy from oligarchic and U.S. national security interests and a highly articulated, strategic vision to maintain the military's institutionality and protect the State from Opponents. Despite fears and insecurities with regard to democracy, officers loyal to the Thesis of National Stability believe that a protected democracy must be attained through the largesse of the armed forces as the ultimate constructors of the state and as the final arbiters of the boundaries of lawful opposition. As Gramajo has stated, "We believe with much modesty that we are the stabilizing institution in the transition. We are the institution that gives force to democracy."

Although officers are taught to perceive of conflict and dissent as inevitable, inherently negative, and in need of control in most, if not all, military academies throughout Latin America (cf. Stepan 1988) as well as in other parts of the world, Guatemalan military officers recognize the need to generate a new and more stable source of legitimacy. The Thesis parts from national security doctrine by arguing *sui generis* that this military is not interested in controlling conflict for the sake of control, but for the sake of development and, by extension, state stability. Yet the Thesis retains, by way of its schema of Opponents of the State, an alarmist worldview of inexorable threats—ranging from delinquency, public disorder, and strikes to general agitation, violent demonstrations, and armed conflict—that continue to justify in officers' minds repressive police-military operations for the "next twenty to twenty-five years of the transition." It is a low-profile but powerfully repressive scheme for the political management of opponents of the ever-vulnerable State that serves to provide an institutional basis for military intervention. It wages a permanent and selective war on those potential dissidents who need not have actually acted on their beliefs but, it is assumed, will inevitably act on them in the near or distant future. To not allow political space for "innocent dissent" even if one has a recognized legitimate complaint signifies that the military must always assume complicity of its citizens in "manipulated dissent." The logic is that war against one's Opponents never ends because the State can never be totally secured. If there is no peace, which is the "climate of justice," then *one must opt for order within a war of minimum force.* Different modalities of repression then are viewed as necessarily intrinsic to the transition for the advancement to a secure democracy: the very language the military uses to describe those who dare to dissent—Opponents of the State—should serve as the central counterpoint to the military's espousal for tolerance and respect for democratic freedoms. The Thesis thus dramatically exposes the crisis of credibility and

representative governance in Guatemala after decades of self-serving paranoia of a predatory military-police security apparatus. With the military
believing it is the protector of the state as well as the necessary creator of
democracy because "somebody had to do it," it utilizes psychological warfare, evangelicalism, Ixil cosmology, and Catholicism among Civil Affairs
Units; it also uses democratic and human rights language in Geneva, New
York, and Washington, usurping a vocabulary of reason and right to create
hazardous securitized rights. In the end, securing the state against its opponents supersedes any provision for full political participation or even a partial accounting for the thousands killed by security forces. Because the military sees itself as mostly unaffected by each new presidential administration,
it remains unconcerned with how its own view of the operational aspects of
law and definitions of those "outside the law" may erode the very rule of law
it proclaims to uphold. Under these circumstances, this hybrid, diffuse co-
governance continues to limit and stigmatize dissent and rely upon efficient, coercive dominance to the point of murderous violence. Nevertheless, despite its optimism in having achieved infrastructural electoral and
judicial reform as well as the power to reach down to the village level,
officers are much less certain as to their abilities to "penetrate" hearts and
minds to achieve ideological control. In evaluating the 14 Points, Gramajo
expresses disappointment with point 1: "To make citizens feel that the authorities are at the service of the *pueblo* and not that the *pueblo* is at the
service of the authorities" has only been fulfilled 60 percent. Regarding
point 9: "To stimulate in the national leadership of the different pressure
groups a new developmentalist, reformist, and nationalist thinking" only 60
percent. Such uncertainty and lack of complete control further fuel and
justify "preventive measures" in these officers' minds against a remote future of subversion.

Is Guatemala a Democracy?

Popular misconceptions associate civilian rule with democracy and military
rule with authoritarianism (belying a serious misunderstanding about the
nature of the State in Guatemala). As a way to counter such misconceptions,
debates about a typology of democracies — such as representative, minimal-
ist, delegative, or low-intensity democracies, polyarchies, or democracies by
default (cf. Karl 1990; Dahl 1971) — as well as analyses of democratic transitions and consolidations (cf. O'Donnell et al. 1986; Mainwaring et al.
1992) — underscore the need to understand the strategic choices and calculated interactions of those in power. Despite these typological and interac-
tionist approaches, though, it continues to be difficult to "place" Guatemala
within the spectrum of transition-democracy types. Civilian regimes have
shifted with each election since 1985 in Guatemala, to be sure, with a particular tacking of presidential personalities; there has even been a signifi-

cant expansion of political space, especially since 1994. But the peculiarly collaborationist politico-military project integral to state and political affairs as delineated in both the Thesis and the Strategy of National Stability indicates neither a substantial nor incremental diminishing of military power; on the contrary, despite an insistence on playing a professional, nondeliberative role, military oversight has been expanded and championed. "Our long-term strategy confronts social, economic and political problems" (Mazariegos); "We do interfere a little [in order] to fill the vacuum of power" (Gramajo). Guatemala thus represents a paradox: although the military project may actively maintain itself "independent of whomever wins the elections," its capacity to incorporate both state apparatuses and political parties into its plans for a "strategic democracy" represents yet another historic opportunity for this institution to reconstitute itself for future crises, while the nature of the civilian regimes elected into office remain fundamentally the same. This raises the question: Whose institution, in the end, is being strengthened by democratic processes?

The case of Guatemala thus forces us to rethink the traditional questions of how a military can accommodate itself to civilian rule and to what extent demilitarization is accomplished when a military (with a strong sense of politico-militarism) "prepares the environment" for elections by way of "pacification," and immerses state security into both the constitution and the presidency with few protections for human rights. It is not a question of when the military can be made to return to the barracks, retreat from power, or be made accountable to civilian rule, but rather, to what extent it has been able to "delete the hyphen between civil-military relations," with the full collaboration, if not complicity, of its civilian presidents. As Vinicio Cerezo stated in June 1987, "The army does not necessarily have to return to the barracks, which is an age-old Latin American concept — a concept established in the U.S. It should be an army deeply responsible for the guidance of the country's social and political processes, in fulfillment of its duties."[1]

Within this national strategy, civilian rule is eclipsed by a military institution strong enough to make civilian rule count in some realms while ensuring that it remains irrelevant in others. The gamble of "accepting the game proposed by those in power in order to beat them at their own game" (Rouquié 1986: 136) forces us to also rethink the nature and purposes of such *concertación*: "Up to what point does one compromise democracy all away?" mused one member of the Guatemalan Human Rights Commission in the late 1980s. Cerezo's advance-retreat strategy assumed continual compromise, and even that was perceived by some military hardliners as too lenient — resulting in two coup attempts. These *intentos*, in turn, provided the Cerezo-Gramajo *cúpula* a unique opportunity to approach Washington for more aid, and to purge several of the military hard-liners, while narrowing the already tightened political space. But the Christian Democrats and (what some Guatemalans refer to as) the subsequent "genuflexus presidents" censored themselves far more than even the Army High Command expected — getting "two out of five years" from his regime for their own purposes (Gramajo, interview).

Such *concertación*, I believe, is the dual intent of military fundamentalism: to at once control and eliminate Opponents of the State and distance the military from responsibility and blame for political problems, most especially human rights, by placing the blame squarely on the self-restraining civilian executive's shoulders ("I informed Cerezo of all the activities of Intelligence when I was Minister [of Defense] so that he would take the blame, not me!") — to create, in short, a co-governing but not co-responsible partnership. The *cúpula* kept the original 1982 politico-military project right on track: the establishment of a co-governance that championed civilian presidentialism and the administration of the state and an increase in civilian responsibility for international purposes, coupled with an expansion of military-political managerialism and oversight in Guatemalan society, especially with regard to development and intelligence activities. With democratic rhetoric far surpassing their ability and willingness to act, the Christian Democrats committed the fatal error of moral bankruptcy. Perhaps a transition policy that more directly created a modernized economy with wage pacts and agrarian reform would have been better than doing nothing; at least the coup attempts that these reforms would most certainly have aroused would have been against a regime run by a party committed to something other than itself. The contradiction of being a long-term transitional regime that lacked the political resolve to confront the real economic and political crises and that maintained the status quo may have been too great, as the 1988 and 1989 coup attempts and general social agitation bear out.

Both Cerezo and Gramajo argue in interviews that the long-term transition is necessary to "neutralize" military hardliners and the extreme right on the one hand and leftist guerrillas on the other by drawing them all into the electoral-institutionalist project. Meanwhile, their collaborative project did not "forge" democratic discipline, but rather failed the country by purposefully not actively combating impunity and stopping the killing by a known "handful" at La Dos ("They are powerful and we have to use that power") — seriously debilitating faith in the rule of law and participatory democracy. Nevertheless, Cerezo remains optimistic that this collaboration will eventually force the army to convert itself "into an instrument of the institutionality; it will be at the orders of the institutionality." Yet we don't know if and to what extent this collaboration can actually be translated into a democratic order because no civilian president has as yet tested the army's limits of tolerance. The fact that serious human rights violations have continued at alarming rates under such collaborative regimes (Gramajo admitted in a 1991 article that "unsolved political assassinations" remained the main feature of the electoral process [1991b: 45]), makes *both* military and civilians, rather than just the military, party to an active omission to acknowledge and redress past horrors, as well as to a *continuismo* based on an official contempt for the fundamental rights of Guatemalan citizens, most especially the right to life. Such co-governance gives new meaning to "civilian oversight" as purposeful blindness to violations — creating the extraordinary situation that human rights groups, and the popular movement in general, have had to challenge *both structures of power*: the military State and the civilian regime.

Lessons and Ironies

Such a hybrid military-initiated, civilian-headed electoral regime can serve as a lesson to those (including a number of people in the U.S. Congress, State Department, U.S. Embassy in Guatemala, and CIA) who contend that (1) counterinsurgency campaigns against guerrilla forces in "civil wars" do not constitute massive human rights violations as long as operations are carried out by "moderate" forces within the bounds of formal electoral structures, and (2) these "moderate forces" must be "professionalized" and courted with training, equipment, and funding (e.g., as assets and liaisons). First, to say that the campaigns of pacification were part of a "civil war" is erroneous: State policy of systematic violence for the last four decades overwhelmingly against unarmed civilians has few parallels given its length, dimensions, and extreme cruelty in Latin America (as Aguilera argued in 1983, and it bears repeating [1983: 85]). Second, the *concientización* among some officers in the late 1970s and early 1980s was a recognition of the poverty and misery of the majority of the indigenous population. But to say that it liberalized the institutionalist-developmentalist *línea* of the military toward democracy and human rights is to completely overstate the situation: their consciousness led them to realize that to maintain solid control of highland villages from insurgency forces in the future, they not only had to go "to the origin, to the cause of the conflict" in order to massacre, but they also had to maintain a permanent presence (*aniquilar y recuperar*). They built military garrisons in almost all departments, stationing as many military troops and linguistically skilled (and increasingly in the 1990s, female *indígenas*) *especialistas* trained in Civil Affairs and located in as many locales in the "conflictive zones" as possible to inhibit potential conflict or dissent through intimidation, threats, disappearances, and massive and selective killings. There is no moral dilemma here with regard to killing for either faction of the military: both the intransigent and "less intransigent" officers, as former President Cerezo refers to the institutionalists, very much believe in the doctrine and use of force. It is not the issue of killing that divides them but the dilemma that once the decision is made that it is necessary to do so in order to maintain order, there is a lack of strategic planning for and control over those who do the killing ("We aren't renouncing the use of force [but] you needn't kill everyone to complete the job").

Moreover, a mythical language of camouflage and conjuring tricks that hides its intentions and fabricates an innocent world that denies the consequences of an operational language of action and duty figures prominently in this military's narrative. Both languages engender a Prototype of Sanctioned Mayanism emptied of memory and replaced by a creation myth of the subversive past. What some call mythmaking or "reorganized truth" (Graziano 1992), others refer to as irony, and still others, hypocrisy. However named, this narrative is particularly salient with regard to the following issues.

Command Structure

In countering severe human rights criticisms of the 1982–83 campaign, High Command officers claim there was little control over local commanders, with individual "abuses" and "excesses" but no overarching policy, and that the calculations of victims and survivors are vague but lower than the figures proffered by human rights groups. Yet the picture drawn from these interviews is one of a strategically and scientifically calculated 30/70 percent massacre *campaign* choreographed out of the Army General Staff's offices in the Palacio Nacional, down to the last detail with regard to major Task Force operations, calculations of village sympathies, and logs of the numbers of victims caught in each sweep. We are told in interviews how distinctive these 30/70 sweep campaigns in 1982 are from the mere tactical, reactive operations of the Lucas García regime, which did not sufficiently annihilate the guerrilla before Civil Patrols were established nor recuperate those left behind. We are further informed that military discipline and the reestablishment of the hierarchical command structure after the 1982 coup were paramount in restoring the institutionality of the armed forces (to counter the insubordination of the young *golpistas* of 1982 and several mini-rebellions of *luquista* officers in the field).

Incompetent or Crack Civil Affairs Units?

At the same time that a military spokesman blames the killing of eleven peasants and the wounding of thirty other returning refugees at Xamán in 1995 on the internal "incompetence" of one young commander of the army patrol, he concurs with the opinion that the Sargentos Mayores Especialistas of the Civil Affairs Units (which constituted this very patrol) are "the secret weapon" of the military in "winning the war." The manuals of both Civil Affairs and the Thesis of National Stability (with its schema of Opponents of the State) reveal the military's formulation of a long-term, low-profile methodology utilized by in situ Civil Affairs Units to attack and eliminate conflict "in its infancy."

Guilt and Amnesty

As part of its psychological warfare strategy, the military has blamed the guerrilla for placing the indigenous community "between two fires" and razing 440 villages, at the same time that it blames the indigenous population in the highlands for having brought such destruction on itself by letting itself be deceived (*engañado*) by false promises of the insurgency. Yet admissions are made in these and other interviews that no distinction was made at the time between combatants and noncombatants: "We killed them all," one colonel remarks. Gramajo, too, asserts that "We won't return to the killing zones (*matazonas*)" and a Civil Affairs *jefe* states that "The army is no longer killing Indians." Girón Tánchez justifies the 1986 amnesty law for "violent acts" committed between 23 March 1982 and 14 January 1986 by saying, "Yes, [the military and guerrillas] have committed political . . . crimes and for this reason they are all responsible." We are told the 1986 amnesty decree-law is merely an extension of one passed in 1963, indicating the length of the military's impunity: "I thought it convenient to protect my men," Head of State Mejía Víctores remarks. These admissions give lie to the army's denials of responsibility for the massacre campaigns, with amnesty, ironically, their most salient expression of guilt and impunity. To say that it was a war with guilt either equally divided or placed solely on the shoulders of the deceived Indian soldiers and Civil Patrollers is mistaken. The guerrillas are not blameless, clearly; nor are many of the army-appointed *soldados regulares locales* and *jefes* of Civil Patrols. But it is the military that refuses to accept its own historical responsibility for genocide.

Army impunity was further institutionalized with the legislating of yet another general amnesty law in December 1996. Passed with extreme rapidity by the conservative majority (Ríos Montt's Guatemalan Republican Front), together with President Alvaro Arzú's Party of National Advancement in the Guatemalan Congress by illegally shutting out the public, Article 5 of this Law of National Reconciliation states that "all criminal responsibility for crimes of a political nature is dissolved. Those who committed, were accomplices in or covered up these crimes during the internal armed confrontation, did so to prevent, impede, pursue or repress political and common crimes. Victims have ten days to prove that it was not a common crime." The fact that military intelligence now includes a Juridical Advisory Office staffed not by military lawyers but civilian ones, "so we can know what our best strategy is in civilian courts" (Captain Yon Rivera, interview), is a manifestation of the military's nervous preparation for potential forthcoming human rights trials, and the maintenance of impunity under a civilian regime (see Figure 21). The issue is thus not one of complying with the law or carrying out the law — that is, putting into practice what is legally proscribed — but of impunity by law.

Intelligence Apparatuses

The final and perhaps most critical irony of this *proyecto* for democracy and human rights has been the centralization of command within army intelligence and its shifts in methods and operations. Like the overall *proyecto*, these changes have not meant the demise or even the diminishing of the powerful autonomy of La Dos. Adjustments under the Gramajo-Cerezo *cúpula* were made not to purge G-2 of its heinous deeds or make it more accountable to the civilian regime, but to reconfigure its bureaucracy and perfect its clandestine functioning by professionalizing its agents and continuing to modernize and refine its archives for the purposes of improving the management, control, and elimination of Opponents of the State. While Gramajo claims he had little control over G-2 and was being "tested" by a "handful" of the "hardliners" who had "bad habits," lives were protected when the credibility of the Defense Minister was at stake, or when a human rights monitor (e.g., CERJ) had powerful connections with the Washington community. Abducted, disappeared individuals were somehow "found" and released. But these are exceptions to the rule in military intelligence operations: in interviews, Gramajo and Cerezo admit that G-2 is responsible for "most of the killings." Gramajo, for his part, states that it was his "duty to control La Dos" as chief of the National Defense Staff and defense minister; later in a 1993 interview, he assumed full responsibility for violations incurred during his tenure as defense minister.

Moreover the CIA was fully aware of the "reprehensible" and "ongoing" abuses of kidnapping, torture, and assassination by "assets and liaisons," including those by senior officers of D-2 and Archivos, "some of the stations' closest contacts." Yet it was willing to ignore the fact that "the army acted with total impunity in the 1980s" and that "human rights problems, including cases involving U.S. citizens, remain a serious concern" in the 1990s, to the point of intentionally misleading Congressional Oversight Committees as to the status of human rights in Guatemala (IOB Report 1996: 6, 19, 20; CIA Inspector General Report 1995: 2). The CIA provided computers, communications gear, special firearms, and specialists for intelligence training throughout the 1980s and into the 1990s for a more modernized, "professional" effort that "would not harm the country's image" (Gramajo, interview). It financed a new intelligence school at which in 1996, along with courses called "Threats," exactly one course on human rights was being taught. The new methodology that "penetrates, discredits, and buys off" still requires threats, surveillance, abduction, imprisonment, and interroga-

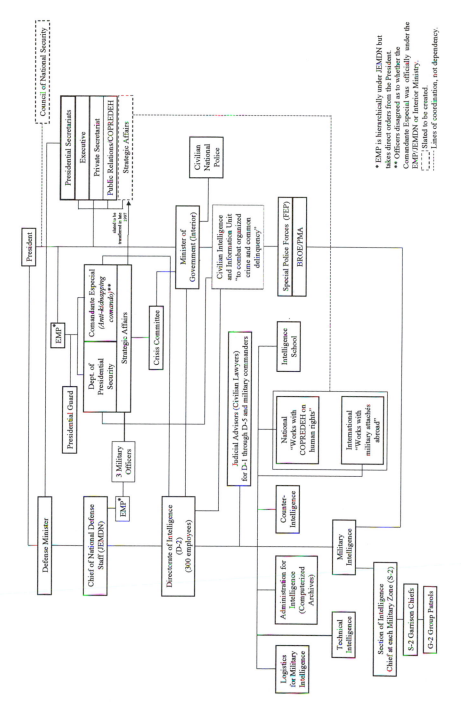

Figure 21. Convergence of military and civilian intelligence to create "Strategic Intelligence," as drawn by intelligence officers, November 1996.

tion in secret cells (using more psychological than physical torture measures) in order to create a network of informants released back into society; those who do not cooperate are "kill[ed] with justice." Such "minimum force" or more selective persuasion and elimination tactics are preferred. "That way they [the international community] cannot say then that you are using force" (Gramajo, interview). The consequence for human rights protections has been further to institutionalize impunity: despite detailed evidence gathered by National Police detectives, numerous human rights organizations, and G-2/EMP officers themselves, the report is either placed in a "dead case file," as in the killing of Christian Democrat Barillas, or in the wastebasket, as in the case of the American innkeeper Michael Devine. Moreover, to avoid the chance of being recognized or to quell demands by relatives of the disappeared, G-2 *especialistas* who are linked to abductions are transferred to another post, as after the GAM killings. No senior officer has ever been indicted for human rights violations (an admission found in the IOB Report despite the CIA's claim for "some improvement" in the military's accountability). The underlying fears that provided the impetus for this systematic centralization in the management of repression could be summarized as: "We won't be caught again with our eyes closed" (regarding the rebirth of the insurgency) in 1982 and "We won't be skinned alive like the Argentine generals!" (concerning the maintenance of impunity under civilian presidents) in 1986 (Gramajo, interview).

In January 1994, when President deLeón Carpio announced the dissolution of the Office of Intelligence and the destruction of its files within the Presidential General Staff, it was reported that the files were merely transferred back to the G-2. "We at G-2 will not interfere with civilian intelligence," one general stated without apparent irony (Letona, 1995 interview). One year later, a civilian Secretariat of Strategic Affairs (which includes the Crisis Committee within the Presidential Office) was awaiting congressional approval and funding. In a November 1996 interview, however, Lieutenant Colonel-engineer Carlos Alberto Villagrán, the director of the "all-civilian" Secretariat of Strategic Affairs (one of three military officers who work full-time with the eighty civilian *analistas* of the national and international sections), admitted that the Intelligence Office still effectively operates out of the Estado Mayor Presidencial. It is slated to become a Secretariat "once Congress makes them all legal and approves the Q90 million budget." When asked whether the CIA had funded the construction of the modern, six-story building with high-tech computers and brand new office furniture just two blocks from the National Palace, he responded elliptically that while such support was welcome, it could not be made public as it would strain Guatemalans' sense of sovereignty. He described the "three parallel levels" of intelligence: military intelligence, the office of civilian intelligence of the Government Ministry (yet to be established), and the Secretariat of Strategic Affairs (see Figure 21).

The Army and the Peace Accords

With the signing of the Peace Accords on 29 December 1996, what are the possibilities in the future for diminishing military power and establishing civilian oversight? To what extent is the notorious military intelligence being brought under civilian control and made accountable for its operations? After eight years of attempts to initiate government-guerrilla peace talks, it was not until January 1994 that an intensive round of negotiations resulted in eight substantive issues and operative agreements: (1) the Framework Agreement of 10 January 1994, which incorporated the earlier eleven-point Mexico Accord and assigned Jean Arnault as UN Moderator; (2) the Comprehensive Agreement on Human Rights, which established MINUGUA, 29 March 1994; (3) the Agreement for the Resettlement of Populations Uprooted by the Armed Conflict of 17 June 1994, which included the involvement of UNESCO and the UNDP; (4) the Agreement for the Establishment of the Commission for the Clarification of Human Rights Violations and Violent Acts that have Caused Suffering to the Guatemalan Population of 23 June 1994; (5) the Agreement on the Identity and Rights of Indigenous Peoples of 31 March 1995; (6) the Agreement on Socio-Economic Aspects and the Agrarian Situation of 6 May 1996; (7) the Agreement on the Strengthening of Civilian Power and the Role of the Army in a Democratic Society of 19 September 1996; and (8) the Agreement for a Firm and Lasting Peace of 29 December 1996.

"Operative Aspects Derived from the End of the Armed Conflict" of the 19 September 1996 Accord are intended to initiate "a progressive process" that will conclude in having (1) reorganized deployment of military forces in the national territory during 1997, arranging their location in line with national defense, border patrols, coastal vigilance, and air defense; (2) reduced the total figure of 38,000 army troops and *especialistas*, 2100 officers, and 1000 Kaibils by 33 percent in 1997; (3) reduced its budget 33 percent by 1999, freeing those revenues for programs in education, health, and citizen security; and (4) adapted and transformed the content of counterinsurgency courses to be congruent with a new military education system and the guarantee of human rights.

In limiting the military to external defensive operations, the extraneous counterinsurgent security forces to be dismantled by the implementation of the Accord include: (1) the network of military *comisionados* first established in the 1960s and decreed to be dismantled by President de León Carpio in September 1995. There was no mention of disarmament; (2) all Civil Patrols of Self-Defense. The PACS began to be disarmed and demobilized throughout the countryside in 1996, even though the agreement calls only for their demobilization thirty days after congressional dissolution of the decree that established the Patrols in 1983. "The Patrols will cease all institutional relation with the army and will not be converted in a manner that would reconstitute this relation"; and (3) Mobile Military Police forces (both PMA *or-dinaria* and *extraordinaria*) stationed throughout the country. The PMA are scheduled to be "dissolved" and "demobilized" by the end of 1997. Like the *comisionados* there is no mention of disarmament.

From October–November 1996 interviews with several more High Command officers, it becomes clear that these agreements, particularly the Accord on the Strengthening of Civilian Power and the Role of the Army in a Democratic Society, represent for the army the final institutionalization of their strategic project to win the war militarily and politically by "neutralizing" and reinserting the guerrilla into political life. In particular, it appears that the Army is playing games with the demobilization of its paramilitary units notorious for grave human rights violations in the countryside. Despite the September 1995 presidential decree to demobilize the 33,000 military commissioners, for example, a Staff document of March 1996 flies in the face of the decree by calling "for maintaining relations with the personnel of the demobilized military commissioners with the objective of organizing whatever type of group to be allied with the army in order to develop all class of activities that promote the integration of this personnel and its unrestricted support to the armed institution" (Ejército 1996a: Annex B, 7–8). The lack of mention of disarmament of the *comisionados* in the Agreement of September 1996 is thus very significant. Also, as noted in the 1995 and 1996 MINUGUA reports, Civil Patrols are being formed into other kinds of groups. Based on these documents, the intelligence web of commissioners and patrols, it seems, has merely been shifted from an officially recognized "grouping" to an unofficially recognized one.

This maintenance of military and social intelligence networks in the countryside flatly contradicts the Accords' intention of strengthening civilian power and control over military hegemony. This is especially worrisome in the rural areas where Civil Affairs Units maintain "a close relationship with the rural population," as officers proudly point out, apparently oblivious to how this presence contradicts the "external defense" clause of the agreement. The longer the army's presence and meddling is maintained in these areas, the greater the potential for repressive action.

With regard to "Information and Intelligence-gathering by Organisms of Intelligence of the State," the September Accord reiterates that military intelligence be "circumscribed" to defend the Constitution and provide external defense only. In this vein, a Civilian Intelligence and Information Analysis Unit is slated to be created within the Ministry of Government to "combat organized crime and common delinquency" by means of a civilian National Police force. The degree of independence of the police from the army, however, has been seriously weakened in the subsequent law legislating the September Accord. In addition, a Secretariat of Strategic Affairs serves to "inform and advise the President regarding the anticipation, prevention and resolution of situations of risk or threats of a distinct nature for the democratic state." All three organisms — military intelligence, civilian intelligence, and the Secretariat — "integrated" under the National Security Council, "will strictly respect the separation of functions of intelligence, information and operations that take place. The responsibility of acting operationally to confront threats lie with the executive office." Unlike the other two entities, the "strictly civilian" Secretariat cannot mount clandestine operations.

Nevertheless, when "the ordinary means of maintaining internal peace" are inadequate, the president may temporarily place the army at the disposal of a civilian authority in order to restore internal public order. At this stage, the army is limited in time and form of activities that are "strictly necessary for such actions," with the president informing Congress, and Congress, in turn, capable of ending such activities at any time. Ideally, these safeguards would prevent army intelligence from operating like the repressive secret police it has been since the 1960s. But while there has been a decrease in political assassinations and disappearances, these intended safeguards and oversight of the Accord continue to be thwarted. For example, in response to an ominous rise in car thefts, robberies, and "rapid kidnappings" in Guatemala City by organized crime, cashiered police officers, and G-2 operatives (with the parallel ominous rise in private security firms, some of them run by retired and "standby" officers), the response of the Arzú government has been to become increasingly dependent on G-2's technical and operational expertise.

Although the G-2 is not supposed to involve itself with internal defense, Presidential Accord No. 90-96 of 17 March 1996 officially established a direct link between the Secretariat of Strategic Affairs, the Government Ministry (with its Anti-Kidnapping Comando of the National Police) and with military intelligence in order "to combat organized crime and common delinquency" (Presidencia de la Republica 1996). (One Guatemalan daily reported that, despite all the monies going into training this civilian National Police, its Anti-Kidnapping Comando office was operating with only one telephone and one defunct patrol car [*Prensa Libre*, 27 October 1996].) In November 1996, this situation had not only not changed since the September signing, but "oversight" by G-2 of the Government Ministry's targeting of organized crime, kidnapping, and common delinquency operations had become so routine that officers continued to refer to a "medium-range" figure of twenty to twenty-five years of army intelligence expertise being "on loan" because of the "inherent ineptness" of the police and Ministry itself. "Do we just leave the state unprotected?" one G-2 colonel asked, echoing General Gramajo's comments in a 1990 interview. This hybrid parallel and integrated military-civilian intelligence web thus enhances the power of La Dos. It is an implicit recognition of who is in control, who is initiating and perpetrating the violence, who decides whether to "discover" or bury the identity of the culprits, and who can match violence with violence. "In the future," one intelligence colonel remarked proudly in an interview, "we will be regularly loaned out to the civilian intelligence service as advisors, just as FBI and CIA agents are loaned out to the U.S. Army, and German army intelligence officers are loaned out to the German government." The autonomy of the intelligence apparatuses—be they military or civilian-dependent-upon-military intelligence—remains the real test for this new democracy in Guatemala. Whether the U.S. intelligence community allows for a truly independent civilian government to be built is also in question.

Pressure from the U.S. intelligence and military community is a significant factor in maintaining this culture that breeds contempt for accountability. The tremendous pressure by the DEA to combat drug trafficking continues to pull G-2, Navy intelligence and operations, and the Treasury Police dangerously back into the quagmire the Peace Accords are trying to draw them out of. "It would be a lot cheaper for us if they would just take this whole thing over," the Defense Attaché at the U.S. Embassy in Guatemala stated with regard to DEA-directed operations in the country (1996 interview). With the armed forces trying to control the use of drugs among its own troops, with officers deeply implicated in drug trafficking (according to interviews), and with impunity prevailing for continuing death threats, torture, disappearance, and assassination, how wise is it to reinforce the role of the military as internal and external Guardians of the State?

This same lack of civilian oversight holds for the "purges" of the army and the police in 1995 and 1996, even though President Arzú has taken credit and has been applauded for this action. Nevertheless, most, if not all, of these could be described as self-purges by the military to accomplish two things: First, before the signing of the Accords, purging was used to pre-empt further discussion at the negotiating table. As one colonel averred, "We must purge the officers ourselves; we can't wait until they hand us a list. As Gramajo would tell officers, 'Shall we clean our own house or have no house to clean?'" (interview). Given the institutionalist ascendancy within the army, most of those officers purged were hardliners and/or more than borderline corrupt. (For example, the arrest by the Arzú government in fall 1996 of contraband mafioso/former G-2 operative, Alfredo Moreno and the dismissal of dozens of military and police officers, including the Defense Vice Minister and military attaché in Washington, who were thought to form part of the contraband network within customs, may have been more of an astute political move to eclipse Moreno's friend—the FRG presidential candidate Alfonso Portillo, who had lost by 50,000 votes to Arzú—than an attempt to control the army. Also, the immediate increase in customs revenues arising from these arrests bolstered government and investor confidence [Holiday 1997].) Second, the self-purge intended to keep the army in charge of how its purged officers were and continue to be treated: many were not summarily cashiered but made *disponible*, or placed on standby status, continued to draw pay, and face obligatory retirement in two years.

Colonel Alpírez and Colonel García Catalán, connected to the murders of Americans and their relatives, as well as former G-2/EMP chief General Ortega Menaldo, under investigation for corruption, were on "standby" status until at least April 1997, if not beyond. (By going back on duty for even a day or two, an officer can restart the two-year clock of *disponibilidad*.) Other officers were offered a buyout, or an early retirement package of fifteen months salary (*un quince*) and a thirty-three-year full army pension supplemented by presidential slush funds. By way of this rapid self-purge, the institutionalist wing of the army has seen to it that many of the *ultras* officers of the G-2 brotherhood have been removed but not indicted for either corruption or human rights violations—similar to the hands-off treatment of *luquista* officers spared the wrath of angry *golpista* officers in 1982. With the new law of general amnesty, signed just before the Final Accord, it will apparently remain that way.

Not surprisingly, the military's repressive habit of mind has already found its next target, as one intelligence colonel remarked. "We don't know who our next enemy will be, but we are told that, traditionally, one must consider peasants as potential enemies in the immediate future."[2] Drug trafficking, too, is considered a menace in the long term, not for reasons of U.S. consumption but "because, unlike communism, it delivers" (Camargo, interview). Such autonomy of purpose and hubris of control is also clear with regard to the definition of "Threats" as taught at the army's School of Intelligence, and is apparent in the National Defense Staff's National Strategic Analysis for 1996 when it speaks of "eliminating and/or neutralizing adverse factors for the Guatemalan State." These adverse factors include "the repatriated," whose poor living conditions allow them to "maintain their connection to terrorist groups, providing human resources and materials for their survival, and from there, the logic is to continue organizing groups to re-establish themselves in the areas of armed skirmishes (*enfrentamientos*)" (Ejército 1996a: 79). Interests of nongovernmental groups are seen as "supporting the cause of the armed opponent in the areas of skirmishes" and "supporting the absence of governmental authorities in areas of re-settlement" (99). Other adverse factors include the emergence of a Pan-Mayan movement which "for the next five to six years will only be run by Mayan intellectuals and academics, but in the medium term of twenty to twenty-five years, if it succeeds in homogenizing the differences within the Mayan community and creates conditions for leadership, could become a political movement that forms the basis for a new political party in the twenty-first century" (Lieutenant Colonel in the Defense Ministry, interview). Other officers voiced their fears that the movement could easily be taken over by former *guerrilleros* being reinserted into political life with the Accords: "Now, everyone's Mayan, or ethnic, or whatever they call themselves" (DIDE Lieutenant Colonel, interview). These categorical imperatives continue to form part of the military's new arsenal of subjugation in the 1990s and beyond. This mindset should alert us to the fact that even if a military institution is "professionalized" (such as Gramajo's attempt to reform La Dos), it does not necessarily make it in the least democratically minded.

In many ways, the initial period of negotiation was the easy part; now begins the difficult task of implementation of the Peace Accords. The first difficulty is compliance: Once the Accords were underway, the military was not going to serve as an obstacle (and as an easy target of criticism internationally); but documents and interviews at this stage reveal that the military will not concede in practice to all the conditions of peace, particularly with regard to the internal/external security distinctions. But there is another obstacle: even if the Accords are implemented and verified by constitutional and legislative reform, they do not sufficiently restructure the State to rid Guatemala of military hegemony. Indubitably, MINUGUA's presence has had a firm, dissuasive effect on human rights violations by the Army. But given the murderous history of La Dos, and the enormous influence that the Army still wields over criminal investigations and the judicial system, especially in cases involving military officers, the Guatemalan government's public indifference to the UN Verification Mission's repeated recommendations in its five reports against impunity,[3] portends an ominous lack of effective subordination of military power to civilian authority. Whether these Accords can and will make military intelligence — the heart of the heart of this repressive democracy — accountable and submissive to civilian control, and whether civilian regimes, in turn, do not come to depend upon G-2 to deal with "permanent crises," rendering even minimum standards of accountability and submission void, is still the central question for the attainment of sustainable democracy in Guatemala. Unless the military, and most especially army intelligence, is made fully accountable for its past and present crimes and forced to rigorously comply with its own self-proclaimed allegiance to effective democratic freedoms and human rights, their repressive habits of mind, and hegemonic power within a State of their own crafting will continue to haunt Guatemalans into the twenty-first century, managing a violence that is a democracy only in name.

Appendix 1. Interview List

Much of the material for this book is derived from interviews conducted between 1984 and 1997 with more than fifty military officers involved in both the construction and the articulation of the 1982–97 politico-military project, as well as in its attempted destruction with the 1988 and 1989 coup attempts. In addition, interviews with President Cerezo, two presidential secretaries (of Cerezo and Serrano), government ministers, and many Guatemalan analysts were conducted during this same period. Almost all interviews were taped, in each case with the consent of the informant.

Military Heads of State

General Efraín Ríos Montt (ret.), President, 1982–83 (July 1991)
General Humberto Mejía Víctores (ret.), President, 1983–85 (August 1990)
Colonel Francisco Luis Gordillo Martínez (ret.), member of the 1982 Junta (August 1988)

Defense Ministers, Chiefs, and Deputy Chiefs of the National Defense Staff

General Héctor Alejandro Gramajo Morales, Defense Minister between 1987 and May 1990 (14 interviews, June 1990–March 1991, January 1994)
General Juan Leonel Bolaños Chávez, Defense Minister (August 1990)
General Roberto Matta Gálvez, Deputy Chief of National Defense Staff (August 1990)
General José García Samayoa, Deputy Chief of National Defense Staff (July 1991) and Defense Minister (May 1993)
General Héctor Mario López Fuentes (ret.), Army Chief of Staff under Ríos Montt (August 1988)
General José Luis Quilo Ayuso, Chief of National Defense Staff (January 1994)

General Sergio Arnoldo Camargo Muralles, Military Zone Commander, Cuartel General (January 1994)

General Julio Balconi Turcios, Defense Minister (November 1996)

Air Force Colonel-Lawyer Manuel de Jesús Girón Tánchez, Presidential Private Secretary to Ríos Montt and General Secretary of the Chief of State of Mejía Víctores (2 interviews, January 1986)

General Otto Pérez Molina, Army Inspector General (April 1997)

Colonel Carlos Fernando Durán Hernández, Personal Chief of Staff to Minister of Defense Bolaños Chávez (August 1990)

Lieutenant Colonel Héctor Mauricio López Bonilla, Personal Chief of Staff to Minister of Defense General Balconi Turcio (4, 13 November 1996)

Captain Alfredo Herrera Cabrera, Personal Secretary to Chief of National Defense Staff, General Quilo Ayuso (January 1994)

Civil Affairs Chiefs and Chiefs of Committees of National Reconstruction

Air Force Colonel Herman Grotewald Cerezo, Executive Director of the National Reconstruction Committee (19 January 1986)

Air Force Colonel Eduardo Wohlers, Director, Plan of Assistance to Conflict Areas (January 1986)

Army Reservist Major-Doctor Luis Vladimiro Sieckavizza Alvarez, lecturer, CEM (January 1986)

Colonel Homero García Carillo, Director, Civil Affairs (August 1988; Colonel Mario Rolando Terraza-Pinot, Captain Echeverría, and a colonel sat in on the meeting and made occasional remarks)

Colonel in Civil Affairs who requested anonymity (August 1988)

Colonel Javier Schaeffer Paz, Deputy Director, Civil Affairs (January 1994)

Anonymous military zone commander (January 1994)

Colonel Olmedo Vázquez Toledo, Director, Civil Affairs (January 1994)

Several *comandantes* of model villages at the Pole of Development, Ixil Triangle (January 1986)

Civil Patrol leaders and patrollers in the department of El Quiché (January 1986)

Military Attachés

Colonel Marco Tulio Espinosa Contreras, Military Attaché, Washington, D.C. and Boston (March 1993)

Colonel Benjamín Godoy Búrbano, Military Attaché, Washington, D.C. (November 1993)

Colonel-General Roberto Eduardo Letona Hora, Director, Civil Affairs (August 1990); Military Attaché, Washington, D.C. (November 1995)

Army Relations

Colonel Otto Noack, former human rights spokesman for President Ramiro de León Carpio, 1994–95 (December 1995); DIDE spokesman, 1996–97 (October, November 1996)
Lieutenant Colonel Carlos Humberto Avila, Chief of Public Relations (5 November 1996)
Colonel Edgar Noé, Deputy Chief of DIDE (4, 5 November 1996)
Colonel Luis Arturo Isaacs Palacios Rodríguez, Chief of DIDE (August 1988)
Lieutenant who requested anonymity, DIDE officer

Officers of the Mountain

Major Gustavo Díaz López (September 1988)
Captain Luis Antonio García (September 1988)

Center for Military Studies

Navy Captain Jorge Arturo Mazariegos Aquirre, Director, CEM (August 1990)
General Ricardo P. Peralta Méndez, former Director of CEM and CRN (2 interviews, April, July 1991)
Colonel Oscar Hugo Alvarez Gómez, instructor, CEM (January 1986)
Lieutenant Colonel R. González Centeno, psychologist-historian, CEM/DIDE (January 1986)

Military Intelligence/Presidential Chief of Staff

G-2 *especialista* (2 interviews, July, August 1992)
General Luis Francisco Ortega Menaldo, former G-2 Chief and Staff Director, Inter-American Defense Board (November 1993)
Navy Captain Edwin Guzmán, National Defense Staff (2 interviews, December 1995; February 1996)
National Police officer who requested anonymity (2 interviews, May 1992)
Four G-2 officers who requested anonymity (1988, 1990, 1995)
Lieutenant Colonel-engineer Carlos Alberto Villagrán, "military advisor," EMP/Secretariat of Strategic Affairs (November 1996)
Navy Captain Julio Alberto Yon Rivero, Director of Army Intelligence (November 1996)
Lieutenant Colonel José Luis Fernández Ligorría, Deputy Director, School of Intelligence (November 1996)

Kaibil Training and Special Operations Center, El Petén

Director, Kaibil School (November 1996)
Deputy Director, Kaibil School (November 1996)

ESTNA

Colonel Félix Armando Baeza Cortéz (ret.), Academic Advisor, 1989–90
   ESTNA Course (August 1990)
Alfonso Yurrita, architect, ESTNA Academic Director, COPREDEH Aca-
   demic Advisor (August 1990)
Francisco Beltranena Falla, adviser and later director, ESTNA (August 1990;
   June 1991)
José María Argueta, political scientist, economist, Director, ESTNA (August
   1990; June 1991)

Retired Officers and Analysts

Colonel-lawyer Armando Diéguez Pilón (ret.) (August 1988)
Lieutenant Colonel José Luis Cruz Salazar, (ret.) political scientist (January
   1986; August 1988)

Civilians

Vinicio Cerezo Arévalo, former President of Guatemala (July 1991)
Ramiro deLeón Carpio, lawyer (Human Rights Ombudsman, appointed
   President 1993) (January 1986)
Andrade Díaz-Durán, lawyer, Foreign Minister during Mejía regime (June
   1991)
Juan José Rodil Peralta, lawyer, Government Minister during Carezo regime
   (January 1986)
Colonel Roberto Valle Valdizán, lawyer, Government Minister (August 1988)
Ricardo Sagastume Viduarre, Supreme Court Justice (January 1986)
Edmundo Vázquez Martínez, Supreme Court Justice (1986, 1988)
Six other ministers under Cerezo regime
Three Human Rights Ombudsmen (1988, 1990, 1991, 1993)
Several advisors to President Serrano and his private secretary
Two civilian members of the National Reconstruction Committee (January
   1986)

CACIF

Edgar Heinemann, businessman (August 1990)
Gustavo Vielmann Anzueto, architect, Air Force Reserve (June 1991)

U.S. Embassy in Guatemala and State Department Personnel

Dr. Cesar Sereseres, counterinsurgency expert, Office of Policy, Planning, and Coordination of the State Department's Bureau of Inter-American Affairs (March 1986)

James Canon, Guatemalan Desk Officer (March 1986)

Phillip Taylor, Chargé d'Affaires officer (with Political and Labor Affairs officers) (August 1990)

Ambassador Marilyn McAfee and George Chester, Political Affairs officer (January 1994)

Retired colonel, former U.S. military attaché (April 1995)

Colonel Dennis Keller, U.S. Military and Defense Attaché, U.S. Embassy (November 1996)

Others

Over 100 interviews with Guatemalan congressional deputies, lawyers, judges, journalists, social scientists and human rights activists were conducted throughout the country between 1984 and 1996.

Appendix 2. Documents and Interview

Manifesto of the 13 of November 1960 Rebel Officers

Interpreting the feelings of our *pueblo*, all the *jefes*, officers, and troops of the General Luis García León military zone at Puerto Barrios declare our decision to openly rebel against the government of General Ydígoras Fuentes. We take this decision by virtue of the evident incapacity the government has demonstrated since it came to power, bringing total political and economic chaos to Guatemala, as has been widely discussed in the press and over the radio.

Aware that only the Army can understand and cooperate with *el pueblo*, we are ready to sacrifice ourselves, if necessary, to destroy the man who not only didn't know how to respond to the aspirations of Guatemalans, but in fact totally defrauded them. We know that *el pueblo* will know how to respond to this crisis, as they always have, by backing this movement that has no other goal than to save Guatemala from such a painful disaster, and to install a regime of social justice in which wealth belongs to those who work and not to those who exploit: those who starve the people and those imperialist *gringos*.

Guatemalans: this is a supreme movement in our national life; you now have the unique opportunity to choose the road that the country will be bound to follow. Poverty, chaos, exploitation, on the one hand, or well-being, social justice, a fair distribution of national wealth, on the other — a progress to which we pledge everything.

We are not alone, the entire pueblo is with us: intellectuals, workers, students, in short, all the life forces of the country. Moreover, we count on the cooperation and help of a country, free and sovereign of truth, that, shoulder to shoulder with Guatemalan workers and other Central American countries, will help us, the true representatives of the army, to expulse from the land of our forefathers the exploiters who take everything and leave us with only hunger and misery.

Within the military, all the *jefes*, officers and soldiers are with us; this is not an isolated movement. In the capital and in all the military zones, all the *jefes*, officers, and our brave soldiers, legitimate sons of *el pueblo*, are waiting for the moment to act. This assures us that our movement is a movement of the people.

Today begins an era of social justice for Guatemala. We are certain of triumph. Guatemalans: onward! We need our determination and your bravery. In a few hours or a few days at the most, we will have banished from Guatemala and Central America those military men who hold the power and enrich themselves at the cost of the people—a people who will know how to honor their bayonets by assassinating today these military men and their allies.

Guatemalans! Central Americans! To a great and strong country with an army of the people, by the people and for the people; to a wealth of the people, by the people and for the people; and to a land of the people, by the people and for the people.

Strategic Analysis: Command and General Staff Course, Center of Military Studies, May–June 1980

General Conclusion

The geographic factor is positive given the resource potential; the economic area, in spite of recent deterioration, has high expectations for the short term (three years) . . . even though this depends in large part on the capacities of the leaders to achieve political stability, or at least to prevent a deterioration to an intolerable level. In the military area, no significant problems are foreseen in the short term (three years), although these could crop up in moments of crisis. . . . The political and psycho-social factors are vulnerabilities for the Guatemalan State. The political factor currently suffers internal and external depressions that put to the test the flexibility of the system, the qualities, capacities and goodwill of the current leaders as much as the Government and opposition groups and parties . . .

5. Recommendations

5.a. *For Immediate Action*:
To strengthen the maintenance of the present system and structure of Government:
5.a.1. It is necessary to seek national harmony by holding elections that are democratic. In order to achieve this end, a plan must be conceived, elaborated, and executed that
5.a.1.a. eliminates or decreases the current violence
5.a.1.b. provides the people with a relative degree of security

5.a.1.c. ensures the massive participation of the citizens in the electoral process

5.a.1.d. guarantees and convinces the voting citizen that his vote will be respected; this will be achieved more easily if there are no military candidates in the elections.

5.a.2. As a way to contain the economic deterioration and achieve the planned goals of development while integrating particular strategies of the larger national strategy, *a Supra-Ministerial* commission should be implemented that defines the national strategy for the long term (20 years), medium term (15 years), and short term (5 years). This organism must be planner, coordinator, supervisor, and funder of the *Integrated* strategies of development and security . . .

5.a.3. To resolve the current situation of violence, a series of intelligent measures (Economic, Social, Political, and Military) can be taken; but these will not produce satisfactory results if no laws exist that provide the basis and legal weapons for the fight against the subversion. Indispensable then are:

5.a.3.a. Adequate legislation for combating acts of violence

5.a.3.b. Consolidation of the judicial organism with efficient functionaries and workers to gain credibility of an impartial justice

5.a.3.c. Augment the personnel and technological capacities of the groups of security of the State

5.a.3.d. To encourage consciousness within the population to respect law as the only alternative for the maintenance of peace

5.b. *For Immediate Action*

(within the next 3 years, the time period of the problem)

To strengthen the Political, Psycho-social, and Military Factors, it is recommended that:

5.b.1. Education programs at all levels consider respecting national traditions and symbols, prepare Bilingual Teachers who originate from the region and ethnic group with whom they will be working, create adequate jobs for these teachers to integrate into programs of systematic Spanish instruction, and include coordination with the universities to achieve in the medium term an effective technological education.

5.b.2. To carry out educational plans directed at eradicating illiteracy which will help consolidate the moral and civic principles of the nation, and integrate them into one nationalism.

5.b.3. It is necessary to develop a national campaign so that these groups do not feel isolated, emphasizing that we are all Guatemalans, that Guatemala is our country, and that we have the same ideals for which to fight, to integrate the *indígena* into national development in every sense of the word and prevent the separation of the *indígena* and the ladino.

5.b.4. To revise the current levels of all classes of supplies, to maintain quantities that allow for a sufficient reserve to carry out operations during the time period of the problem (the next 3 years).

5.b.5. With respect to Belize, it is recommended the current negotiations be maintained; in complying with the above recommendations, the internal tensions will decrease as will the possibility of having to confront an internal (subversion) and external front simultaneously, that is, a military confrontation with England.

Strategic Evaluation and 14 Fundamental Points from the National Plan of Security and Development (PNSD-01-82, Guatemala City 01ABR82, RLHGCC-82)

Current National Objectives

1.0 *Basic Concepts*
1.1. *General Strategic Concept*
Guatemala will promote and undertake, in the short and medium term, administrative, functional, and juridical reforms of the structure and functioning of the organs of the State, employing the corresponding branches of public authority, and will coordinate and integrate antisubversive programs at the level of all political bodies of the nation; this action will be supported, assuring the optimum working of economic structures and activities and giving special attention to the economic problems of the people; guaranteeing the implementation of programs designed to shape and maintain a concept of nationalism compatible with the traditions of the country; assuring the adaption of the structures and functioning of the Army of Guatemala and internal security forces in order to efficiently confront and combat subversive movements and groups; programs will be put into effect which aim to improve living conditions for the dispossessed classes, and finally, efforts will be made to improve the image of Guatemala abroad, based on clearly defined and aggressive diplomatic actions.
1.2. *Strategic Military Areas*
1.2.a. The Areas of Conflict are understood to be all of the national territory, principally the area of influence of the EGP in the departments of Huehuetenango, El Quiché, Alta Verapaz, Sololá, Chimaltenango, and part of the south coast in Escuintla, Suchitepéquez, Retalhuleu, the department of Guatemala, and the center-west of Petén; the area of influence of ORPA, understood as the departments of Sololá, San Marcos, Quezaltenango, with projections toward the south coast, where the following dominant pressures are manifest:
1) Disfavorable psycho-social and economic conditions that constitute fertile ground for the subversion.
2) Politico-military action of the subversive organizations of communist orientation that try to achieve power and eliminate the administrative-political structures and our democratic system.
1.3. *Goals and Policies to Achieve*

1.3.1. Eradication of the subversion, promoting conditions of security, peace, and tranquility that guarantee normal life for Guatemalans and integral development of the country by way of *efficient employment of military power, supported by other governmental actions*.

1.3.2. Cementing civic value in order to deny subversive ideological indoctrination, making the inhabitants aware of the advantages of the democratic system.

1.4. *Strategic Value of the Geographic Zones*

1.4.1. With its unexplored resources and demographic level, the northwest region has value for the nation, [and] would make a big contribution to the economy; at the same time, the irregular topography favors subversive operations.

1.4.2. The southwest region in which ORPA operates has great potential for becoming the most developed and economically powerful zone of the country. On this basis, we reiterate our Permanent National Objectives:

1.5. *Permanent National Objectives*

1.5.1. To maintain independence and total sovereignty.

1.5.2. To maintain territorial integrity.

1.5.3. To optimize general social well-being.

1.5.4. Institutional stability.

1.5.5. Economic development of the country.

1.5.6. More equiminious distribution of wealth.

1.6. *14 Fundamental Points of the Military Government*[1]

1.6.1. *Adminstrative*

1.6.1.a. To make citizens feel that authority is at the service of the people and not that people are at the service of authority. [60 percent]

1.6.1.b. To eradicate administrative corruption and to encourage among State employees a genuine spirit of public service to act as the basis of a national government. [40 percent]

1.6.1.c. To reorganize public administration with the goal of invigorating the execution of governmental programs, making them efficient, regulating their operation, and avoiding administrative anarchy. [10 percent]

1.6.2. *Legal*

1.6.2.a. To bring about individual security and tranquility on the basis of absolute respect for human rights. [40 percent]

1.6.2.b. To restructure the judiciary with the participation of the legal profession, to have it meet the demands of the current situation and guarantee its ethical, moral, and juridical functions. [80 percent]

1.6.2.c. To reestablish constitutional rule in the country as a matter of urgency in order that Guatemalans may know and demand their duties and obligations within the free play of the democratic process. [100 percent]

1.6.3. *Social*

1.6.3.a. To achieve the reconciliation of the Guatemalan family in order to favor national peace and harmony. [60 percent]

1.6.3.b. To recover individual and national dignity. [30 percent]

1.6.3.c. To establish a nationalistic spirit and to lay the foundations for the participation and integration of the different ethnic groups which make up our nationality. [60 percent]

1.6.4. *Economic*

1.6.4.a. To improve the standard of living of the population in order to diminish existing contradictions. [30 percent]

1.6.4.b. To achieve economic recovery within the system of free enterprise in accordance with those controls made necessary by the prevailing national situation. [70 percent]

1.6.4.c. To strengthen national integration, taking effective advantage of cooperation with other countries and international organizations, at the same time projecting the problems of the [Guatemalan] State abroad. [70 percent]

1.6.5. *Political*

1.6.5.a. To restructure the electoral system so that, as the fruits of a genuine democracy, there will be respect for political participation and avoidance of frustration among the people. [100 percent]

1.6.5.b. To stimulate among the various pressure groups which represent the activity of the nation a new way of thinking: developmentalist, reformist, and nationalist . . . [60 percent]

Abbreviated Interview with a G-2 Torturer

He began as a First Sergeant at fifteen and then at sixteen was asked if he wanted to be a G-2 investigator. The majority of soldiers who go to work for the G-2 have "the minimum rank of Corporal or Sergeant, given the close connections they have with the second lieutenant in charge of a Company." He voluntarily entered the G-2 where "there are no ranks. There is only a *comandante* of a *patrulla*, who is a major or captain, and each *patrulla* (with its *jefe* and four to eight *elementos*) takes orders only from that *comandante*. . . . In that Intelligence Service where I worked [for eleven years between 1978 and 1987], it is not obligatory for anyone to work there. Many young people like ourselves who enjoy living in a better environment, [who enjoy being] able to drive cars and carry pistols, well, we try to get ourselves assigned to the section called G-2. But if you don't want to serve, then you are under no obligation."

"Training" for Coldbloodedness

To become an *elemento* of the G-2, one must go through a course, to be trained. So one goes but [he hesitates], [it is a] training course in which one is taken to one of the cells (we call them *calabozos*) where they have people destined to be killed, okay? The major or captain (never a colonel) takes you to the cell, gives you a knife and throws you together to see how, how you react against that person, while he watches.

Q: As a kind of training exercise?

Yes, in other words, it is to prove your tolerance for such things, to prove that you are cold-blooded, if you have sufficient courage to torture and kill any person.

Q: With a knife?

With a knife, with whatever [they give you]. But there [in the cell], the only thing they give you is a knife, nothing else, and one has to figure out for oneself how to torture that person, how to kill that person and if you have enough courage to do so. . . . And then, from there, you begin to do your work, making pieces of that person, to do it like one cuts up an animal. And if one does [the job] well and they think you have enough courage to do these things, then they give you a position. . . . This lasts only one or two hours. It makes me uneasy at times to relate this. I have always asked God's forgiveness and the forgiveness of some of the people I've killed for what I've done.

Q: What do they tell you about these people in the cells? Who are they?

Frankly, when one is doing this [work], one isn't interested whether the person is a *guerrillero* or not.

Q: It doesn't matter?

It doesn't matter because you must demonstrate your courage in how one kills a person. So, one goes to the General Barracks (*Cuartel General*) in Guatemala City, to prepare oneself [for this work]. . . . When you arrive at this section, they tell you that if they ordered you to kill your mother, you would have to go and kill her. Or your father, or your uncles, or your brothers, or any friend or relative — you couldn't refuse. You must go and kill them. But whenever they gave a reason or some information about the job, they would say "That guy there is a *guerrillero* and that guy is my uncle . . ." and then my *comandante* would say, "You are the *comandante* of this *patrulla*. Go find two or three more *elementos* and kidnap me that person and then pull out all the truth (*sacar toda la verdad*)." That person could be useful for the army, he could be used as a guide to find guerrilla encampments or to find collaborators of the guerrilla, if they let him live, of course (*si les da vida pues*). Now, if those people can't say anything [of value] because they are innocent or because they are rebels and they don't want to say anything, then those people are strangled, tortured, and finally assassinated.

Each military zone and garrison has a G-2 section and secret torture cells. . . . At the garrison level, with an order signed by the commanding officer one goes out to kidnap or investigate a person. The mission is to bring that person back alive to base headquarters, where he will be tortured. If that person resists with gunshots, then one can assassinate that person then and there.

Q: You mentioned patrols?

A G-2 *patrulla* can consist of four *elementos* [men] or it can be up to eight. Almost always four, though; not too big. So they get a car, and four [men] go to bring back such-and-such a person. Or if one knows that that person will resist and is well armed, then they get two cars and take along eight *elementos*. So, each *comisionsita* is usually a minimum of four persons, no more than eight.

Q: A *comisionsita* is a G-2 mission to kidnap?

There exist various types of *comisiones*. It can consist of being ordered to just investigate. That's when one works in civilian clothes, drinks beer with those close to the person or directly with him if possible. You never say "I'm from the G-2"; on the contrary, you say, "I don't work with either the Army or the Police, I don't work for anyone. I work with the guerrilla, or that one is a criminal (*asaltante*) and that one is looking for one or two people to collaborate with [on a crime], something like that." . . . When one goes to kidnap a person it is also a *comisión*: one's mission is to bring this person back alive, or if they resist, dead. But if he doesn't resist, then that person comes in alive.

Q: So, one goes out in civilian clothes?

Yes, tennis shoes, regular shoes . . .

Q: In private cars?

Civilian cars of the government of whatever color. But it must be large, with six or eight cylinders, in case it is pursued.

Q: At night?

At any hour. This [work] has no [fixed] hour.

Q: How does one enter a house to kidnap someone?

It's not easy. You don't say, "I've come to kidnap you." That's because you've already been there and investigated [the scene].

Q: But aren't there witnesses?

Yes, many people see what is going on when one does one's job, but they cannot say that it is the G-2. Because one is in civilian clothes. So people can say it is criminals, guerrillas, or the army. But who is going to say, who would *dare* say: "It was the army, it was G-2"? No one. Everyone says, "Well, there were some civilians who came, entered [the house], and took him away."

9mm: Weapon of the G-2

Q: What kind of pistol does G-2 use?

A very important question: the 9mm.

Q: So, when one reads in the newspaper that . . .

someone was shot with a 9mm, then one can say "This was the G-2." Only the G-2 and military officers can use this type of weapon. Not even the National Police can use the 9mm.

The G-2 Is a Death Squad

The reason G-2 *exists* is to kidnap and torture until our subjects are wretched and maimed. Then they are assassinated, thrown in a ravine, buried, or left by the side of the road. That's the work we do.

Q: Are you saying it is the same thing as a death squad?

G-2 *is* a death squad; it is a squad that is directly for killing. . . . It is in effect an opportunity for an individual to do wretched things with impunity. . . . We torture whoever are guerrillas no matter what kind. They can even be American, Cuban, Irish, they can be from any part of the world. They can be Guatemalan, Indian, or non-Indian. It can be any person, you understand; we torture everyone the same. There are persons who have been grabbed (*agarrado*) and killed who are white, tall and everything, and many times one believes they are Americans. But legally, one doesn't know where they come from because their identification is never revealed.

Q: How do you know they are guerrillas?

We kidnap, we torture. Frankly, we aren't very interested in their identity.

Q: Were your victims from all walks of life: students, workers?

There are many students who aren't students, who go to the university to infiltrate subversive propaganda, as we call it, and to form other guerrilla bands (*bandos*). I know because as a member of G-2, I had the opportunity to investigate or torture a person of ORPA, Organización Revolucionaria del Pueblo en Armas. And another who was with ESA, Ejército Secreto Anti-comunista. [ed. note: this is a rightwing death squad.]

Q: But how did you know they were *guerrilleros*? Did the officers tell you this?

They were people who had been captured by troops and brought to us to torture.

Q: Ah, so you didn't have a hand in the kidnapping? Only in the torture?

That's right, we only had to deal with those they captured in combat or those who were captured taking food to the guerrilla, or were fingered by an ex-guerrillero who would tell us "This one gave us food, this one gave us medicine, and him over there gave us money." This person would be grabbed and it was our job *sacarle toda la informacion posible* (to pull out all the information possible) with such questions as, "Where are your *compañeros*, your *campamento*, who give you food, medicines and money so you can survive?" And when this guerrilla who perhaps was deceived or forced to join *el bando* falls into the hands of the army and has the opportunity to live, he freely gives up every little thing he knows.

Torture Methods

Q: What kinds of torture methods does G-2 use?

We use the most painful we can find in order to pull out [as much] information from the person: sewing needles, electric cables; one places an electric battery in water and electrifies the water; there are many forms . . . pulling out fingernails.

Q: Who decides which methods to use?

It depends on the person [being tortured]. There are persons who one has only to prick them with a needle and he says, "*Un momento, no me matan* (don't kill me). I'm going to help you." So one stops torturing that person. Only two or three more kicks and that person remains there. You give them an opportunity [to talk]. But there are persons who say, "No, son of such-and-such, I am a *guerrillero*, I'm not going to squeal on anyone. The mission of a *guerrillero* is to leave and return alive or dead but never to say anything." When they say no, they give no information. It's someone who you cut off at least a finger and he says, "Kill me, I will say nothing." Then you cut off an ear and he still refuses to speak; you cut off another finger, and he still refuses. And you realize that you could cut this person into a thousand pieces and he won't give you anything (*este no da nada*). So, why bother torturing him? So in one stroke you eliminate him.

Q: And are there times when the *jefe del cuartel* or *jefe del destacamento* (G-2 military zone or garrison chief) comes in when you are torturing to see how you are doing your job? Does he supervise?

Yes, sometimes. And at times, when he sees that one is trying to tear out information from a person that is giving us nothing, he says, "No, this one will give [up] nothing," and he pulls out his 9mm gun, grabs the prisoner, and shoots him in the head right there. And he says, "Go on and throw this one away . . ."

Q: So he makes the decision [about the prisoner]?

Yes, sometimes; other times they leave the *elementos* to do whatever they want with their prisoner, they let them work with whatever they have. . . . That's why we exist: to torture that person [who gives up no information] and do the most horrible things to him and after all this, he is assassinated and thrown in a ravine, buried or thrown by the side of the highway or wherever. That's the work then that one does in G-2.

Women Raped and Tortured

Q: As a G-2 *elemento*, did torturing a woman include raping her?

Yes, this is normal. But it depends on the women, too. Because there are many women who aren't worth the effort to look at. Some even make you sick. But at times, the opportunity arose to be able to kidnap a young woman, to investigate a young woman, or for a young woman combatant to be wounded in combat, or an excellent woman. . . . Well, that woman couldn't escape. That woman, the first, the first, the first thing would be to rape her, right? That's the very first thing!

Q: By everyone?

Yes. Everyone. Ay! *El jefe* is the first [laughs]. And then the lieutenant or *el comandante* of G-2 or *el jefe de la patrulla*. If I were *el jefe de la patrulla*, then it would be my turn. Ay! This woman I like and so I would tell them, "Leave her over here" or "Cover me." [laughs] Yes, the rapes occur [as normal procedure].

The Need to "Cleanse" Members of the Group of Mutual Support

Many times members of the GAM [Group of Mutual Support] were kidnapped by the G-2 because they knew too much; they had to be cleansed (*limpiado*).
Q: What do you mean "to be cleansed"?
To eliminate them so that [their] investigations [of the G-2] didn't continue. There are many kidnapped persons who have not reappeared in my country in ten or fifteen years. But they are persons who have been assassinated and buried, and the graves will never be found. These are the secrets kept by G-2.
Q: Is the G-2 afraid that these investigations will be conducted?
As long as GAM is free to investigate, it is very dangerous. Such an investigation could end with the zone commander in jail; so many people can't fall victim to this! But it is very difficult to prove a kidnapping by G-2 because the G-2 is very smart.
Q: You mean it works to keep its secret, and when a person is getting too close, it is better to eliminate that person?
Yes . . . but I was never investigated. Never, my section, in all the sections where I've been [around the country]. . . . GAM staged hunger strikes to demand their [disappeared] relatives from the government because they didn't know who had been responsible (*el promotor*) of all this [abduction]. They believe that it is the government and many times there are kidnappings based on orders from the same garrison where one is assigned. And those who stage hunger strikes demand that they return the person alive and want the government to stop all that. The government could say "It must stop." They could say that, but the G-2 *elementos* have grown accustomed to kidnapping and killing and continue to do so. They continue to do so.

Are Military Officers Tortured?

Q: Are military officers ever tortured?
Never. Unless he was seen operating with the other side (*el otro bando*), then he would have his wings clipped. He would be told, "You're going to the *calabozo* and you're going to be investigated." But these *calabozos* aren't used for military men to be tortured. They release a soldier who needs discipline into the countryside to punish him, to do exercises, to run, and so forth. But these aren't mortal punishments (*castigos mortales*) that they give to someone who has been investigated as being in collaboration with the guerrilla.

G-2 Operatives Often Contract Out and Sell Drugs

Q: Was there much drug trafficking within G-2?

Yes, we would sell it, we would smoke marijuana and take cocaine. We often went to the border checkpoint where they wouldn't register our cars or our drugs. . . . We would also contract out to kill and rob. Friends would approach us *elementos* for this work since we can walk around armed anywhere in the country and no institution has the right to disarm us.

Q: Would officers do the same?

No, they earned enough and were more centered on their own affairs. One or two were corrupt, but the majority weren't.

Q: How much did you earn?

Only Q250 a month between 1978 and 1985. This was doubled in 1985, they told us, because we were *una sección especialista*: we had to earn more than soldiers because we didn't use uniforms; we were different. Besides, our work was dangerous, with groups of only four to eight people, it is *trabajo bien delicado* (very delicate work).

Changed Methods Under Ríos Montt

Q: Did the methods of G-2 change with Ríos Montt?

Yes. The people were killed but they were no longer thrown into the streets; they were buried. In the period of Lucas one used to leave four here, four there, and another four over there. Up to twenty. On one road of fifteen kilometers, from one *pueblo* to another, one would find twenty cadavers. With Ríos Montt, the order was given that we could no longer assassinate people in public view nor assassinate them and leave them thrown onto the streets. Instead, people had to be assassinated outside of town — that is, at the *destacamento*, but without alarming people, without them knowing. And likewise, to bury the cadavers without people noticing.

For decades, G-2 agents and officers have been transferred after "an incident" of human rights violations, while the victim's family members are told the culprit has been jailed or killed for their crime.

Sometimes I would kill a person who was innocent. Then her family would come to see the zone commander and tell him that they had seen me assassinate her. The [G-2] major would tell me, "You have to go to another *destacamento*." He would then tell the family, "All right, we're going to throw him in jail" or "We're going to kill him, too." So, I was transferred to the other end of the country so that these people wouldn't see me. That's how changes were made. I wasn't in any zone for very long: at times three months, other times six months. Only in one zone — 1316 of Mazatlán in Suchitepéquez — did I last two years.

Q: Is it possible for a general, say, of the Cuartel General of Zone 1 to not know about these operations of the G-2?

No, he knows because he's passed through all of this himself: in order to be a general, he had to reach the rank of captain and major when he is made commander of one of the sections: S-1, S-2, S-3, S-4, or S-5 in one of the military zones. Then, as lieutenant colonel, he is commander of all of these sections together within one military zone. So, the general would have already been through the activities of the G-2.

Opportunities for a Better Lifestyle, and for Revenge

With G-2 membership, one doesn't pay hotel fees, or entry fees to dances; one doesn't pay anything. If you enter a party and show one's card, one gets in free.

Q: What kind of ID is this?

There are two institutions in my country which give ID cards to those who work in G-2: INDE and GUATEL. The money is the same, the only difference is who issues the checks. Imagine if one had an ID card that said G-2: right then and there they'd tear you to pieces.

[Once one is in the G-2], you can use pistols, you can walk anywhere you please out of uniform, armed with guns, using any car and doing [these] things. But many also take on other work outside of the work of G-2, and it is these people they bring in in order to torture the *guerrilleros*. . . . There are always opportunities and no one investigates the killings. There is no risk involved. . . . The fact is we enjoyed our work. At least that was true for me; I liked it because I brought to it much of the resentment from my earlier life when I was younger. So, I'll tell you, placing myself in the G-2 I thought to myself, "I'm going to have the opportunity to revenge myself [on others], to kill people [to get back at] those who had killed my parents."

Q: Did you have any dealings with the CIA?

Only high-ranking officers (*gente grande*) went to the CIA.

"You Know Too Much"

But the message, I, _____,[1] want to give to those who don't know anything about G-2 is this: don't allow your relatives or your sons to be converted into a killer like myself. . . . If I could ask forgiveness from those I hurt, I would do so, including those many people I robbed. But there are wounds I cannot repair. I can't very well go to the house of a *señora* and say, "*Señora*, look, I assassinated your son and I've come here so you can forgive me." This woman, if she had a gun, would probably shoot me, or if she had a machete, she would kill me. So, all I can do now is ask God's forgiveness only because I can't go directly to her and ask for it. . . . If I could change my personality, I would leave all of this. But at thirty-one years old, I'm too old for this. People start putting on weight and can't act fast. I never saw anyone over forty in this *sección*.

That's why when one enters G-2, they tell you to forget about your family, to forget about retiring from this job to lead a tranquil life. They tell you: "When you no longer are serviceable to this section, your own *compañeros* will be the ones who are going to kill you."

Q: Because you know too much?

Of course, because you know too much.

Comunicados/Communiqués of the Officers of the Mountain and the White Hand Death Squad, 1988–1989

Comunicado 1

OFFICERS, SPECIALISTS AND TROOPS; DIGNIFIED SOLDIERS OF THE ARMY OF GUATEMALA; those inspired by the highest patriotic values that demand total and unconditional loyalty for the maintenance of the independence, sovereignty, and honor of Guatemala, the integrity of the territory, peace, and internal and external security.

TO THE PEOPLE OF GUATEMALA

the reason for our existence, sovereign, and authentic supreme Commander of our Institution; arising in arms to entreat freedom

WE PROCLAIM

FIRST: That in support of a constitutional framework that we contribute to forge with enthusiasm, nonpartisanship, and patriotism, the authorities have falsified and corrupted the process of democratization of the country, by constructing bases in which to install a dictatorship of the party against the national interest and to benefit a corrupt and unscrupulous political inner circle of the Christian Democratic Party; [by] using for such crooked ends the money of the people, the resources and institutions and organisms of the State as a gigantic and unnecessary propagandistic apparatus in charge of deceiving the international community by projecting a false image of a nonexistent pluralistic, participatory democracy in which the noble people of Guatemala were blackmailed by the manipulation of the term "democracy" and the threat of losing economic aid supposedly supplied by friendly countries.

SECOND: That the government of the Christian Democratic Party can be characterized by its constant and innumerable violations of the Constitution of the Republic: total subordination of the Legislative and Judicial organisms to the dictates of the Executive; lack of respect for the Human Rights Ombudsman and Court of Constitutionality; permanent actions to silence and eliminate the Independent Press; the positioning of known members of the Marxist-Leninist groups in important government posts; nepotism; general corruption; abuse of power; illicit enrichment; absolute lack of ethics and morality; the squandering of resources of the people on trips and unnecessary activities; an alarming increase in criminality; a constant battle for the seat of power in the mentioned party; anachronistic judicial system; a marked lack of interest in solving the problems of the people; an increase in the electoral bureaucracy; unemployment; high cost of living; lack of housing, water, public transport, and other essential services; worsening medical care and lack of all medicines in the national hospitals; lack of Teachers and Schools; a salary increase for functionaries of the DCG [Christian Democratic Party] while the majority scarcely survive on miserable salaries; a permanent campaign to politicize and neutralize the Army and the National Police; the involvement of the highest functionaries of government and the DCG Party in drug trafficking, whose only product is the debasement and destruction of our youth.

THIRD: All of the above has produced a state of anarchy and social decomposition which has taken Guatemala to the edge of civil war, the very government of the Republic [has been] inciting the class struggle which has been provoked by the stemming of economic activity and the virtual disappearance of the middle strata [leading] to the impoverishment of Guatemalan society — a situation which could not have been possible without the support and complicity of the Minister of National Defense, the Chief of Staff of National Defense, and a small group of opportunist and corrupt commanders.

FOURTH: Responding to the commanding need to avoid . . . the resurgence and consolidation of the terrorist factions that had only recently been destroyed in a bloody war, little by little, [these factions] have succeeded in infiltrating the highest political and governmental levels; they have taken advantage of the organization and various resources of many ministries and entities of the State in order to indoctrinate the population and restructure their military unities and political groups; they have obtained undeserved national and international recognition and have succeeded in legalizing themselves under the protection of respectable union organizations — extremist groups that at other times were clandestine; their only goal is their sudden ascent to power and the installation of a totalitarian regime contrary to the interests and the Christian faith of the people of Guatemala.

FIFTH: Heeding the cry of the people that has come from many different sources and has demanded the action that today we save Guatemala from the political, social, and economic anarchy caused by the DCG regime . . .

Based on Article 45 of the Constitution of the Republic which establishes that "RESISTANCE OF THE PEOPLE IS LEGITIMATE FOR THE

PROTECTION AND DEFENSE OF THE RIGHTS AND GUARANTEES WITHIN THE CONSTITUTION":

Today 5 of April 1988 we have decided to denounce and depose the government of the Guatemalan Christian Democratic Party and to relieve the command of the military *cúpula* for TREASON TO THE COUNTRY AND TO THE DEMOCRATIC INSTITUTIONS, for having diminished the aspirations of the national promise of work, peace, and freedom which the people of Guatemala had previously enjoyed.

AS SUCH:

This day we restore a new government of national unity that has an honest and absolute devotion to the law as its frame of reference, and as such, responds to the interests and legitimate aspirations of the people of Guatemala.

SIXTH: By virtue of the preceding, in this hour of need for the dignity and honor of our people, we appeal to the citizenry in general, asking for their prudence, comprehension, and faith in the divine mercifulness of God and confidence in the professionalism of the Guatemalan soldier and his love of country.

Guatemala 5 of April of 1988
[unsigned]

Comunicado de La Mano Blanca

In the presence of a series of events which have been developing in the country, among which is a group reduced to betraying countries (Marxist-Leninists: URNG/RUOG) by trying to install a communist dictatorship in Guatemala supported by the leadership of the Christian Democrats, who, as part of an interim plan, are creating the conditions for the return to their country's soil all the assassins who try to hand over our country to "international communism," sheltering themselves in the poorly named "democratic *apertura*." . . . Elements of the PGT, ORPA, FAR, EGP who, after having hidden like rats during these past years when the Marxist insurrection was crushed in Guatemala, now try to return to occupy the high positions in the government, seats in Congress, receiving international support for the formation of political parties which allows them to openly support international communism and their shadow organizations; and all of this as though nothing were happening, with the masquerade already in place in the executive, legislative, judicial [branches], and in the court of constitutionality. . . . Next time we will present a detailed list of the organizations and groups that utilize [this masquerade] to deceive Guatemalan society (groups such as the PSD, CUC, FUR, UNSITRAGUA, AEU, GAM,[2] and some sectors of the "progressive" church, isn't that right, [Bishop] Gerardi y Flores? As such:

The Mano Blanca returns to combative life in Guatemala raising the flags of Western civilization and Christianity—against the new Marxist avalanche that has accompanied the two agencies of communist spies, *Tass* and *Prensa Latina*, for whom we also have a surprise at an opportune moment; for that reason, in the presence of the imminent arrival of the leadership (URNG-RUOG) who were invited by the country-betrayers Chea, the Mano Blanca warns them that if they stay in the country, they will be presented with an action that the Marxist Guatemalans will never forget; we call upon all Guatemalans to avoid being close to these Marxist guerrillas as we do not wish for other respectable and mentally sound persons to suffer the consequences of actions we are contemplating against them and their guides.

> FOR GUATEMALA, BASTION OF ANTI-COMMUNISM IN AMERICA
> THE WHITE HAND
> GUATEMALA 14 APRIL 1988

Comunicado 15

NATIONAL COMMAND AND GENERAL STAFF OF THE OFFICERS OF THE MOUNTAIN

Given the tendencious declarations of Commander Ramón [Cerezo], who is trying to diminish the purity of our movement and to defend the armed spokesman of the DC, Gramajo Morales, we feel obligated to make the following declarations:

1. That the recent movement of the 9th of May [1989] was an action eminently military intended to rescue the dignity of the Army and the principles inculcated in our Glorious and Centenarian Escuela Politécnica which is now being sold to and put at the service of a political party by the traitors Gramajo Morales and all the generals who are arranging for the destruction of our Army.

2. The movement of the 9th of May was directed against Gramajo and the High Command acting in concert (*la cúpula concertada*).

3. It tried and continues to try to put an end to so much corruption, to the socialist penetration which is the goal of the officers through their wives.

4. To rescue the Glorious and Centenarian Politécnica which is directed by an absolute crazy of Gramajo who allows for the wounding and raping of our Alma Mater to occur such that it serves the likes of Mario Monteforte Toledo, Jorge Mario García Laguardia, Ballsels [sic] Tojo, Marco Antonio Villamar Contreras, all the members of the PGT [Guatemalan Workers Party] and those directly responsible for the bloodshed Guatemala has suffered for so many years.

5. Although we did not achieve our objective of eradicating the socialist

cancer which each day penetrates the country even more, we will continue to denounce all of their acts and all of those who consent to it. . . .

8. We express our satisfaction with the liberation of our 10 *compañeros* last Friday. We warn the Auditor de Guerra [Military Court Judge], the puppet Ramón Pantaleón, that we will remain vigilant regarding the form that the process takes against the rest of our *compañeros* and we have noted all the foul play and anomalies (as he himself informed the press, saying that he received his orders directly from Gramajo) for which we warn him that if he continues using this type of manuevers, such as the delivery of the processes to the traitor Gramajo in order to receive his instructions, he will soon be in for a disagreeable surprise. From our Intelligence Service, we know that the corrupt Gramajo has assembled a team of juridical advisers in order to try to drastically punish the highest number of our *compañeros* who have been captured. We give a severe warning to those lawyers they don't get too enthusiastic with the money and the orders of the traitor gramajo [sic] because not even the defense minister can guarantee your personal safety. Be forewarned: [Supreme Court Justice] Edmundo Vázquez Martínez, the stranglers (*los garrotes*) Marroquín, Julio Ernesto Morales, Carlos (bulletproof vest) Díaz Durán, Apollo Mazariegos, Mario Chacón [former Supreme Court Justice] Ricardo Sagastume Vidaurre, Donaldo García Peláez and [former government minister] Juan José Rodil [Peralta]. We also know that Gramajo assigned the eunuch Fernando Linares Beltranena to act as lawyer for Lieutenant Colonel Corzo Rodas only to worsen the defense of all the indicted officers. He is forewarned that soon he will receive a gift to remember.

9. To gramajo [sic], Callejas, de la Cruz, we want to remind them that in one year and a half, at most, the three will be retired and in such a situation not even their mothers will be able to protect them. You understand us, right?

10. To the traitor gramajo [sic] we say that he convinced no one in his clownish interview on Channel 7, and that it only demonstrated that he is the only one who believed his classes on Marxism at the CEM [Center for Military Studies], which allowed us to hear a lexicon only appropriate for convinced socialists. The most interesting thing is to see how, of his wartime experience, he cannot boast of any medal of combat or anything that would identify him as a warrior officer (*oficial guerrero*) who fought against the subversion (whom he defends now more openly than before) — he considers [warrior officers] as reactionaries, to use one of his words, officers with fialty to the oath of the Escuela Politécnica who continue defending our Patria from the sudden communist attacks. This is the hour gramajo morales [sic] stops repeating the lessons and words of priest Pellecer Faena who is one of their principle analysts of the "brilliant" team of Marxists that he has. To this penitent Jesuit who knows how to take advantage of his situation, we will one of these days teach him what should have been done to him a long time ago.

11. The traitor gramajo qualifies as those [officers and troops] in combat as reactionaries. just like the leaders of the URNG do. Has the Defense Minister begun to make the postulates of the guerrilla his own? Who will serve this traitor?

12. This traitor is very correct in affirming that the guerrilla is extinct as an armed branch of the URNG; their existence as combatants has been annulled because of the political power they have gained and which they are consolidating in having reached major governmental positions and intermediate groups (President of the republic, post office Ramón, Raquel Blandón [First Lady], commander Carlota, Catalina Soberanis, Alfonso Cabrera . . . Cifuentes (PGT) in the National Police, [Development Minister] René Deleón [*sic*] . . . [Labor Minister] Rodolfo Maldonado, Arturo de Cid, M13N[ovember] companion of Gramajo, [Government Minister] Roberto Valle Valdizán and his wife Beatriz . . . [Finance Minister] Lizardo Sosa . . .

13. To those Officers, above all Junior Officers, who have not been involved in this state of affairs, we ask that you be analytical and that you don't allow yourselves to be permeated by the verbosity of the post office ramón [Cerezo] and the traitor gramajo morales who are very able in presenting their ideas about the national reality, but they lie and they hide [the reality]. We refer to the letter sent by Cerezo to his comrade Napoleon Duarte in which he revealed his intentions to annihilate the army. Democracy for these drug traffickers is only a form of personal enrichment and one to take us into a totalitarian State. The future of Guatemala cannot be based on [relations] between Cuba and Mexico. What must be very carefully analyzed by the officers who are still indecisive is to ask about the lack of character of [Chief of Staff] Callejas: why did he stop the Task Forces Kaibil and Xancatal — especially the latter when it was just at the point of dealing the final blow to ORPA leader Pancho Palma Lau on the outskirts of Pochuta? The retreat of our Task Forces [from the field] was anticipated by the lack of action of the sad Plan Cloud-Sun (*Plan Nube-Sol*). The indecisive officers must choose between remaining [on the sidelines] with their arms crossed seeing the destruction of the Armed Institution and watching them give the Nobel Prize to the countrywoman [Rigoberta] Menchú whose only virtue has been to present us before the whole world as a genocidal and cannabilistic army.

Our struggle to maintain the Patria free from totalitarianism must continue. The blood of our fallen *compañeros* in combat must inspire us not to let our guard down for one instant. We are at war against a powerful enemy, but we have always come away victorious and now we won't fail. It is only a matter of time before we will vindicate the army's dignity and glory because a Guatemalan soldier has never been defeated.

NATIONAL COMMAND OF THE OFFICERS OFFICERS [*sic*] OF THE MOUNTAIN
Guatemala 29th of May 1989

Notes

Introduction

1. As Chilean politico-legal analyst Herman Montealegre has pointed out, the national security argument used by various Latin American governments "has led [them] to adopt the extraordinary means established by law to confront dangers to public order: declaration of a national state of war, indictment of citizens on the charge of treason, and attribution of the legal status of enemies of the state to certain persons or organs of the nation. This has resulted in an unprecedented and permanent application of traditional provisions of the legal system . . . contained in the juridical codes in Latin America which hitherto had only been employed in cases of actual war between the states [and] are certainly illegal, since the circumstances which led to their implementation are not those foreseen by the codes" (1979: 3).

2. E.g., Fukuyama 1992.

3. During the long period of compilation of materials and writing of this book, several controversies arose as to this lack of boundaries of national security prerogatives of the U.S. intelligence community: the Iran-contra hearings resulted in the indictment of several Reagan administration officials and the questioning of several CIA officials; the controversial appointments of several new CIA directors; and the investigation by the Intelligence Oversight Board and the CIA Inspector General into the DeVine and Bámaca killings in Guatemala led to the dismissal of the CIA chief of Covert Operations, Latin American Division, Terry Ward, and the 1990–93 Guatemalan station chief, Fred Bruegger, and the sanctioning of other CIA officers (CIA Inspector General Report 1995).

4. See, for example, Zagorski 1992.

5. Gramajo may be the "granddaddy," but General Manuel Antonio Callejas y Callejas was considered the "godfather" of military intelligence in the late 1970s and throughout the 1980s.

Chapter 1

1. "Professional" should not be confused with "nonpolitical," as Adams has pointed out (1970: 239): "The tendency of some contemporary writers on the military in Latin America to equate professionalism with nonpolitical concern is misleading in Guatemala. The position taken here is that men of any profession may also be political."

2. Quoted in Cruz Salazar 1970: 74–98; this section draws heavily on Cruz Salazar's very interesting article, generously provided by the author.

3. Nevertheless, several older officers complained bitterly in interviews about being discouraged by both ranking officers and university students from seeking a university education.

4. Albizúrez 1989: 43–45. General Gramajo also recognized this same contradiction:

> The 1945 Constitution committed a big mistake: for the first time it said that the army was apolitical and nondeliberative, but at the same time they organized a Consejo Nacional de la Defensa, which was elective! It is against the nature of a military to vote. And the only interests represented [in these elections] are of those politicians out of office. So the government uses the army for its own problems of domestic politics, with the army becoming politicized against the constitution! ... Then came the problem with the prohibition of the Communist Party in the 1956 Constitution. The communists wanted to be able to vote, and that united the capitalists with the army [politicizing the army once again]. But the 1956 Constitution corrected the first two mistakes by stating that the Army was apolitical and nondeliberative. [The constitutions] always say that [now], but at least there is no longer a Consejo de Defensa (interview).

5. See Carlos Wer's bitter account as one of the rebellious cadets of 2 August 1954 (1992).

6. In 1970, I interviewed peasants, many in their late fifties and sixties, in the department of Escuintla, who had received small allotments in 1954. With tears in their eyes, these older *campesinos* would speak fiercely and lovingly of "nuestro Presidente Arbenz."

7. The Army's Constitutive Law remained essentially the same between 1944 and 1985:

    a. 1944 Constitution, Art, 149: The Army . . . is subject to the laws and military regulations.

    b. 1956 Constitution, Art. 180: [The Army] is governed by the laws and military regulations.

    c. 1965 Constitution, Art. 220: The Army of Guatemala is governed by its Constitutive Law, laws, and military regulations.

    d. 1982 Fundamental Statute of Government, Art. 93: The Army of Guatemala is governed by the norms of the Statute and its Constitutive Law, laws, and Military Regulations.

8. Although a good 50 percent of the officer corps were involved in plotting the coup, only about 120 participated, presumably because the date had been moved up (Cifuentes 1993). Gramajo provided the figure 21 percent of the number of officers who were forced to leave the army after the rebellion (interview).

9. Admission to the Escuela is a "transcendent" event for most officers, as it means a significant upward shift in social status; graduation is "to enter a band of brothers, an elite born of a special demanding common experience, one bonded by ties in which no civilian could share, with great external morale and group loyalty, and a personal sense of destiny" (Patterson 1988: 374, 367). This fierce bonding is based on what officers refer to as *la fibra* or a culture of discipline, intense loyalty, and secrecy.

10. Gramajo believes these two officers rebelled partly because they were cuckolded by their fiancées while training in the United States.

11. In 1980, according to Gramajo, his brother-in-law, rector of the National University in Quezaltenango, was shot, his sister was wounded, and a bullet barely missed

his mother. As defense minister in 1987, Gramajo ordered a secret investigation that determined that an agent of the National Police had been responsible. "But I did nothing" (interview).

12. "Speech on the 117th Anniversary of the Founding of the Guatemalan Army" (1988d).

13. Oil- and mineral-rich properties in the Northern Transversal Strip, bought or expropriated by the state and passed on to key officers, became known as the Generals' Corner; Lucas García himself was reported to own 40,000 *hectares*. (It is unclear, however, given his wealthy family background in Cobán as "cardamon growers" whether some of this land was from his family. "Lucas gave away land to officers as favors even before he became general," Gramajo stated in interview.) Lucrative arms deals in which eight generals overcharged the government millions of dollars were also exposed in the early 1980s (Nyrop 1984: 134).

14. The checks were sent either from INDE (Instituto Nacional de Electrificación/National Institute of Electrification) or INGUAT (Instituto Guatemalteco de Turismo/Guatemalan Institute of Tourism) (G-2 operative, interview).

15. "*Apreciación estratégica del estado de Guatemala,* parte del curso no. 6 para comandantes y oficiales impartido por el CEM 25 de mayo–27 de junio 1980." Ríos Montt, like Gramajo, was relegated to Washington "for having opposed the hardline generals in succeeding themselves militarily in power, and in insisting upon the institutional role of the army in upholding the constitution," according to former President Cerezo in a 1991 interview.

16. He first offered the candidacy to congressional deputy Dr. Alfonso Ponce Archila, an ophthalmologist from Alta Verapaz and a close friend of the general's. "But the risks were very high at the time for anyone, particularly a civilian, to participate in politics" (Beltranena 1992: 16).

17. Ríos Montt was supported by the MLN-CAN (National Liberation Movement and Authentic Nationalist Center) party coalition and junior officers (many of whom had been his students at the CEM). His military status at this time was a form of *disponibilidad,* unassigned status or inactive reserve. This term refers to the flexible situation of an officer who has not reached the appropriate age for retirement, yet is not on active duty; he is free from military duties, yet bound by a military code of conduct and continues to receive basic pay. This status is often applied as a sanction for political reasons, yet indicates how well the military old-boy network of *promoción* takes care of their own. Ríos Montt, for his part, had won the election for president as a Christian Democratic candidate in 1974, but had it taken from him by the army to install General Kjell Laugerud and had been in disfavor with the military *camarilla* (inner circle) ever since.

18. Colonel Gordillo recounts Ríos Montt's hubris:

From the first moment of the coup, Ríos Montt used very intelligent methods no one could counter; he had hegemony over us. He said "I am the oldest general here . . . The situation in Guatemala is very difficult. The country is in a state of insecurity. We need to gain control of it: the Army, the Police, and the Communications. I'm going to control the Army, Maldonado the Police, and you, Gordillo, the communications." So, we began by reorganizing the military sectors. . . . And with a group of advisers, we devised a plan [that] delivered the country into the present circumstances of government. [This plan] had its advantages in a country as divided as ours was and in which political parties were small entities only interested in power. (1988 interview)

19. Several officers and civilians interviewed said they had seen, or heard through army intelligence, that the MLN had infiltrated the army to give money to officers,

including General Ríos Montt, to stage the coup. Gramajo confirmed this. "This was proven, and I took charge of those who we proved had received money enthusiastically; only two escaped [my efforts to purge these officers]. [Such activity of receiving money] is the most lamentable. You [as an officer] can participate [in something] for ideological reasons, or for free, but for money, you must then give up being an officer" (interview).

20. Gramajo later gives the young officers more credit in his book, detailing how young rebel officers at the Quelzaltenango military base fired upon the base commander, attempting to assassinate him (1995: 164–67).

21. Gramajo claims that the military government at this time "sought communication through the diplomatic representation of countries known to have open communication with representatives of the Guatemalan armed insurgency in the form of a dialogue to save lives and resources. Hostilities had to cease to bring peace to the country. The insurgents, with a very haughty attitude, openly rejected this." (1991a: 15). Ríos Montt has made the same claim in interview. I have not verified this from the guerrilla side.

22. (1988d).

23. Gramajo explains that "there were only military officers involved in drawing up the Plan, but in the end, to be certain [of some of the points], we brought in some select members from the Secretariat for Social and Economic Developmental Planning (SEGEPLAN) to look over the aspects of economic planning and they said it made sense [to them]" (interview).

24. It was reported at the time that the MLN (National Liberation Movement), CAN (Authentic Nationalist Central Party), DCG (Christian Democratic Party of Guatemala), and PNR (National Renovation Party), boycotted the Council. Vinicio Cerezo is quoted as saying "There is no reason to participate as long as there is no political freedom or right of expression" (*Cadena de Emisoras Unidas*, 25 August 1982).

25. In a later interview, Girón Tánchez complained, "Of course, no one believed us because they believed that we were trying to perpetuate ourselves in power perhaps in the style of General Pinochet. This, of course, we did not do" (1986 interview).

26. The Guatemalan weekly *Crónica*, credits Ríos Montt's advisor, American evangelical Harris Whitbeck with the catchy names Frijoles y Fusiles and Techo, Tortilla, y Trabajo (29 June 1990: 16); Beltranena believes the advertising professional Alvaro Contreras Valladares, an elder of the Church of the Word, to be the spinmaster (1992: 164).

27. See chapter 3 for estimated figures of human rights violations during the period.

28. Manuel Ayau is the former rector of the most conservative private university in Guatemala, the Universidad Francisco Marroquín.

29. Elders and other members of Ríos Montt's evangelical church had taken control of several programs in the national government. Gramajo confirms that the high number of relatives of army officers and evangelicals employed in the Ministry of Social Welfare was one of the factors in the officers' removal of Ríos Montt at this time (interview).

30. Four of the officers' demands were: fire Ríos's evangelical advisors; cease his Sunday television evangelical *discursos*, dissolve La Juntita, which consisted of many young officers in the Presidential General Staff; and take no reprisals against the *golpistas* (coup plotters). Ríos agreed, but by late July 1983 he was already breaking this agreement.

31. Also at this time, Mejía having graduated from the Mexican military academy, renamed the Army General Staff (Estado Mayor General del Ejército) the National

Defense Staff (Estado Mayor de la Defensa Nacional) with Decree-Law 28-83 (Mejía, 1990 interview).

32. Mejía is quoted in *Revista Cultural del Ejército* in 1985: "The function of the Army is not only to defend the sovereignty of the Nation, but to contribute to its construction" (Ejército 1985a: 4).

33. This is the same desk officer who stated in a 1986 interview with the author that "no one wants the job of Human Rights Ombudsman in Guatemala because they're afraid of being knocked off!" He then slapped the arm of his chair and roared with laughter.

Chapter 2

1. On seeing a draft of the transcribed tape interview for the *Harvard International Review*, Gramajo first suggested that "kill" be changed to "violently repress," and later to "coerce."

2. Arias argues that the burning alive of a group of indigenous peasants who had peacefully occupied the Spanish Embassy after both President Lucas and the Congress had refused to listen to their pleas to stop the repression in the Ixil area was a watershed event for most Indians: "For them, there were now no options left other than to join the popular war being waged against the reactionary regime" (1990: 254). For the military, this event has been interpreted as an assault on an embassy by "a guerrilla commando, dressed in indigenous dress from El Quiché, who were following the Sandinista example in the taking of the National Palace in Nicaragua on August 22, 1978" (Cifuentes, "El secuestro," *Revista Militar* No. 29, May–August 1983: 59).

3. These are towns only forty minutes by car from downtown Guatemala City.

4. For example, at this time when an officer died, his wife received his pension, unless she herself worked for government. She had to choose between her job or his pension, "reducing the family income by half," one officer's wife told me, angry at "the socialist statutes" (1986 interview; Gramajo, interview). With the 1982 coup, the Fondo de Protección Militar was broadened to allow widows to receive pensions and continue to work at government jobs (Decree-Law 55-82, Recopilador de Leyes 1982: 221).

5. Mariscal Zavala and Guardia de Honor are the two major brigades in Guatemala City.

6. Gramajo refers to this Task Force as Cumarcaj (1995: 182), while other officers, including those who drew up Figure 7 (p. xvii), refer to it as Humarcaj.

7. Gramajo admits that this attempt at dialogue was "psychological warfare, but it was also a real effort to dialogue. The guerrillas refused because they thought they were in a very strong position, and we were not" (interview).

8. Gramajo describes how he saw the problem: "The ethnic groups were infiltrated by the subversion, and the first thing they did was replace the traditional leadership, the elders (*ancianos*). It's difficult for us *ladinos* to understand, but once it's understood, one can see that this infiltration wasn't well done. What the subversion did was choose a young leader, ideologize him, take the authority away from the elder, polarizing *indígena* and ladino, and deliver the *indígena población* to the subversion. The villages were *indígena*, the town (*municipio*) ladino. There were many cases in which the *indígenas* united and burned down the *municipio*. But it was done within a polarization *induced* by the subversive. Our approach was to reestablish normalcy, and normalcy is having the *ancianos* in control, not the [subversive] ones."

9. Amnesty International estimates that troops killed 15 peasants and burned 4 others alive in Estancia de la Virgen on 31 March 1982 (1982), while another report

estimates that on 7 April 1982, 250 were massacred by the army in all the villages and hamlets mentioned by Gramajo in this interview as well as several others in the same municipality (ICADIS 1982: 2–3; Falla 1983: 86; 1984: 203). The level of violence is estimated to have been as high in Chimaltenango as in the Ixil, with at least 20 percent of the population displaced in that *departamento* (PAVA 1984).

10. Author of this interview with Gramajo in the early 1990s wishes to remain anonymous.

11. The documentation of massive and systematic atrocities by the Guatemalan military against the noncombatant indigenous population is overwhelming. See Comité Pro-Justicia y Paz 1982 through 1992; Amnesty International 1981 and 1982; Americas Watch de Guatemala Reports 1982 and 1983; Falla 1983, 1984, 1994, among others.

12. *Kaibil* is a Mayan term loosely translated as "warrior" or "strategist." Kaibils are special forces units from the Jungle Training School in the Petén.

13. Aguilera Peralta has divided the attacks into three categories: a) preventive terror: public executions of persons selected at random to prevent guerrilla support; b) selective repression of local community and regional leaders to eliminate that part of the population suspected of being or that already is part of the guerrilla irregulars; c) massive repression aimed at punishing a major portion of the population that, according to the regular forces, is collaborating collectively with the guerrilla (1983: 98 fn. 44).

14. All six departments included in the TOSO campaign, for example, had originally been covered by the Quezaltenango zone commander (Gramajo 1995: 205).

15. This last figure is from the Conference of Catholic Bishops report, summer 1982. The Ríos Montt government dismissed this estimate as an exaggeration.

16. With the March 1982 coup, many of the officers in very high positions in the Lucas García government were transferred out to serve the war effort in the mountains, while the Ríos Montt officers were "gathered around the Presidential palace enjoying power," one officer explained (interview).

17. The Special Tribunals were secret antiterrorist courts for summary executions (see chapter 6 on law).

18. Stoll has argued that solidarity explanations for the violence "systematically elide the provocative role of the guerrillas." Regardless of the structural factors at work that encouraged political violence in Guatemala, he says, "the chronology of events shows that army repression began in reaction to guerrilla actions" with the guerrillas minimizing their own responsibility for triggering the escalation of military violence (1993: 91).

Chapter 3

1. "Somos bien masacre" (We are well massacred) is a phrase used by many indigenous campesinos in the conflict areas after 1984 (anonymous source, 1986 interview).

2. US-AID funded a survey of the effects of the violence in the departments of Chimaltenango, Huehuetenango, and Quiché by PAVA (Programa de Ayuda para los Vecinos del Altiplano), a Guatemalan-based private voluntary organization. The survey was conducted between August 1983 and February 1984.

3. According to officers, of the Q368 million ($61,333,333) needed to implement all the plans, only Q14 million ($2,333,333) were available from more than a dozen State organizations. This original budget was "thrown into the wastebasket" and 90 percent of the funds needed were supplied by foreign assistance with no new taxes or

foreign loans ("Guatemala: Acción cívica militar en la guerra de contrainsurgencia."
1985: 5). Demands throughout the 1980s for tax reform — an increase from 5 percent to 7 percent — to fund such development projects were rejected outright by the
business confederations, CADIF.

4. The parallels between the army's national strategy of security and development
and US-AID's projects for "integrated development" are striking.

5. From AVANCSO 1988.

6. "La Perla" references the *latifundia* in the Ixil area where much of the land
would have come from. U.S. Embassy report, *Land and Labor in Guatemala* (October
1982) published in Spanish in *Polémica* 17, 18; ICADIS 1983.

7. Cf. Severo Martínez Peláez, *La patria del criollo* (1973).

8. "Informe de Asuntos Civiles del Estado Mayor de la Defensa Nacional (S-5),"
Diario de Centroamérica, 29 June 1984, quoted in Centro de Estudios de la Realidad
Guatemalteca 1985: 17.

9. Highlands Agricultural Development, Grant 5200274, FY 83-93. This grant was
extended "to construct 800 additional kilometers."

10. The MLN badly lost the April 1988 municipal elections, thus increasing their
fears of Army-Christian Democratic control.

11. As Head of Civil Affairs in 1988, Colonel García, stated:

> The politicians have allowed the functions of government to become unglued. . . .
> It is a novelty, really, for our Republic that the present government has created a
> ministry especially for development. I believe this is very interesting for the con-
> cept it has. They consider it an activity which they must direct from only one place,
> and I believe that the divergences could mean [disaster]. . . . For me, and this is only
> my personal opinion now, development is an activity concurrent with all else going
> on in the country. Everything is connected to it. And in some way, he who attends
> to the problems of labor, health, and the economic administration of this country,
> is intimately tied in with the concept of well-being and development. (interview)

Chapter 4

1. The amnesty also applied to security personnel who had broken the law while
engaged in counterinsurgency — effectively an admission by the military that massive
human rights violations had been perpetrated by security forces.

2. This fear of arming former guerrillas reflects two currents in military thinking:
Indians are deemed to be part of a dangerous rural populace of Indians and ladinos,
but it is the Indian, in the end, who is unteachable, disobedient, and untrustworthy.
Gramajo's point that they could be "rescued" and formed into "civilized" units
echoes the one hundred-year history since the emergence of Indian soldiers and the
argument that not only was the Indian good for the army, but that the army would be
good for the Indian (Adams 1994: 16). Turn-of-the-century discussions favoring
Indian participation in the army were couched in terms of specific virtues of Indian
soldiers: "obedience, docility, endurance, subordination, loyalty, cheap food, no
shoes, tenacious fighters" (36). Nonetheless, even among the Indian regional militias such as the Momostecos who in 1920 refused to "obey anyone other than their
own sergeants and didn't acknowledge any other authority," the question of loyalty
appears to never have been fully resolved. As Adams writes, "The questions concerning the aptness of the use of Indians was framed in terms of their loyalty to the
nation, ability as fighters, cheapness of maintenance, and . . . competitive need for
farm labor" (19–22). Moreover, Indian noncommissioned officers (as well as auxili-

ary municipal officers) were preferred because "they had better communication with their subordinates" than did ladino officers (29).

3. According to Sereseres, "This was partly racist because the military doesn't want Indians with guns, nor do they want Civil Patrols in fatigues" (interview). As the previous note points out, the ladino fear of Indian rebellion has a long history (cf. Smith 1990a: 161). This fear, in turn, reflects the army's recognition of the indigenous population's hatred toward them. As Colonel Gordillo admitted in 1988, "People are very wounded with lost loved ones; there are still very bloody memories, which means one cannot give in to the guerrillas just yet" (interview).

4. In his book, Gramajo details two "losses": one in the military garrison at Nebaj when a "recruit" deliberately released a hand grenade, killing himself and wounding six of his companions, and the other in Uspantán, where one person was killed (1995: 196).

5. Promulgated on 29 December 1983 (*Diario de Centroamérica*, 3 January 1984).

6. The full quote is under the subheading "But What to Do in the Absence of Leadership?": "The Guatemalan Army, facing that enormous but at the same time ennobling task, sought [to establish] direct, friendly relations with the population. As a result of this communication, among other things, a petition arose by general consensus that the Army provide training and basic weapons to all these peasants to enable them to defend their homes and communities, *thus making them responsible for their own defense needs.* . . . The self-defense Civil Patrols arose *spontaneously* in the rural communities. The objective is to organize the population civically and politically . . . to come to know, study and understand how they were deceived and how to be prepared not to fall again into the same trap . . .;*to report to the authorities any persons, facts or situations that appear to be unusual or suspicious as far as their lives and communities are concerned*" (emphasis added).

7. Earlier, Civil Patrollers could not leave their village for work on the south coast; later, they gained a restricted leave of four to five weeks (in contrast to the four to five months many had spent working on the coast previously). Women and children were given more freedom of movement, resulting in families being split up (whereas before, whole families would migrate together).

8. Despite this initial coercive selection of mayors in the highlands by the Ríos Montt regime to maintain army control and surveillance, it has had an ironic effect on indigenous-ladino relations. For example, in Nebaj in 1982, the Ríos Montt regime appointed an Ixil mayor. Since then, ladino candidates have been defeated by Ixils running on a Christian Democratic ticket. The three mayors of Nebaj up to 1992 have all been bilingual *promotores* from a US-AID pre-primary program to help Mayan children learn Spanish (Stoll 1993: 7).

9. For Gramajo, Santiago represents "a strategic place [for the guerrilla] . . . where all the money of Guatemala is located: coffee, sugar, cotton, everything!" He sketches while he talks, "Here are the mountains, the lake, and here is Santiago — *la tierra fría* with food, with [clandestine] hospitals and here is where the subversive is located. *La guerrilla* must come to Santiago: while he works on the coast, and lives in the mountains, he eats and is cured [of his wounds] in Santiago. This is [then] the strategic place."

10. CERJ *denuncia* to the Procuraduría Auxiliar del Procurador del Derechos Humanos, Santa Cruz del Quiché, 1 June 1991.

11. In January 1989, Army Public Relations Chief Colonel Isaacs held a press conference at which a former GAM member, Miguel Angel Reyes Melgar, claimed to be a guerrilla defector. He declared that several human rights groups, including CERJ president, Amílcar Méndez and GAM president, Nineth de García, were agents of the EGP and ORPA respectively. No supporting evidence for these accusations was

provided. Reyes repeated his accusations in the Public Relations Secretariat of President Cerezo (*El Gráfico* 25, 27 January 1989).

12. *La Hora* article, "Patrulleros condenados a 20 años" (14 May 1986) reports the 20-year sentencing and Q1000 fine of four patrollers for the beating and shooting death of another patroller in Alta Verapaz.

Chapter 5

1. Generally, the Ixils have not served in the army mainly because the army has forcibly recruited in other regions where, as Cifuentes states in this document, "the character of the *indígena* is more inclined to military discipline" (36).

2. The 11 special companies were expanded to 17 to serve in as many departments by 1986. A company contains 120 soldiers.

3. Civil Affairs chiefs Colonel Homero García Carillo (1988 interview); Colonel Olmedo Vázquez Toledo and Deputy Chief (and later Chief) Colonel Javier Schaeffer Paz (1994 interviews).

4. "In accordance with the mandates contained in Articles 34, 35, 135, and 245 of the Constitution and with a basis in Articles 1, 2, 22, 90 and 91 of Decree-Law 26-86 (Ley Constitutiva del Ejército) and Decree-Law 19-86, in the creation of the PACs, the Civil Affairs units will advise the communities in the organization, functioning and control of the PACs. . . . The cooperation of the PACs in all aspects will be sought, as much in the passive activities, the vigilance, the collection of intelligence, as in the active civil defense in the prevention of sabotage of installations and units of production" (Ejército 1987a: 28–30). (Article 244 of the Constitution and Article 1 of the Constitutive Law are one and the same.)

5. According to Gramajo, "target audiences" are "nothing more than the term used in psychological operations for directing a message to the population, to the subversive, or to the soldiers. It depends on who you want to receive the message. You must target those you most want to influence" (interview).

6. One colonel made the interesting point that "using Marxists' own methodology of historical materialism, we can see [given the fall of the Soviet Union], that communism itself is not inevitable." Yet, in the same breath, he contradicted his previous methodological analysis by saying, "there is always Cuba; thus, there will always be subversion" (1990 interview). This reveals an understanding of Marxist terminology as well as the ideological opportunism in using it. Words have "use-value" for officers only in particular contexts, and the use-value of Marxist language, it seems, is only for critiquing Marxists.

7. Colonel-lawyer Girón Tánchez also referred to the Special Tribunals promulgated in 1982 and dissolved in 1983 because of international pressures as "born dead" (1986 interview).

8. "Lobos con piel de oveja" (wolves in sheep's clothing) (interview with Gramajo), *Suplemento Domingo Prensa Libre* 397, 4 September 1988: 55. The previous month, President Cerezo declared that within eight months "a total of 4,500 subversives had been brought in by the amnesty" (*La Hora*, 3 August 1989, all above quoted in AVANCSO 1990: 25).

9. Usually the first encounter with an authority for the displaced was with a Civil Affairs Unit or Civil Patrol, and during the first few days, they were placed under military supervision and required to reveal information. One returning Kekchí stated: "They asked us if we had arms or equipment. If we did, then we must go fetch them. If there are others [out there], we must tell them to turn themselves in. [They told us] 'We can no longer kill people; that is very dangerous [to do].' . . . The

lieutenant took down everyone's name. They gave speeches: 'Don't be afraid, be calm.' They showed [us] pictures" (AVANCSO 1990: 27).

10. Testimony from refugees in the Ixcán verifies this:

I remember three or four days after the army had entered our area. . . , a civilian helicopter arrived and started to shout overhead with a loudspeaker: "Brother Guatemalans, don't be afraid. The government is no longer killing people or making threats. Your lives have been pardoned, you must deliver yourselves to [Pole of Development] Playa Grande. Don't worry, we will be there to receive you. First they spoke in Spanish and then in different Indian dialects. . . . About fifteen minutes later, the bombing started." ("Testimony from the Ixcán," Comité Pro-Justicia y Paz, March 1988: 16)

11. As we saw in Chapter 4, relations between the army and the Ministry of Development under President Cerezo were less than cordial, partly because of the army's underlying bias toward "lazy civilians."

12. The government Institute of Agrarian Transformation.

Chapter 6

1. Interview on the Televisión Española program *La religión que vino del norte*, quoted in *Crónica*, 26 January 1989: 14, his emphasis.

2. A military lawyer, involved in military politics for years, stated humorously: "Normally, the military is in agreement with the political climate [in the country], but military discipline does not allow it to meddle in political affairs as such. There was a very indirect means by which one did not meddle. That is to say, one didn't meddle because one was already meddling! Or one meddled in other ways," he said, laughing (1988 interview).

3. The three-man junta-style government under General Mejía Víctores as Chief of State included Mejía, Colonel-lawyer Girón Tánchez and civilian lawyer Fernando Andrade Díaz-Durán (who served as Foreign Minister and who would stand as a presidential candidate in the 1995 elections).

4. The Fundamental Statute was written by Colonel Girón Tánchez, together with civilian lawyers "Licenciados Mario Quiñónes Azmequita and [Juan José] Rodil Peralta, among others" (Gramajo, interview; anonymous, 1988 interview).

5. For this revelation, Congressional Deputy García Bauer was ostracized by his colleagues in a vote of censure with possible legal action against him. The house of his parents was ransacked, with servants beaten by heavily armed men (*La Hora*, 16, 17, 21 and 24 June 1986). A Christian Democratic Deputy subsequently admitted that under the General Lucas García regime all Christian Democratic deputies each received Q1,000 (approximately $160) as "honorable businessmen" after approving a certain law. FUR president Licenciado Toledo Peñate confirmed that the National Constituent Assembly of 1963–65, of which Colonel Girón Tánchez was a member and which wrote the 1965 constitution, was also rife with pressures from powerful economic groups (*La Hora*, 24 June 1986; interview).

6. Ríos Montt selected the president of the Supreme Electoral Council (interview).

7. Its intention was to "make a space in which to create a National Assembly to make all the decisions. The last decision of the Army was to create the Assembly" (Gramajo, interview).

8. I find *self-referential* to be a better descriptive term than *autistic* or *self-centered*, as Ietswaart describes Argentine military legal discourse (1980).

9. Licenciado Alfred Balsells Tojo, *La Hora*, 14 January 1986.

10. Andrade also comments that the reason for dropping for good a plan for a population registry (*cedulación*) is that it "could have prolonged the state of things unduly" (1988: 5).

11. Lukes uses the term "imposed consensus" (1974: 47); however, in the case of the Guatemalan military, "coercive consensus" seems more apt.

12. General Gramajo was not the only high-ranking officer to speak of this constitutional mandate at the army's first National Forum on Counterinsurgency entitled "27 Years of Fighting for Freedom". General Callejas y Callejas, National Defense Chief of Staff (and Chief of Army Intelligence under Lucas García), stated in his introductory remarks:

The responsibility which the Magna Carta assigns us has far-reaching significance . . . principally with regard to the current circumstances in which terrorist delinquents are promoting an ideological and armed struggle, and in their eagerness to take power, they provoke death, desolation, destruction and pain in the Guatemalan family. (1987: 1)

General Juan Leonel Bolaños Chávez, Deputy Chief of Staff at the time (and later Defense Minister), also stated:

The Army, as an institution of the State, offers within the strategic concept contained in [the Constitution] the maintenance of constitutional order by way of permanent military presence in all the national territory as a means by which to reach stability which generates well-being among Guatemalans. We are conscious as an institution that we are accomplishing our mission imposed on us by the political Constitution of the State, and as a derivation of such action, the People support their army. (1987: 5, 6)

13. This assumption that "illegal" dissenters — i.e., those outside the boundaries of law — are within the bounds of justifiable killing has been echoed by the civilian presidents. At a public, on-the-record talk in Washington, D.C., President Serrano asserted that "We have documented CERJ's relations with the insurgency" (30 September 1991, author's notes). At a later meeting, he contradicted himself by stating that "CERJ was within the law. . . . I am saying that with their political actions they are supporting the insurgency, and the insurgency is outside the law" (Washington Office on Latin America 1992: 10).

14. Mathews refers to the remote future mentality of the South African military apparatus under the apartheid government in which the "guilty mind" (*mens rea*) is connected to the "potential criminal deed" (*actus reus*) (Mathews 1986: 233). That is, one may be sanctioned *before* going outside the law, as criminality can be *imputed* by the legal arbiter — in this case, the security forces.

15. Gramajo has stated, for example, "The minorities do whatever they want and since they operate within a double standard, they support law when it's convenient to them and act outside of it when it's not" (speech to the Mobile Military Police, *Prensa Libre*, 22 April 1988: 2).

16. Decree-Laws 61-82, 71-82, 76-82 sustained a state of siege in Guatemala between the March 1982 coup until 29 June 1983, when a state of alarm was put into effect with little change in the protection of rights (Recopilador de Leyes, Volumes 1, 2, and 3, 1982, 1983, and 1984 respectively).

17. Cf. Alonso 1986 concerning a lawyer's personal account of defending Secret Tribunal prisoners; see also Schirmer 1996.

18. Ríos Montt referred to them as "Knowers of the Law" (*Conocedores del Derecho*) (interview).

19. Several sources pointed to civilian lawyer and President of the Guatemalan Bar Association in 1982–83, Licenciado Juan José Rodil Peralta (who was Minister of the Interior under the Cerezo government and Supreme Court Justice under President Serrano). They claim he helped write the Decree-Law 42-82 establishing the Special Tribunals and, according to Ríos Montt's testimony in the Inter-American Court of Human Rights, served as one of the secret judges. Rodil, in turn, says that although he advised Ríos Montt, he opposed the Special Tribunals but supported the death penalty (Washington Office on Latin America 1992: 33; 1986 interview).

20. In a 1988 speech, Andrade referred to the Special Tribunals as "returning to past stages in juridical evolution . . . that [were] totally unacceptable in a modern democracy." Yet, as the speech proceeds, Andrade complains of the need to "[simplify [legal] things . . . in order to facilitate the [democratic] process" (1988: 9).

21. Asked the reason for the amnesty decree if the army had acted within the law, Defense Minister Jaime Hernández responded elliptically that it was probably a decision intended to invite equal treatment to the military, given that the subversive elements had the opportunity of being amnestied by the past government as well (*La Hora*, 21 March 1986).

22. "There has been enormous attention paid to the fact that various military officers visited congressional deputies in order to provide them with their point of view about the necessity for an amnesty" ("Militares analiza con diputados la nueva ley de amnistía," *La Hora*, 30 May 1988; "Proyecto aún estancado," *Prensa Libre*, 31 May 1988: 15).

23. It was precisely the phrase "*delitos políticos y comunes conexos*" (linked political and common crimes) that was claimed by congressional deputies as not appearing in either the Penal Code or the Constitution.

24. "244 campesinos se acogieron a protección del ejército," *El Gráfico*, 27 May 1988.

25. Despite evidence of the army's control of police investigations and despite the army's disdain for judges, Colonel Gordillo stated that "The police many, many times make fun of the law. They believe that judges are bad and they terrorize them about a case, and if the judge acts [on the case], they kill him. The question [for them] is: 'what could be easier: to kill a person who may send you to jail for eight months?' " (interview).

Chapter 7

1. Gramajo has admitted in several interviews that "the G-2 archives are lists of Guatemalans and foreigners who have participated in illicit activities against the State. Ideological opinions are not so much taken into account as their behavior or attitude, which have been typified as [those of] Opponents of the State" (*El Gráfico*, 11 July 1986; "Gral. Gramajo dice que archivos son públicos," *La Hora*, 10 July 1986: 1).

2. Interviews with several officers confirmed that with information provided by the computerized archival system of G-1, as well as an order signed by the zone commander (in this case, Military Headquarters Zone 1, in Guatemala City, Cuartel General), G-2 would kidnap or "investigate" a particular person who they were informed had been doing "certain subversive things."

3. No one but army personnel are allowed to enter these cells: "Wives or brothers or army collaborators are *never* allowed to enter these *calabozos*. *Never*." While each military zone garrison has a G-2 section and secret cells, it is in the Cuartel General where new G-2 agents take a course "to prepare oneself on how to kill people."

Secret cells near the soccer field are used for torture (see appendix 2, regarding his training to kill).

4. Cf. *Crónica*, 24 May 1991: 15 regarding Dinora Pérez's killing.

5. Reportedly, the first victims were twenty-eight people disappeared by members of the army and police between December 1965 and March 1966. The corpses of some of the victims were thrown into the sea (Guatemalan Human Rights Commission, "Clandestine Agencies of Repression in Guatemala" [trans.], July 1988: 2–3).

6. FUR leader Manuel Colóm Argueta held a press conference to denounce the Policía Regional as a secret police force closely linked to disappearances and political assassinations. To facilitate investigations, he named the leaders of this organization during the last three governments as Major Rolando Archila under Méndez Montenegro, Colonel Elias Ramírez under Arana, and Colonel Ramón Quinteros and Major Byron Lima under Kjell Laugerud (McClintock 1985: 171). Only days later Colóm was assassinated in broad daylight on a major avenue in Guatemala City. Between 1978 and 1981, 20 leaders of the FUR, 16 PSD politicians and 70 PDCG activists met the same fate (Black, et al. 1982: 42).

7. With the exception of the National Police director, the security force chiefs were not soldiers; nevertheless, "they nominated themselves colonels and all the junior officers resented that" (Gramajo, interview w/o attribution). It is interesting to note that omitted from Gramajo's account is the fact that the Defense Minister and the Army Chief of Staff also attended these CRIO meetings, according to guerrilla infiltrator and Lucas's personal secretary, Elias Barahona (1984).

8. During this same time period, August 1981, the CIA and the Special Assistant to the U.S. Secretary of State (and former CIA Deputy Director), U.S. Ambassador-at-Large Vernon Walters arranged a meeting in Guatemala City to merge former Somoza Guardsmen into the *contras* and for Argentine military officers to serve as advisors and trainers (who were later replaced with CIA personnel) (affidavit of *contra* defector Edgar Chamorro, *Nicaragua v. United States of America*, International Court of Justice, 5 September 1985: 4, 5, 7). In late September 1981, moreover, Walters reportedly met with President Lucas García while U.S. Navy Captain John Thurber met with Chief of Staff Benedicto Lucas García (Televisora Nacional, 28 September 1981).

9. Many sources report that the Israelis funded, designed, and staffed an Army School of Transmission and Electronics in November 1981 to teach the monitoring and ciphering of radio transmissions. Tadiran Israel Electronics Industries Ltd. installed all of the army's computer service, including one to monitor passengers at the airport (*Israeli Foreign Affairs* 1, 1 (December 1984): 8; John Rettie, *Guardian* (London) 29 December 1981; *NACLA* 21, no. 2 (March–April 1987); cf. Beit-Hallahmi 1987, Bahbah 1986). Both institutionalist and hard-line officers are nevertheless, critical of Israel's role: "Maybe some Israelis taught us intelligence but for reasons of business. . . . We had Israeli trainers in computer processing" but "it was all a bluff: they sold us very old computers with punch cards. And we had a major train our pilots to fly the Arava [troop transport plane]. . . . The hawks [arms merchants] took advantage of us [in the late seventies, early eighties], selling us equipment at triple the price," stated Gramajo angrily (interview).

10. Jesuit priest Father Luis Eduardo Pellecer was kidnapped 9 June 1981. He reappeared after three months to "confess" his defection from the EGP. On 3 December, the EGP took over four radio stations to broadcast a statement by leader Emeterio Toj, who, like Father Pellecer, had been presented as an EGP defector. Toj detailed how he had been forced to "confess" to revolutionary activity under torture and threats to his family (*New York Times*, 7 December 1981, 18 December 1981).

11. *Golpista* officers accused President Cerezo of destroying CRIO (interview), not

Ríos Montt, as Gramajo states in interview and in his book (1995). In January 1994, the author witnessed several PMA units in full riot gear practice advancing in formation, with shield and shock baton held high, in the soccer field of the Cuartel General, their headquarters. When asked what they were doing, the officer in charge responded, "Preparing ourselves for street demonstrations" (*preparándonos para las manifestaciones*).

12. Together with Colonel Jaime Rabanales Reyes, Colonel Argueta had worked as an instructor at the Command and General Staff School under Colonel Gramajo's directorship at the Center for Military Studies in 1980 and had helped formulate the Strategic Appraisal.

13. Reportedly, a *patrulla* headed by DIT Chief of the Homicide Division, Jaime Martínez Jiménez (supervised by Army Lieutenant Colonel Juan Méndez), acted on orders from the highest level of government and relayed by G-2 commander Colonel Carlos Dorantes Marroquín to abduct and assassinate baker and GAM public relations director, Héctor Gómez and one of the more outspoken leaders, María Rosario Godoy de Cuevas. He was abducted from a bus stop on 31 March 1985, and later found by the side of the road: his tongue had been torn out, burn marks on his body suggested the use of a blow torch, and the back of his head had been crushed (Amnesty International 1987). She was abducted on 4 April with her younger brother and two-year-old son. They were later found killed; the baby's fingernails had been torn out (Nairn and Simon 1986: 19; cf. Schirmer 1988).

14. Nuíla had served as chief of the secret police under General Arana and as founder and first director of the Kaibil special forces school under General Kjell Laugerud. As *jefe* of the Mobile Military Police in 1982, he was responsible for much of the psychological warfare under General Ríos Montt, according to Barahona (1984: 5–6). Later, he was "Mejía's chief of the presidential staff" (Gramajo, interview).

15. Several officers explained that the training of Guatemalan officers had shifted to Chile, Brazil, Israel, and Argentina between 1978 and 1982 (interviews). This does not exclude, however, the assignment of Green Beret officers to the Military Academy after 1978 to instruct in "direct action destruction patrols" and helicopter "assault tactics" (Allan Nairn, *Washington Post*, 21 October 1982: 1). Nor does it exclude the Green Beret training of recruits at the Regional Center of Military Training (CREM) in Puerto Castilla, Honduras, during the *contra* war (Barahona 1984: 5) or the training of elite forces at Fort Bragg "at least once or twice a year, although they would never admit it," throughout the 1980s and early 1990s (intelligence source, interview).

16. Callejas was chief of the Treasury Police under Mejía and was known for his corruption. Although involved in the 1988 coup attempt, he later aligned himself with Gramajo, which allowed him to complete his thirty years of service. He gained the highest rank in the Guatemalan army: División General. According to some G-2 officers, he is purportedly considered to be "the godfather" of G-2 (interviews).

17. Gramajo: "I had a lot of contact with South Africa, exchanging intelligence methods and techniques . . . as a way of studying how Cubans fought [in Angola] and how Cuban intelligence operated, but only three or four individuals knew this. The finance minister provided us money, but the National Defense staff didn't have to know many things."
Q: "So, the finance minister has two budgets: one military and one civilian?"
"No, they are one and the same. It only says 'expenses,' but it doesn't say what the money is for. When one is in the High Command, one has one's programs of crosscheck. You don't trust everyone; nor do you want everyone to know what you're doing" (interview).

18. The CIA station chiefs in the U.S. Embassy in Guatemala between 1977 and

1995 were: V. Harwood "Vinx" Blocker III (1977–80), whom apparently Gramajo met at Fort Benning, Georgia, while Gramajo was taking the 1960 Ranger course at the U.S. Army Infantry School; Barry Royden (1980); Robert Hultlander (1981–83); Vincent M. Shields (1983–84); Jack McCavitt (1984–86); Rafael Mariani (1987–88); Alfonso Sapia-Bosch (1988–91) (Gramajo met Sapia earlier when Sapia worked as Reagan's chief adviser on Central American affairs and worked on the National Security Council with Oliver North in 1982–83); Fredric Brugger (1991–93) who Gramajo may have met when he was military attaché to the Guatemalan Embassy in El Salvador when Brugger was deputy station chief there; and Dan Donahue (1993– 95) (anonymous intelligence source, interview; Allan Nairn, "The Country Team" *Nation*, 5 June 1995). Gramajo also described meeting "a lot of majors and lieuten- ant colonels when I was a student at Fort Benning, Georgia," in 1969. Also, "because they had a lot of cross-training, I met a lot of people training from government, a lot of people from other agencies. . . . Remember Malcolm X and the Symbionese Army? People from [U.S.] military intelligence were working with the police in California, looking for terrorist groups" (interview without attribution).

19. This may well have included videocamera equipment for the army and security forces (DIC and PMA) to record forced "guerrilla confessions" for television broad- cast (cf. Americas Watch, "Clandestine Detention in Guatemala" 5, 2 [March 1993]).

20. "The CIA station chief would fly" Defense Minister Gramajo to Washington to meet with the CIA second-in-command, or to meet with a Nicaraguan defector at a hotel in Maryland (Gramajo, interview without attribution).

21. When I confronted the Chargé d'Affaires, political and labor officers at the U.S. Embassy in Guatemala with this admission in 1991, the Charge d'Affaires said, "Well, you know as well as I do that we never know what the CIA is up to, and even if we did, we couldn't comment on it." In a 1996 visit to the school, the first plaque remains; the second has been removed from the entrance.

22. Cf. Millman, "Taiwan's Central American Links," *Jane's Defence Weekly*, 26 No- vember 1988: 1330. Officers such as future Defense Ministers García Samayoa and Mendoza attended the Taiwan course (Gramajo, interview).

23. For example, Colonel Ramón Quinteros (G-2 Chief for Kjell Laugerud [1973– 78]), was named commander of a base; *luquista* General de la Cruz was appointed Vice Minister of Defense. Both officers were of Gramajo's graduating class of 1959. However, when Quinteros supported the 1989 coup, Gramajo "exiled" him to the Central American Defense Board (interview).

24. Díaz Urquizú, the head of *grupos de acción*, or the repressive organism of Archivo, was implicated in a number of abductions and killings of students in con- nection with a white van.

25. According to one source, when National Police Director, Colonel Caballeros confronted Cerezo with a detailed report providing evidence of Díaz Urquizú's in- volvement in the abductions and killings, the President pleaded with Caballeros and Gramajo not to prosecute him. A few weeks later, Díaz Urquizú was working as a personal bodyguard for Christian Democratic presidential candidate Alfonso Cabrera (anonymous source, interview).

26. Barillas served as former ambassador to Spain, where he participated in initial peace talks with the URNG. President Cerezo publicly accused "right-wing extrem- ists" for his murder (*Miami Herald*, 2 August 1989).

27. Colonel Caballeros was replaced by Navy Captain Romeo Guevara, who was replaced in June 1989 (after Guevara's participation in the coup attempt) by Colo- nel Byron Valerio Cárdenas, described as "an expert in security matters." DIC and the Office of Professional Responsibility (for internal police discipline) were also headed by G-2 officers, although both ICITAP and the Administration of Justice Program at Harvard protested over these appointments in September 1989, which

reportedly resulted in their replacement by civilians (Washington Office on Latin America memo, 18 September 1989).

28. Anthropologist Myrna Mack Chang, a founding member of AVANCSO (Association for the Advancement of Social Science) was stabbed to death on a Guatemala City street on 11 September 1990 by two men, one of whom was Archivo Sargento Mayor Especialista Noel de Jesús Beteta. On 28 April 1993, the Appeals Court ruled out any judicial investigations of Beteta's superiors and suspected intellectual authors of the killing: former EMP chief, retired General Augusto Godoy Gaitán, Archivo *jefe* Colonel Juan Valencia Osorio and his immediate Archivo superior, Lieutenant Colonel Guillermo Oliva Carrera.

29. For example, in the case of the abduction, rape, and torture of the American Ursuline nun Diana Ortiz reportedly by G-2, Gramajo blamed the victim for being involved in a "lesbian love triangle." Although he later retracted this story (which was being repeated by U.S. Embassy staff to journalists at the time), he said he "got involved" with this case "to defend Cerezo" and "the State of Guatemala" (interview without attribution).

30. "Liaison" is a relation for exchanging information between institutions; it represents a policy decision on the part of two governments. "Asset" is a specific individual who is paid for information about whatever is of interest to the CIA. A particular individual may serve the CIA in both capacities, though not necessarily (U.S. sources familiar with CIA operations and terminology). In reviewing the CIA Directorate of Operations "asset validation system," the IOB determined that many assets in Guatemala were acquired less for informational purposes ("[the] information was not worth the payments they received") than for CIA "internal performance appraisal and rewards" (IOB 1996: 15, 24). In other words, the more assets a CIA handler acquired (and paid), even if this information was irrelevant or false, the more likely she or he would be given a raise or a promotion.

Chapter 8

1. All quotes of Cerezo are from the author's July 1991 interview unless otherwise indicated.

2. Aguilera Peralta, quoted in Montenegro Ríos 1980: 57. Much of the following analysis of the PDCG is based on both Carlos Roberto Montenegro Ríos's 1980 comprehensive thesis and AVANCSO's 1988 report.

3. His pamphlet was printed in *Diario La Hora*, 25 and 26 July 1975.

4. The Committee of Santa Fe included L. Francis Bouchey, Roger Fontaine (National Security Council's Latin American specialist), David Jordan, Lieutenant General Gordon Sumner (ret.; Inter-American Defense Chief and Special Advisor to the Assistant Secretary of State for Inter-American Affairs), and Lewis Tambs (editor).

5. Attending the meeting were two of President Reagan's advisors, Roger Fontaine and Jeanne Kirkpatrick, as well as Aristides Calvani and Ricardo Arias of the Christian Democratic Organizations, and René de León Schlotter, honorary president of the Guatemalan PDCG and president of the World Christian Democratic Union. Cerezo has stated he did not attend this meeting.

6. Gramajo, interview by Cruz Salazar (1988a: 1). He contends that, contrary to the rumors, he had not spoken with Cerezo before he won the elections on 8 December 1985 at 8 P.M. "It was the second round of voting, and it was Mejía Víctores's birthday, and I arrived two hours late because I had been speaking with Cerezo" (interview). Cerezo, on the other hand, has stated that there were occasional informal meetings with Gramajo for "an exchange of ideas" before the 1985 elections.

7. In one of Gramajo's academic papers, "Consolidation of a Democratic Transi-

tion," he outlines his points this way: "*Objective*: To hold elections. *Strategy*: Quick short-term solutions for problems to allow the event [elections] to take place. Accept the challenge of national polarization. Identify our name and doctrine with the Roman Catholic [Church]. *Tactics*: Use incumbent Cerezo. Main communicator, *shock absorber*. Face-to-face campaign" (1990, emphasis added).

8. This was also confirmed by a civilian who is close to military circles (interview).

9. "Since [the time that] the subbasement of the National Police was sealed off, [the police] have been using apartments and houses in the city, where they take students and street kids to torture and kill. Guatemala has a lot of problems with demonstrations, and that's why they needed SIPROCI" (National Police interview).

10. Former Assistant Secretary of State for Inter-American Affairs Elliott Abrams has stated in an interview that "I think it's fair to say, after the second coup, [Cerezo] gave up being president" (Lundberg, quoted in Rosenthal 1992: 90).

11. Serrano and Gramajo worked together in Washington (during Gramajo's "exile" under Lucas García), successfully lobbying for pesticide-laden beef exports from Guatemala to enter the United States in the late 1970s.

12. The Electoral Council (Tribunal Electoral) decided in August 1990 that Ríos Montt could not run for President because the Constitution does not allow (1) the reelection of past presidents or (2) those who have participated in coups to run for any elected office (see Chapter 6).

13. Gramajo is not referring here to security vis-à-vis human rights violations. He told me later, "the most significant security issue in Guatemala [today] is twofold": (1) the organized crime of Peruvians and Nicaraguans (i.e., more immigration control needs to be implemented) and (2) common crime for which "we need to create a new, more efficient judicial police force. Judges do nothing and blame the police for being so inept" (interview).

Chapter 9

1. Gustavo Anzueto Vielman is an architect, the former head of UNAGRO (representing radical rightwing agro-business interests), Minister of Communications under President Arana, former presidential candidate for CAN (Central Auténtica Nacionalista), and lieutenant in the army reserve. Mario David García is the owner and director of the rightwing news show *Aquí el Mundo*. Danilo Roca (a.k.a. Edmundo Deantes), a columnist for *Prensa Libre Domingo*, was a central figure in the 1982 coup, who wrote in support of the 1988 *intento*.

2. Speculations were made in the press as to how much money the *golpistas* received from agro-businessmen: Gramajo placed the figure at Q3 million; Cerezo estimated Q6 million (*La Época*, 3 June 1988). The head of CACIF, Edgar Heinemann, another officer surmised, collected "Q40 million for the coup attempt altogether," even though "UNAGRO couldn't buy many officers" (interviews).

3. Lieutenant Colonel D'jalma Domínguez, the Chief of Intelligence under Mejía, was sacked by Chief of Staff Lobos Zamora because "[EMP Chief] Colonel Nuíla reported a telephone conversation to Mejía in which D'jalma spoke critically of Mejía *over the telephone*! So, Lobos Zamora sacked both him and Nuíla" (interview). A cousin of Cerezo, D'jalma thought that when Cerezo became President he would regain his rank. He had to go to a judge, however, to have his office returned to him, but he was never able to reenter the army. When complaints within the army rose to a pitch with the tax reform, it is believed that it was D'jalma who provided the military terminology for the *comunicados* of the Officers of the Mountain.

4. Defense Minister Bolaños complained in August 1990 of the fiscal crisis of the armed forces (interview).

5. This is also according to Lieutenant Colonel-political scientist Cruz Salazar (1988 interview).

6. Major Díaz López was accompanied by Captain Vielman García at a three-hour taped interview in my hotel room. The captain first asked whether I was a journalist and if I had been in the highlands during the counterinsurgency war between 1981 and 1983. He then checked the room for bugs in the lamps, telephone, under the bed, in the closet, behind the toilet, and under the sink. He checked out on the patio and insisted on opening the door quickly to the maid and bellboy. These fears of microphones and surveillance were warranted: Gramajo later stated that G-2 officers loyal to him were watching the *oficiales'* every move.

7. I met Captain Vielman García (who would later introduce me to Major Díaz López) at the house of the former Army Chief of Staff and MLN presidential candidate retired General López Fuentes, when he arrived with MLN Congressional Deputy Simons for a meeting. When I asked for a copy of the *oficiales'* communiqués, the general went into a back room and quickly returned with a fresh copy of No. 9 dated the day before. Regarding MLN-army relations, see Figures 16 and 17.

8. Díaz López claimed that the High Command "*has* tried to put a stop to the clandestine distribution of the *comunicados/* for two years now but they cant'! . . . Because it is something too large within the army" (interview). This may have been the case, or it confirms Gramajo's calculated tactic of ignoring them in order to diminish their importance.

9. The legalization of CUC is later mentioned in *Comunicado* 10 of 3 November 1988 as one of the reasons for the 11 May coup.

10. In 1990, Mario Sandoval Alarcón spoke out in favor of conversations with the guerrilla leading to a peace accord (1990: 13–14).

11. Much of this account of the first coup is a combination of information from interviews, *Inforpress Centroaméricana, Crónica,* and the thick description in Iglesias and Varley's 1989 unpublished paper.

12. *Unscrupulous* is the word the Officers of the Mountain used in their first *comunicado* of 5 April 1988 to describe "the corrupt inner political circle of the Christian Democratic Party." Gramajo's use of the term points to a game of psychological warfare to target troops and officers.

13. Apparently, the interrogating court official never asked the names of these callers (Iglesias and Varley 1989).

14. See also note 1. Padilla admitted knowing Vielman because he had on previous occasions "collaborated with the army in combating the subversives, arranging financial assistance, and securing necessary resources" (anonymous source, interview). Padilla knew Mario David García as a classmate at the Instituto Adolfo Hall in Jutiapa. Dr. Mario Castejón was a partisan of Ríos Montt's regime. Nicolas Buonafina was a wealthy *latifundista* and regular columnist for two dailies; he served as an economic adviser for Ríos Montt. Díaz López was dismissed from the army on 22 June 1987 on charges of "blind nihilism." He claims that he was dismissed because he tried to expose wrongdoing by some other intelligence officers (interview).

15. Two days later, *El Gráfico* printed a document sent by the Secret Anticommunist Army (ESA), claiming responsibility for the grenade attack "to express our repudiation of measures to socialize Guatemala. . . . we of the ESA do not want war. We want peace, but the government is itself inciting a revolution in Guatemala, and if they want war, they will have war because we are committed to giving our lives in the war against communists everywhere" (20 May 1988). On this same day, a bomb exploded outside the gymnasium where the Association of University Students was commemorating its sixty-eighth anniversary.

16. As reported in *El Gráfico* and *Prensa Libre,* 8 June 1988. These threats stopped as soon as the defendants were released.

17. *La Época* decided not to reopen.

18. *Comunicado 14* asserted that the riot was staged by the PDCG on orders of the Medellín cartel so that two Colombian drug traffickers could escape (11 May 1989).

19. In one of the first interviews with a guerrilla leader published in a Guatemalan newspaper, EGP *Comandante* Pablo Monsanto claimed that at least 50 Guatemalan army officers had died in 1988, with 1200 soldiers wounded. He stated, "When we have caused casualties, and the command demands that soldiers advance, we know [from radio transmissions] that the soldiers have refused, demanding 'Why don't you come over here and do it yourselves?' " (*Prensa Libre Domingo*, 28 August 1988).

20. Gramajo, Castellanos Góngora, and Quinteros were classmates of the same 1957 graduating class (*Promoción 59*). Quinteros is also godfather to Gramajo's oldest child. (When asked if he thought Quinteros would have killed his family, Gramajo shrugged, "I don't think so, but maybe the others.") But because of this connection, "he thought I owed him a position. I wanted to work with him but he is an extremist. I made him Guatemalan representative on the Central American Defense Board. . . . I ignore him, and he joins forces to organize the second coup" (interview).

21. Those dismissed from the army one year earlier were Lieutenant Colonel Gustavo Adolfo Padilla Morales, former subcommander of the Retalhuleu military zone, Air Force Lieutenant Colonel Carlos Mazariegos Ramírez, and Major Gustavo Adolfo Díaz López, who were all tried but absolved for lack of evidence; and Captain Allan Castellanos Reyes, who was mysteriously never brought to trial, and who was in hiding after the 1989 coup. The five high-ranking officers who were displaced without the command of troops were Air Force Colonel Juan Adenolfo Gálvez del Cid, former military attaché to Uruguay, who would be sent tin the same capacity to Panama, Colonel Francisco Castellanos Góngora, FYDEP (who was in hiding after the coup), Colonel Raúl Dehesa Oliva (of COPECODECA, or Consejo Permanente de Defensa Centroamérica), and former director of the National Police, Naval Captain Romero Guevara Reyes. Finally, the active-duty officers were Captain Jesús Adalberto de la Peña Corado, Air Force pilot Colonel Julio Padilla González, Second Commander of the Air Tactical Security Group of the Air Force (who was in charge of all planes and who was considered a confidante of Gramajo), and Army Reserve Lieutenant Colonel Oscar Augusto Méndez Tobias, high ranking in the Cuartel General. Other officers implicated were Lieutenant Jaime David Funes, Lieutenant Eduardo Izaguirre Cambara, Major Byron Barrientos, Captain Carlos Alberto Arriaga López, Sublieutenant Ariel José Paiz, and Lieutenant Miguel Angel Acevedo (interviews; *Crónica*, 12 May 1989: 13; *Inforpress Centroaméricana*, 11 May 1989: 13).

22. Yet, the first press bulletin from the President's Public Relations office stated that "a group of retired officers and civilians" had participated in the coup (*Crónica*, 12 May 1989: 13).

23. *Comunicado 15* states that "from our Intelligence Service, we can see that the corrupt gramajo [*sic*] assembled a team of juridical advisors in order to severely punish a major number of our captured *compañeros*. We severely warn these lawyers not to get too enthusiastic with the money and the orders of the traitor gramajo [*sic*] because not even the Defense Minister can guarantee your personal safety" (29 May 1989). It then proceeds to list names of lawyers, including the Supreme Court Justice Vázquez Martínez.

24. Navy Captain Jorge Mazariegos, Director of the CEM, cited a lower number. "There were twenty officers indicted, so it was less than 0.01% [of the army]. . . . On the whole, everyone has adapted [to the Thesis]" (1990 interview).

25. Colonel Lima, General Nuíla, Major Díaz López, Colonel Quinteros, Colonel D'jalma, as well as Colonel Romeo Guevara and Major Byron Humberto Barrientos of the reserves were all apparently army intelligence officers.

26. This is according to former Assistant Secretary of State for Inter-American affairs, Elliott Abrams (Lundberg interviews quoted in Rosenthal 1992: 110).

27. Nine million dollars, U.S. Ambassador Thomas Stroock has said, "is serious money to . . . this army," as it covers the costs of critical replacement parts for its U.S.-manufactured helicopters (Lundberg interview, quoted in Rosenthal 1992: 111).

Chapter 10

1. Gramajo's Army Day speech, 30 June 1988 (1988d).

2. Gramajo apologized for the outdated description "Marxist-Leninist," explaining that the Thesis was written before the demise of the Cold War; he said it was being updated.

3. Mazariegos added that the PMA "are in areas where the National Police don't go; there they prevent crime." Interior Minister Valle Valdizán explained that the PMA "rents its services out to private companies, such as a bank that needs security, or a mill that needs a watchman. They are certainly better than the National Police, and they are better paid. They provide services to the civilian community, and for that reason alone they are incorporated into SIPROCI" (interview). He failed to distinguish the elite *ordinaria* PMA commandos from the less-trained PMA *extraordinaria* that are used as watchman at banks and stores.

4. CACIF is Guatemala's largest and most prominent business confederation.

5. The last paragraph of the Thesis emphasizes that "in spite of the efforts the majority of Guatemalans make, we will always be exposed in this initial period to the actions of the Opponents of the Guatemalan State who want to obtain power for power's sake, without thinking about progress or peace and tranquility for Guatemalans, and they will participate within the legal structure with attitudes and proposals that favor illegality" (51–52).

6. CERJ estimated that up to July 1991, at least twenty-five of its members had been killed by security forces; GAM estimated that at least ten of its members had been killed, and many more threatened (interviews).

7. Federation of union and popular groups.

8. For example, in July 1987, Colonels Bolaños, Wohlers, Ruano, and de la Cruz became generals. In October 1987 Colonels Nuíla and Marroquín, both opposed to the Thesis, were promoted: Nuíla was sent out of the country; Marroquín became Chief of the National Defense Staff but was forced out when his "careerism" in working with Jorge Carpio's political campaign became too blatant for institutionalist Defense Minister Bolaños. In January 1988, Colonel Matta was promoted to general.

9. Under the Esquipulas II accords, a delegation from the National Commission of Reconciliation of Guatemala (CNR) met with representatives of the Guatemalan National Revolutionary Unity (URNG) on 30 March 1990 in Oslo to negotiate an agreement for peace.

10. These are thousands of internal refugees who fled to the impenetrable Ixcán to escape army violence and organized themselves into cooperatives. The army continued to stage bombing raids throughout the region against these groups in the early to mid-1990s.

11. Several professionals interviewed spoke of how "uncomfortable" they felt entering the "very militarized" environment of ESTNA and wondered why the army, if so concerned with improving its image, located the Center there; as a consequence, some refused to participate in the ESTNA sessions (interviews).

12. Social pressure groups, or *grupos populares*, invited to the courses at the military think tank ESTNA included UNSITRAGUA (federation of union and popular

groups). "We did not directly invite CERJ or GAM because they are not represen- tative. But UNSITRAGUA, which is the federation of all of them, of Marxism in Guatemala, we invited them, and they didn't show up" (Gramajo, interview).

13. As Gordillo added, "I'm going to be frank with you. We cannot allow for democracy [in Guatemala] because we don't have the layers of experience as in Switzerland. Above all, we must put into place preventive measures because there is much democracy within these *focos* [subversive cells] that provokes much insecurity among the masses" (interview).

Chapter 11

1. (FBIS Reports, Central America, 18 June 1987: G3). Seventeen-year veteran director of Policy, Planning, and Coordination of the Bureau of Inter-American Affairs of the U.S. State Department, Luigi Einaudi, has remarked: "It is possible to build a democracy without the military in Guatemala, but it is hard to *consolidate* democracy without drawing them in. The military [acting] as the guarantors of democracy does not equal their right to decide what kind of democracy should be established — but the military have rights, too. The problem is how [such a consol- idation] is to be achieved" (April 1991 Latin American Studies Association meeting panel, author's notes).

2. Sereseres commented in a 1986 interview with the author: "I told one colonel I know in the highlands, after he had boasted of the success of the counterinsurgency, that Indians have a unique ability to absorb foreign concepts and survive. I warned him they would be back [as insurgents] in the next generation or two."

3. The National Defense Chief of Staff's National Strategic Analysis of 1996 refers to the MINUGUA reports, "in which a decrease in the pointing to the government for human rights violations can be perceived; the reports are more objective, impar- tial, and point to the URNG as one of the generators of human rights violations." Despite "an improvement of state efforts to comply with the constitutional mandate to guarantee individual rights," MINUGUA "points to state functionaries, security elements, and members of the army as violators of human rights. . . . It is estimated that its reports will continue being objective; yet with each new report, they will exert pressure for legal action to be taken against all violators of human rights" (Ejército nacional, National Defense Staff 1996a: 97).

Appendix 1

1. Percentiles at the end of each Point are General Gramajo's estimation of how much the military had achieved by 1990 (interview). In the original document each point is preceded by a Mayan numeral.

Appendix 2

1. He had originally insisted that his real name be used in the publication of this interview for the book "so they will know who is speaking."

2. PSD = Democratic Socialist Party; CUC = Committee of Peasant Unity; FUR = Front of Revolutionary Union; UNSITRAGUA = Trade Union Unity of Guatemalan Workers; AEU = Association of University Students; GAM = Group of Mutual Sup- port for the Reappearance of Our Sons, Fathers, Husbands, and Brothers.

Bibliography

Adams, Richard. 1970. *Cruxifiction by Power: Essays on Guatemalan National Social Structure, 1944–1966*. Austin: University of Texas Press.

———. 1994. *Ethnicidad en el ejército de la Guatemala liberal (1870–1915)*. Manuscript draft published in 1995 as *Debate 30*. Guatemala: FLACSO.

Aguilera Peralta, Gabriel. 1972. "El proceso de terror en Guatemala." *Aportes* 24: 117–36.

———. 1978. "La tragicomedia electoral de la burguesía." *Política y Sociedad* (*Revista de la Escuela de Ciencia Política de la USAC*).

———. 1979. "The Massacre at Panzós and Capitalist Development in Guatemala." *Monthly Review* (December).

———. 1983. "Informe sobre el ejército guatemalteco." Tribunal Permanente de los Pueblos. Sesión Guatemala, Madrid, 27–31 January 1983. Madrid: Iepala Editorial, pp. 95–98.

———. 1986. "La guerra oculta: La Campaña contrainsurgente en Guatemala." Instituto Centroaméricano de Documentación e Investigación Social. Paper presented at conference, "The U.S. and Central America: A Five-Year Assessment, 1980–85." Los Angeles, 20–22 February.

———. 1989. *El fusil y el olivo: La cuestión militar en Centroamérica*. San José: Editorial DEI.

Aguilera Peralta, Gabriel, Jorge Romero Imery, et al. 1981. *Dialéctica del terror en Guatemala*. Guatemala: Editorial Universitaria Centroaméricana.

Alonso, Conrado. 1986. *15 fusilados al alba: Repaso histórico jurídico sobre los Tribunales de Fuero Especial*. Guatemala: Serviprensa Centroaméricana.

Alvarez Gómez, Col. de Art. DEM Oscar Hugo. 1984. "Seguridad nacional y la política de desarrollo nacional," *Revista Militar* 33 (September–December): 5–9.

———. 1985. "Seguridad nacional y objectivos nacionales." *Revista Militar* 35 (May–August: 5–8.

Albizurez, Miguel Angel. 1989. "Recuerdos de la revolución (III y final): Entrevista con el coronel Carlos Paz Tejada." *La Otra Guatemala* 7–8 (July).

American Association for the International Commission of Jurists. 1987. "Guatemala: A New Beginning." Report of a Mission by the Honorable G. C. Edwards and Wm. Butler, Esq. New York, April.

Americas Watch. 1982. *Human Rights in Guatemala: No Neutrals Allowed*. New York: Americas Watch.

———. 1989. *Persecuting Human Rights Monitors: The CERJ in Guatemala*, May. New York: Americas Watch.

———. 1993. "Clandestine Detention in Guatemala." *Americas Watch* 5, 2 (March).

Americas Watch and British Parliamentarian Group. 1987. *Human Rights in Guatemala During Cerezo's First Year.* New York: Americas Watch.

Americas Watch and Physicians for Human Rights. 1991. *Guatemala: Getting Away with Murder.* New York: Americas Watch.

Amnesty International. 1981. *Guatemala: A Government Program of Political Murder.* London: Amnesty International Publications.

———. 1982. "Guatemala: Massive Extrajudicial Executions in Rural Areas Under the Government of General Efraín Ríos Montt." July. Special Briefing.

———. 1984. *Torture in the Eighties.* London: Amnesty International Publications.

———. 1987. *Guatemala: The Human Rights Record.* London: Amnesty International Publications.

———. 1992. *Report on Human Rights Violations Around the World.* London: Amnesty International Publications.

Anderson, Ken and A. Anderson. 1985. "Limitations of the Liberal-Legal Model of International Human Rights: Six Lessons from El Salvador." *Telos* 64 (Summer): 9–104.

Andrade Díaz-Durán, Fernando. 1988. "Transición política en Guatemala, naturaleza, alcances y perspectivas." Speech given to IV Seminario Sobre la Realidad Nacional, "Transición política, Diálogo nacional y Pacto social en Guatemala" organized by Asociación de Investigación y Estudios Sociales (ASIES), May 23–25.

Arias, Arturo. 1988. "La respuesta del poder 1982–1986." In *Guatemala: Polos de desarrollo.* Guatemala: CEIDEC, pp. 169–220.

———. 1990. "Changing Indian Identity: Guatemala's Violent Transition to Modernity." In *Guatemalan Indians and the State, 1540 to 1988,* ed. Carol A. Smith. Austin: University of Texas Press, pp. 230–57.

Arriagada Herrera, Genaro. 1985. *El pensamiento político los militares.* Santiago: Centro de Investigaciones Socioeconómicas (CISEC), Asamblea Nacional.

Austin, John L. 1975. *How To Do Things with Words.* Oxford: Clarendon Press.

AVANCSO (Asociación para el Avance de las Ciencias Sociales en Guatemala). 1988a. "La Política de desarrollo del Estado guatemalteco, 1986–87." *Cuadernos de Investigación* 2 (April).

———. 1988b. "On Their Own: A Preliminary Study of Youth Gangs in Guatemala City." *Cuardernos de Investigación* 4.

———. 1990. "Política institucional hácia el desplazado interno en Guatemala." *Cuadernos de Investigación* 6.

Bahbah, Bishara. 1986. *Israel and Latin America: The Military Connection.* New York: St. Martin's Press in association with the Institute for Palestinian Studies, Washington, D.C.

Barahona, Elias. 1984. "Testimonio." Tribunal Permanente de los Pueblos, Sesión Guatemala. Madrid, January 27–31, 1983. Madrid: Iepala Editorial, pp. 106–8.

Barnett, Frank R., B. Hugh Tovar, and Richard H. Schultz, eds. 1984. *Special Operations in U.S. Strategy.* National Defense University Press in cooperation with National Strategy Information Center. Washington, D.C.: U.S. Government Printing Office.

Barry, Tom, 1986. *Guatemala: The Politics of Counterinsurgency.* Albuquerque, N.M.: Inter-Hemispheric Education Resource Center.

Barry, Tom, Beth Wood, and Deb Preusch. 1983. *Dollars and Dictators: A Guide to Central America.* Albuquerque, N.M: Inter-American Education Resource Center; New York: Grove Press.

Barthes, Roland. 1972. *Mythologies.* New York: Hill and Wang.

Beit-Hallahmi, Benjamin. 1987. *The Israeli Connection: Who Israel Arms and Why.* New York: Pantheon Books.

Beltranena Falla, Francisco Fernando. 1992. "Guatemala: Pretorianismo y democracia estratégica." Thesis, Instituto de Estudios Políticos, Universidad Francisco Marroquín, Guatemala.

Berganzo, Gustavo and Evelyn Klussman. 1987. "El Ejército está en proceso de cambio." Interview with Gramajo. *Prensa Libre*.

Black, George. 1985. "Under the Gun." *NACLA Report on the Americas* 29, 6 (November/December): 10–25.

———. 1989. "Military Rule in Guatemala." In *The Politics of Antipolitics: The Military in Latin America*, ed. Brian Loveman and Thomas M. Davies, Jr. 2nd ed. Lincoln: University of Nebraska Press, pp. 509–12.

Black, George with Milton Jamail and Norma Stoltz Chinchilla. 1984. *Garrison Guatemala*. New York: Monthly Review Press.

Cain, Maureen. 1982. "Gramsci, the State and the Place of Law." In *Legality, Ideology, and the State*, ed. David Sugarman. London: Academic Press: pp. 95–118.

Carmack, Robert M., ed. 1988. *Harvest of Violence: The Maya Indians and the Guatemalan Crisis*. Norman: University of Oklahoma Press.

Castañeda, Gabriel Angel. 1982. "Guatemalidad y autodefensa civil." *Revista Militar* 27 (September–December): 5–14.

Center for Democratic Education Research. 1994. *Guatemala's Social Funds. A Report and Guide for Practitioners*. Washington, D.C.: Center for Democratic Education Research.

Centro de Estudios Integrales de Desarrollo Comunal (CEIDEC). 1988, 1990. *Guatemala: Polos de desarrollo*. 2 vols. Guatemala: CEIDEC.

Centro de Estudios Militares. 1980. *Apreciación estratégica del estado de Guatemala*. Parte del curso no. 6 para comandantes y oficiales impartido por el CEM 25 de mayo–27 de junio. Mimeo.

Centro de Estudios de la Realidad Guatemalteca. 1985. "Contrainsurgencia y régimen constitucional." *Temas* 1, 1 (October–December).

Centro de Investigación y Documentación Centroaméricana. 1980. *Violencia y contraviolencia: Desarrollo histórico de la violencia institucional en Guatemala*. Editorial Universitaria de Guatemala (Universidad de San Carlos). Guatemala: Centro de Investigación.

Cerezo, Vinicio. 1975. "Segunda petición de la D.C. al Golpe de Estado I y II." *Diario La Hora*, 25, 26 July.

CIA Inspector General. 1995. "Summary of CIA Inspector General Report Relating to Agency Activities in Guatemala." July 26.

Cifuentes H., Capt. de Navío DEMN Juan Fernando. 1982. "Operación Ixil." *Revista Militar* 27 (September–December): 25–72.

———. 1983. "El Secuestro." *Revista Militar* 29 (May–August): IV Epoca.

———. 1993. "Causas y consecuencias del alzamiento del 13 de noviembre de 1960." *Crónica*, 19 November, p. 34.

———. 1994. "Operación Latigo." *Crónica*, 11 February, p. 48.

Clark, Gordon L. and Michael Dear. 1984. *State Apparatus: Structures and Language of Legitimacy*. Boston: Allen and Unwin.

Colegio de México. 1980. *Centroamérica en crisis*. México: Colegio de México.

Comisión Multipartita. 1991. "CPR de la Sierra. Comunidades de Población en Resistencia. Informe de la Visita Realizada a la CPR de la Sierra los Días 27 y 28 de febrero." No publisher given.

Comité Pro-Justicia y Paz de Guatemala. 1982–92. "Human Rights in Guatemala." Annual Reports prepared and published with the support of the World Council of Churches.

Commission for Restoration of Areas. 1988. *Impact Evaluation*. Research Triangle

Institute, Research Triangle, N.C., September 20. U.S. AID-funded study on El Salvador.

Commission on Integrated Long-Term Strategy. 1988. *Discriminate Deterrence: Report of the Commission on Integrated Long-Term Strategy, with a Memorandum for the Secretary of Defense and Assistant to the President for National Security Affairs*. Washington, D.C.: U.S. Government Printing Office.

Committee of Santa Fe. 1980. *A New Inter-American Policy for the Eighties*. Washington, D.C.: Council for Inter-American Security.

———. 1989. *Santa Fe II: A Strategy for Latin America in the Nineties*. Washington, D.C.: Council for Inter-American Security.

Constituyente de Guatemala. 1985. *Constitución política de la República de Guatemala*. Guatemala: Ayala Jiménez Editores.

"Contra las patrullas civiles." 1989. *La Otra Guatemala*, January, p. 13.

Cruz Salazar, Lt. Col. José Luis. 1980. "El Ejército como una fuerza política." *Estudios Políticos*, pp. 74–98.

———. 1975. "Postura política de los oficiales de ejército guatemalteco." With Fernando Hoyos. *Estudios Sociales*, pp. 96–118.

———. 1982. "Democracia, participación y partidos I y II." *Prensa Libre*, March.

———. 1987. "Tema: Asuntos civiles." Opus 16, 19 March, 1987. Fuente: D-5, Ejército. Unpublished notes.

———. 1988a. "Perfiles militares: Entrevista con el Ministro de la Defensa Nacional 12.1.88." Unpublished interview.

———. 1988b. "El espacio político se fractura." Unpublished talk. June.

Dahl, Robert A. 1971. *Polyarchy: Participation and Opposition*. New Haven, Conn.: Yale University Press.

Damaška, Mirjan. 1986. *The Faces of Justice and State Authority*. New Haven, Conn.: Yale University Press.

Davis, Shelton. 1988. "Introduction: Sowing the Seeds of Violence." In *Harvest of Violence: The Maya Indians and the Guatemalan Crisis*, ed. Robert M. Carmack. Norman: University of Oklahoma Press, pp. 3–38.

Dunckerley, James. 1988. *Power in the Isthmus: A Political History of Modern Central America*. New York: Verso.

Ejército de Guatemala. 1982a. *Plan nacional de seguridad y desarrollo*. PNSD-01-82 Guatemala City CEM 01ABR82 RLHGCC-82.

———. 1982b. "Appendix H." Standing orders for the development of anti-subversive operations to the Victoria 82 Plan of Campaign. LEMG-1800. 160800JUL82. Army General Staff.

———. 1984a. *Polos de desarrollo*. Guatemala: Editorial del Ejército.

———. 1984b. "Pensamiento y cultura." *Revista Cultural del Ejército*. Edición especialmente dedicada a la labor institucional del CRN.

———. 1984c. *Las patrullas de autodefensa civil: La respuesta popular al proceso de integración socio-economico-político en la Guatemala actual*. Guatemala: Editorial del Ejército.

———. 1984d. "Polos de desarrollo." *Revista Militar* 31 (January–April).

———. 1985a. "Polos de desarrollo." *Revista Cultural del Ejército* (January–February).

———. 1985b. "Polos de desarrollo y servicio." *Revista Militar* (February).

———. 1986. *Informe de la obra realizada por el Gobierno Militar, periódo del 8 August 1983–31 December 1985*. 14 January. Guatemala: Editorial del Ejército.

———. 1987a. *Forjar y libertar: Asuntos Civiles*. Guatemala: Editorial del Ejército.

———. 1987b. *Foro Nacional*. "27 años de lucha por la libertad." Una presentación oficial del Ejército de Guatemala. Organizado por el Consejo Empresarial. 12 August. Tape transcription.

———. 1988. *Army Bulletin*, 1 January. Guatemala: Departamento de Información y Divulgación.

———. 1994. *Historia del ejército, 1981–1984*. Guatemala: Departamento de Información y Divulgación, Sección de Relaciones Nacionales e Internacionales.

———. 1996a. *Análisis estratégico nacional, 1996*. January. National Defense Staff.

———. 1996b. *Plan de Campaña Integración '96*. 060800MAR96.

———. 1996c. "Proceso de paz en Guatemala: Fortalección del poder civil y function del ejército en una sociedad democrática. Lograr la paz es tarea de todos." September. Guatemala: Departamento de Información y Divulgación.

———. n.d. "Estratégia actual de la guerrilla contrasubversiva del Ejército de Guatemala." Tesis de Ascenso, Curso de Comando y Estado Mayor. Guatemala: Centro de Estudios Militares.

Ejército Nacional de Guatemala, Departamento de Información y Divulgación (RR.PP. del Ejército). 1984. "Pensamiento y cultura." *Revista Cultural del Ejército*. Edicion especialmente dedicada a la labor institucional del CRN.

Equipo de Antropología Forense de Guatemala. 1997. *Las massacres en Rabinal: estudio histórico-antropológico de las massacres de Plan de Sánchez, Chichupac, y Río Negro*. Guatemala: EAFG.

Falla, Ricardo. 1983. *Voices of the Survivors: The Massacre at Finca San Francisco, Guatemala*. Boston: Cultural Survival and Anthropology Resource Center.

———. 1984. "Testimony." Tribunal Permanente de los Pueblos. Sesión Guatemala, 27–31 January, 1983. Madrid: Iepala Editorial, pp. 177–208.

———. 1994. *Massacres in the Jungle: Ixcán, Guatemala, 1975–1982*. Boulder, Colo.: Westview Press.

Figueroa Ibarra, Carlos. 1991. *El recurso del miedo: Ensayo sobre el estado y el terror en Guatemala*. Serie Investigaciones 5. Programa Centroamericano de Investigaciones, Secretaría General de CSUCA. San José: Editorial Universitaria Centroamericana.

Fine, Bob. 1984. *Democracy and the Rule of Law*. London: Pluto Press.

Fitch, Samuel and Andrés Fontana. 1990. *Military Politics and Democratic Consolidation in Latin America*. Buenos Aires: CEDES.

Fix Zamudio, Héctor. 1983. *Estado social de derecho y cambio constitucional*. México: UNAM.

Fuentes y Guzmán, Antonio de. 1933. *Recordación Florida*. Vol. 3. Madrid: Navarro, 1882–83. Reprint Biblioteca "Goathemala" Sociedad de Geografía e Historia 8. Guatemala: Sociedad de Geografía e Historia.

Fukuyama, Francis. 1992. *The End of History and the Last Man*. New York: Free Press.

Fundación para el Desarrollo Institucional de Guatemala (DIG). 1991. "Curso 1991. Centro de Estudios Estratégicos para la Estabilidad Nacional." Guatemala: CENTRO ESTNA.

García Laguardia, Jorge Mario and Edmundo Vázquez Martínez. 1984. *Constitución y orden democrático*. Guatemala: Editorial Universitaria de Guatemala, Universidad de San Carlos de Guatemala.

Gaspar, Gabriel. 1985. "The Strategy of Christian Democracy in Central America." ACEN-SIAG, 18 November, pp. 13–14.

Girón Tánchez, Col.-Lic. Manuel de Jesús. 1983. "Poder y justicia." *Revista Militar* (January–April): 9–15.

Gleijeses, Piero. 1991. *Shattered Hope: The Guatemalan Revolution and the United States, 1944–1954*. Princeton, N.J.: Princeton University Press.

Gluckman, Max. 1965. *Politics, Law, and Ritual in Tribal Society*. Chicago: Aldine.

Gobierno de Guatemala. 1989. "Guatemala: Human Rights." Report presented to UN Human Rights Commission, Geneva, 26 January.

González, Edward. 1983. *Caribbean Basin Study on U.S.-Guatemalan Relations*. Washington, D.C.: Rand Corporation.

Gramajo Morales, General Héctor Alejandro. 1987. "Discurso al 10a promoción del Curso de Comando y Estado Mayor, Centro de Estudios Militares." April 30.

———. 1988a. "Impondremos la paz." Interview. *Prensa Libre*, 22 April.

———. 1988b. "El ejército es el garante de la democracia." Interview. *Crónica*, 19 May, pp. 21–24.

———. 1988c. Address to graduating cadets, Escuela Politécnica.

———. 1988d. Speech on the 117th Anniversary of the Founding of the Guatemalan Army. Suplemento Aniversario del Ejército de Guatemala. *Prensa Libre*, 3 July.

———. 1989a. "Contrainsurgencia en Guatemala: Un caso de estudio." *Revista Militar* 39 (September 1986–April 1987).

———. 1989b. *La Tesis de la estabilidad nacional*. Guatemala: Editorial del Ejército.

———. 1990a. *Liderazgo militar y el futuro del ejército de Guatemala*. Guatemala: Editorial del Ejército.

———. 1990b. "Discurso oficial." May. Gramajo's last speech.

———. 1990c. "Consolidation of a Democratic Way of Life: Guatemala, the Next 12 Months." Paper prepared for political science class, Kennedy School, Harvard University.

———. 1991a, b. "Political Transition in Guatemala (1980–1990): A Perspective from Inside Guatemala's Armed Forces." Two drafts edited separately for *Democratic Transitions in Central America and Panama*, ed. Jorge Domínguez and Marc Lindenburg.

———. 1991c. "The Role of the Armed Forces in the Process of Transition Towards Democracy." Paper presented to American University Conference on "Civil-Military Relations and Democracy in Latin America" (16–21 May.

———. 1991d. "¿Hay condiciones para una paz duradera en Guatemala?" Paper presented to conference, "Violence and Democracy in Central America: El Salvador and Guatemala," Inter-American Dialogue and Graduate School of International Studies, Miami, 13–15 June.

———. 1995. *De la guerra . . . a la guerra: La difícil transición política en Guatemala*. Guatemala: Fondo de Cultura Editorial.

Graziano, Frank. 1992. *Divine Violence: Spectacle, Psychosexuality, and Radical Christianity in the Argentine "Dirty War."* Boulder, Colo.: Westview Press.

"Guatemala: Acción cívica militar en la guerra de contrainsurgencia." 1985. March 2. ACEN-SIAG 34.

Guatemalan Human Rights Commission (Mexico). 1984. "Guatemala."

Guatemala Human Rights Commission (Washington). 1995. *Guatemalan Human Rights Commission Report* 13: 1, 2.

Guatemalan Human Rights Ombudsman Office (Guatemala). 1996. 1996 Report.

Gutiérrez, Edgar. 1990. "Transición política y sistema de poder en Guatemala." Instituto AVANCSO, August.

Handy, Jim. 1984. *Gift of the Devil: A History of Guatemala*. Boston: South End Press.

Harnecker, Marta. 1984. *Pueblos en armas*. Interview with guerrilla Pablo Monsanto. México: Era.

Hart, Herbert L. A. 1961. *The Concept of Law*. Oxford: Clarendon Press.

Holiday, David. 1997. "Guatemala's Long Road to Peace." *Current History* (February).

Horwitz, M. J. 1977. *The Transformation of American Law, 1789–1860*. Cambridge, Mass.: Harvard University Press.

Huntington, Samuel. 1968. *Political Order in Changing Societies*. New Haven, Conn.: Yale University Press.

———. 1991. *The Third Wave: Democratization in the Late Twentieth Century*. Norman: University of Oklahoma Press.

Instituto Centro-Américano de Investigaciones Sociales (ICADIS). 1982. "La gran matanza." *Coyuntura*, p. 2.

———. 1983. "Tierra y trabajo en Guatemala: Una evaluación." U.S.-AID proposal published in *Polémica* 17–18 (1987).

———. 1987. "La contrainsurgencia rural en Guatemala." In *Centroamérica: La guerra de baja intensidad*. San José: Editorial DEI, pp. 51–68.

Ietswaart, Helen F. P. 1980. "The Discourse of Summary Justice and the Discourse of Popular Justice: An Analysis of Legal Rhetoric in Argentina." In *The Politics of Informal Justice,* ed. Richard L. Abel. Vol. 2. New York: Academic Press.

Iglesias, Elizabeth M. and Pamela Varley. 1989. "The 1988 Coup Attempt." Unpublished paper for Phil Heymann, Harvard Law School.

Immerman, Richard H. 1982. *The CIA in Guatemala: The Foreign Policy of Intervention*. Austin: University of Texas Press.

Inforpress Centroaméricana. 1985. "Guatemala: Elections 1985." Guatemala.

Intelligence Oversight Board. 1996. Report on *The Guatemala Review.* June 28.

International Human Rights Law Group. 1989. *Maximizing Deniability: The Justice System and Human Rights in Guatemala*. Report prepared by Kenneth Anderson. Washington, D.C.: International Human Rights Law Group.

Janowitz, Morris. 1964. *The Military in the Political Development of New Nations*. Chicago: University of Chicago Press.

Jiménez de Arechaga, Eduardo. 1985. "El derecho y la justicia, resguardos de la libertad." *Revista IIDH* 1 (January–June): 25–38.

Jonas, Susanne. 1984. "The Complicity of the U.S. Government and U.S. Capital in the Violation of Human Rights in Guatemala." In *Guatemala—Tyranny on Trial: Testimony of the Permanent People's Tribunal,* ed. Jonas, Ed McCaughan, and Elizabeth Sutherland Martínez. San Francisco: Synthesis Publications, pp. 188–99.

Junta Militar de Gobierno. 1982. *Objetivos nacionales actuales*. 23 March. Guatemala: Tipografía Nacional.

Karl, Terry. 1990. "Dilemmas of Democratization in Latin America." *Comparative Politics* 23, 1 (October): 1–21.

Keefe, Eugene K. 1984. "National Security." In *Guatemala: A Country Study,* ed. Richard F. Nyrop. Area Handbook Series, American University. Washington, D.C.: U.S. Government Printing Office, pp. 177–218.

Kirkpatrick, Jeane. 1979. "Dictatorships and Double Standards." *Commentary* (November).

———. 1982. *Dictatorships and Double Standards: Rationalism and Reason in Politics*. American Enterprise Institute. New York: Simon and Schuster.

Kitson, Brig. Gen. Frank. 1971. *Low Intensity Operations: Subversion, Insurgency, Peace-Keeping*. Mechanicsburg, Pa.: Stackpole Books.

Kobrak, Paul. 1994. "Support for the Civil Patrols in Aguacatán, Guatemala." Paper presented at the LASA Meetings, Atlanta.

LeBot, Yvon. 1992a. *La guerre en terre maya*. Paris: Editions Karthala.

———. 1992b. "Guatemala: Violencia, Revolución y Democracia." Debate 15. Guatemala: FLACSO.

Leiken, Robert S. and Barry Rubin, eds. 1987. *The Central American Crisis Reader*. New York: Summit Books.

Letona, Lt. Col. Roberto E. 1989. "Guatemalan Counterinsurgency Strategy." U.S. Army War College Study Project, 7 April. Carlisle Barracks, Pennsylvania.

Linares Morales, Lic. Arquiles. 1985. "La Constitución guatemalteca de 1985." CITGUA (Ciencia y Tecnología para Guatemala), Cuadernos 7, Year 2, October. México.

Lukes, Steven. 1974. *Power: A Radical View*. London and New York: Macmillan.

Lundberg, Kirsten. 1990. *U.S.-Guatemalan Relations: The Struggle over Human Rights*. Case Program. Cambridge, Mass.: Kennedy School of Government, Harvard University.

Mainwaring, Scott, Guillermo O'Donnell, and J. Samuel Valenzuela. 1992. *Issues in*

Democratic Consolidation: The New South American Democracy in Comparative Perspective. Notre Dame, Ind.: University of Notre Dame Press.

Martínez Peláez, Severo. 1973. *La patria del criollo: Ensayo de interpretación de la realidad colonial gualtemalteca.* San José: Editorial Universitaria Centroamericana, EDUCA.

Mathews, Anthony. 1986. *Freedom, State Security, and the Rule of Law.* Cape Town: Juta and Co.

Mazariegos, Jorge A. (Capt. de Navío DEMN). 1990. *El Estado, su estabilidad y el desarrollo de una estratégia nacional.* Guatemala: Editorial del Ejército.

McClintock, Michael. 1985. *The American Connection: State Terror and Popular Resistance in Guatemala.* Vol. 2. London: Zed Press.

Mensch, Elizabeth. 1982. "The History of Mainstream Legal Thought." In *The Politics of Law,* ed. David Kearys. New York: Pantheon Books.

Montealegre Klenner, Hernán. 1979. *La seguridad del estado y los derechos humanos.* Santiago: Academia de Humanismo Cristiano.

Montejo, Victor. 1993. *Testimonio: Muerte de una comunidad indígena en Guatemala.* Guatemala: Editorial Universitaria, Universidad de San Carlos.

Montenegro Ríos, Carlos Roberto. 1980. "El partido demócrata cristiano guatemalteco y su desarrollo político e ideológico." Tesis para el grado de Licenciado en Sociología, Facultad de Ciencias Sociales, Universidad de Costa Rica.

Nairn, Allan. 1982. "Back in Guatemala Again." *Washington Post,* 21 October.

———. 1995a. "CIA Death Squads." *The Nation,* 17 April, pp. 511–13.

———. 1995b. "The Country Team." *The Nation,* 5 June, p. 780.

Nairn, Allan and Jean-Marie Simon. 1986. "Bureaucracy of Death." *New Republic,* 30 June, pp. 13–17.

Novoa Monreal, Eduardo. 1983. *El derecho como obstáculo y el cambio social.* 6th ed. México: Siglo Veintiuno Editores.

Nyrop, Richard E., ed. 1984. *Guatemala: A Country Study.* Area Handbook Series, American University. Washington, D.C.: U.S. Government Printing Office.

O'Donnell, Guillermo. 1986. "The U.S., Latin America, Democracy: Variations on a Very Old Theme." In *The United States and Latin America in the 1980s,* ed. Kevin J. Middlebrook and Carlos Rico. Pittsburgh: University of Pittsburgh Press.

O'Donnell, Guillermo, Philippe Schmitter, and Laurence Whitehead, eds. 1986. *Transitions from Authoritarian Rule: Comparative Perspectives.* Baltimore: Johns Hopkins University Press.

Palencia Prado, Tania. 1996. *Peace in the Making: Civil Groups in Guatemala.* Trans. David Holiday and Matthew Creelman. London: Catholic Institute for International Relations.

Patterson, Franklin. 1988. "The Guatemalan Military and the Escuela Politécnica." *Armed Forces and Society* 14, 3 (Spring).

PAVA (Programa de Ayuda para los Vecinos del Altiplano). 1984. Final Report, US-AID project DR-520-84-04. March.

Payeras, Mario. 1983. *Days of the Jungle: The Testimony of a Guatemalan Guerrillero, 1972–1976.* New York: Monthly Review Press.

———. 1991. *Los fusiles de Octubre.* Ed. Juan Pablos. México: Editorial Juan Pablos.

Peckenham, Nancy. 1983. "Guatemala 1983: A Report to the American Friends Service Committee." Philadelphia: AFSC.

Peralta Méndez, Gen. (ret.) Ricardo. 1986a. "Los militares y el congreso." *Prensa Libre,* 12 December, p. 11.

———. 1986b. "Los militares y la sociedad." *La Hora,* 14 August, pp. 1, 3.

———. 1986c. "Las causas de la subversion." *La Hora,* 17 August, pp. 1, 11.

———. 1986d. "Militares y democracía I y II." *La Hora,* 30 October, 2 November, pp. 1, 11.

———. 1989. "El Generalato." *La Hora,* 6 April, pp. 2, 23.

——. 1990. "Los militares y las elecciones generales." *Crónica*, 14 September, p. 39.

Petersen, Kurt. 1992. "The Maquiladora Revolution in Guatemala." Occasional Paper Series 2. Orville H. Schell, Jr. Center for International Human Rights, Yale Law School, Yale University.

Recopilador de Leyes. 1982–84. *Estatuto fundamental del Goberno: Decretos-Leyes I, II, III*. Guatemala: Ministerio de Gobernación.

Reina, Carlos R. 1985. "Derechos humanos y seguridad del estado en Centroamérica: Su situación actual." II Seminario Interamericano Sobre Seguridad del Estado, Derecho Humanitario y Derechos Humanos en Centroamérica," Comité Internacional de la Cruz Roja and Instituto Interamericano de Derechos Humanos, San José.

Richards, Michael. 1985. "Cosmopolitan Worldview and Counterinsurgency in Guatemala." *Anthropological Quarterly* 58, 3 (July): 90–107.

Robinson, Barry. 1988. "La guerra continúa en el Triángulo Ixil. *Crónica*, 22 September, pp. 14–17.

Rosada Granados, Héctor. 1985. "Guatemala 1984 elecciones para Asamblea Nacional Constituyente." #2. Cuadernos de CAPEL (Instituto Interaméricano de Derechos Humanos, Centro de Asesoría y Promoción Electoral), San José.

——. 1988. "El rol de nuestros partidos políticos." *Crónica*, 3 November.

——. 1992. "Fuerzas armadas, sociedad y defensa nacional: Proyector en Guatemala." Unpublished talk, Consejo Latinoaméricano de Ciencias Sociales, 6 November.

Rosenthal, Stephen. 1992. "The Missing Piece: The Role of the United States in Supporting Civilian Control over the Militaries in El Salvador and Guatemala." Bachelor of Arts Honors Thesis, Department of Government, Harvard College.

Rouquié, Alain. 1986. "Demilitarization and the Institutionalization of Military-Dominated Politics in Latin America." In *Transitions from Authoritarian Rule: Comparative Perspectives*, ed. Guillermo O'Donnell, Philippe Schmitter, and Laurence Whitehead. Baltimore: Johns Hopkins University Press.

——. 1984. *El estado militar en América latina*. Vol. 2. Buenos Aires: Emecé Editores.

Sandoval Alarcón, Mario. 1990. "Entrevista con el General Ricardo Peralta Méndez: El golpe militar está descartado por el grado profesional del ejército" *Revista Elecciones '90*, 28 June, pp. 13–14.

Sarti Castañeda, Carlos. 1986. "La democracia en Guatemala: Sus contradicciones, limites y perspectivas." *Democracia y autoritarismo*. Cuadernos de Critica 3. México: Universidad Autónoma Puebla.

Schirmer, Jennifer. 1988. "'Those Who Die for Life Cannot Be Called Dead': Women and Human Rights Protest in Latin America." *Harvard Human Rights Yearbook/Journal* 1 (Spring): 41–76.

——. 1990. "Rule of Law or Law of Rule? Guatemalan Military Attitudes Toward Law, National Security and Human Rights." Special Issue on Guatemala: *Lateinamerika. Analysen. Daten. Dokumentation: Journal of the Institut für Iberoamerika-Kunde* (June): 53–60.

——. 1991. "The Guatemalan Military Project: An Interview with Gen. Héctor Gramajo." *Harvard International Review* 13, 3 (Spring): 10–13.

——. 1992. "Guatemala: Los militares y la Tesis de Estabilidad Nacional." In *América latina: Militares y sociedad*, 2 vols., ed. Dirk Kruijt and Edelberto Torres-Rivas. San José: Facultad Latinoaméricana de Ciencias Sociales (Latin American Institute of the Social Sciences), pp. 183–220.

——. 1996a. "The Looting of Democratic Discourse by the Guatemalan Military: Implications for Human Rights." In *Constructing Democracy: Human Rights, Citizenship and Society*, ed. Elizabeth Jelin and Eric Hershberg. Boulder, Colo.: Westview Press, pp. 84–96. (Spanish edition Buenos Aires: Editorial NVa. Sociedad.)

———. 1996b. "Universal and Sustainable Human Rights? Special Tribunals in Guatemala." In *Human Rights, Culture and Context: Anthropological Perspectives*, ed. Richard A. Wilson. London: Pluto Press, pp. 215–46.

Schlesinger, Stephen and Stephen Kinzer. 1983. *Bitter Fruit: The Untold Story of the American Coup in Guatemala*. New York: Doubleday.

Schoultz, Lars. 1981. *Human Rights and U.S. Policy Toward Latin America*. Princeton, N.J.: Princeton University Press.

———. 1987. *National Security and United States Policy Toward Latin America*. Princeton, N.J.: Princeton University Press.

Secretaría Ejecutiva Permanente. 1987. "XVII Conferencia de Ejércitos Américanos, Buenos Aires, Argentina." 17–19 November. Report.

Sereseres, Cesár D. 1978. "Guatemalan Paramilitary Forces, Internal Security and Politics." In *Supplementary Military Forces, Reserves, Militias, Auxiliaries*, vol. 8, ed. Louis A. Zurcher and Gwyn Harries-Jenkins. London: Sage, pp. 179–99.

———. 1982. "Guatemala: Not Just Another Coup." *Los Angeles Times*, 31 March, OpEd pages.

———. 1984. "The Guatemalan Legacy: Radical Challengers and Military Politics." Report on Guatemala. SAIS Papers. In International Affairs No. 7. Boulder, Colo.: Westview Press with the Foreign Policy Institute, Johns Hopkins University, pp. 17–49.

———. 1985. "The Highlands War in Guatemala." In *Latin American Insurgencies*, ed. Georges A. Fauriol. Georgetown University Center for Strategic and International Studies and National Defense University. Washington, D.C.: U.S. Government Printing Office.

Sheehan, Michael A. 1989. "Comparative Counterinsurgency Strategies: Guatemala and El Salvador." *Conflict* 9: 127–54.

Shklar, Judith N. 1964. *Law, Morals, and Political Trials*. Cambridge, Mass.: Harvard University Press.

Smith, Carol A. 1990a. *Guatemalan Indians and the State, 1540–1988*. Austin: University of Texas Press.

———. 1990b. "The Militarization of Civil Society in Guatemala: Economic Reorganization as a Continuation of War." *Latin American Perspectives* 17, 4, iss. 67 (Fall): 8–41.

Smyth, Frank. 1987. "El Salvador's Forgotten War." *The Progressive*, August, pp. 26–28.

Solórzano Martínez, Mario. 1983. "Centroamérica: Democracias de fachada." *Polémica* 12 (November–December): 41–55.

Soto, Carlos Rafael. 1988. "Bajo los pies, el abismo." *El Gráfico* (*La Revista*), 3 July, pp. 26–27, 50.

Stepan, Alfred. 1971. *The Military in Politics*. Princeton, N.J.: Princeton University Press.

———. 1988. *Rethinking Military Politics: Brazil and the Southern Cone*. Princeton, N.J.: Princeton University Press.

Stoll, David. 1993. *Between Two Armies in the Ixil Towns of Guatemala*. New York: Columbia University Press.

Sumner, Colin. 1982. "Law, Legitimation and the Advanced Capitalist State: The Jurisprudence and Social Theory of Jürgen Habermas." In *Legality, Ideology and the State*, ed. David Sugarman. London: Academic Press, pp. 119–58.

Tapper, C. F. H. 1973. "Powers and Secondary Rules of Change." In *Oxford Essays in Jurisprudence*, ed. A. W. B. Simpson. Oxford: Clarendon Press.

Thompson, Robert. 1967. *Defeating Communist Insurgency*. London: Chatto and Windus.

Toledo Peñate, Cesár A. 1985. "Olvidé mi bola de cristal." *Prensa Libre*, 23 June, p. 3.

Tomuschat, Christian. 1992. Report of the Independent Expert, Mr. Christian Tomuschat, on the Situation of Human Rights in Guatemala. United Nations Economic and Social Council, January 21. Official English version.

Torres-Rivas, Edelberto. 1980. "Vida y muerte en Guatemala: Reflexiones sobre la crisis y la violencia política." In *Centroamérica en crisis*. Centro de Estudios Internacionales, El Colegio de México, pp. 29–54.

——. 1986. "Comment: Constraints on Policies Regarding Human Rights and Democracy." In *The United States and Latin America in the 1980s*, ed. Kevin J. Middlebrook and Carlos Rico. Pittsburgh: University of Pittsburgh Press, pp. 469–79.

Tribunales Permanentes de Los Pueblos. 1983. Sesión Guatemala. Madrid, 27–31 January. Madrid: Iepala Editorial.

Troy, Pablo. 1984. "Columna de Troy." *Diario de Centroamérica* (Guatemala), 7 May.

——. 1985. "Orden, libertad, seguridad y desarrollo." *Revista Cultural del Ejército* (January–February): 70.

Trudeau, Robert. 1989. "The Guatemalan Election of 1985: Prospects for Democracy." In *Elections and Democracy in Central America*, ed. John A. Booth and Mitchell A. Seligman. Chapel Hill: University of North Carolina Press, pp. 93–125.

U.S. Embassy in Guatemala. 1986. "Labor Trends in Guatemala." U.S. Government Publication, August.

Valencia-Tovar, Alvaro. 1985. "Why Is Guatemala the Target of a Communist Attack?" *Revista Militar* (May–August): 4–8.

Vargas, Jacobo Foronda. 1984. *Guatemala: Sus recursos naturales, el militarismo, y el imperialismo*. México: Claves Latinoaméricanos.

Warren, Kay. 1992. "Transforming Memories and Histories: Meanings of Ethnic Resurgence for Mayan Indians." In *Americas: New Interpretive Essays*, ed. Alfred Stepan. Oxford: Oxford University Press, pp. 189–219.

——. 1993. "Interpreting *la Violencia* in Guatemala: Shapes of Kaqchikel Resistance and Silence." In *The Violence Within: Cultural and Political Opposition in Divided Nations*, ed. Kay B. Warren. Boulder, Colo.: Westview Press, pp. 25–26.

Washington Office on Latin America. 1989. *The Administration of Injustice: Military Accountability in Guatemala*. Washington, D.C.: Washington Office on Latin America.

Washington Office on Latin America and International Human Rights Law Group, with John A. Booth. 1985. *The 1985 Guatemalan Elections: Will the Military Relinquish Power?* Report of the Delegation. Washington, D.C.: Washington Office on Latin America.

Washington Office on Latin America, with Chris Krueger and Kjell I. Enge. 1985. *Security and Development Conditions in the Guatemalan Highlands*. Report on a Mission of Inquiry, August. Washington, D.C.: Washington Office on Latin America.

Washington Office on Latin America, with Bonnie Tenneriello. 1992. *Habits of Repression: Military Accountability for Human Rights Abuse Under the Serrano Government in Guatemala 1991–1992*. Washington, D.C.: Washington Office on Latin America.

Wer, Carlos. 1992. "En Guatemala los héroes tienen 15 años." *Crítica*, 31 July and 14 August.

Wiarda, Howard. 1982. *Politics and Social Change in Latin America*. Amherst: University of Massachusetts Press.

Wilson, Richard. 1991. "Machine Guns and Mountain Spirits: The Cultural Effects of State Repression Among the Q'eqchi'," *Critique of Anthropology* 11, 1: 33–61.

Wickham-Crowley, Timothy P. 1992. *Guerrillas and Revolution in Latin America: A Comparative Study of Insurgents and Regimes Since 1956*. Princeton, N.J.: Princeton University Press.

Yurrita, Alfonso. 1989. "La transición del gobierno militar a civil en Guatemala." In *The Military and Democracy: The Future of Civil-Military Relations in Latin America*, ed.

Louis W. Goodman, Johanna S. R. Mendelson, and Juan Rial. Lexington, Mass.: Lexington Books.

Zagorski, Paul W. 1992. *Democracy vs. National Security: Civil-Military Relations in Latin America*. Boulder, Colo.: Lynne Reinner.

Newspapers, Weeklies, and Reports Cited

ACEN-SIAG (Agencia Centroamericana de Noticias) *Weekly Reports* (Mexico and Guatemala cities)

Americas Watch, reports

Amnesty International, reports

Aportes (Guatemala)

Central America Report / Inforpress Centroaméricana (Guatemala)

Christian Science Monitor Television, interviews

Comisión de Derechos Humanos Guatemaltecos (CDHG) (México), reports

Comité Pro-Justicia y Paz (México), annual reports

Crítica (Guatemala)

Crónica (Guatemala)

El Día (Mexico)

Diario de Centroamérica (Gobierno de Guatemala)

La Época (Guatemala)

El Gráfico (Guatemala)

La Hora (Guatemala)

Jane's Defence Weekly

Israeli Foreign Affairs Latin American Regional Reports

Miami Herald

NACLA (North American Congress on Latin America)

New York Times

Notícias de Guatemala (Mexico)

El Nuevo Diario (Guatemala)

La Otra Guatemala (Mexico)

La Palabra (Guatemala)

Polémica (Costa Rica)

Prensa Libre (Guatemala)

Index